The Impact of the Current 4Cs Skills Gap in Organizations

The shortage of skills in the workforce is one of the major problems facing enterprises today. How American businesses and organizations intend to deal with these issues and operate in a global market under strong competition is one of their primary worries. The only logical and tangible solution to this issue is for the educational system and major businesses and organizations to begin making investments in educating more children and young adults in soft skills like the 21st-century 4Cs skills (critical thinking, communication, creativity, and collaboration) to prepare them to meet the challenges of emerging businesses and technologies.

The 21st century has witnessed a rapid transformation in the global workforce and the skills required to thrive in it. Traditional knowledge-based skills alone are no longer sufficient to succeed in today's complex and dynamic business environment. Instead, organizations increasingly value what is known as the "4Cs" skills: communication, collaboration, critical thinking, and creativity. However, a significant skills gap exists, where many employees lack these crucial abilities. This book explores the impact of the 21st-century 4Cs skills gap in organizations and how it affects their performance, innovation, and competitiveness.

The 21st-century 4Cs skills gap poses a significant challenge for organizations across industries. The inability to communicate effectively, collaborate seamlessly, think critically, and foster creativity can hinder productivity, innovation, and competitiveness. As the business landscape continues to evolve, addressing this skills gap is not only a necessity but also a strategic imperative for organizations looking to thrive in the 21st century. Bridging the gap through training, recruitment, and a commitment to a learning culture will be essential for success in the increasingly complex and interconnected world of business.

The Impact of the Current 4Cs Skills Gap in Organizations

Using Emotional Intelligence to Develop Competencies

Behnam Bakhshandeh, PhD

Foreword by William J. Rothwell

Routledge
Taylor & Francis Group

A PRODUCTIVITY PRESS BOOK

First published 2025
by Routledge
605 Third Avenue, New York, NY 10158

and by Routledge
4 Park Square, Milton Park, Abingdon, Oxon, OX14 4RN

Routledge is an imprint of the Taylor & Francis Group, an informa business

ISBN: 978-1-032-61163-1 (hbk)
ISBN: 978-1-032-61162-4 (pbk)
ISBN: 978-1-003-46231-6 (ebk)

DOI: 10.4324/9781003462316

Typeset in Garamond
by Deanta Global Publishing Services, Chennai, India

I dedicate this book to all hardworking workforces in the
United States of America who have contributed to developing this great
nation as one of the most advanced industries around the world.

Contents

Foreword

I am honored to write this book's Foreword. As a skilled talent developer and organization development consultant with 50 years of experience in government, multinational businesses, and small businesses, I am qualified to write about this book because I know the author and the subject very well. I have published 161 books on human resources and related fields (training, workforce development, and Organization Development), some translated into seven different languages, and given 1,500 professional presentations in 15 nations over 30 years.

In the rapidly evolving landscape of the 21st century, the dynamics of the workplace are undergoing a profound transformation. As organizations strive to navigate the complex interplay of technological advancements, shifting demographics, and global connectivity, a critical challenge emerges from the widening gap between the skills demanded by the contemporary workplace and those possessed by the workforce. Dr. Behnam Bakhshandeh's insightful work, *The Impact of the Current 4Cs Skills Gap in Organizations: Using Emotional Intelligence to Develop Competencies*, serves as a beacon of understanding and guidance in addressing this pressing issue. The title itself encapsulates the essence of the book's mission—a comprehensive exploration of the 4Cs skills gap and a strategic roadmap that leverages emotional intelligence as a catalyst for developing the competencies necessary for success. In a world dominated by automation, artificial intelligence, and an ever-accelerating pace of change, the 4Cs—Critical Thinking, Communication, Collaboration, and Creativity—have emerged as the linchpin competencies that define the modern professional landscape.

I met Behnam when he decided to expand his organization development and change interventions knowledge and continued his graduate studies at Penn State University to earn a Master of Professional Study in Organizational Development and Change, which was immediately followed up by his Doctorate in Workforce Education and Development with a concentration on Human Resources Development and Organization Development at Penn State. Behnam enjoyed expanding into psychology as an addition to his already strong background in philosophy and ontology. He particularly enjoyed and was inspired by the Emotional Intelligence, Positive Psychology, and Humanistic Psychology approach to empowering individuals and teams.

Behnam is an accomplished business manager known widely as a dynamic writer, speaker, personal and professional development coach, and trainer. I chaired Behnam's Ph.D. committee at Penn State University, where Behnam's topic was the subject of this book. Since then, we have published numerous books on performance coaching, transformational coaching, and supervisory leadership. We have also co-presented as webinar partners for various professional groups. He was my student and now a trusting friend, co-author, coaching college, co-consultant, and co-researcher.

Behnam is the consummate organization development professional. He knows how to conduct himself professionally, provide leadership quality performance and put everyone at ease in his training seminars and workshops. He is diligent about collecting and analyzing information and insists on developing custom reports to give a very informative and helpful presentation. Behnam always indicates the practical applications organization development work has for organizations, plus growth and development of current and future workforce and management. Behnam brings a wealth of knowledge and expertise to the forefront, drawing upon his extensive background in psychology, organizational development, and emotional intelligence. His interdisciplinary approach lays the foundation for a nuanced understanding of organizations' challenges in bridging the 4Cs skills gap and emotional intelligence's pivotal role in surmounting these hurdles.

The book begins by meticulously dissecting the nuances of the 4Cs, unraveling their interconnectedness, and emphasizing their indispensable role in fostering innovation, adaptability, and resilience. Dr. Bakhshandeh's exploration transcends the mere identification of skills; it delves into the intricacies of how these skills manifest in the day-to-day operations of diverse organizational contexts. One of the book's most compelling aspects is its emphasis on emotional intelligence as the linchpin in addressing the 4Cs skills gap. In an era dominated by technological prowess, it is easy to overlook the profound impact of human emotions on individual and collective success. Dr. Bakhshandeh deftly elucidates how emotional intelligence serves as the bedrock for cultivating the 4Cs, amplifying their effectiveness, and ensuring their sustainable integration into organizational culture.

Upskilling. Reskilling. Cross-skilling. New skilling. These words are like magical words for managing the present and future workforce. And there are good reasons why: At least 54 percent of all employees in the near future will require major reskilling and upskilling (Go-globe, no date). Of these employees, approximately 35 percent are likely to require extra training lasting up to six months, 9 percent will require reskilling lasting six to twelve months, and 10 percent will require additional skills training lasting more than a year. Approximately 57 percent of American workers desire to improve their abilities, and 48 percent would consider changing employment to do so. Furthermore, 71 percent of workers say that training and development boosts their engagement, while 61 percent say upskilling possibilities are an essential reason to stay at their employer (Go-globe, no date). Furthermore, research suggests that 94 percent of employees would stay with their current employers if their employers engaged in their development.

It is easy to see why upskilling, reskilling, cross-skilling, and new skilling are needed. The advent of artificial intelligence (AI) threatens employment for many Americans. Employers globally see it as one solution of many to chronic and acute labor shortages. In 2022, 19 percent of American workers were in jobs that were most vulnerable to AI, meaning that the most vital tasks might be replaced or aided by AI. Twenty-three percent of people have professions that are least exposed to AI, with the most vital operations being out of AI's reach. Jobs lending themselves to a high level of AI exposure are typically in higher-paying areas where a college education and analytical skills can be advantageous (Pew Research Center, 2023). Workers with a bachelor's degree or more (27 percent) are more than twice as likely as those with a high school diploma only (12 percent) to see the most exposure. A greater share of women (21 percent) than men (17 percent) are likely to see the most exposure to AI. That is because of differences in the types of jobs held by men and women (Pew Research Center, 2023).

It is just a matter of time before self-learning (generative) AI is paired with robots to burst on the labor scene. Imagine self-propelled AI machines that are smarter than humans and are nearly immortal. When that happens, many workers could be displaced. And it could lead to massive needs for those magic words, upskilling, reskilling, cross-skilling, and new skilling, that opened this Foreword.

As readers embark on this intellectual journey, they will encounter a rich tapestry of real-world case studies, illuminating anecdotes, and practical strategies that seamlessly weave theory into actionable insights. Behnam's ability to distill complex concepts into accessible narratives ensures that the book is not merely a scholarly exploration but a practical guide for leaders, educators, and individuals committed to navigating the challenges of the contemporary workplace. Moreover, *The Impact of the Current 4Cs Skills Gap in Organizations: Using Emotional Intelligence to Develop Competencies* transcends the boundaries of a traditional business or psychology book. It is a call to action for leaders to rethink their approach to talent development, for educators to recalibrate their curricula, and for individuals to embark on a journey of self-discovery and growth. The book is not just a diagnosis of the skills gap but a prescription for a future where organizations and individuals can thrive amidst the uncertainties of our rapidly changing world.

The Impact of the Current 4Cs Skills Gap in Organizations: Using Emotional Intelligence to Develop Competencies is a guide for employers on how to navigate the shoals of upskilling, reskilling, cross-skilling, and new skilling. It identifies the key skills that will need to be the focus of attention for future employers in guiding efforts to re-tool their workforce. It also helps individual workers reflect on how they can remain competitive by focusing their attention on continuous learning around key skills of essential value to present and future employers.

This book focuses on the 21st-century 4Cs skills gap, organizations' expectations of their workforces, the reality of situations caused by the 4Cs skills gap, the impact of such a gap on organizations, and how using emotional intelligence can help develop training for increasing the level of 4Cs skills among the workforces. It addresses how to raise awareness and the reality of the skills gap in the workforce, provides research-based data on the impact of the 4Cs skill gap on employee performance and productivity, provides ideas for developing 4Cs skills for the 21st century, shows organizations how to use Emotional Intelligence to help their staff acquire the 4Cs and other soft skills, and outline strategies for managers and supervisors to use in directing staff to learn more about the 4Cs and other soft skills with a growth attitude.

In conclusion, Dr. Bakhshandeh's work stands as a testament to the transformative power of emotional intelligence in addressing the challenges posed by the 4Cs skills gap. As we navigate the uncharted waters of the 21st century, this book serves as a compass, guiding us toward a future where individuals and organizations are not merely equipped to survive but empowered to thrive in the face of unprecedented change.

Employers can read this book with a view in mind on how to launch upgrading skills; individuals can read this book with a view in mind of how to shelter themselves from future job loss by upgrading their present skills at a time when all human knowledge is out of date every 3.3 to 19 years (depending on specialty) (Neimeyer, Taylor, & Rozensky, 2014). All employers—and all workers—need this book to guide their thinking for continuous learning in the future.

With great anticipation and excitement, I recommend this book to all organizations and those seeking a deeper understanding of the dynamics shaping the future of work and a roadmap for unlocking the full potential of human capital.

William J. Rothwell
Distinguished Professor
The Pennsylvania State University
State College, Pennsylvania
February 2024

References

Go-globe. (no date). The importance of job-reskilling: Statistics and trends. See: https://www.go-globe.com/the-importance-of-job-re-skilling-statistics-and-trends-infographic/#:~:text=At%20least%2054%25%20of%20all,of%20more%20than%20a%20year.

Neimeyer, G., Taylor, J., & Rozensky, R. (2014). The diminishing durability of knowledge in professional psychology: A Delphi Poll of specialties and proficiencies. *APA PsycNet*. See: https://psycnet.apa.org/record/2014-13439-002

Pew Research Center. (2023, July 26). Which U.S. workers are more exposed to AI on their jobs? See: https://www.pewresearch.org/social-trends/2023/07/26/which-u-s-workers-are-more-exposed-to-ai-on-their-jobs/

Preface

Welcome to *The Impact of the Current 4Cs Skills Gap in Organizations: Using Emotional Intelligence to Develop Competencies.*

The 21st century has witnessed a rapid transformation in the global workforce and the skills required to thrive in it. Traditional knowledge-based skills alone are no longer sufficient to succeed in today's complex and dynamic business environment. Instead, organizations increasingly value what are known as the "4Cs" skills: communication, collaboration, critical thinking, and creativity. However, a significant skills gap exists, where many employees lack these crucial abilities. This book explores the impact of the 21st-century 4Cs skills gap in organizations and how it affects their performance, innovation, and competitiveness.

The following elements are some of the major topics which are covered in 21 chapters within five parts:

The 21st-Century 4Cs Framework. Before delving into the impact of the 4Cs skills gap, it's essential to understand what these skills entail.

The Prevalence of the 21st-Century 4Cs Skills Gap. Despite the increasing importance of these skills, a significant gap exists between the demand for and the supply of the 4Cs skills in the workforce. This book will cover several factors contributing to this gap.

Impact on Organizational Performance. The 4Cs skills gap has a profound impact on organizational performance. This book will cover the nature of many such impacts.

The Competitive Landscape. In a globalized and highly competitive business environment, organizations that can adapt quickly and leverage the 4Cs skills are more likely to succeed. Those with a skills gap may find themselves falling behind competitors. This book will shed light on many of such issues throughout the book.

Bridging the 21st-Century 4Cs Skills Gap. To address the 4Cs skills gap, organizations must take proactive steps. This book points out several solutions for such proactive actions.

Use of Emotional Intelligence (EI) for Training and Development in 4Cs. In this book the author suggests using emotional intelligence and its related clusters as a platform for providing workforces with training and development in 4Cs skills.

Various Forms of Incorporating EI into 4Cs Skills Training. This book suggests some ways and applications of incorporating EI into 4Cs skills training and development.

This book is constructed in 21 chapters under five parts. The book starts with Chapter 1, "Overview and Background of Study," as an independent chapter (not part of the following five parts). Chapter 1 covers the book's overview and background study that unveiled the present and pressing the 4Cs skills gap among organizations and gives readers the perspective of the problem. The rest of the book is organized as follows.

Part I—Recognizing the Problem, and the Role of 4Cs Skills Gap in the Economy

In the first part of this book, we define the 4Cs framework in business and industries and examine how external factors have affected the workforce 4Cs skills gap. We also face the dimensions of this skills gap and its effects on firms' operations, performance, and production. This problem appears to affect the national and worldwide economy. Part I contains four chapters: Chapter 2, "Understanding the 21st-Century 4Cs Skills," explains the 4Cs skills in respect to business and gives instances of their use; Chapter 3, "The External Elements Impacting the Skills Gap," explores exogenous theories and notions that directly cause the labor skills gap; Chapter 4, "4Cs Skills Gap: A Present and Persistent Problem for Organizations—A Brief Literature Review," is a brief literature analysis on how long the 4Cs skills gap has been a concern for companies and cites academic and professional studies and evidence on how different variables contribute to the problem; and Chapter 5, "Impact of 4Cs Skills Gap on the Economy," analyzes the economic consequences of the 4Cs skills gap. Competencies help recruit and retain top talent who boost corporate performance.

Part II—Diagnosing the 4Cs Skills Gap and Evaluating Employees

Part II of this book uses current models to diagnose, analyze, and evaluate the workforce's 4Cs skills gap and how it affects their businesses in their sectors. This section also examines methods to assess and help students learn 4Cs before entering the job. Part II contains three chapters: Chapter 6, "Role of Needs Assessment in Competencies and Skills Development," is about how organizations can use a needs assessment approach to identify the 4Cs skills gap among their workforces; Chapter 7, "Identifying 4Cs Skills Gap Using Organization Diagnosis Models," is about how organizations may utilize diagnostic models to identify a 4Cs skills gap in their workforces and prolong their growth or identify which skills require extra training; and Chapter 8, "Evaluating and Supporting Students and Workforce on Their Progress," is about how to help and evaluate students before joining the workforce and the existing workforce to assess preparedness and competency.

Part III—Identifying What Is Real and Present in Organizations

Part III of his book reviews quantitative data to present the actual research findings, which are a series of themes and sub-themes based on interviews with business professional contributors (senior managers, middle- and lower-tier managers, supervisors, and line managers) to identify the real scenarios and what is present in organizations and their workforces regarding the 21st-century 4Cs skills. Part III contains four chapters: Chapter 9, "Values Placed on 4Cs Skills by Organizations," presents the research findings on what level of values organizations place on the 4Cs skills among their workforces; Chapter 10, "Impact of 4Cs Skills Gap on Team Performance," discovers the perspectives of business professionals about the influence of the 4Cs skills gap on organizations regarding team performance; Chapter 11, "Effective 4Cs Skills Training and Development," reveals business professionals' perspectives of what is good and effective training for developing 4Cs skills among their workforces; and Chapter 12, "Essence of Cohesiveness and Workability," presents business professionals' extra information regarding 4Cs abilities in their organization or workforce that they would like to share or add to the interview.

Part IV—Use Emotional Intelligence to Create Competency-Based Training

This part discusses emotional intelligence clusters, competences, traits, and attributes, and how they connect to 4Cs skills. EI coaching for individuals and teams, including competency-based training for 4Cs skills development, is covered in this part. This part concludes with the steps needed to implement and manage training and development. Part IV contains the following five chapters: Chapter 13, "Emotional Intelligence: The Key to Personal and Professional Success," breaks down the EI clusters and all corresponding competencies; Chapter 14, "Application of Emotional Intelligence Coaching," looks at elements of the EI coaching process and the competencies of an EI coach; Chapter 15, "4Cs Skills Competency-Based Training and Development via EI," covers several competency-based training and development approaches to increase 4Cs skills among individuals and teams; Chapter 16, "Implementation and Management of Training and Development," looks at implementation and management systems to ensure the quality of design and presentation and manage the progress process; and Chapter 17, "Emotional Intelligence Coach," looks at what it takes for a coach to be qualified to be an EI coach.

Part V—Foresight, Summary, and Final Thoughts

This part looks at implications, suggestions for use and future research, and study limitations. This part continues with the book summary, a brief conclusion, final thoughts, and details of demographics of the study. Part V contains four chapters: Chapter 18, "Upskilling, Reskilling, and Cross-Skilling Your Workforce," talks about how employers can effectively counteract what is predicted to become an enduring skills shortage using both of these tactics; Chapter 19, "Implications, Suggestions, and Restrictions," briefly addresses various training initiatives and their potential impacts on corporations, the current workforce, educational institutions, workforce education professionals, and local, state, and federal governments. Research restrictions are also covered in this chapter; Chapter 20, "Summary and Final Thoughts," represents the overall summary of the book, a brief conclusion, and final thoughts by the researcher; and Chapter 21, "Elements and Demographics of Study," presents all the related elements and demographics of our study.

The Primary Focus

This book will address the following elements regarding 4Cs skills gap: organizations' expectation of their workforce, the reality of situations caused by 4Cs skills gap, the impact of such gap on organizations, and how using EI can help to develop training for increasing level of 4Cs skills among workforces:

- Establish understanding and awareness regarding the reality of the skills gap among the workforces.
- Provide research-based information on the impact of 4Cs skills gap on employee performance and productivity.
- Provide strategies and practices for developing 21st-century 4Cs skills.
- Direct organizations on how to utilize emotional intelligence to develop 4Cs and other soft skills among their employees.

■ Present practices for managers and supervisors to direct employees in learning more about 4Cs and other soft skills with a growth mindset.

The Target Audience for the Book

Senior executives, senior and middle managers, supervisors and line managers in organizations, human resource (HR) leaders, human resources development (HRD) managers, organization development (OD) practitioners, workplace learning and performance (WLP) practitioners, and consultants, business coaches, and talent development practitioners are the book's main target audiences.

Academic environments including faculties, instructors, undergraduate and graduate students, researchers, and university libraries, make up the bulk of this book's target readership.

Benefits for Readers

This book provides the following information and abilities for their readers and its target audience:

■ Gives readers access to understand the importance of 21st-century 4Cs skills and overall soft skills for a 21st-century workforce.
■ Guides managers and supervisors on how to recognize the lack of 4Cs skills among their employees.
■ Recognizes the source of 4Cs skills gap and the way they show up at the workplace.
■ Recognizes the hidden themes at the workplace caused by 4Cs skills gap.
■ Explains how to use emotional intelligence and its clusters to recognize the areas that employees need to pay attention to in order to develop a deeper understanding of their 4Cs skills gap.
■ Creates practices based on emotional intelligence to increase employees' awareness of their 4Cs skills gap and establishes interest to develop competencies around the apparent gap.
■ Designs workshops to develop competencies among employees using emotional intelligence clusters and attributions.

Conclusion

The 21st-century 4Cs skills gap poses a significant challenge for organizations across industries. The inability to communicate effectively, collaborate seamlessly, think critically, and foster creativity can hinder productivity, innovation, and competitiveness. As the business landscape continues to evolve, addressing this skills gap is not only a necessity but also a strategic imperative for organizations looking to thrive in the 21st century. Bridging the gap through training, recruitment, and a commitment to a learning culture will be essential for success in the increasingly complex and interconnected world of business.

I hope you enjoy reading this research-based book as much as I enjoyed the research and writing of it.

Behnam Bakhshandeh

Acknowledgments

At the heart of every successful organization lies a workforce that is the backbone of its achievements. I would like to acknowledge the workforce's unwavering commitment, tireless efforts, and unyielding dedication, which are the cornerstones upon which organizations' collective success is built. Here and now, I am expressing our heartfelt gratitude and admiration for your enduring contributions.

Additionally, I would like to acknowledge and express my appreciation to all the organizations from seven different industries and all the business professionals who contributed to the related study and assisted me in collecting the data set and coming up with this great book related to 21st-century 4Cs skills.

Finally, I would like to express my gratitude and acknowledge Dr. William J. Rothwell for accepting my invitation to write a foreword for this book.

Behnam Bakhshandeh
Greenfield Township, Pennsylvania
February 2024

Advance Organizer

Complete the following Organizer before you read the book. Use it as a diagnostic tool to help you assess what you most want to know about *The Impact of the Current 4Cs Skills Gap in Organizations: Using Emotional Intelligence to Develop Competencies*—and where you can find it in this book fast.

The Organizer

Directions

Spend about ten minutes on the Organizer and read each item thoroughly. Think of *The Impact of the Current 4Cs Skills Gap in Organizations: Using Emotional Intelligence to Develop Competencies* as you would like to practice it for yourself and how you want to develop others in a leadership position. Be honest and indicate your level of knowledge on a Likert scale of 1–5, with "1" having little to no knowledge and "5" being very knowledgeable. When you finish, score and interpret the results using the instructions appearing at the end of the Organizer. To learn more about any item below, refer to the right-hand column referencing the specific chapter.

I would like to develop myself on:						
Level of knowledge No knowledge ------- knowledgeable					**The area of knowledge, understanding, and development**	**Chapter #**
1	**2**	**3**	**4**	**5**		
					Background of skills gap in the market	1
					4Cs skills in context of business	2
					The external elements that are impacting the skills gap	3
					Skills gap as a present and persistent problem in organizations	4
					Impact of 4Cs skills gap in economy	5
					Role of needs assessment in competencies and skills development	6

					Identifying 4Cs skills gap using organization diagnosis models	7
					Evaluating and supporting employees in their progress	8
					Values placed on 4Cs skills by organizations	9
					Impact of 4Cs skills gap on team performance	10
					Effective 4Cs skills training and development	11
					Essence of cohesiveness and workability	12
					Emotional intelligence and its clusters	13
					Application of emotional intelligence coaching	14
					4Cs skills competency-based training and development via emotional intelligence	15
					Implementation and management of training and development	16
					Emotional intelligence coach and skills	17
					Upskilling, reskilling, and cross-skilling your workforce	18
Total						

Scoring and Interpreting the Organizer

Give yourself 1 point for each Y and a 0 for each N or N/A listed above. Total the points from the Y column and place the sum in the line opposite to the word Total above. Then interpret your score below.

Score

- **1–45 points** = Congratulations! This book is just what you need. Read the chapters you marked 2 or 1.
- **46–60 points** = You have great skills in understanding the impact of current 4Cs skills gap in organizations already, but you also have areas where you could develop professionally. Read the chapters you marked 2 or 1.
- **61–75 points** = You have skills in understanding the impact of current 4Cs skills gap in organizations, but you could still benefit from building skills in selected areas.
- **76–90 points** = You believe you need little development in understanding the impact of current 4Cs skills gap in organizations. Ask others—such as mentors—to see if they agree.

About the Author

Behnam Bakhshandeh, Ph.D., MPS, is an accomplished business manager known widely as a dynamic writer, speaker, personal and professional development coach, and trainer. Implementing his skills as a passionate, visionary leader, he produces extraordinary results in record time. Behnam brings his broad experience and successful track record to each project, whether it involves personal development, implementing customer-focused programs, integrating technologies, redesigning operational core processes, or delivering strategic initiatives.

Dr. Bakhshandeh's formal education includes a Ph.D. in Workforce Education and Development (WFED) with a concentration on Organization Development (OD) and Human Resources Development (HRD) from the Pennsylvania State University, a master's degree in Professional Studies in Organization Development and Change (OD&C) from the Pennsylvania State University, World Campus, and a bachelor's degree in psychology from the University of Phoenix.

He is also the founder and president of Primeco Education, Inc. (www.PrimecoEducation .com), a coaching and consulting company that has been working with individuals, teams, and organizations on their personal and professional development since 1993. He has authored and published many personal and professional development books. Some of his latest books include: on the genre of coaching, *Building an Organizational Coaching Culture* (Taylor & Francis Group, 2024); on the genre of supervisory, *Successful Supervisory Leadership, Exerting Positive Influence While Leading People* (CDC, 2023); and another on the genre of coaching, *Transformational Coaching for Effective Leadership* (Routledge, 2023).

Before these, Bakhshandeh published two books on the genre of organization development: *High-Performance Coaching for Managers* (Routledge, 2022) and *Organization Development Interventions* (Taylor & Francis Group, 2021). His other two titles are *Anatomy of Upset; Restoring Harmony* (Primeco Education, 2015) and *Conspiracy for Greatness: Mastery of Love Within* (Primeco Education, 2009). Besides these books, he has designed and facilitated 17 coaching modules for individuals, couples, the public, teams, and organizations, 9 audio/video workshops, 16 articles on personal and professional development topics, and 21 seminars and workshops.

Before designing Primeco Education technology, he led educational programs and later managed operations for a global education organization based in two major US cities. During these seven years, he was manager of the overall operations for the staff and their team of over 400 volunteers, who served an annual client base of over 10,000. He enjoyed expanding into psychology as an addition to his already strong background in philosophy and ontology. He particularly enjoyed and was inspired by applicative inquiry, positive psychology, and humanistic psychology.

He consistently delivers and works with others to produce results beyond what was predicted or expected. This exceptional rate of business and personal growth is the result of his high integrity, unprecedented teamwork, open communication, and a contagious, unflinching commitment to excellence in all business operations, personal relationships, and professional interactions. Behnam is a shining example of how combining vision and goals with hard work consistently pays off beyond even the highest expectations. His work with businesses has resulted in successful team building, companies that grow through a shared vision, efficient process redevelopment, increased revenues, and work environments that support employee satisfaction and retention.

Behnam is widely known for his commitment to making a difference in every life he touches. He is distinguished in his field for delivering outcomes that leave all his clients fulfilled in realizing their dreams. His rigor ensures that results are produced while his compassion and sense of humor bring play to every working relationship.

Chapter 1

Overview and Background of Study

Introduction

The shortage of skills in the workforce is one of the major problems facing enterprises today. How American businesses and organizations intend to deal with this issue and operate in a global market under strong competition is one of their primary worries. The only logical and tangible solution to this issue is for the educational system and major businesses and organizations to begin making investments in educating more children and young adults in soft skills like the 21st-century 4Cs skills (critical thinking, communication, creativity, and collaboration) in order to prepare them to meet the challenges of emerging businesses and technologies.

This author has carried out an applied qualitative study among 17 private-sector firms in the state of Pennsylvania, the United States, to better understand the importance of 21st-century 4Cs skills and know how these firms' workforce deficit impacts enterprises. By highlighting the complexity of soft skills, including the 4Cs, and the ways in which companies employ them, this research begins by outlining the general problem of the soft skills gap, including the 4Cs skills, both in the United States and on a global scale for businesses and enterprises.

The data collection method for this study included interviewing participants, conducting coding, identifying emerging themes and sub-themes, and eventually arriving at several primary themes. As a result of this research, emotional intelligence clusters and related competencies that correspond to the key emerging themes will be introduced. Additionally, this study offers recommendations and proposals based on the effects of those themes and competency-based training for emotional intelligence on businesses, their present workforce, educators, trainers, and developmental programs.

For national and multinational companies, the lack of skills and competencies within today's workforce has turned into a serious issue. Businesses in the 21st-century sectors are going through significant transformations (Longmore, Grant, & Golnaraghi, 2018). How is the United States preparing to replace the massive exodus of baby boomers from the labor market while still keeping up with the expansion of domestic and overseas jobs? The United States' educational system and leading organizations must begin preparing more American students with the required education (academic and vocational) and skills in order to meet the requirements of a workforce for the

DOI: 10.4324/9781003462316-1

21st century, that is, one with the 4Cs and soft skills to fulfill these 21st-century jobs (Gordon, 2009). This is the only logical and obvious solution.

Organizations are focusing on offering exceptional services in the new global economy while utilizing the most recent knowledge, technology, and information. The capacity of organizations and enterprises to effectively compete in their markets and even to survive the severe national and international competition is increasingly dependent on having talented and competent staff (Longmore et al., 2018). The significance of workforce development coupled with a college degree has been highlighted by the growing need for locating and obtaining trained and competent individuals. Even newly employed college graduates, according to a recent study, lack the abilities that employers need for the sustainability and compatibility of their businesses (Ng et al., 2021; PACTT, 2018; Boyles, 2012).

This chapter covers the following elements:

- The Knowledge Base.
- Background of the Study.

The Knowledge Base

There is a clear problem facing educational institutions and companies in the job market today. Whether high school graduates intend to join the workforce immediately after graduation, after attending vocational schools, or after earning a college degree, they must exhibit certain skills in order to be productive employees or even to be considered as a new hire. They must possess the ability to think critically, be creative, communicate effectively, and solve problems in both their professional and personal lives (Ng et. al., 2021; Martz et al., 2016; Soulé & Warrick, 2015).

Soft skills are crucial and required for the growth and effectiveness of the workforce in the 21st century in addition to the 4Cs. Interpersonal competencies are crucial for creating a positive work environment and are considered to be soft skills (Handley, 2017). Due to their complexity and nebulous conceptualization, interpersonal abilities are difficult to describe. The broad ideas of interpersonal abilities are difficult to condense into one or two descriptions. The nomenclature used and the core qualities of the ideas being investigated frequently diverge in attempts to characterize or explain interpersonal abilities (Handley, 2017). Terminologies like emotional intelligence, social intelligence, communication ability, management interaction ability, composure, and many more that are fundamental characteristics of motivation, knowledge, and skill are all trait characteristics that attempt to describe interpersonal competencies (Handley, 2017). To put it simply, it is quite challenging to limit the concept of soft skills to only interpersonal or people abilities.

Absence of 4Cs Training in Schools

In order to meet this urgent requirement, academic and educational institutions such as high schools, colleges, and technical vocational schools need to adapt their curricula to include 21st-century skills in their instruction (Greer, Brown, & Raimondo, 2020; Martz, Hughes, & Braun, 2016). Organizations in the 21st century seek employees who not only have the necessary technical skills or subject-matter knowledge but who also possess contemporary skills like critical thinking, taking initiative, problem-solving, adaptability, agility, communication, and the capacity for teamwork (Ng et al., 2021; Longmore et al., 2018). According to studies, business education institutions are under fire for not producing a workforce that can fulfill the 21st-century need for skilled labor as a result of these fundamental professional demands (Longmore et al., 2018). The information given above and the conclusions about the fundamental requirements (critical thinking, taking initiative, problem-solving, adaptability, agility, communication, and collaborative ability) can help in a more thorough understanding of the effects of the "Workforce Skills Gap in 21st Century Skills" in the United States.

Along with these contemporary talents, skills development is often divided into two primary categories: hard skills and soft skills. While soft skills pertain to people's attitudes, personal behaviors, and social/interpersonal habits, hard skills often refer to more of the duties, technical, and administrative components of a firm (Ibrahim, Boerhannoeddin, & Bakare, 2017). When combined with hard talents, soft skills may increase a person's competitiveness in the workplace and make them more appealing for employment and promotions. According to Ibrahim et al. (2017), "It is often said that hard skills get one a job, but soft skills keep one in the job" (p. 389).

Problem Facing the Job Market

According to Soulé and Warrick (2015), "These are today's survival skills—not only for career success but also for a quality personal and civic life" (p. 178). Numerous studies (Nizami et al., 2022; Longmore et al., 2018; Robb, 2017; Soulé & Warrick, 2015) have been undertaken to highlight the impact of the lack of abilities and competencies in general and 21st-century skills (4Cs), particularly given the relevance of these skills. Meanwhile, a lot of research has been conducted (Longmore et al., 2018; Ibrahim et al., 2017; Martz et al., 2016; Soulé & Warrick, 2015) on the necessity of further developing such skills, not just the 4Cs but also soft skills and other skills required by employers like knowledge, skills, and abilities (KSAs). The P21 Model 2009 ("Partnership for 21st Century Learning," n.d.) is one such study and proposal. It is a 21st-century learning framework that aids practitioners in integrating these skills in schools to make learning about them more pertinent to students' future endeavors in higher education and the workforce.

Thousands of educators in the United States and elsewhere have utilized this framework model to apply a combination of particular skill sets, content knowledge, competencies, and literacies, among other conventional learning disciplines for the benefit of students (Soulé & Warrick, 2015). The phrase "Framework for 21st Century Learning" has been credited by Soule and Warrick (2015) because it has been described as a significant resolution for integrating learning for the demands of today's students and the workforce in their daily lives at home and more generally as a member of society.

Background of the Study

Businesses and organizations have had to adapt to a completely new learning process in order to remain competitive and succeed in this new environment since the beginning of the 21st century as compared to earlier decades (Soulé & Warrick, 2015). Organizational leaders grew more interested in a workforce with more than only technical abilities and industry expertise as a result of these changes in the business and market contexts (Longmore et al., 2018). Critical thinking skills, good communication skills, access to creativity, the capacity to solve problems, and a desire to work with people were all highly regarded qualities. A workforce that can solve problems, take the initiative, and practice adaptation in the workplace is built on these abilities and skills (Longmore et al., 2018). According to the American Management Association's (AMA) 2010

Critical Skills Survey, which polled 2,115 executive and senior manager participants, *communication* and *critical thinking* skills were the top two skills required when hiring new employees and the first and second most important skills in their organizations, respectively (Martz et al., 2016).

Generation Gaps

The youthful workforce has a lot to offer enterprises, including new ideas, uplifting energy, technological know-how, and new views, as noted by Tulgan (2015). However, a large number of them are unable to relate to the older generation due to their lack of soft skills, and this gap is producing conflict in the workplace. The other half of the problem is that older workers are impatient and intolerant in dealing with new hires.

The various non-technical talents referred to as soft skills by Tulgan (2015) include people skills, collaboration, self-awareness, and more. In addition to the aforementioned soft skills, Robles (2012) added the following components, which refer to the top ten qualities that business executives look for in either new hires or current employees: "integrity, communication, courtesy, responsibility, social skills, positive attitude, professionalism, flexibility, teamwork, and work ethic" (p. 453). The definition of soft talents is vague or unclear. Despite the multiplicity of explanations, descriptions, and classifications for these talents, this ambiguity is still acceptable. Charoensap-Kelly, Broussard, Lindsly, and Troy (2016) classified soft skills into categories including self-regulation, self-awareness, empathy, motivation, and social skills and identified soft skills as being related to emotional intelligence.

Soft Skills and Personal Traits

Additionally, Charoensap-Kelly et al. (2016) connected soft skills to a number of professional attributes and abilities, including customer service, teamwork, communication, and problem-solving. Levasseur (2013) characterized soft skills as categories of abilities and competencies as self-awareness, communication, leadership, interpersonal skills, and teamwork, which is very similar to Charoensap-Kelly et al. (2016). According to Levasseur (2013), these soft skill characteristics are crucial to and consistent with attempts to build skills, manage change, and manage organizations. Anthony and Garner (2016) discussed the several definitions and components of soft skills as well as how they differ significantly from hard skills and technical aptitudes. Anthony and Garner (2016) identified a number of personal traits and attitudes that would fit under the category of soft skills, including empathy, collaboration, teamwork, listening, professionalism, etiquette, motivation, politeness, and social intelligence. According to Ibrahim et al. (2017), a set of behaviors, habits, attributes, attitudes, social skills, and personality traits known as soft skills are necessary for employability in both a professional job and in everyday life.

Soft Skills and Employability

The Pennsylvania Academic & Career/Technical Training Alliance (PACTT) (2018) published the *Employability and Soft Skills Manual*, which lists 27 crucial competencies under five general headings, which include the following:

1) Career awareness and exploration.
2) Job search skills.
3) Job retention and career advancement skills.

4) Life skills.
5) Personal and social development.

It's interesting to note that the bulk of these 27 abilities falls within the 4Cs and soft skills criteria. Additionally, according to PACTT Alliance (2018), these competencies are not meant to be all-inclusive to future employment but rather reflect the minimal set of abilities that students must be trained in and have developed as their foundation for a successful profession.

It is obvious that every company needs the technological know-how, talents, and aptitude of the employees in addition to their expertise in their crafts. It would be challenging for any business, nevertheless, to disagree with the significance of having workers who are equipped with cooperation, communication, critical thinking, and creativity skills and competencies (Rampasso et al., 2021; Martz et al., 2016). One set of abilities cannot take the place of another. The 4Cs promote the growth of problem-solving skills, which serve as a foundation for other crucial talents like math, correspondence, and cooperation. New and creative educational programs and ways for developing the 4Cs in schools and colleges are increasingly necessary due to the rise in interest and demand for these skills and abilities, as well as an organization's appeal to recruits who exhibit these competencies (David, et al., 2021).

Up to this point, a lot of criticism has been directed at educational systems and business education for failing to fully develop a skilled workforce with competencies able to meet employers' demands for employees who are capable of using 21st-century skills (Longmore et al., 2018). As a prerequisite for training and development, firms that want to thrive in the current climate of severe national and international competition must provide their staff with both soft skills and hard skills (Ibrahim et al., 2017).

Purpose, Intention, and Guidance

This applied qualitative study's goal was to examine, explore, and describe private sector employers' perceptions of the 21st-century 4Cs skills gap and how it affects their productivity. The previously identified 4Cs skills should be in accordance with the productivity and professional development goals of business and industry to serve as a foundation for the future needs of the 4Cs skills gap.

The purpose of this study and its literature review is to highlight and clarify the detrimental effects that a workforce without 21st-century skills have on productivity growth and the viability of firms. In addition to introducing the idea of 21st-century skills, this study and its literary review will examine the impact of the 21st-century 4Cs on employment, productivity, turnover, and employer–employee relationships.

The following topics are the main intention of this study, which is to find the private-sector and non-profit organizations' views on these areas:

1. Values placed on 4Cs skills by organizations.
2. Impact of 4Cs skills gap on team performance.
3. Effective 4Cs skills training and development.

What Is Next?

Now that we talked about the purpose of the research and all the relevant aspects of the research, we continue our work in Part I of the book "Recognizing the Problem, and the Role of 4Cs Skills

Gap in the Economy." The next chapter, "Understanding the 21st-Century 4Cs Skills," briefly explains what the 4Cs skills are in relation to a business operation and gives readers some examples of skills and abilities of those with such skills.

References

Anthony, S. & Garner, B. (2016). Teaching soft skills to business students: An analysis of multiple pedagogical methods. *Business and Professional Communication Quarterly, 79*(3), 360–370. https://doi.org/10.1177/2329490616642247.

Boyles, T. (2012). 21st century knowledge, skills, and abilities and entrepreneurial competencies: A model for undergraduate entrepreneurship education. *Journal of Entrepreneurship Education, 15*, 41–55. Retrieved from https://www.abacademies.org/articles/jeevol152012.pdf#page=47.

Charoensap-Kelly, P., Broussard, L., Lindsly, M., & Troy, M. (2016). Evaluation of a soft skills training program. *Business and Professional Communication Quarterly, 79*(2), 154–179. https://doi.org/10.1177/2329490615602090.

David, M. E., David, F. R., & David, F. R. (2021). Closing the gap between graduates' skills and employers' requirements: A focus on the strategic management capstone business course. *Administrative Sciences, 11*(1), 10. https://doi.org/10.3390/admsci11010010.

Gordon, E. E. (2009). The future of jobs and careers. *Techniques: Connecting Education and Careers, 84*(6), 28–31. Retrieved from https://eric.ed.gov/?id=EJ858227.

Greer, S., Brown, K., & Raimondo, M. (2020). Gap bridgers: Teaching skills to cross lines of difference. *Journal of College and Character, 21*(3), 221–233. https://doi.org/10.1080/2194587X.2020.1781664.

Handley, M. (2017). *An Interpersonal Behavioral Framework for Early-Career Engineers Demonstrating Engineering Leadership Characteristics across Three Engineering Companies.* (Published doctoral dissertation). Sate Collage, PA: The Pennsylvania State University.

Ibrahim, R., Boerhannoeddin, A., & Bakare, K. K. (2017). The effect of soft skills and training methodology on employee performance. *European Journal of Training and Development, 41*(4), 388–406. https://doi.org/10.1108/EJTD-08-2016-0066.

Levasseur, R. (2013). People skills: developing soft skills—A change management perspective. *Interfaces, 43*(6), 566–571. https://doi.org/10.1287/inte.2013.0703.

Longmore, A.-L., Grant, G., & Golnaraghi, G. (2018). Closing the 21st-century knowledge gap: Reconceptualizing teaching and learning to transform business education. *Journal of Transformative Education, 16*(3), 197–219. https://doi.org/10.1177/1541344617738514.

Martz, B., Hughes, J., & Braun, F. (2016). Creativity and problem-solving: Closing the skills gap. *The Journal of Computer Information Systems, 57*(1), 39–48. doi: 10.1080/08874417.2016.118149.

Ng, P. M. L., Chan, J. K. Y., Wut, T. M., Lo, M. F., & Szeto, I. (2021). What makes better career opportunities for young graduates? Examining acquired employability skills in higher education institutions. *Education & Training, 63*(6), 852–871. https://doi.org/10.1108/ET-08-2020-0231.

Nizami, N., Tripathi, T., & Mohan, M. (2022). Transforming skill gap crisis into opportunity for upskilling in India's IT-BPM sector. *Indian Journal of Laboure Economics, 65*(3), 845–862. https://doi.org/10.1007/s41027-022-00383-9.

PACTT Alliance (Pennsylvania Academic & Career/Technical Training Alliance). (2018). Employability and soft skills manual, forth version. Retrieved from http://www.pactt-alliance.org/Pages/PACTT-Employability-Soft-Skills.aspx.

Partnership for 21st Century Learning. (n.d.) website. *Framework for 21st Century Learning: Communication and Collaboration. Retrieved from www.p21.org/about-us/p21 framework/261.*

Rampasso, I. S., Mello, S. L. M., Walker, R., Simão, V. G., Araújo, R., Chagas, J., Quelhas, O. L. G., & Anholon, R. (2021). An investigation of research gaps in reported skills required for industry 4.0 readiness of Brazilian undergraduate students. *Higher Education, Skills and Work-Based Learning, 11*(1), 34–47. https://doi.org/10.1108/HESWBL-10-2019-0131.

Robb, L. (2017). Read talk write: Developing 21st-century skills. *Voices from the Middle, 24*(4), 19–23. Retrieved from http://www.ncte.org/library/NCTEFiles/Resources/Journals/VM/0244may2017/VM0244Leading.pdf.

Robles, M. M. (2012). Executive perceptions of the top 10 soft skills needed in today's workplace. *Business Communication Quarterly, 75*(4), 453–465. https://doi.org/10.1177/1080569912460400.

Soulé, H. & Warrick, T. (2015). Defining 21st century readiness for all students: What we know and how to get there. *Psychology of Aesthetics, Creativity, and the Arts, 9*(2), 178–186. https://doi.org/10.1037/aca0000017.

Tulgan, B. (2015). *Bridging the Soft Skills Gap: How to Teach the Missing Basics to Today's Young Talent.* Hoboken, NJ. John Willey & Sons, Inc. https://doi.org/10.1002/9781119171409.

RECOGNIZING THE PROBLEM, AND THE ROLE OF 4CS SKILLS GAP IN THE ECONOMY

In the first part of this book, we attempt to describe the 4Cs framework in the context of business and industries and also look into what other external elements have impacted or have a role in the 4Cs skills gap among workforces. Furthermore, we confront the dimensions of this skills gap and the related problems it is causing in organizations' operation, performance, and productivity. Nevertheless, it appears that this problem directly impacts the national and international economy.

Chapter 2: Understanding the 21st-Century 4Cs Skills

This chapter will briefly explain the place of 4Cs skills in the context of business operation and gives readers some examples of skills and abilities of individuals with such skills.

Chapter 3: The External Elements Impacting the Skills Gap

This chapter explores some external theories and concepts that have a direct impact on causing the skills gap in the workforce.

DOI: 10.4324/9781003462316-2

Chapter 4: 4Cs Skills Gap: A Present and Persistent Problem for Organizations—A Brief Literature Review

A brief literature review on how long the 4Cs skills gap has been a problem for organizations points toward academic and professional research and evidence, examining the role of different variables in raising the skills gap problem.

Chapter 5: Impact of 4Cs Skills Gap on the Economy

This chapter discusses the impact of the 4Cs skills gap on the economy. Organizations are becoming aware of the value of competencies and how they play a part in attracting and keeping excellent people who positively influence the success of their businesses.

Chapter 2

Understanding the 21st-Century 4Cs Skills

Introduction

This chapter will explore broad notions and descriptions of critical thinking, creativity, communication, collaboration, soft skills, and people skills as part of soft skills in order to provide the reader with a better grasp of the 4Cs and soft skills required in the 21st century. It is important to note that scholars and management professionals have a wide range of descriptions and definitions of soft skills. These descriptions and definitions may be found in a wide number of contexts. It is unclear where the phrase "soft skills" originated.

According to Charoensap-Kelly et al. (2016), however, the oldest mention of the use of this word dates back to the year 1972, when Whitmore and Fry conducted a study on the subject of leadership for the US Army. Robles (2012) demonstrated the connection between people skills and soft skills by proving that in today's culture while attempting to define soft skills, most people also refer to them as people skills, which are a major aspect of soft skills. This chapter will explore the relationship between people skills and soft skills.

This chapter will look at:

- What Are Soft Skills?
- The 21st-Century 4Cs Skills in Business Context.
- Collaboration.

What Are Soft Skills?

As mentioned above, the first time this phrase was used was in 1972 when Fry and Whitmore investigated leadership in the US Army (Charoensap-Kelly et al., 2016).

According to Charoensap-Kelly et al. (2016):

- Whitmore and Fry (1972) defined the term soft skills as "important job-related skills that involve little or no interaction with machines and can be applied in a variety of job contexts" (p. 155).

DOI: 10.4324/9781003462316-3

■ Several researchers have used and defined the term soft skills since the 1990s. The relationship between soft skills and emotional intelligence, which is defined by five key components, including self-awareness, self-regulation, motivation, empathy, and social skills (p. 155), is undisputed.

■ Team skills, communication skills, leadership skills, customer service skills, and problem-solving skills are examples of assigned professional attributes that are included in soft skills (p. 155).

Robles (2012) used the example of how, in today's culture, the majority of people also use the term "people skills," a key component of soft skills, to highlight the connection between soft skills and people skills. Additionally, Robles (2012) noted that an individual's interactions with other people are illustrated by their people skills. He emphasizes it as one of the most crucial workplace competencies. "While many authors equate interpersonal skills with soft skills, interpersonal skills are only one facet of soft skills" (Robles, 2012, p. 457). Soft skills are personal aptitudes and character attributes that go beyond interpersonal skills, such as time management, personality, and organizational skills. In addition, leadership skills, communication proficiency, a collaborative spirit, and a commitment to providing excellent customer service may all be considered professional and career attributes (Robles, 2012).

The 21st-Century 4Cs Skills in Business Context

This section will explore the fundamental concepts and definitions of critical thinking, creativity, communication, collaboration, soft skills, and people skills as parts of soft skills in order to have a better knowledge of the 4Cs and soft skills for the 21st century. It is important to note that the aforementioned sections of this study indicated the wide range of descriptions and definitions of soft skills used by researchers and management experts (see Figure 2.1). It is significant to note that the definition of 21st-century talents (4Cs) and soft skills used in this research is consistent with descriptions and basic understandings used nationally and globally.

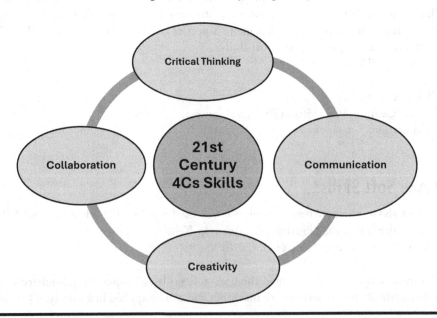

Figure 2.1   21st-century 4Cs skills. © Bakhshandeh 2024.

Critical Thinking

The following are some definitions of critical thinking:

- "the objective analysis and evaluation of an issue in order to form a judgment" (Oxford Language, 2023c, n.p.).
- "Critical thinking is that mode of thinking—about any subject, content, or problem—in which the thinker improves the quality of his or her thinking by skillfully taking charge of the structures inherent in thinking and imposing intellectual standards upon them" (The Foundation of Critical Thinking, 2019, n.p.).
- "Critical thinking is the intellectually disciplined process of actively and skillfully conceptualizing, applying, analyzing, synthesizing, and/or evaluating information gathered from, or generated by, observation, experience, reflection, reasoning, or communication, as a guide to belief and action" (Scriven & Paul, 2003, n.p., in University of Minnesota, 2023).

Moore (2013) did research to analyze conceptions of critical thinking in the context of academics from three disciplines:

1) Philosophy.
2) History.
3) Cultural studies.

In this section, this book aims to briefly define and explain what critical thinking is. In a study conducted by Moore (2013) entitled "Critical Thinking: Seven Definitions in Search of a Concept," he presented seven elements that described and defined critical thinking as "(i) judgment; (ii) skepticism; (iii) simple originality; (iv) sensitive readings; (v) rationality; (vi) an activist engagement with knowledge; and (vii) self-reflexivity" (p. 506). The Moore (2013) study was a component of a research project that involved interviewing university students from a range of academic fields, including history, philosophy, and literary and cultural studies.

Given their importance to educational sagacity, Moore (2013) purposefully chose these fields. According to Moore (2013), these meanings have a big impact on how schools and institutions teach and learn. When hiring college graduates for professional positions, companies seek skills in critical thinking and problem-solving (one of its outputs). The American Management Association (AMA) asked 2,115 executives and senior managers to rate the top talents they seek when recruiting new employees as part of its Critical Talents Survey in 2010. The most sought talent was communication skills, with critical thinking coming in second (Martz et al., 2016).

It makes sense that employers seek candidates with technical expertise as well as other job-related characteristics and talents when hiring new employees. But many businesses view the ability to solve problems as being just as important as mathematics knowledge, written communication, and collaboration among their employees. These two sets of talents complement one another and are necessary for success in the labor market of the 21st century (Martz et al., 2016).

According to many business professionals and researchers, there are several imperial skills that would assist an individual to practice and express critical thinking. Figure 2.2 displays some of these skills based on this author's professional experience.

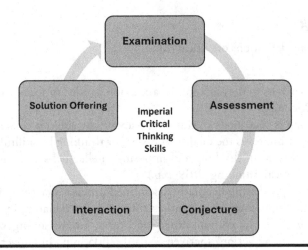

Figure 2.2 Imperial skills of critical thinking. © Bakhshandeh 2024.

- **Examination.** The capacity to recognize and anticipate possibilities, challenges, and potential solutions.
- **Assessment.** The process of collecting, comprehending, and analyzing various types of data and information.
- **Conjecture.** Concluding anything after considering the pertinent data, information, as well as one's own personal expertise and experience.
- **Interaction.** Exchanging information with other people vocally, non-verbally, and in writing, as well as receiving information from other people.
- **Solution Offering.** The process of obtaining information, interpreting that information, and disseminating it in order to discover problems and find solutions to those problems.

Communication

The following are some definitions of communication:

- "means of sending or receiving information, such as phone lines or computers" (Oxford Language, 2023a).
- "a process by which information is exchanged between individuals through a common system of symbols, signs, or behavior" (Merriam-Webster, 2023b).
- "Communication is the act of giving, receiving, and sharing information—in other words, talking or writing, and listening or reading. Good communicators listen carefully, speak or write clearly, and respect different opinions" (Common Sense Media, 2020).
- "The root of the word 'communication' in Latin is *communicare*, which means to share, or to make common (Weekley, 1967). Communication is defined as the process of understanding and sharing meaning (Pearson & Nelson, 2000)" (University of Minnesota, 2023).

According to Steinfatt (2009), "The central thrust of human communication concerns mutually understood symbolic exchange" (p. 295). This is how he sees communication and its crucial part in human connectivity. Although Steinfatt's definition of communication may not be widely embraced, it does highlight the significance of this crucial ability. This is how Steinfatt (2009) outlined the purposes of communication, along with its definition, message, channel, and receiver components.

The term "communication" is employed in a variety of contexts, from the straightforward definition of speaking and interacting with others via language to the sophisticated technological applications in information technology and everything in between (Steinfatt, 2009). However, in both personal and professional contexts, the term "communication" is generally used to describe the flow of information from one person to another. The idea of communication is essential to human connection, given that people may chat and utilize language as a tool for communication with others (Steinfatt, 2009). This is especially true for the development of professional skills and teamwork in order to boost accuracy, save time, and increase productivity.

One of the ideas that has been and continues to be the subject of several theories and studies regarding the human connection is communication. Humans communicate their intents and messages via a variety of non-verbal cues, including body language, noises, and visual cues. Through applications and platforms for voice and visual communication, people and organizations may interact quickly in today's electronic and technical world (Jones, 2015a).

Figure 2.3 displays some of communication skills and competencies that are essential to present a skillful communication. There are more skills related to effective communication, but based on this author's professional experience, the following are the foundation of an individual with communication skills.

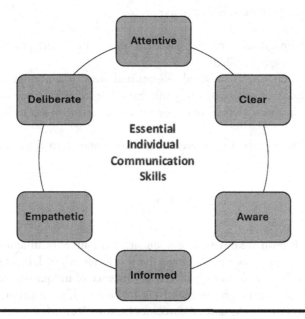

Figure 2.3 Essential communication skills needed for individuals. © Bakhshandeh 2024.

■ **Aware.** Be mindful of your facial expressions and body language. A key component of being a successful communicator is your body language. Although words are vital, your tone, eye contact, facial emotions, and hand gestures are more crucial. Hand movements signify bravery and confidence.

■ **Attentive.** You will comprehend more if you listen attentively. Even when speakers are not very successful, those who pay attention to what they are saying can still grasp their message. Additionally, by paying attention and participating, you show respect for others.

- **Clear.** When communicating, be specific and straightforward. Your audience will understand you more clearly if you deliver a specific message. Giving clear explanations of the information you are conveying, together with numbers and statistics, just makes it easier for others to comprehend you.
- **Informed.** Know your subject well, educate yourself, and gather information about the subject you plan to discuss. The topic should be clear to your target audience. Having a good understanding of the conversation will be beneficial. Additionally, it will make it simple for them to understand your message.
- **Deliberate.** Make sure to fully explain the communication's aim, to provide the conversation's points one at a time in order of relevance to the purpose, and to logically link and deduce these points within the sentences.
- **Empathetic.** Empathy is the act of comprehending. Your ideas or statements may occasionally conflict with those within or outside the core audience. But you shouldn't feel furious or upset in this circumstance. Instead, accept their viewpoints and be inspired by their bravery to communicate and express their comments or criticisms.

Creativity

The following are some definitions of creativity:

- "the use of the imagination or original ideas, especially in the production of an artistic work" (Oxford Language, 2023b).
- "the ability to produce or use original and unusual ideas" (Cambridge Dictionary, 2023).
- "the ability to make or otherwise bring into existence something new, whether a new solution to a problem, a new method or device, or a new artistic object or form" (Kerr, 2023).

Runco and Jaeger (2012) stated that there are two components to the conventional notion of creativity:

1) Effectiveness.
2) Uniqueness.

Some could question if both are essential components. Undoubtedly, uniqueness is necessary for creativity. An idea, concept, or action is not creative if it is not original, unusual, or rare. Instead, it is ordinary, conventional, and unoriginal. The significance of uniqueness and creativity is supported by the second component, effectiveness. It is not creative if the concept, thinking, or action is ineffective or fails to provide the desired outcomes from such creativity and uniqueness (Runco & Jaeger, 2012).

An increase in enthusiasm over the past few years has resulted in the inclusion of creativity as a subject of study in schools. This interest is a result of more people becoming aware of how critical competencies and abilities are for the present and future workforce. However, other studies have examined the challenges teachers encounter when integrating creativity into their lesson plans because of overstuffed class schedules that prevent them from adopting the 4Cs and the necessary abilities (Ahmadi & Besançon, 2017).

Figure 2.4 displays some examples of how individuals can use creativity to make a difference in expanding leadership skills and have a positive influence on businesses.

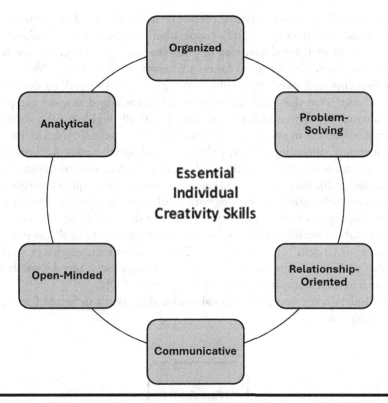

Figure 2.4   Essential aspects of individuals with creativity skills. © Bakhshandeh 2024.

- **Organized.** Ability to come up with innovative structures and action plans for implementing new ideas.
- **Analytical.** Ability to investigate issues first, before coming to immediate conclusions.
- **Open-Minded.** Ability to look outside of the box and think of options that are not being considered by others.
- **Relationship-Oriented.** Ability to create opportunities to expand on internal and external interpersonal relationships.
- **Communicative.** Ability to listen without prenotions and perceptions and ask a series of creative questions.
- **Problem-Solving.** Ability to come up with creative ideas for solving issues before they escalate.

Collaboration

The following are some definitions of collaboration:

- "to work jointly with others or together especially in an intellectual endeavor" (Merriam-Webster, 2023a).
- "the action of working with someone to produce or create something" (Oxford Language, 2023d).
- "Collaboration is a working practice whereby individuals work together for a common purpose to achieve business benefit. Collaboration enables individuals to work together to achieve a defined and common business purpose" (AIIM, 2023).

Collaboration is not only a talent for the 21st century; it is also a method of instruction in schools. According to Ahmadi and Besançon (2017), cooperation is a talent that will help working teams in businesses come up with novel solutions to problems and deliver speedier outcomes among students in the classroom. Collaboration fosters a diversity of viewpoints, allows for the expression of such viewpoints, and speeds up problem-solving compared to working alone. Ahmadi and Besançon (2017) countered that while cooperation is acknowledged as a key component in the development of creativity, there is little research that specifically highlights this connection.

The majority of learners in today's culture, according to Jones (2015b), are linked primarily through "collaborators" including tablets, cellphones, and social media platforms. By utilizing their digital awareness to foster cooperation and increase productivity, educators and businesses may take advantage of this phenomenon and construct projects that require students or employees to work together. As with instructors working with children to improve their fluency in other topics like a foreign language, arithmetic, physics, or creativity, the Global Digital Citizen Foundation refers to this as collaborative fluency (Jones, 2015b). "Simply put, better collaborators make better students—and better citizens" (Jones, 2015b, p. 24). Communities, neighbors, and co-workers working together without self-interest, prejudice, or political or social agendas will benefit society whether they do it at their workplaces or from home (Jones, 2015b).

Figure 2.5 displays some examples of collaborative skills that can be used and practiced by those in their workplace.

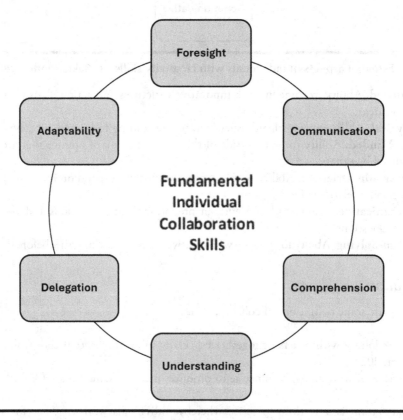

Figure 2.5 Fundamental elements of individuals with collaboration skills. © Bakhshandeh 2024.

- **Foresight.** In every team environment, the capacity to unify the team behind a single goal is crucial for collaboration. The criteria for what constitutes a company's purpose vary. Leveraging many areas of knowledge will lead to speedier results and better outcomes if you have a great vision for the big picture.
- **Communication.** If you want other employees to benefit from your expertise and experience, it is imperative that you communicate properly. In your written, verbal, and non-verbal communication, convey ideas and information that are clear and concrete.
- **Comprehension.** Listening and comprehension abilities are as important as communication skills. To make sure you understand your coworkers' perspectives completely, you should attentively listen without passing judgment and, if required, ask for clarification.
- **Understanding.** You may recognize when a coworker is in pain and know how to respond if you have empathy and compassion. Your coworker could want you to listen to them talk about a problem they are having at home or with a particular project.
- **Delegation.** The best collaboration happens when duties and responsibilities are outlined and incorporated into routine activities. You risk upsetting and weakening your employees' feelings of responsibility and accountability if you often coordinate and reassign assignments and responsibilities.
- **Adaptability.** Adaptability is a quality of both management and employees in a truly collaborative organization. When completing any project, unforeseen issues might include delays, shifting priorities, a lack of funding, etc. Experience is necessary to think quickly and creatively under pressure.

What Is Next?

We just briefly explained the 4Cs skills in the context of business and how they are being used in business operations with individuals who have a clear understanding of these skills. Chapter 3, "The External Elements Impacting the Skills Gap," explores some external theories and concepts that have a direct impact on causing the skills gap in the workforce.

References

Ahmadi, N. & Besançon, M. (2017). Creativity as a steppingstone towards developing other competencies in classrooms. *Education Research International, 2017*, 1–9. https://doi.org/10.1155/2017/1357456.

AIIM. (2023). Association for Information and Image Management. Retrieved from https://www.aiim.org/what-is-collaboration#:~:text=Collaboration.

Cambridge Dictionary. (2023). Creativity. Retrieved from https://dictionary.cambridge.org/us/dictionary/english/creativity.

Charoensap-Kelly, P., Broussard, L., Lindsly, M., & Troy, M. (2016). Evaluation of a soft skills training program. *Business and Professional Communication Quarterly, 79*(2), 154–179. https://doi.org/10.1177/2329490615602090.

Common Sense Media. (2020). What is communication? Retrieved from https://www.commonsensemedia.org/articles/what-is-communication.

Jones, V. R. (2015a, December). 21st century skills: Communication. *Children's Technology and Engineering, 20*(2), 28–29. Retrieved from https://www.iteea.org/Publications/Journals/ESCJournal/CTEDecember2015.aspx?.source.

Jones, V. R. (2015b, September). 21st century skills: Collaboration. *Children's Technology and Engineering, 20*(1), 24–26. Retrieved from https://www.iteea.org/CTESeptember2015.aspx.

Kerr, Barbara. (2023). Creativity. *Britannica*. Retrieved from https://www.britannica.com/topic/creativity.

Martz, B., Hughes, J., & Braun, F. (2016). Creativity and problem-solving: Closing the skills gap. *The Journal of Computer Information Systems, 57*(1), 39–48. https://doi.org/10.1080/08874417.2016.118149.

Merriam-Webster. (2023a). Collaboration. Retrieved from https://www.merriam-webster.com/dictionary/collaboration.

Merriam-Webster. (2023b). Communication. Retrieved from https://www.merriam-webster.com/dictionary/communication.

Moore, T. (2013). Critical thinking: Seven definitions in search of a concept. *Studies in Higher Education, 38*(4), 506–522. https://doi.org/10.1080/03075079.2011.586995.

Oxford Language. (2023a). Communication. Oxford University Press. Retrieved from https://languages.oup.com/google-dictionary-en/.

Oxford Language. (2023b). Creativity. Oxford University Press. Retrieved from https://languages.oup.com/google-dictionary-en/.

Oxford Language. (2023c). Critical Thinking. Oxford University Press. Retrieved from https://languages.oup.com/google-dictionary-en/.

Oxford Language. (2023d). Collaboration. Oxford University Press. Retrieved from https://languages.oup.com/google-dictionary-en/.

Pearson, J. & Nelson, P. (2000). *An Introduction to Human Communication: Understanding and Sharing (p. 6)*. Boston, MA: McGraw-Hill.

Robles, M. M. (2012). Executive perceptions of the top 10 soft skills needed in today's workplace. *Business Communication Quarterly, 75*(4), 453–465. https://doi.org/10.1177/1080569912460400.

Runco, M. A. & Jaeger, G. J. (2012). The standard definition of creativity. *Creativity Research Journal, 24*(1), 92–96. https://doi.org/10.1080/10400419.2012.650092.

Scriven, M. & Paul, R. (2003). Defining critical thinking: A statement prepared for the National Council for Excellence in Critical Thinking Instruction. In *8th Annual International Conference on Critical Thinking and Education Reform*, Summer 1987.

Steinfatt, T. (2009). Definitions of communication. In S. W. Littlejohn & K. A. Foss (Eds.), *Encyclopedia of Communication Theory* (Vol. 1, pp. 295–299). Thousand Oaks, CA: Sage Publication, Inc. https://doi.org/10.4135/9781412959384.n108.

The Foundation of Critical Thinking. (2019). Define critical thinking. Retrieved from https://www.critical-thinking.org/pages/defining-critical-thinking/766.

University of Minnesota. (2023). Libraries. What is communication. Retrieved from https://open.lib.umn.edu/businesscommunication/chapter/1-2-what-is-communication/.

Weekley, E. (1967). *An Etymological Dictionary of Modern English* (Vol. 1, p. 338). New York, NY: Dover Publications.

Whitmore, P. G. & Fry, J. P. (1972). What are soft skills. In *CONARC Soft Skills Conference*. Texas: Fort Bliss.

Chapter 3

The External Elements Impacting the Skills Gap

Introduction

This chapter looks at some of the theoretical frameworks and challenges that are connected to external influential forces such as the family, society, policies, learning, educational systems, and organizations on the apparent 4Cs skills gap that is now present in the labor market.

- External Elements with Impact on Causing 4Cs Skills Gap.
    - Motivation and Behavior Theories.
    - Educational System and Learning Theories.
    - Political Policies and Theories.
    - Family and Society Theories.
    - Other Relevant Issues.

External Elements with Impact on Causing 4Cs Skills Gap

Figure 3.1 provides a representation of some of the theoretical framework and issues as they relate to influential forces such as the family, society, policies, learning, educational system, and organizations on the apparent 4Cs skills gap in the labor market. Please note that the order of issues on display does not correspond to any sort of order of importance or influence. Several of these external concerns will be highlighted in the next section.

DOI: 10.4324/9781003462316-4

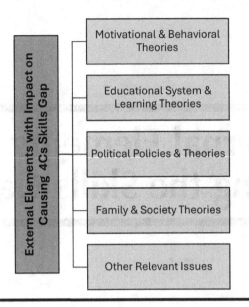

Figure 3.1   External elements with impact on causing 4Cs skills gap. © Bakhshandeh 2024.

Motivational and Behavioral Theories

To begin with, let's investigate where the word "motivation" came from in the English language. The word comes from the Latin word "*movere*," which literally means "to move." To put it more succinctly, motivation may be defined as the force that causes individuals to act from within themselves or that motivates them to work in some way (Mitchell, 1997). Industrial and Organization (I/O) psychologists defined motivation as "those psychological processes involved with the arousal, direction, intensity, and persistence of voluntary actions that are goal-directed" (Mitchell, 1997, p. 60).

Figure 3.2 represents three theories connected to and supporting the motivation and behavior theory.

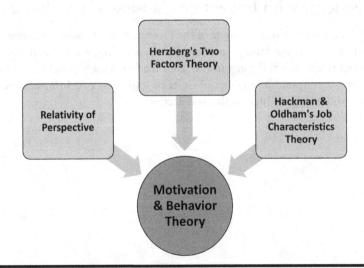

Figure 3.2   Three theories connected to motivation and behavior theory. © Bakhshandeh 2024.

Relativity of Perspective

According to this notion, every individual is born into a certain family, culture, society, tradition, and time period. According to this idea, these factors influence how people form their habits and understanding of the world, shape how people perceive the world, and perpetuate those beliefs into adulthood (Mar, 2004). Because people might decide that timeliness is not necessary or develop some resistance to it since childhood, we are applying this notion here.

The human mind is driven, motivated, and capable of creating stories and tales based on interpretations and their perception of reality as they are observed and understood, as Mar (2004) highlighted. Mar (2004) also noted that people employ these realities and beliefs in a variety of domestic and professional contexts, including the workplace. Possessing abilities and completing tasks accurately and on time are two essential components of productivity, whether on a personal or professional level. As a result, someone's degree of timeliness will be affected if, for whatever reason relating to their former upbringing—their family, culture, or background—they do not believe in growing and acquiring abilities.

Herzberg's Two Factors Theory

The working environment is split into two distinct parts according to this theory:

- **Hygiene Factors.** According to Herzberg, Mausner, and Snyderman (1959), hygiene factors are aspects of the workplace context that are linked to the intrinsic qualities of the job itself, such as pay, employment benefits, supervision structure, the relationships between employees and co-workers, organizational procedures, and HR policies.
- **Motivators.** The inherent qualities of the job, such as the number of difficulties, the employees' direct responsibility at work, their level of autonomy, and the possibilities available to them in their position, are motivators (Herzberg et al., 1959). Some people may not care about doing good work if they are unhappy with some of these employment features. No matter how the organization offers appropriate salary or helpful management and a nice work environment, Herzberg et al. (1959) argued that these hygienic aspects could not independently generate and source motivation among the workers.

In the best case, hygiene issues can only prevent employees from becoming unhappy at work, not the other way around. Herzberg et al. (1959) also described their idea for motivating the workforce, which would involve organizations providing the right levels of motivators like more interesting and engaging jobs, more recognition and empowerment, a stimulating work environment, and high accountability and autonomy. According to Herzberg, businesses should focus more on creating fulfilling occupations and work conditions while trying to preserve production and profitability.

Hackman and Oldham's Job Characteristics Theory

The factors that comprise a job have a direct bearing on employees' levels of contentment in their positions, which in turn influences the quality of their time spent working and their level of output (Spector & Jex, 1991).

According to research conducted by Spector and Jex (1991), there is a correlation between work satisfaction and the five factors listed below:

1) Skill variability.
2) Task distinctiveness.

3) Task significance.
4) Autonomy.
5) Feedback.

Nevertheless, there are a few other elements that impact job satisfaction, such as:

1) The condition of the work.
2) The degree of stress associated with the job.
3) The social interactions with co-workers.

(Spector & Jex, 1991)

I chose this idea since it directly relates to employees' conduct at work and their level of job satisfaction. This idea may also be applied to the training and development of staff members to increase their level of engagement at work. Job characteristics are another component in developing a pleasant and effective work attitude, much like job satisfaction. In accordance with Zhao et al. (2016), "Job characteristics are the motivational dimensions that affect employees' experiences of meaningfulness, responsibility, and knowledge relating to work activities" (p. 27). These motivational dimensions are seen as specific traits that enunciate and quantify the work characteristics of employees.

It is obvious that their job characteristics, such as the availability of skill variability, task distinctiveness, the level of task significance, work autonomy, and the potential feedback they are receiving (Spector & Jex, 1991), along with some other factors like work conditions, the level of stress and workload, and social relationships with co-workers, would be relevant among people caring about being motivated or being careless about their work.

Educational System and Learning Theories

The following three models and the theories of teaching and learning have a direct influence on the way in which younger generations are gaining the skills and knowledge necessary to apply such skills to a real-life or job context.

Figure 3.3 represents three theories and issues connected to and supporting the educational system and learning theories.

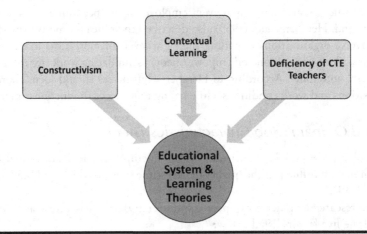

Figure 3.3 Three theories and issues connected to the educational system and learning theories. © Bakhshandeh 2024.

Constructivism

Education professionals refer to constructivism as a set of conventions regarding the nature of human learning that guide constructivist learning philosophies, theories, and teaching techniques while valuing developmentally appropriate teacher-supported learning models that come from the students (Gordon, 2014). "The theory of constructivism rests on the notion that there is an inherent human drive to make sense of the world" (Gordon, 2014, p. 391). Gordon (2014) asserts that constructivist theories are important to and have an influence on the information learning sector in the current educational system.

As Parnell (1996) highlighted, the academic education perspective and philosophy has been "learning to know is most important; application can come later" (p. 19). According to Parnell and other career technical education (CTE) experts, "Learning to do is most important; knowledge will somehow seep into the process" (p. 19). Instead of assigning assignments to students, CTE professionals and instructors can rather create experiences that will allow them to expand their learning horizons and deepen their comprehension of the subject matter (Gordon, 2014).

Contextual Learning

Contextual learning is described by Gordon (2014) as:

> teaching and learning conceptions that would help teachers or facilitators link and create relevance among the content of the subject matter at hand with real-world situations and allow students to develop their own experience of how the subject matter is working or not working in the real world.

Problem-solving and critical thinking are two of the key contextual learning processes, according to Gordon (2014). According to several study findings, not all pupils will benefit equally from the abstract approach of teaching and learning. In actuality, Gordon (2014) and Gardner (2006) found that the majority of people learn through contextual encounters in informal settings and immersive situations.

Deficiency of Career and Technical Education Teachers

According to Gordon's (2014) research, there was at least a 10% decline in higher education institutions offering CTE teacher preparation programs between 1991 and 2001. As a result of the absence of CTE teacher preparation programs at their state's colleges and institutions, several local and statewide communities are also experiencing an alarming degree of CTE teacher shortages (Carl D. Perkins Career and Technical Education Act of 2006) (Gordon, 2014).

Gordon (2014) cited the National Association of State Directors of Career and Technical Education (2012) and claimed that the three industries and groups with the greatest shortages of CTE teachers in 2012 were Science, Technology, Engineering, and Math (STEM), Health Science, and Manufacturing. The Strengthening Career and Technical Education for the 21st Century Act, often known as Perkins V., was passed in 2018.

Political Policies and Theories

The local, state, and federal governments' policies and laws, as well as the manner in which these policies and legislation have been continued or increased, have a direct influence on the amount of skilled labor that is available on the labor market. The following are some but not all instances of such policies:

Figure 3.4 represents three theories and issues connected to and supporting the political policies and theories.

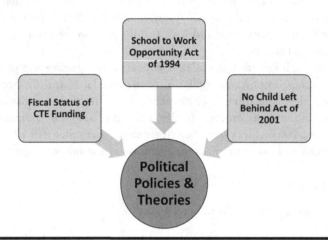

Figure 3.4 Three theories and issues connected to and supporting political policies and theories. © Bakhshandeh 2024.

Fiscal Status of CTE Funding

The "Carl D. Perkins Vocational Education Act of 1984" was modified and extended by the "Carl D. Perkins Vocational and Applied Technology Education Act of 1990" (Gordon, 2014). According to Baxter (2012), the primary funding source for local public vocational education programs that integrate CTE with real-world professions for program participants is the Perkins Act.

Additionally, CTE plays a crucial role in preparing the workforce by giving students the information, abilities, and skills they need to succeed in the job market (Baxter, 2012). Regrettably, in 2011, the Perkins Act budget/funding was lowered to $140.2 million. In addition to $37.3 million in reductions for Basic State Grants, this significant budget decrease resulted in the termination of the Tech Prep program. Additionally, Baxter (2012) predicted budget and funding reductions for CTE in the near future.

School-to-Work Opportunities Act of 1994

The School-to-Work Act (STWOA) was created and enacted by Congress to solve the national shortage of skilled workers by applying a model of education to build a qualified workforce for the US economy by forming alliances and bringing together educators and companies (Gordon, 2014). To prepare students for the labor market and the transition from school to post-school employment in their local work market in partnership with local businesses and organizations, the STWOA is designed to equip them with the necessary competencies, skills, abilities, and knowledge about professions and occupations (Gordon, 2014).

No Child Left Behind Act of 2001

President George W. Bush signed the No Child Left Behind Act (NCLB) of 2001 in January 2002. The Elementary and Secondary Education Act (ESEA) was renewed by this statute (Gordon, 2014). This rule recalls a remarkable agreement on how to increase student performance at the elementary and secondary school levels in the US educational system. At the same time, this law's ability to prevent any primary or secondary student from remaining in a failed institution is crucial (Gordon, 2014).

According to Gordon (2014), opponents of the NCLB said that the law gave standardized testing an excessively high priority for assessing kids' learning and performance. Subsequently, the No Child Left Behind law was amended, modified, and reauthorized in 2015 (US Department of Education). The new law is referred to as the "Every Student Succeeds Act, 2015."

Family and Society Theories

The families of the people in the workforce, the upbringing they received, the society in which they participate, and the relationships they have all have an influence and effect on the ways in which they behave while at work and the decisions they make there. This portion of the study will examine some of the factors that have contributed to these impacts.

Figure 3.5 represents three theories and issues connected to and supporting the family and society theories.

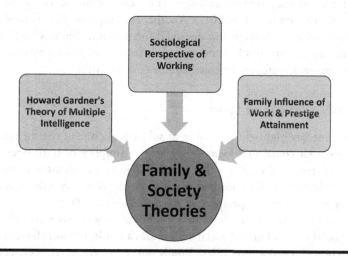

Figure 3.5   Three theories and issues connected to and supporting families and society theories. © Bakhshandeh 2024.

Howard Gardner's Theory of Multiple Intelligence

In 1983, an American developmental psychologist by the name of Howard Gardner proclaimed the nine different forms of intelligence that may be found in human beings (Vital, 2019):

1) Naturalist or nature smart.
2) Musical or sound smart.

3) Logical–mathematical or number and reasoning smart.
4) Existential or life smart.
5) Interpersonal or people smart.
6) Bodily-kinesthetic or body smart.
7) Linguistic or word smart.
8) Intrapersonal, or self-smart.
9) Spatial, or picture smart.

Of the above nine bits of intelligence, only interpersonal and intrapersonal intelligence and skills will be highlighted in this research. All nine bits of intelligence and skills are useful and intriguing to identify and relate to the growth of the workforce's abilities. The capacity to see, comprehend, and engage successfully with others is known as interpersonal intelligence.

A person with interpersonal skills may effectively communicate with others via both verbal and non-verbal means while taking note of their differences. They have the capacity to demonstrate sensitivity to the attitudes and personalities of others and to take into account different points of view that are raised throughout any discourse (Vital, 2019). Simply said, those who possess interpersonal skills are able to communicate and connect with others with ease as well as respect and comprehend those around them (Silberman, 2001). Interpersonally intelligent and skilled individuals frequently perform well in team and group contexts and communicate with others without difficulty (Gardner, 2006).

Intrapersonal intelligence is a set of abilities and capacities that serve as the foundation for growth and development. They are acknowledged as the core components and admirable traits of one's leadership abilities (Sheck & Lin, 2015). Another technique to differentiate and define self-awareness or introspection is through intrapersonal intelligence. Those with high intrapersonal intelligence are the most aware and in tune with their intents, motives, emotions, and beliefs, as well as possessing goal- and outcome-oriented abilities (Vital, 2019).

Sociological Perspectives of Work

Basic sociological concepts highlight a number of subjects. As one of the themes, proponents of this concept suggest that contextual factors may help to simplify or limit one's behavior (Gray & Herr, 1998). "The structural elements that influence human decisions and their effects on the network of roles in which labor is performed, as well as who plays what roles and why, are among the emphasis areas of a sociological perspective" (Gray & Herr, 1998, p. 92).

This viewpoint, which is a basic tenet in sociological viewpoints on work, maintains that labor is a type of social institution and social activity. As a result, the workforce is carrying out its tasks inside a web of social tasks and duties. Simply put, every employee is engaged in a network of interactions at any given time, directly with co-workers, managers, supervisors, or clients, and indirectly with shareholders and investors they don't see or interact with on a daily basis (Gray & Herr, 1998).

Family Influences of Work and Prestige Attainment

Numerous study findings, according to Gray and Herr (1998), indicated and suggested that a family's socioeconomic situation is profoundly significant and connected to the development of careers, professional choices, and socialization of children. According to Hotchkiss, Borow, and Brooks (1990, p. 267), as stated in Gray and Herr (1998, p. 105), "The social status of one's parents affects the level of schooling one achieves, which in turn affects the occupational level that one may achieve."

Families' socioeconomic status has an impact on the knowledge they acquire about employment, working, and the kinds of jobs they will be able to access. Additionally, the financial level of a family has an impact on an individual's advancement of professional preconceptions, which will have an impact on the development of occupational interests (Gray & Herr, 1998).

Other Relevant Issues

There are other difficulties that should be brought up in addition to all of the ideas and problems mentioned above that are confronted by the labor force and employers.

Figure 3.6 represents three theories and issues connected and supporting the other relevant issues.

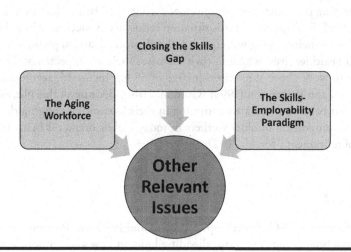

Figure 3.6 Three theories and issues connected to and supporting the other relevant issues.
© Bakhshandeh 2024.

Closing the Skills Gap

Many studies (Reese, 2011; Shatkin, 2011; US Chamber of Commerce Institute for a Competitive Workforce, 2012) have revealed that there is a skills gap between the workforce's talents and the skills that employers are looking for, according to Gordon (2014). According to a 2013 article by "Manpower Group" forecasting bleak employment prospects for the newest members of the workforce, as many as 39% of persons under the age of 25 were either jobless or underemployed (Gordon, 2014, p. 389). In this regard, Gordon (2014) cited Yang's (2013) speculation that more than half of the positions and vocations in the professional industries now did not exist 25 years ago. "How do you prepare students for jobs that don't exist today?" (Gordon, 2014, p. 389). The US economy and sectors would require at least 4.7 million skilled workers with postsecondary qualifications by 2018, according to Gordon (2014), who cites a study report by Carnevale, Smith, and Strohl (2010).

The Skills-Employability Paradigm

According to Gordon (2014), all industrialized countries adopted the idea of a skills-employability paradigm by the end of the 19th and the beginning of the 20th centuries, which connected work training and growth with personal independence and social integration. It is impossible to over-state this paradigm's strength and beneficial effect. One of the main reasons workforce educa-tion—in this example, employment and training programs—figures prominently in practically every social program globally is the conviction in the "skills-employability" paradigm (Gordon, 2014, p. 9). Notably, workforce education may be found all over the world in schools, prisons, wel-fare program training, for displaced workers, and for individuals with disabilities (Gordon, 2014).

The Aging Workforce

One of the biggest possibilities and difficulties for the workforce and companies in the US is the increase in the aging population (Gordon, 2014). The growth of elder population cohorts is "a sig-nificant factor shaping the future demographics of the US population" (Gordon, 2014, p. 295). In this regard, Gordon (2014) noted that this situation is due to advancements in public health issues and more effective medicine, along with quick technological advances, giving the US older popu-lation better and healthier lives, which in turn increases their life expectancy. The desire of older adult Americans to work above the retirement age of 65 has increased, according to the Centers for Disease Control and Prevention (1999) (Gordon, 2014). Because of this phenomenon, experts are discovering that baby boomers are continuing in their jobs and prolonging their employment. The growth in the proportion of older workers in today's labor market is being impacted by this postponement of retirement (Toossi, 2012).

What Is Next?

We move on to Chapter 4, "4Cs Skills Gap: A Present and Persistent Problem for Organizations." Chapter 4 acts as a brief literature review, shedding light on how and for how long the 4Cs skills gap is a problem for organizations, pointing out academic and professional research and evidence, examining the role of educational systems and other aspects of private and government sectors in the raising of such a problem.

References

Baxter, J. (2012). C.T.E. funding: An uphill battle. *Techniques, 87*(2), 20–23. Retrieved from https://search
    -proquest-com.ezaccess.libraries.psu.edu/docview/927664723/C9249CC16C594E50PQ.
Carnevale, A. P., Smith, N., & Strohl, J. (2010). *Help Wanted: Projections of Job and Education Requirements
    Through 2018*. Lumina Foundation.
Gardner, H. (2006). *Multiple Intelligences: New Horizons*. New York, NY: Basic Books.
Gordon, H. R. D. (2014). *The History and Growth of Career and Technical Education in America* (4th ed.).
    Long Grove, IL: Waveland Press, Inc.
Gray, K. C. & Herr, E. L. (1998). *Workforce Education: The Basics*. Boston, MA: Allyn & Bacon.
Herzberg, F., Mausner, B., & Snyderman, B. (1959). *The Motivation to Work*. New York: John Wiley &
    Sons, Inc.
Hotchkiss, L., Borow, H., Brown, D., & Brooks, L. (1990). *Career Choice and Development*. Newbury Park,
    CA: Sage Publications, Inc.

Mar, R. A. (2004). The neuropsychology of narrative: Story comprehension, story production and their interrelation. *Neuropsychologia, 42*(10), 1414–1434. https://doi.org/10.1016/j.neuropsychologia.2003 .12.016.

Mitchell, T. R. (1997). Matching motivational strategies with organizational contexts. *Research in Organizational Behavior, 19,* 57–149.

Parnell, D. (1996). Cerebral context. *Vocational Education Journal, 71*(3), 18. Retrieved from https://eric.ed .gov/?id=EJ519286.

Reese, W. J. (2011). *America's Public Schools: From the Common School to "No Child Left Behind".* Baltimore, MD: Johns Hopkins University Press.

Shatkin, G. (2011). Planning privatopolis: Representation and contestation in the development of urban integrated mega-projects. In A. Roy & A. Ong (Eds.), *Worlding Cities: Asian Experiments and the Art of Being Global* (pp. 77–97). Chichester: Blackwell.

Sheck, Daniel T. L. & Lin, L. (2015). Intrapersonal competencies and service leadership. *International Journal of Disability Human Development, 14*(3), 255–263. https://doi.org/10.1515/ijdhd-2015-0406.

Silberman, M. (2001). Developing interpersonal intelligence in the workplace. *Industrial and Commercial Training, 33*(6), 266–269. Retrieved from https://search-proquest-com.ezaccess.libraries.psu.edu/ docview/214108163.

Spector, P. E. & Jex, S. M. (1991). Relations of job characteristics from multiple data sources with employee affect, absence, turnover intentions, and health. *Journal of Applied Psychology, 76*(1), 46–53. https:// doi.org/10.1037/0021-9010.76.1.46.

Toossi, M. (2012, January). Labor force projections to 2020: A more slowly growing workforce. *Monthly Labor Review,* 43–64. Retrieved from http://www.jstor.org/stable/monthlylaborrev.2012.01.043.

US Chamber of Commerce, Institute for a Competitive Workforce. (2012). Institute for a competitive workforce highlights link between education, national security. Retrieved from https://www.uscham-ber.com/press-release/institute-competitive-workforce-highlights-link-between-education-national -security.

US Department of Education. (2015). Every Student Succeeds Act (Reauthorization of Elementary and Secondary Education Act of 1965), Pub. L. No. 114-95, S. 1177.

Vital, M. (2019). Nine types of intelligence. Infographic. Adioma website. Retrieved from https://blog.adi-oma.com/9-types-of-intelligence-infographic/.

Yang, D. (2013, August). Can we fix the skills gap? [Web log post]. Retrieved from http://www.forbes.com /sites/groupthink/2013/08/02/can-we-fix-the-skills-gap/.

Zhao, X., Ghiselli. R., Law, R., & Ma, J. (2016). Motivating frontline employees: Role of job characteristics in work and life satisfaction. *Journal of Hospitality and Tourism Management, 27,* 27–38. https://doi .org/10.1016/j.jhtm.2016.01.010.

Chapter 4

4Cs Skills Gap: A Present and Persistent Problem for Organizations—A Brief Literature Review

Introduction

Skills like critical thinking, communication, creativity, collaboration, and teamwork are not new to the world of work or organizations in the context of business and productivity. However, they are significantly more in demand among new employees in the 21st century (Soulé & Warrick, 2015). Employers that are searching for candidates who can do more than simply a routine job or task strongly encourage and demand the capacity to accomplish a variety of non-routine jobs in the highly technological and fast-paced work environment (Boyles, 2012). A key requirement for success on an individual level, as well as in teams and organizations as a whole, is having competence in these areas (Boyles, 2012).

It is essential for recent high school graduates to have a fundamental knowledge of these critical abilities, given that firms want to hire candidates who are equipped with 21st-century 4Cs. They must develop the habit of thinking critically about their future planning and communicating effectively and skillfully during their hiring or administration interviews, regardless of whether they want to attend college, a vocational school, a university, or immediately enter the workforce after high school (Soulé & Warrick, 2015). Students have a higher chance of competing for employment in the market if they acquire cooperation as a talent. Critical thinking and problem-solving abilities are also referred to as survival skills by Soulé and Warrick (2015), not only for success in one's profession or job but also for one's personal and social survival.

This chapter explores the following topics:

- What Is the Problem?
- Is This Problem a Failure of the Education System?
- Soft Skills Are as Important as Cognitive Skills.
- Help from the 21st Century Teaching and Learning Environment.

DOI: 10.4324/9781003462316-5

- Strategies for Integration of Soft Skills and 4Cs Skills.
- Student-Centered Approach and Developing Soft Skills and 4Cs Skills.

What Is the Problem?

According to Cappelli (2015), the arguments that are connected to the current difficulties regarding the availability of talent in the labor market may be broken down into the following three categories:

Skills Gap

The main gripe is the assertion that the vast shortage of workers with the most basic abilities is due to new hires rather than the existing labor force. This argument's proponents blame the deficiencies and breakdowns in the present educational system, particularly difficulties with K–12 public education, for this shortage (Cappelli, 2015).

Skills Shortage

The criticism places emphasis on job and task-related abilities that are tied to specific vocations, such as a complaint about the lack of engineers and professionals working in information technology in the United States (Cappelli, 2015).

Skills Problems

Most people outside the United States have voiced worry about this. People who are upset about this believe that there is always a risk of an imbalance between the supply and demand for skilled labor, leading to either an overstock or an undersupply. According to educational qualifications and the nation's development level, this problem frequently arises in a particular job market (Cappelli, 2015).

Is This Problem a Failure of the Education System?

In their article about the framework of Partnership for 21st Century Learning, or P21, Soulé and Warrick (2015) pointed to what they called a "widespread consensus" regarding how the education structure has failed to make students ready for critical 21st-century skills needed in order to succeed in school and work, as well as in life and citizenship in general. "Low performance across core content areas persists according to data for fourth and eighth graders for the 2011 National Assessment of Educational Progress" (Soulé & Warrick, 2015, p. 178).

P21 Approach

The Partnership for 21st Century Learning (P21), according to Soulé and Warrick (2015), is a top non-profit organization dedicated to fostering collaboration with the educational system, educators, business leaders, and policymakers to develop strategies and policies that will better prepare students to meet the rising global demand for skilled workers and citizens equipped with 21st-century skills. "P21 is a coalition of education, business, community, and government leaders working to help build a broader awareness of the importance of a 21st century education system" (Soulé & Warrick, 2015, p. 178).

Math Proficiency

Only 34% of fourth and eighth graders achieved proficiency in reading, according to Soulé and Warrick (2015), who used data from the Institute of Education Sciences (2011). In contrast, 40% of fourth graders and 35% of eighth graders achieved proficiency in arithmetic. In a similar vein, just 32% of eighth-grade pupils were considered to be adept in scientific studies. The worrying reality is that, regrettably, there hasn't been a significant shift in the statistics over the past ten years. Knowing that the data was just based on fundamental skills raises the worrying fear that these students may struggle in their further education programs or that there is now a significant need for qualified workers across all industries (Soulé & Warrick, 2015).

Push for College

When Hirsch and Alliance (2017) mentioned that there is a big effort to attract high school kids to attend college, they also highlighted this issue. A college education is supposed to expand students' knowledge, intellectual capacity, and skill sets, positioning them for future employment opportunities with high compensation. But few students enroll in college or finish their degrees. Only 30% of Black and Hispanic students enroll in college within the first two years of graduating from high school, and only about 20% earn an associate degree or higher by the time they are in their twenties, according to findings of a national analysis of study data correlated to these students (Hirsch & Alliance, 2017).

Need More Than Career Technical Programs

Additionally, Hirsch and Alliance (2017) noted that career–technical programs account for the majority of efforts made in today's high schools to prepare students for the workforce. Despite initiatives to combine academic and professional–technical learning, such as "career academies," high schools continue to emphasize trade skills as a pathway to future employment prospects. "Students in academic tracks receive little or no job preparation. In part, this reflects the enormous cultural gap between academic and career-technical tracks. Those who teach traditional academic courses often don't see a fit with trade skills" (Hirsch & Alliance 2017, p. 13).

Lack of Urgency

The aforementioned worry was also expressed by Martz et al. (2016), who highlighted the findings' inconsistency with a pressing call for the requirement to teach students critical thinking and problem-solving skills and expressed their concern with the findings of recent studies on the lack of skills in students and the workforce. Two studies that show the skills gap and the need for skills training among students and the workforce were also mentioned by Martz et al. (2016). The International Data Corporation (IDC) conducted the study, "Skills Requirements for Tomorrow's Best Jobs," in 2013. In this study, the researchers examined 14.6 million job placements where companies sought candidates with the necessary qualifications to fill high-growth, high-paying roles (Martz et al., 2016).

Over 50% of the high-growth, high-wage occupations assessed by IDC identified problem-solving abilities as "cross-functional" competencies necessary for success. Additionally, America's Skills Challenge performed the Educational Testing Service (ETS) research in 2015, comparing American 16–35-year-olds to similar age groups abroad. According to the ETS study, among a total of 21 sets of groups from various nations, the American group came in at number 20 in terms of preparation for critical thinking and problem-solving abilities (Martz et al., 2016).

Essentials for Senior Management

The organization's interest in 21st-century skills is further evidenced by survey and research findings. Robles (2012) performed a study to ascertain what employers needed from their workforces in terms of critical soft skills. These can be created and added to the curriculum by an expert in business and career development. Robles (2012) utilized 45 students from a junior-level business communication class for his study. Each student was requested to interview two company leaders and then send the executives a "Thank You" card and an assessment form that the course instructors had created. The students also included a self-addressed stamped envelope for the executives' convenience and to guarantee that they would get the survey back.

In addition to asking executives to comment on how well students performed during the interview process, the survey also asked executives to list the top 10 essential and desired soft skills they wished to see among the workforce in their organizations (Robles, 2012). Forty-nine company leaders out of a total of 90 responded to the poll (54%). After deleting duplicate abilities from the list of 517 reported soft talents (some CEOs reported more than 10 soft skills), 490 of them were gathered. After coding with related phrases and concepts, the final selection of 26 soft talents was made. The following are the top 10 soft talents chosen by business executives: "integrity, communication, courtesy, responsibility, social skills, positive attitude, professionalism, flexibility, teamwork, and work ethic" (Robles, 2012, p. 454).

Soft Skills Are as Important as Cognitive Skills

Soft skills, according to Robles (2012), are as important as cognitive skills. Soft skills development gives students a significantly higher chance of landing a job in their selected sector. Students who possess technical expertise and professional abilities but lack people skills may find their career chances severely hampered by a lack of soft skills. Robles (2012) went on to say that effective managers who were promoted and had continuing progress in their businesses have both hard and soft talents, particularly the attitude and capacity to work well with others. According to Robles (2012) and the National Union of Students in the UK, employers throughout the country are becoming increasingly concerned about the lack of soft skills among recent high school graduates.

Seventy percent of high school graduates lack professionalism and work ethic in the job, according to a 2007 poll of 400 managers from US firms. Robles (2012) also cited a different survey from the US Department of Labor, which showed that despite corporate managers' interest in and value for interpersonal skills, new hires, recent college graduates, and labor they are recruiting do not share these beliefs. Employers are still concerned about the shortage of soft skills.

Help from the 21st-Century Teaching and Learning Environment

Mr. Matsuda, the superintendent of the Anaheim Union High School District (AUHSD) in California, presented his insights about the administration recruitment process in 2016. He added that one of the most crucial inquiries they ask prospective employees is, "Can you please describe a 21st century learning environment?" (Matsuda, 2017, p. 26). The majority of candidates who were interviewed for possible administrator positions related the idea of 21st-century teaching and learning to the "fields of information technology, electronic devices, internet use, and communication methods via smart devices" (Matsuda, 2017, p. 26).

Implementing Technology

This phenomenon, which Matsuda (2017) referred to as an urban educational myth, requires additional clarification and discussion. Candidates occasionally mention pedagogy as a means of imparting the 4Cs, but technology should be viewed as a means of enhancing and developing abilities other than the 4Cs, such as reading, writing, listening, and speaking. However, those applicants frequently fail to capture the full scope of the "Partnership for 21st Century Learning," or P21 initiative, in their descriptions of 21st-century education, teaching, and learning environments ("Partnership for 21st Century Learning," 2016; Matsuda, 2017).

P21 Challenging 21st-Century Education

Regarding the validity and viability of P21 (2016) programs, Matsuda (2017) discussed how P21 programs force 21st-century educationalists to consider the goal of American K–12 education in a world beset by ambiguity and confusion regarding numerous global issues, including but not limited to, climate issues, geopolitical skirmishes, alternative energy to fossil fuels, health care, and workable economies. P21 (2016) urges teachers to address fascinating issues like "How are we going to prepare the next generation of Americans to meet the challenges of an increasingly complex and interconnected global society? What are the skills, dispositions, and knowledge needed to get there?" (Matsuda, 2017, p. 26).

The P21 programs are increasingly emphasizing critical thinking, creativity, communication, and teamwork (Jones, 2015). In order to emphasize the critical role of 4Cs skill education in daily pedagogy and instruction in school systems, the P21 program foundation has done so (Matsuda, 2017). P21 encourages students to access a far wider range of subjects than only testing, assessments, and passing examinations, such as math, the arts, language, music, and more. The 4Cs are being pushed into the existing educational curricula by P21 (Matsuda, 2017).

Recognizing the Value of Soft Skills

Schweppe and Geigel (2011) noted the growing importance and acceptance of soft skills in recent years at the same time. For instance, to improve students' preparation for the actual business world, numerous worldwide academic institutions have advocated on integrating soft skills into technical programs and subjects, including accounting, engineering, computer graphics, and information technology (Schweppe & Geigel, 2011). According to Charoensap-Kelly et al. (2016), from the perspective of human resource management, integrating soft skills into the workforce will enable all employees, including supervisors and coworkers, to collaborate more effectively. Learning, putting into practice, and honing social, practical, and soft skills foster a welcoming and secure work environment that boosts productivity and enables employees to excel in their jobs (Charoensap-Kelly et al., 2016).

According to Hirsch and Alliance (2017), instructors have the capacity to help students enhance their soft skills: "Teachers may not be aware that they are teaching a variety of important soft skills in their classes" (p. 17). If professional development sessions were implemented, teachers would be better able to recognize the need for both hard and soft skills in the workplace and, as a result, teach the same abilities to their students in the classrooms (Hirsch & Alliance, 2017).

Strategies for Integration of Soft Skills and 4Cs Skills

According to a literature review conducted by Levin-Goldberg (2012), "Teaching Generation TechX with the 4Cs: Using Technology to Integrate 21st Century Skills," the author offered several pedagogical suggestions that teachers and educators may use to integrate the 4Cs along with other important abilities like innovation and problem-solving into the curriculum at their respective schools. These techniques, when combined with technology, can produce a more thorough teaching and learning environment and create an area where 21st-century abilities can be fostered (Levin-Goldberg, 2012).

Readiness

According to Levin-Goldberg (2012), the following strategies will serve as the most comprehensive, natural, and real examples of preparation for the twenty-first century: "(a) becoming cognizant and literate in Web 2.0 tools; (b) assigning real-world problems and issues for students to resolve using technology; and (c) creating collaborative problem-based learning experiences utilizing the resources available via the Web" (p. 61).

This finding was part of the overall findings of a survey conducted of over 400 organization executives about the significance of the 4Cs to their organizations and their desire to hire a workforce with the 4Cs skills, according to Levin-Goldberg (2012). The survey was steered by a coalition of several organizations, including the Corporate Voices for Working Families, The Conference Board, the Partnership for 21st Century Skills, and the Society for Human Resource Management. Nearly 50% of new graduates, according to participants, lacked the following:

a) The ability to communicate effectively orally as well as in writing.
b) An ethical and professional approach to work and the workplace.
c) The ability to analyze critically and solve problems.

Leadership Skills

In addition to this survey, Levin-Goldberg (2012) noted that the American Society of Training and Development polled some executives and higher managers in 2009, and the results showed that 50% of respondents thought their workforces lacked the most insufficient level of leadership skills in relation to decision-making, goal-setting, ethical judgment, motivation, and team-building. In the same survey, 46% of participants selected fundamental abilities like critical thinking and problem-solving as most compatible with the abilities they want in their existing employees or prospective hires. Additionally, according to 97% of employers who took part in a survey by The

Conference Board in 2011 about employees' skills, creativity is one of the executive positions that is most in-demand when it comes to hiring new employees (Levin-Goldberg, 2012).

Variety of Soft Skills

The relevant subjects are being attempted to be covered by teachers in their curricula (Robles, 2012). Given that the majority of instructors already have to cope with a constrained program schedule, asking them to add another topic, like soft skills, to their class schedule might be challenging (Robles, 2012). What can schools do, then, to prepare children for interpersonal professional connections, office work (soft skills), and high-tech/high-paying employment (hard skills)? He suggested instructing students with some strategies listed below, which include soft skills into the already hectic school curriculum by dispersing the material throughout the course of the semester:

a) Teaching students fundamental social skills such as how to interact with and get along with others.
b) Introducing customer service abilities that are fundamentally straightforward.
c) Gaining a grasp of the process of problem-solving and having a debate about it through role-playing real-life events.
d) Working with other people by demonstrating how the interpersonal skills they've acquired may be applied in a professional setting.

A developmental program for teaching soft skills is necessary beyond the school environment to help students apply their learning at work, as well as at home and in society. This will help students acquire these skills. "Research indicates that the typical learning styles of all students are not necessarily suited to the acquisition of generic skills" (Robles, 2012, p. 462).

Student-Centered Approach and Developing Soft Skills and 4Cs Skills

The value of teaching the 4Cs skills and soft skills in today's schools cannot be overstated. Giving students real-world experiences would improve their understanding of these crucial abilities (Robb, 2017). She stressed the significance of this strategy by emphasizing that all activities children engage in while in school should contribute to the development of the 4Cs. According to Robb (2017) and Soulé and Warrick (2015), this strategy would aid in the development of interpersonal and analytical skills to help people shape their minds to solve problems in their immediate surroundings as well as in national and international issues like clean water, clean air, climate change, immigration, and many other problems facing humanity.

Debates and Discussions

By fostering learning via conversations, debates, and reflections rather than in a regimented classroom setting with exams, assignments, quizzes, and presentations of questions with a single correct response, schools may create the 4Cs curriculum with a student-centered approach. Daily sessions in the classroom can include open conversations led by students and assisted by qualified teachers (Robb, 2017). College graduates believe they are prepared for employment and ready to join the professional workforce since they have developed and acquired the necessary abilities. This theory might not hold true, though, when it comes to soft talents. Many college graduates, including some MBA graduates, have shown a lack of critical soft skills in their written and verbal communication as well as in their interpersonal relationships with their coworkers, according to several reports (Anthony & Garner, 2016; Charoensap-Kelly et al., 2016; Stewart et al., 2016).

Collaborating Groups

Robb (2017) proposed that in these kinds of learning environments, students will establish a collaborative group or choose one or more partners to compose a conversation by formulating questions or inquiries. This will boost the efficacy of students' communication abilities. Typically, the group or partners decide on a timeframe for the discussion, select a student facilitator to keep things on track, and ensure that the conversation is constructive (Robb, 2017). She also mentioned that during conversations, pupils are in direct contact with one another. According to Robb (2017), Soulé and Warrick (2015), and Moore (2013), it is they who direct the discourse and present their views in a way that their peers can understand, relate to, and listen to (Robb, 2017).

Students will remember details of their discussions and what other students say during the dialogue as a result of these expressive conversations, as well as the meaningful and authentic learning environment, and they will be able to cite examples that will support their way of thinking and how they express their ideas (Robb, 2017).

What Is Next?

Now that we conducted a brief literature review on the actual problem and what would help resolve such a problem, we continue to Chapter 5 and discuss the impact of the 4Cs skills gap in the economy.

References

Anthony, S. & Garner, B. (2016). Teaching soft skills to business students: An analysis of multiple pedagogical methods. *Business and Professional Communication Quarterly, 79*(3), 360–370. https://doi.org/10.1177/2329490616642247.

Boyles, T. (2012). 21st century knowledge, skills, and abilities and entrepreneurial competencies: A model for undergraduate entrepreneurship education. *Journal of Entrepreneurship Education, 15*, 41–55. Retrieved from https://www.abacademies.org/articles/jeevol152012.pdf#page=47.

Cappelli, P. H. (2015). Skill gaps, skill shortages, and skill mismatches: Evidence and arguments for the United States. *ILR Review, 68*(2), 251–290. https://doi.org/10.1177/0019793914564961.

Charoensap-Kelly, P., Broussard, L., Lindsly, M., & Troy, M. (2016). Evaluation of a soft skills training program. *Business and Professional Communication Quarterly, 79*(2), 154–179. https://doi.org/10.1177/2329490615602090.

Hirsch, B. & Alliance, D. (2017). Wanted: Soft skills for today's jobs. *The Phi Delta Kappan, 98*(5), 12–17. https://doi.org/10.1177/0031721717690359.

Jones, V. R. (2015, September). 21st century skills: Collaboration. *Children's Technology and Engineering, 20*(1), 24–26. Retrieved from https://www.iteea.org/CTESeptember2015.aspx.

Levin-Goldberg, J. (2012). Teaching generation techX with the 4Cs: Using technology to Integrate 21st century skills. *Journal of Instructional Research*, 1, 59–66. Retrieved from https://eric.ed.gov/?id =EJ1127608.

Martz, B., Hughes, J., & Braun, F. (2016). Creativity and problem-solving: Closing the skills gap. *The Journal of Computer Information Systems*, *57*(1), 39–48. https://doi.org/10.1080/08874417.2016 .118149.

Matsuda, M. (2017). Global education in the 21st century. *Social Studies Review*, 55, 26–30. Retrieved from http://ezaccess.libraries.psu.edu/login?url=https://search-proquest-com.ezaccess.libraries.psu .edu/docview/1896260514?accountid=13158.

Moore, T. (2013). Critical thinking: Seven definitions in search of a concept. *Studies in Higher Education*, *38*(4), 506–522. doi: 10.1080/03075079.2011.586995.

Partnership for 21st Century Learning (2016). Framework for 21st century learning: Communication and collaboration. Retrieved from www.p21.org/about-us/p21framework/261.

Robb, L. (2017). Read talk write: Developing 21st-century skills. *Voices from the Middle*, *24*(4), 19–23. Retrieved from http://www.ncte.org/library/NCTEFiles/Resources/Journals/VM/0244-may2017/ VM0244Leading.pdf.

Robles, M. M. (2012). Executive perceptions of the top 10 soft skills needed in today's workplace. *Business Communication Quarterly*, *75*(4), 453–465. https://doi.org/10.1177/1080569912460400.

Schweppe, M. & Geigel, J. (2011). Live theater on a virtual stage: Incorporating soft skills and teamwork in computer graphics education. *IEEE Computer Graphics and Applications*, *31*(1), 85–89. https://doi .org/10.1109/MCG.2011.9.

Soulé, H. & Warrick, T. (2015). Defining 21st century readiness for all students: What we know and how to get there. *Psychology of Aesthetics, Creativity, and the Arts*, *9*(2), 178–186. https://doi.org/10.1037/ aca0000017.

Stewart, C., Wall, A., & Marciniec, S. (2016). Mixed signals: Do college graduates have the soft skills that employers want? *Competition Forum*, *14*(2), 276–281. Retrieved from https://search.proquest.com/ openview/fa7c5369a44d3fc071a43203a1ef6d5e/1?pq-origsite=gscholarcbl=39801.

Chapter 5

Impact of 4Cs Skills Gap on the Economy

Introduction

When compared to the economies of the 20th or 19th centuries, the 21st-century economy has grown more swiftly and furiously than is typical (Tindowen, Bassig, & Cagurangan, 2017). The social and economic fabric of the workforce and organizations have changed as a result of the rapid advancement of technology, the rapid growth of the global economy, and severe rivalry on both a national and worldwide scale (Soulé & Warrick, 2015). Organizations are becoming more and more aware of the value of competencies and abilities and how they play a part in finding, attracting, and keeping excellent people who have a positive influence on the expansion and success of their businesses.

Tulgan (2015) suggested that compared to hard talents, soft skills may be seen as being less tangible and more difficult to define and quantify. However, soft skills are essential to one's personal and professional success or failure in the workplace. They also have an indirect impact on companies, costs, employee growth, and stability. Tulgan (2015) also voiced concern that it would be too late to address and improve these issues by the time the younger generation entered the workforce and employers realized their lack of soft skills.

The skills gap is a problem that affects the entire world, not just the United States and other countries separately. There are many more countries where a lack of education and, eventually, a trained labor force is causing social problems.

This chapter briefly explores the following elements:

- Distinguishing Skills, Competencies, and Training.
- The 21st-Century Economy Link to 4Cs and Soft Skills Gap.
- Position of Competencies and Skills in Economy.
- Competencies in Performance Gap.

Distinguishing Skills, Competencies, and Training

This section defines and describes several key terminologies in the context of professional business and organization development and training to help readers better understand the differences

DOI: 10.4324/9781003462316-6

between the terms, particularly in relation to the development of the 4Cs through conducting training.

Skills

The talent and knowledge needed to carry out a job or complete a task are called skills. Skills are what give people the self-assurance they need to succeed in their endeavors. Almost every ability can be learned, developed, and improved, albeit doing so does need practice and willpower (Donahue, 2018). According to Rothwell (2015), competence is the capacity to carry out an activity or job with predetermined results within a predetermined amount of time.

An individual's personal characteristics, knowledge, and talents are combined into a skillset during the course of their personal and professional lives. Two categories of talents are often included: soft skills and hard skills.

Soft Skills

Interpersonal or people abilities are included in this list. These abilities are hard to measure, but in a broad sense, they constitute the individuals' personalities and capacities for collaboration. The ability to think critically, solve problems, communicate effectively, listen objectively, show empathy, and many other qualities are among these.

Hard Skills

These abilities are observable and measurable. They contain a few particular technical and profession-related skills and information needed to complete a task or job. Accounting, computer programming, mathematics, and data analysis are examples of hard talents.

Competencies

Competency has been used frequently without a clear understanding of what it means or the context in which it is employed. The term "competence" refers to a level of individual proficiency in the contexts of business and education, such as knowledge, abilities, attitudes, and behaviors measured against a set of rules and accepted norms (Donahue, 2018). Competency and competence are frequently used synonymously in certain older writings. Organizations rely on the skills of their employees, but over time, there appeared to be a shift in workplace learning that emphasized both individual and organizational competencies (Newhard, 2010).

The following are some of the definitions of competencies by professionals and academia:

- "measurable and observable knowledge, skills, attitudes, and behaviors (KSABs) critical to successful job performance. Competencies refer to the specific KSABs that a person can readily show. They include not only technical skills but also what are known as soft skills" (Donahue, 2018, p. 21).
- "an underlying characteristic of an individual that is causally related to criterion-referenced effective and or superior performance in a job or situation, where 'criterion-reference' indicates that competency will predict performance" (Spencer & Spencer, 1993, p. 9).

- ■ ""certain characteristics or abilities of the person [that] enable him or her to demonstrate the appropriate specific actions" (Boyatzis, 1982, p. 12).
- ■ "a personal capability that is critical to the production of a quality output or outputs" (McLagan, 1988, p. 374).

According to Spencer and Spencer (1993), who were cited by Newhard (2010), McClelland (1973, pp. 9–11) identified the following five abilities that might help people better comprehend the idea of competency (see Table 5.1).

Table 5.1   Five Abilities of Competency

#	Abilities	Descriptions
1	Motives	The things that a person thinks about or wants on a regular basis and that drive them to behave.
2	Traits	Physical traits as well as reliable responses to different types of information or situations.
3	Self-Concept	The attitudes, values, or a self-image that a person possesses.
4	Knowledge	The information that a person possesses in relation to particular subject areas.
5	Skills	The capacity to successfully carry out a certain mental or physical activity.

Note. Adapted from McClelland (1973, pp. 9–11).

Training

The term "training" has been defined in a variety of ways in professional fields. One of the concepts that apply to the field of organizational development, according to Rothwell and Sredl (2014), is "learning, provided by employers to employees, that is related to their present jobs" (Nadler & Nadler, 1989, pp. 9–10). In addition, Lawrie described it as a "change in skills" (1990), which Rothwell and Sredl noted. Others assert that its primary objective is to provide students with the fundamental information and abilities they need to do everyday activities related to their current employment (Bartz, Schwandt, & Hillman, 1989).

Training is also referred to as a short-term learning intervention with the goal of building people's knowledge, abilities, and attitudes to put together their work requirements at their professions. Knowledge, skills, and individual attitudes are all used to refer to the realities, facts, standards, and information that are necessary for carrying out a job or task in this particular business and organizational context (Rothwell & Sredl, 2014). Individual attitudes are the feelings and emotions that individuals express. "Training helps individuals meet minimally acceptable job requirements or refine, upgrade, and improve what they presently do. When employees finish their training, they should be able to apply it immediately" (Rothwell & Sredl, 2014, p. 9).

The 21st Century Economy Link to the 4Cs and Soft Skills Gap

When compared to the economies of the 20th or 19th centuries, the 21st-century economy has grown more swiftly and furiously than typical (Tindowen et al., 2017). The workforce and organizations' social and economic life have changed as a result of rapid technological advancement, the rapid growth of the global economy, and severe domestic and international rivalry (Soulé & Warrick, 2015). According to Soulé and Warrick (2015), the nature of shifting work settings is real: "The world we live in today has changed dramatically in the last several decades, presaging even more dramatic changes for what our world will look like when today's students enter the workforce" (p. 178).

As of now, workforce preparation for the 21st century is emerging as a crucial component and the focal point of such growth and development that would enable any firm to thrive healthily and sustainably (Soulé & Warrick, 2015). To be able to deliver goods and services that will aid companies in their survival and growth, employment in the 21st century will require workers to possess the skills and competencies of the modern era. Our national and global economies require a workforce that has been educated and equipped with 21st-century skills and competencies, whether it be for boosting the economy, creating a new line of goods for manufacturing, putting in place a national health care system, or generating alternative energy. In order to develop the essential skills and raise our workforce's degree of excellence to a level we haven't seen before, education systems and present and future generations will face obstacles (Soulé & Warrick, 2015).

As we said at the beginning of the chapter, Tindowen et al. (2017) pointed out that the 21st century economy has grown at a much greater rate than the economies of the 20th and 19th centuries. Tulgan (2015) suggested that compared to hard talents, soft skills may be seen as being less tangible and more difficult to define and quantify. However, soft skills are unquestionably essential to one's success or failure in the workplace on a personal and professional level since they indirectly affect businesses, costs, employee growth, and stability. He also voiced concern that it would be too late to correct and develop by the time the younger generation entered the workforce and employers realized their lack of soft skills. Most managers have the mindset that they don't have the time or the willingness to teach the next generation essential soft skills. Because of this, the workforce soft skills gap is widening, regardless of the expense and harm to the company and, therefore, to the regional and global economies (Tulgan, 2015).

The distance between where our pupils are and where we want them to be, however, appears to be rather wide. In this regard, Soulé and Warrick (2015) referred to domestic education statistics that, on the one hand, according to recent trend data, display some improvement but, overall, point to a large gap between where students are and where they need to be—a generation of a highly educated population. This was stated in the Institute of Education Sciences (2011).

The following figures and percentages (see Table 5.2) provide a breakdown by race, comparing the level of competence achieved by pupils of white, Black, and Hispanic backgrounds in the fourth and eighth grades (Soulé & Warrick, 2015).

Table 5.2   Level of Competence. Archived by Students Based on Race

Group		Areas	Proficiency and Race
A	Fourth Grade	Reading	33% of Whites 14% of Blacks 16% of Hispanics
		Mathematics	48% of Whites 16% of Blacks 22% of Hispanics
B	Eighth Grade	Reading	38% of Whites 14% of Blacks 18% of Hispanics
		Mathematics	33% of Whites 12% of Blacks 18% of Hispanics
		Science	43% of Whites 10% of Blacks 16% of Hispanics

Note. IES (2011).

The skills gap is a problem that affects the entire world, not just the United States and other countries separately. There are many more countries where a lack of education and, eventually, a trained labor force, is causing social problems. In every country, especially those in the Third World, education is one of the most important factors in the development of a workforce and a healthy economy (Soulé & Warrick, 2015). The development of skills, knowledge, and competences is becoming more and more crucial for surviving the 21st-century economy as the quick spread of modern communication technologies and economics grow more global. This idea is crucial for emerging nations as much as for wealthy ones. For students in high schools and universities, the task of education on 21st-century skills is becoming considerably more crucial. Recognizing that most third-world nations maintain populations where formal education is a rarity is one of the most difficult truths for comprehending the link between education and economic performance (Tindowen et al., 2017).

The population of these developing nations has trouble comprehending and using the 21st-century abilities that can equip it for the challenges of the 21st-century economy and the pressures of global competitiveness (Tindowen et al., 2017). The Alternative Learning System (ALS) was made available in underdeveloped nations like the Philippines to help people by teaching them through this non-formal education system in order to address this societal challenge connected to job capabilities and education. Living in the 21st century necessitates an integrated awareness that knowledge of the task needs of a specific profession is just as important for both individual and business success as skill sets like the 4Cs. These skill sets include the capacity to think critically, solve problems, offer effective communication, and work with others. These are essentials for leading a fulfilling life and having a successful career (Tindowen et al., 2017). Robles (2012) emphasized the idea of soft skills, their universal applicability, and the fact that they may be applied to any field, occupation, or aspect of daily life. "Unlike hard skills, which are about a person's skill set and ability to perform a certain type of task or activity, soft skills are interpersonal and broadly applicable" (Robles, 2012, p. 457).

Position of Competencies and Skills in Economy

Present-day workplaces place high priority on displaying new and expanding abilities and skills, including the 4Cs, due to concerns about competition for a market share among national and international organizations. In fact, competencies and skills are essential for defining any profession because they give the workforce a common language to define the set of performances that point to the knowledge, abilities, and behaviors that employees, technicians, or practitioners need in order to succeed in their work. The 4C skills are also included in this body of knowledge (Arneson, Rothwell, & Naughton, 2013).

Organizations are becoming more and more aware of the value of competencies and abilities and how they play a part in finding, attracting, and keeping excellent people who have a positive influence on the expansion and success of their businesses. This realization has led to an increase in focus on competency-based learning and development by educational institutions in order to support the demands of a competency-based workforce for the current and future needs of the labor market (Rothwell, Stavros, & Sullivan, 2016; Cummings & Worley, 2015). In addition to the 4Cs of the 21st century, many firms are increasingly evaluating employee knowledge, skills, and abilities (KSA) through competency-based assessments. According to Rothwell et al. (2016), competency-based assessment is being recognized by businesses as a desirable and practical method for evaluating individuals, creating growth plans for them, and incorporating relevant abilities and skills into job descriptions and work duties.

Organizational development (OD) and training are no different from other industries in this sense. Any professionals, including Appreciative Inquiry (AI) coaches and facilitators or any other type of professional coaches and consultants, who practice OD, Workplace Learning and Performance (WLP), Training, Training and Development (T&D), excel at developing their knowledge, skills, and abilities (KSAs) in their careers and in identifying necessary competencies and skills to develop or fine-tune the existing ones.

Competencies in Performance Gap

According to Donahue (2018), the competence gap is defined as the difference between an individual's present competency level and the degree of competency that the business requires or needs. According to the same perspective, a performance gap is a difference between:

- What is occurring now, and
- What should be occurring, or
- What is anticipated to occur.

According to Rothwell (2015), a performance gap is the difference between how things are now and how they should be in light of requirements, goals, plans, or expectations.

What Is Next?

Part II of this book, reviewing models and methods for "Diagnosing the 4Cs Skills Gap and Evaluating Employees," begins with "Role of Needs Assessment in Competencies and Skills Development." In Chapter 6, we look at how organizations can use a needs assessment approach to identify 4Cs skills gap among their workforces.

References

Arneson, J., Rothwell, W., & Naughton, J. (2013). Training and development competencies redefined to create competitive advantage. *T+D, 67*(1), 42–47. Retrieved from https://www.proquest.com/docview /1270282908?accountid=13158&parentSessionId=9XS4yoQK9i61roVdrnDCTZj5BSgICZLEgt2 T2kwY40A%3D&pq-origsite=summon.

Bartz, D. E., Schwandt, D. R., & Hillman, L. W. (1989). Difference between "T" and "D". *Personnel Adm,* 164.

Boyatzis, R. E. (1982). *The Competent Manager: A Model for Effective Performance.* Hoboken, NJ: John Wiley & Sons.

Cummings, T. G. & Worley, C. G. (2015). *Organization Development & Change* (10th ed.). Stamford, CT: Cengage Learning.

Donahue, Wesley, E. (2018). *Building Leadership Competence. A Competency-Based Approach to Building Leadership Ability.* State College, PA: Centerstar Learning.

IES. (2011). Institute of Education Science. US Department of Education. Institute of Education Sciences. www.ies.ed.gov.

Lawrie, John (1990). Prepare for a performance appraisal. *Personnel Journal, 69*(4), 132–136. Retrieved from https://www.proquest.com/docview/219770364?accountid=13158&parentSessionId=mJSAs3 %2BDAnoZqeRO9sfOi7pap2LWKHjCr53ss8bhsVg%3D&pq-origsite=summon&sourcetype =Trade%20Journals.

McClelland, D. C. (1973). Testing for competence rather than for intelligence. *American Psychologist, 28*(1), 1–14.

McLagan, P. (1988). Top management support. *Training, 25*(5), 59–62.

Nadler, L. & Nadler, Z. (1989). *Developing Human Resources* (3rd ed.). San Francisco, CA: Jossey-Bass.

Newhard, Michele L. (2010). *An Exploratory Study of Competencies of Appreciative Inquiry Practitioners: Discovery.* (Published Dissertation). State Collage, PA: The Pennsylvania State University.

Soulé, H. & Warrick, T. (2015). Defining 21st century readiness for all students: What we know and how to get there. *Psychology of Aesthetics, Creativity, and the Arts, 9*(2), 178–186. https://doi.org/10.1037/ aca0000017.

Robles, M. M. (2012). Executive perceptions of the top 10 soft skills needed in today's workplace. *Business Communication Quarterly, 75*(4), 453–465. https://doi.org/10.1177/1080569912460400.

Rothwell, William J. (2015). *Organization Development Fundamentals: Managing Strategic Change.* Alexandria, WV: ATD Press.

Rothwell, William, J. & Sredl, Henry, J. (2014). *Workplace Learning and Performance: Present and Future Roles and Competencies* (Volume 1, 3rd ed.). Amherst, MA: HRD Press.

Rothwell, William J., Stavros, Jacqueline M., & Sullivan, Roland L. (2016). *Practicing Organization Development: Leading Transformation and Change* (4th ed.). Hoboken, NJ: John Wiley & Sons, Inc.

Spencer, L. M. & Spencer, S. M. (1993). *Competence at Work. Models for Superior Performance.* New York, NY: John Wiley and Sons.

Tindowen, C. D. J., Bassig, J. M., & Cagurangan, J. A. (2017). Twenty-first-century skills of alternative learning system learners. *SAGE Open, 7*(3), 1–8. https://doi.org/10.1177/2158244017726116.

Tulgan, B. (2015). *Bridging the Soft Skills Gap: How to Teach the Missing Basics to Today's Young Talent.* Hoboken, NJ. John Willey & Sons, Inc. https://doi.org/10.1002/9781119171409.

DIAGNOSING THE 4CS SKILLS GAP AND EVALUATING EMPLOYEES

Part II of this book is designated to use the existing models of diagnoses, analysis, and evaluation of the workforce on their 4Cs skills gap and how it impacts their organizations in their corresponding industries. Also, this part looks at how to evaluate and support students in acquiring 4Cs skills before joining the workforce.

Chapter 6: Role of Needs Assessment in Competencies and Skills Development

This chapter examines how organizations can use "needs assessment" approach to identify the 4Cs skills gap among their workforces.

Chapter 7: Identifying 4Cs Skills Gap Using Organization Diagnosis Models

This chapter looks at what organizations can use to recognize 4Cs skills gap among their workforces and to extend the workforces' development on 4Cs skills, or understand who needs to be more trained or developed on which of the 4Cs skills.

Chapter 8: Evaluating and Supporting Students and Workforce on Their Progress

This chapter looks at how to support and evaluate students before they enter the labor market, as well as how the existing workforce can determine their readiness and acquisition of 4Cs skills.

DOI: 10.4324/9781003462316-7

DIAGNOSING THE ACS SKILLS GAP AND EVALUATING EMPLOYEES

Chapter 6

Role of Needs Assessment in Competencies and Skills Development

Introduction

Businesses can identify areas within themselves and their operations that have room for growth by conducting a needs assessment. These areas can be in productivity, performance, delivery, customer service, communication, etc. To conduct a needs assessment, there is a need for data analysis and a guide for internal improvements by using a requirements assessment on the procedures that are currently in place. However, it may not always be easy to identify specific areas that may need some improvement. When you are confronted with a number of different opportunities, doing a requirements analysis can assist you in determining the most fruitful areas in which to make improvements.

What Is Needs Assessment?

The gap between the current state of affairs and the ideal state of affairs is referred to as a "need" in the disciplines of organizational development (OD), workforce education, and development (WFED), workplace learning and performance (WLP), and performance consulting. It would not be difficult to utilize the method of needs assessment to establish the degree of the 4Cs possessed by workers and the requirements that must be met for their training. A need is an area in which there is room for development within a certain procedure or system. If you can recognize and address requirements, you will be able to capitalize on potential new possibilities. Some examples of such opportunities include making procedures more effective, simplifying resource allocation, and locating resource gaps in your present workflow (see Figure 6.1).

Some definitions for needs assessment by professionals are as follows:

- "Needs assessment is a process for figuring out how to close a learning or performance gap" (Sleezer, Russ-Eft, & Gupta, 2015, p. 17).

DOI: 10.4324/9781003462316-8

- A needs assessment is a procedure for identifying the requirements, or "gaps," between an existing situation and the intended result. It is a component of strategic planning; simply, a requirements assessment aids in determining how your strategic goals will be achieved (Rothwell, 2015).
- "Needs assessments are tools you can use to gain valuable insights into a company's actions or processes to determine efficiency. This assessment can be part of a company's planning process to determine gaps or needs and how to address areas for improvement" (Indeed, 2022, n.p.).
- The needs assessment is a type of evaluation, and like any other kind of evaluation, it is affected by the manner in which the data is collected and evaluated (Cummings & Worley, 2015).

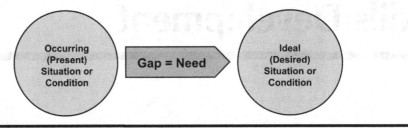

Figure 6.1   What is a need?   Note. Adapted from Sleezer, Russ-Eft, & Gupta (2015, p. 17).

Methods for Conducting Data Collection for Needs Assessment

A wide variety of approaches exist for collecting data, some of which are quantitative, such as surveys, and others, which are qualitative, such as focus groups. Before making a decision, you should consider whose perspective you are seeking because your target demographic may impact the approach you choose. Needs assessments offer teams essential data on the procedures that are currently in place and help them design more efficient methods. The following are some of the most common approaches to data collection for needs assessments (Gupta, Sleezer, & Russ-Eft, 2014; Wilmoth, Prigmore, & Bray, 2014).

Observation

This method is usually quite helpful for figuring out demands. The facilitator can utilize both structured and unstructured observations to enhance the information obtained through other means. You may watch a team meeting, a corporate meeting, an action planning meeting, an objectives review meeting, or simply regular business activities.

Document Review

Reviewing existing documents is one method of gathering data. The records of performance reviews, justifications for promotions or probations, records of training and development classes, manager and supervisor reports, program logs, meeting minutes, newsletters, or human resources policies and records of an individual or organization are a few examples of documents that may be internal or external to the organization. These records might be in physical copy or digital form.

Questionnaires/Surveys

The two most often used techniques for gathering data are questionnaires and interviews. A questionnaire is a simple form that asks broad yes/no questions. This is a fantastic technique to compile data from the responses quickly. Teams frequently use surveys to get outside data on customer experience. Open-ended questions are frequently included in surveys, which means they offer more detailed information than questionnaires. This is a fantastic approach to discovering information quickly and accurately. They are employed in the collection of big, quantitative, insensitive data. It's crucial to create well-considered research questions to get correct data. It's also crucial to confirm the validity and dependability of your survey.

One-on-One Interviews

One-on-one interviews take place in person and are conducted between just the interviewee and one interviewer. These interviews usually follow a simple structure, which is more in line with what candidates anticipate when they are called in for an interview. Thanks to this type of data collection, the interviewer will have access to the interviewee's perspective on the situation and their feedback. For a needs assessment, higher management, stakeholders, or those with direct control over the areas of concern are often interviewed one on one.

Focus Groups

When individuals are gathered together and questioned about their thoughts on a particular subject, focus groups are employed. They are often between five and eight persons; thus, it's critical that the facilitator guiding the group has excellent facilitation abilities. A focus group is an interview with a small group of people who have similar characteristics or experiences. Focus groups give significant information about demands and consumer experience, but they take a lot longer than the other approaches. This is a fantastic technique for compiling comprehensive information.

Existing Data

Finally, evaluating pertinent data such as business plans, mission statements, goals, historical surveys, marketing reports, and more can help appraise the situation. The quantitative or qualitative analysis depends on the type of data. Descriptive statistics assess quantitative data. Qualitative data categorizes interviews, open-ended questions, and notes. Technology and software have improved data analysis.

Advantages and Disadvantages of Data-Collecting Methods

Like any other methods or models, there are always some advantages and disadvantages in using one or the other. Table 6.1 provides brief descriptions of each data-collecting method and briefly mentions their advantages and disadvantages for using them.

Table 6.1   Advantages and Disadvantages of Data-Collecting Methods

Method	Description	Advantages	Disadvantages
Observation	When using this method, the employees' performance is rated based on their supervisors' direct observations of their work.	Produces data that is pertinent to the working environment and reduces the number of disruptions to the working environment.	Demands an astute and experienced observer. The fact that workers are being watched could have an effect on their conduct. In addition to that, it takes a lot of time.
Document Review	Performance reviews, reports, and job descriptions are all examples of documents that may be helpful tools for determining what kinds of training are required.	A reliable source of information on the process, the goal, and objectives.	It's possible that this information is not available, accessible, or genuine; the terminology used may be technical and require an explanation.
Questionnaire	This method is helpful in getting a bigger picture of what a larger number of people on the team have to say about a topic.	Low in cost and able to collect information from a large number of individuals.	Offers only a small amount of information. There is also a worry over the lack of confidentiality.
One-on-One Interviews	In this method, employees' performance is assessed based on their responses to questions that they are asked face to face.	Excellent at unearthing the specifics of the training requirements, and the trainer is able to investigate any issues that come up.	It requires a lot of time and effort to perform an analysis on it. To be successful, you need an interviewer who is skilled.
Focus Group	A moderator leads the participants of an employee focus group through a discussion of their thoughts under their direction.	Beneficial for dealing with complicated or contentious matters that a single individual may be reluctant or unable to investigate.	It is time-consuming to arrange, and disparities in rank or position may prevent people from participating.
Existing Data	Assess the relevant information. A scenario may be evaluated with the use of business plans, mission statements, goals, historical surveys, marketing reports, and other similar documents.	It works well for larger organizations with a large number of employees. This type of data collecting and analysis can be used for research and case studies.	It needs a facilitator with a deep understanding of quantitative and qualitative data categories. Also, it needs relative technology and software to analyze the data.

Note. Adapted from Gupta et al. (2014) and Wilmoth et al. (2014).

What Is Training Needs Assessment (TNA)

The TNAs are only partially focused on the employees' improvement of knowledge, skills, and abilities (KSA) relevant to how they are performing on the job, at work, and on tasks, and how their behaviors and attitudes are influencing their performance, as opposed to OD-related needs assessments, which examine an organization-wide standpoint (Sleezer et al., 2015; Rothwell & Graber, 2010). The needs for 4Cs may also be simply assessed using this specific need statement methodology.

Purpose of TNA

This section aims to identify performance gaps that may be closed by holding training sessions (Rothwell, Stavros, & Sullivan, 2016; Sleezer et al., 2015). The main goal of TNAs, according to the US Office of Personnel Management, is to determine:

a) The organization, occupation, and individual performance requirements, and
b) The knowledge, skills, and abilities (KSAs) required by an organization's workforce to fulfill its work, job, and task requirements.

An efficient and well-designed TNA will help firms to focus resources on the areas that require the right kind of training. "The assessment should address resources needed to fulfill the organizational mission, improve productivity, and provide quality products and services. A needs assessment is the process of identifying the gap between the performance required and the current performance" (US Office of Personnel Management, n.d., para. 1).

Levels of a TNA

Assessments of training needs are now being used to establish an organization's requirements for training and development on three levels of analysis that are directly connected to the growth, productivity, and effective functioning of the organization. According to the findings published by the US Office of Personnel Management (n.d.), there are three levels of TNA:

a) Organization-level assessment.
b) Occupation-level assessment.
c) Individual-level assessment.

Figure 6.2 displays the importance of a good understanding of 4Cs and the role of them on both occupation and individual levels.

Organization-Level Analysis

Analyzing organizational results and anticipating future organizational requirements are the two primary components of the diagnostic process for training needs analysis. When doing an analysis of an organization, it is critical to take into account the ways in which both internal and external factors might influence training. An assessment of the organization's strategic and operational strategies would be the first step in the training requirements analysis that would be performed at this level. This level of research takes into account a wider range of factors, including an organization's culture, its HR goals, and the impact of external factors (Rothwell, Bakhshandeh, & Zaballero, 2023; Gupta et al., 2014).

Occupation-Level Analysis

Reviewing the occupations that are held and the responsibilities that are carried out is the second stage of the analysis of training needs. When employees' abilities in a given job category are compared to the skills required for successful job performance, any skills gaps that need to be filled through training can be identified. Reviewing the competence demands and skill sets of a team compared to the objectives of the team and the intended business objectives is often what is included in this kind of analysis. It will entail taking into consideration the requirements of individuals in addition to everything else that might assist the company in working together in the most efficient manner feasible (Rothwell et al., 2023; Wilmoth et al., 2014).

Individual-Level Analysis

At the third stage of identifying training requirements, the attention shifts to individuals and the manner in which they carry out their work responsibilities. Utilizing data from performance reviews as a basis for determining educational requirements is the individual analysis method that is used most frequently. In the first step of the performance assessment process, a supervisor conducts a formal examination of the employees' work to identify both their areas of strength and those in which they may need improvement (Rothwell et al., 2023; Stahl et al., 2012; Rothwell et al., 2010).

After that, the management will be able to devise a training program that will assist the employees in overcoming their flaws and improving their strengths. It adds to the determination of what needs to be improved, whether via a training program that they are required to complete or through some other kind of continuing professional development. Receiving this sort of information from trainees, who are in a great position to identify training requirements, can assist the training program in acquiring support from those who have a need for training (Rothwell et al., 2023).

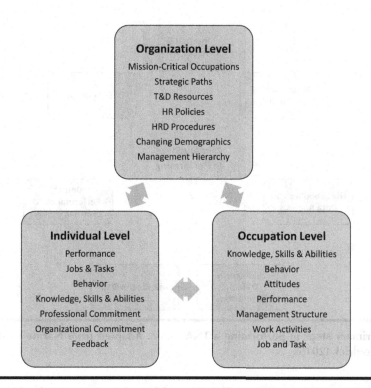

Figure 6.2   Levels of TNA.   Note. Adapted from US Office of Personnel Management (n.d.) and Rothwell et al. (2023).

Primary Steps in Performing a TNA

An in-depth analysis and interpretation of the pertinent data that will play a role in your decision-making may be accomplished very effectively via the use of a requirements assessment. In order to do this, it is necessary for you to have an understanding of the baseline needs of your team, as well as the ultimate desired goal of the process. You should solicit the assistance of important stakeholders, donors, and decision-makers, and you should collect input by holding meetings or brainstorming sessions. According to Narine, Ali, and Hill (2020) and Tobey and McGoldrick (2016), the following are the seven processes to follow while doing a needs assessment (See Figure 6.3).

Figure 6.3 **Primary steps in performing a TNA. Note. Adapted from Narine et al. (2020) and Tobey & McGoldrick (2016).**

Internal and External Audit

Your evaluation will be comprehensive if you examine the internal and external environment and collect data from various sources, such as recent events, annual reports, financial statements, statistics on customer service, strategic plans, and benchmarking.

Data Collecting

The demands of modern organizations may often be broken down into three categories:

- A window of opportunity that has to be exploited, such as a newly discovered product or market.
- An issue that has to be addressed and remedied, such as complaints from customers, subpar product quality, or excessive absenteeism.
- A business plan that requires backing, for instance, a marketing and product strategy that is geared toward a specific age group.

Detect Performance and Learning Needs

To determine learner requirements, desired and current job performance, desired and current skill and knowledge level, and desired and current work performance, several sources of data must be considered. It is likely that each group of requirements will contain some needs caused by a deficiency in workers' knowledge or abilities (needs that may be addressed by training) and needs resulting from other causes that require solutions that do not involve training.

Analyze the Data

The results of data analysis provide crucial information that pinpoints the discrepancies between intended and actual work performance, as well as between wanted and actual levels of knowledge and competence, which ensures that the eventual training design will focus on bridging those discrepancies. The needs assessor also benefits by having a better understanding of the extent of these gaps when it comes to assigning priorities to the many problems that must be fixed.

Distinguish Training Resolutions

At this stage in the procedure, prospective training initiatives have often been identified by the requirements assessor or the client. Sometimes the clients may initiate communication with the needs assessors so that they can share their discoveries, and other times the needs assessors will initiate communication with their clients.

Give Feedback on Data Analysis

The requirements assessor will either give a presentation to the client or produce a report describing data analysis, training suggestions for design and delivery, and non-training recommendations, which are recommendations to remedy issues not caused by knowledge or skill inadequacies. This is an essential phase since acquiring buy-in from relevant parties is essential when it comes to demonstrating why doing a requirements' assessment is important.

Deliver Training Procedure

At this stage, the process will begin to involve design. Suppose the requirements assessment has been done correctly. In that case, the instructional designer will have the knowledge necessary to generate specific learning aims, learning actions, job-related material, and resources to support activities, assessing and appraisal tools, and a learning atmosphere. These things can be produced in a learning environment.

Importance of Competencies for Organizations

This section begins by examining the importance of skills and how they are used by businesses and organizations in order to launch this important investigation. In contrast to job-related activities, Rothwell and Graber (2010) stressed on the importance of competencies and their function in enterprises and organizations. "Competencies concentrate on the traits of individuals who successfully carry out the task. Competencies are a component of individuals, not the tasks they perform. Competencies are more accurate in identifying a person's special qualities that contribute to success" (Rothwell & Graber, 2010, p. 9). Most traditional job descriptions used by businesses and organizations, which typically just use a shortlist of necessary knowledge and skills related to the profession or job tasks included in the 21st-century 4Cs, have neglected and overlooked or, at best, inadequately recognized this crucial distinction (Rothwell et al., 2016; Rothwell & Graber, 2010).

Due to its applicability and capacity to generate more enduring benefits across businesses' workforces, competence modeling is being used more and more frequently. The competency-based performance or competency modeling is being used more and more by specialists and practitioners working with front-line employees, as well as by their supervisors and managers, on learning and performance topics (Cummings & Worley, 2015; Rothwell & Graber, 2010). According to Rothwell and Graber (2010), numerous types of research have shown that some employees at their workplaces may be 20 times more productive than others at the same department or individuals performing the same work or job. This emphasizes the significance of workplace competencies and attempts to match people's competencies with their necessary job competencies. Competency learning does not, in reality, promise a 20-fold increase in worker productivity, but if it is properly implemented and applied by the workforce, it will lead to a shift in employees' behavior (Rothwell et al., 2016; Cummings & Worley, 2015; Rothwell & Graber, 2010). "Competencies are not about duties; they are about people. In that respect, they are different from a job analysis (a process) and its traditional output (a job description)" (Rothwell & Graber, 2010, p. 8).

Competencies for Success in Organization Development

This section briefly reviews the history and research on competency creation and application in organizations and industries. These studies have enlightened academic experts, helped improve competencies' practice, and contributed to OD, training, and related domains (Newhard, 2010; Rothwell, 2015; Rothwell & Lindholm, 1999). Rothwell et al. (2016) cited McClelland's (1973) landmark paper on measuring competence rather than intellect. Professionals agreed in the 1970s to test for intellect, especially anticipated school grades, assuming that intelligence would improve work performance. McClelland questioned this idea by exploring people's drive for personal and professional success and by investigating what genuinely predicts performance (Rothwell et al., 2016).

Cummings and Worley (2015) cited two research studies that defined, classified, and arranged the abilities and knowledge needed for OD experts and practitioners.

A diverse trio of well-known OD practitioners and researchers reviewed, examined, and updated OD practitioner competencies on the first project. This research study produced 187 statements in nine OD practice areas: Entry, start-up, assessment and feedback, action planning, intervention, evaluation, adoption, separation, and general competence. The researchers collected data from 364 OD practitioners and professionals with the following criteria: (1) an average of eight years' experience in OD, (2) a master's degree, and (3) US citizenship. The results produced a list of 23 competencies that demonstrated knowledge and abilities for planned change and, most significantly, the personal traits needed to be an effective OD practitioner (Cummings & Worley, 2015). This list is under the OD competencies area.

The "Organization Development and Change Division of the Academy of Management" (Cummings & Worley, 2015, p. 48) supported the second initiative to generate a list of competencies to guide curriculum development for OD program graduates. According to Cummings and Worley (2015), more than 40 OD professionals and researchers collaborated to create two competency lists for successful OD practitioners (see Cummings & Worley, 2015, p. 13), which included experience and knowledge from organization behavior, organization theories, group dynamics, psychology, management, research methods, and professional business domains.

Leadership Competency Model

Before discussing the necessary abilities for OD, WFED, WLP, and Training, it is crucial to establish a strong framework. "Leadership" is the name of such a situation. There is a need for leadership and professional competencies and proficiencies for designing and implementing any change intervention or leading individuals, teams, departments, or organizations to a successful implementation of any business operation or change intervention, regardless of what type of practitioner or professional is being used or what kind of change intervention is being implemented.

According to Donahue (2018), competencies are a grouping of knowledge, skills, attitudes, and behaviors (KSABs) that can be measured and observed and help people perform better at work and accomplish their personal and professional objectives. Donahue (2018) outlined 35 competencies in five categories that apply to all industries and help people develop in their leadership roles and positions. These competencies also assist managers or supervisors in determining the current proficiency level of employees and the competencies they need to develop.

Essential Competency for Effective Training

A competence model may also be used to help identify future training requirements, such as those for acquiring 4Cs skills. Competencies are acknowledged as essential performance requirements for a particular field, position, or set of duties that an organization would include in its training program (Rothwell et al., 2016). As Rothwell et al. (2016) stated, "To be assessed as competent, a person must demonstrate the ability to perform a job's specific task and develop employee training programs to teach people to understand, model, and exhibit competencies that lead to competent employees" (p. 119).

Essential Skills for a Trainer

Arneson, Rothwell, and Naughton (2013) provided a competency model for the knowledge and skills required for a knowledgeable and skilled trainer to successfully implement training and be able to deliver formal and informal learning platforms in the ASTD Competencies for the Training and Growing Profession as follows:

- Manage the learning environment.
- Prepare for the delivery of training.
- Communicate the goals of the training.
- Align learning solutions with the goals of the course.
- Align learning solutions with the needs of the learners.
- Establish credibility as an instructor.
- Develop a conducive environment for learning.
- Provide a variety of learning approaches.
- Facilitate learning.
- Encourage involvement.
- Build learner motivation.
- Deliver constructive feedback.
- Ensure learning results.
- Evaluate possible solutions.

In addition to the individual abilities, the competencies of the team are also of critical significance. The competencies of the team concern the capacity and competence of the team as a whole, as well as the ability and competence of its members, to deal with a range of challenges and conflicts, as well as how they resolve problems, make choices, and deal with issues that are in front of them. According to Dyer et al. (2013) and Rothwell et al. (2016), team competencies refer to a team's capacity to collectively work together to accomplish their team's goals and to keep the team members motivated and focused on their intended outcomes. According to Donahue (2018), the concept of competency has evolved into something akin to jargon that people use carelessly as if it were something irrelevant. On the other hand, in today's efforts for organization development, competency-based development and education are considered the gateway to the future of educa-tion/learning, team building, and organization development. This is in contrast to the view that traditional education and training methods are the best for these purposes. "Competencies are the measurable and observable knowledge, skills, attitudes, and behaviors (KSABs) critical to success-ful job performance" (21).

What Is Next?

Chapter 7, "Identifying 4Cs Skills Gap Using Organization Diagnosis Models," includes sugges-tions for what organizations can use to recognize a 4Cs skills gap among their workforces and extend the workforces' development on 4Cs skills or understanding of who needs to be more trained or developed on which of the 4Cs skills.

References

Arneson, J., Rothwell, W., & Naughton, J. (2013). Training and development competencies redefined to create competitive advantage. *T+D*, *67*(1), 42–47.

Cummings, T. G. & Worley, C. G. (2015). *Organization Development & Change* (10th ed.). Stamford, CT: Cengage Learning.

Donahue, Wesley E. (2018). *Building Leadership Competence. A Competency-Based Approach to Building Leadership Ability.* State College, PA: Centerstar Learning.

Dyer, Gibb W., Dyer, Jeffrey H., & Dyer, William G. (2013). *Team Building: Proven Strategies for Improving Team Performance* (5th ed.). San Francisco, CA: Jossey-Bass.

Gupta, K., Sleezer, C. M., & Russ-Eft, D. F. (2014). *A Practical Guide to Needs Assessment* (3rd ed.). San Francisco, CA: John Wiley & Sons.

Indeed Editorial Team. (2022). What is need assessment? Retrieved from https://www.indeed.com/career -advice/career-development/needs-assessment.

McClelland, D. C. (1973). Testing for competence rather than for intelligence. *American Psychologist*, *28*(1), 1–14.

Narine, L. K., Ali, A. D., & Hill, P. A. (2020). Application of a three-phase needs assessment framework to identify priority issue areas for extension programming. *The Journal of Extension*, *58*(4), Article 24. Retrieved from https://tigerprints.clemson.edu/joe/vol58/iss4/24.

Newhard, Michele L. (2010). *An Exploratory Study of Competencies of Appreciative Inquiry Practitioners: Discovery.* (Published Dissertation). State College, PA: The Pennsylvania State University.

Rothwell, William J. (2015). *Organization Development Fundamentals: Managing Strategic Change.* Alexandria, WV: ATD Press.

Rothwell, William J., Bakhshandeh, B., & Zaballero, Ailleen G. (2023). *Successful Supervisory Leadership; Exerting Positive Influence While Leading People.* Book 1 of Successful Supervisory Leadership Series. New York, NY: Taylor & Francis Group. Routledge.

Rothwell, William J. & Graber, James M. (2010). *Competency-Based Training Basics.* East Peoria, IL: ASTD Press.

Rothwell, William J. & Lindholm, J. E. (1999). Competency identification, modelling and assessment in the USA. *International Journal of Training and Development*, 3, 90–105. https://doi.org/10.1111/1468 -2419.00069.

Rothwell, William J., Stavros, Jacqueline M., & Sullivan, Roland L. (2016). *Practicing Organization Development: Leading Transformation and Change* (4th ed.). Hoboken, NJ: John Wiley & Sons, Inc.

Sleezer, C. M., Russ-Eft, D. F., & Gupta, K. (2015). Learning, training, and performance timeline: A walk through history. *Performance Improvement*, 54(2), 7–15.

Stahl, G., Björkman, I., Farndale, E., Morris, S. S., Paauwe, J., & Stiles, P. (2012). Six principles of effective global talent management. *MIT Sloan Management Review*, 53(2), 25–32. Retrieved from http://ezaccess.libraries.psu.edu/login?url=https://search-proquest-com.ezaccess.libraries.psu.edu/docview/914408228?accountid=13158 10.1177/2158244017726116.

Tobey, Deborah D. & McGoldrick, B. (2016). *Needs Assessment Basics* (2nd ed.). Alexandria, VA: Association of Talent Development.

Wilmoth, F. S., Prigmore, C., & Bray, M. (2014). HPT models: An overview of the major models in the field. *Performance Improvement (International Society for Performance Improvement)*, 53(9), 31–42. https://doi.org/10.1002/pfi.21440.

US Office of Personnel Management Website. (n.d.). Training and development- planning and evaluating. Retrieved from https://www.opm.gov/policy-data-oversight/training-and-development/planning -evaluating/.

Chapter 7

Identifying 4Cs Skills Gap Using Organization Diagnosis Models

Introduction

This chapter contains our proposals for what businesses may do to detect a 4Cs skills gap among their workforces and expand the workforces' development on 4Cs skills or awareness of who needs to be further trained or developed on which of the 4Cs abilities. Organizations can employ an external organization development (OD) practitioner, use their own internal OD practitioners or human resources development (HRD) professionals, or utilize and implement what is already available to them in the form of elements of organization diagnosis. This simply can redirect the diagnosis on the role and effect of the workforce on an individual and team level. The following explains and describes various possible opportunities for companies to expand their workforces through training and professional growth opportunities.

The OD business has a wide variety of diagnostic models that are offered. According to this researcher, the three organization diagnosis models listed below can be utilized to identify problems with people and teams that have a 4Cs skills gap. The following is an outline of these suggested models:

1) Individual and Group Behavior Model.
2) The Great Place to Work Model.
3) SWOT Analysis.

Given that individuals and teams form organizations, OD and HRD professionals can use the same elements of these diagnoses' models to achieve a better understanding of the issues of individuals, groups, and teams concerning having, utilizing, or lacking the 4Cs skills by utilizing them to achieve minor modifications in language and approach. This is possible because individuals and teams form organizations. These diagnostic models may be used to zero in on the specific challenges that individuals and groups have in terms of their 4Cs skills and determine how they plan to overcome those challenges in order to improve their job performance, increase their level of productivity, and enjoy a more pleasant place of employment.

DOI: 10.4324/9781003462316-9

To have a better grasp on how to use these diagnostic models, it would be very helpful and pertinent to have an understanding of the different diagnosis levels that the organizations have.

a) Organization level.
b) Group and team level.
c) Individual level.

This researcher does not propose doing a diagnostic on all levels of the entire company. Nevertheless, in light of the significant part that individuals and groups play, it would be quite useful to have an understanding of the relevance and connection shared by the three levels.

Organization Diagnosis Levels

Individuals play a significant part in diagnosing organizational problems and understanding those problems, such as determining what kinds of adjustments need to be made or how to build their workforce on 4Cs skills. This is an essential aspect to keep in mind no matter what kind of diagnosis is being carried out, so make sure you don't forget it. "The diagnostic process usually assesses the organization's current condition by guiding what to look at. This is also the first step in selecting the appropriate change strategies and interventions" (Rothwell 2015, p. 15).

The three levels of organization diagnosis and the aspects and locations covered by each of the three levels of diagnosis are shown in Figure 7.1. However, all three levels are connected to one another, and eventually, they will represent an organization in its entirety. While there are variables in each level of organization diagnosis that influence organization development processes and play a substantial role in an organization's successful growth, there are also variables in each level of organization diagnosis that influence organization development processes.

- **Organization Level.** At this stage, the focus is on analyzing human capital, the structure and hierarchy of the organization, HR and HRD practices, the use of information technology, the policies and practices of the organization, as well as the environment, norms, and culture of the company. However, there are some components that are directly associated with workforce education and training and development, such as an organization's practices, environment, norms, and culture. Not all levels of an organization are directly related to the development of the 4Cs skills; however, there are some levels of an organization that are directly related to the development of these abilities.
- **Group and Team Level.** Examining the team format, the team structure and hierarchy, the team composition, the linkages between the team and other groups, the team procedures, behavior, norms, and culture, as well as the use of information and technology by teams, and HR and HRD regulations pertaining to teams and groups are the topics that will be covered in this level. However, certain factors are directly tied to workforce education, training, and development, such as the connections within teams, the behavior of teams and groups, and the culture of norms. As stated before, not all of these group and team levels are directly related to the development of the 4Cs abilities.
- **Individual Level.** This level assesses people's attitudes and behaviors, such as what they value, the principles they follow, their interests, their understanding of self-awareness, their communication style, and their motivations and willingness to work with others. This is the most important level of diagnosis in terms of people.

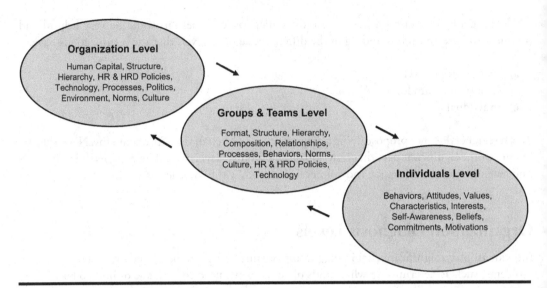

Figure 7.1 Organization diagnosis levels. Note. Adapted from Rothwell, Imroz, & Bakhshandeh (2021) and Rothwell (2015).

Individual and Group Behavior Model

Michael I. Harrison was the one who initially conceived of and constructed this organization diagnostic model in the year 1985. Through the course of Harrison's career, this model has undergone several revisions and has been included in a great number of editions of his work. This model is particularly helpful for analyzing the behavior of people, groups, and teams in order to identify where there may be a gap in their usage of the 4Cs skills, or where there may be a need to create training and development programs for raising all or any of the 4Cs abilities among the workforces. The following are some of the components that Harrison (2005) identified as being part of the Individual and Group Behavior Model (see Figure 7.2).

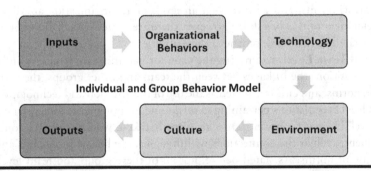

Figure 7.2 Individual and group behavior model. Note. Adapted from Rothwell, Imroz, & Bakhshandeh (2021) and Harrison (2005).

- **Inputs.** These are factors that cover human capital, such as individuals, groups, teams, and the whole workforce, in addition to raw material, supplies, budget, and financial considerations, all of which are intangible parts of a firm.
- **Organizational Behaviors.** This encompasses all of the procedures the organization uses to produce outputs, such as HR and HRD policies, as well as organizational norms, regulations, and laws.
- **Technology.** The systems, production techniques and procedures, equipment, and instruments of the organization are discussed here. These are the things that would turn the company's inputs into outputs.
- **Environment.** There are two environments to consider:
  a) A company's direct rivals, customers, partners, suppliers, and investors are all considered to be part of its close environment.
  b) The local and national political system, the economy and its associated impacts, social structures based on norms and cultures, and technical improvements in the market are all included in the remote environment.
- **Culture.** The values, conventions, beliefs, and behaviors that are prevalent in a society and which also play a role in corporate culture, such as:
  a) The manner in which workers carry out their job responsibilities.
  b) The structure of communications between organizations and how it works.
  c) The manner in which workers interact with their clients.
  d) The manner in which the firm interacts with its workforce.
- **Outputs.** In addition to the contentment and health of the workforce, these are the completed products, goods, and services, and they apply to the workforce as a whole, including all of its groups, teams, and individual members.

The Great Place to Work Model

The Great Place to Work Model is yet another practical and pertinent organization diagnosis model that may assist with understanding the workforce's challenges to comprehend the degree to which 4Cs skills are utilized or are lacking. Michael Burchell and Jennifer Robin conceived this diagnostic approach in 2011 and it was subsequently put into practice. This methodology can provide insight into both an individual's dedication to their job and their organization's commitments. According to Burchell and Robin (2011), this model incorporates the following aspects of the interactions and relationships between people and groups (see Figure 7.3).

Figure 7.3   The Great Place to Work model. Note. Adapted from Rothwell, Imroz, & Bakhshandeh (2021) and Burchell and Robin (2011).

- **Trust.** The quality of trust comprises the people's and teams' trust and respect for each other, as well as fairness among the members of a team, and, ultimately, between the workforce and the business as a whole.
- **Credibility.** Credibility will be achieved when there is open communication among the team members, evidence of proficiency at work, and evidence of members of an organization exercising integrity, responsibility, and accountability.
- **Respect.** One way for people, groups, teams, and organizations to work together to build respect for one another and their own companies is to demonstrate support, collaboration, and thoughtfulness.
- **Fairness.** Attaining this component will need the organization, people, and teams at all levels of the organizational structure, all the way up to the top management, to demonstrate and carry out equality, impartiality, and justice in their daily operations.
- **Pride.** Pride is a personal experience that can be sparked by a variety of factors, including personal accomplishments, the success of one's team, and the standing of the organization in the community.
- **Camaraderie.** Developing a sense of camaraderie in the workplace may be accomplished by activities such as fostering closeness, exhibiting courteous conduct, demonstrating compassion and empathy, being welcoming, and developing a sense of community in the workplace.

SWOT Analysis Model

Practitioners in organizational development, human resource development, and ordinary business consultants employ this model of organization diagnosis rather frequently. The SWOT analysis, which stands for "Strengths, Weaknesses, Opportunities, and Threats," was first developed by

Albert S. Humphrey in the year 1960. The SWOT analysis is aimed at locating the procedural or structural components that establish the primary strengths, weaknesses, opportunities, and threats that are significant to the company under two internal circumstances (strengths and weaknesses) and two external circumstances (opportunities and threats).

However, this diagnosis model can be utilized by organizations in order to gain a better understanding of their workforces, as well as individual and team strengths, weaknesses, opportunities, and threats. These findings can then be used to determine which aspects of the 4Cs skills, or all of the 4Cs skills as a whole, need to be developed among teams or individuals working for the organization. This diagnostic model comprises aspects of the following factors, as stated by Gupta, Sleezer, and Russ-Eft (2014) (see Figure 7.4).

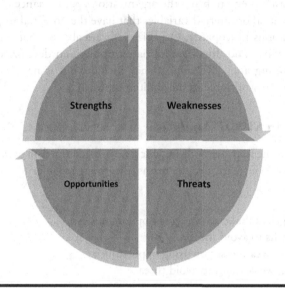

Figure 7.4   SWOT analysis model. Note. Adapted from Rothwell, Imroz, & Bakhshandeh (2021) and Gupta, Sleezer, & Russ-Eft (2014).

According to Gupta et al. (2014) and "SWOT Analysis" (2009):

■ **Strengths.** It's possible that the firms' strengths lie in the distinctiveness of their products, the quality of their customer service, or their formidable market presence. It might also be their ingrained values, their team's cohesiveness, or their management's expertise. The organization has the ability to influence its strengths. At the same time, this aspect of SWOT may be utilized to understand an individual's or a team's strengths, and it can provide managers with access to information about what needs to be done to grow their workforce in the 4Cs skills by utilizing such strengths.

■ **Weaknesses.** The inability of a company to develop, expand, and compete in its market may be attributed to one of its deficiencies, which may include the absence of trained staff, inadequate resources, ineffective tactics, or insufficient amounts of money. An organization's weaknesses are elements that it has influence over. In the same way that the element of weakness may be used to understand an individual or a team's deficiencies, it can also provide managers access to what needs to be done to grow the workforce in the 4Cs skills by having employees focus on improving their weaknesses and increasing the number of strengths they possess.

■ **Opportunities.** Opportunities are factors that make it possible for an organization to enhance its performance and capabilities to compete in the market where it operates. These can be external or internal appealing elements that offer chances for an organization to exist and expand. Opportunities represent prospects for an organization to exist and flourish. Developing and enhancing 4Cs abilities within an organization's workforce is obviously something that businesses can utilize as a chance to grow the 4Cs skills of their individual employees as well as the 4Cs skills of their teams.

■ **Threats.** Threats might originate from people, groups, or other enterprises that are external to the company and intend to bring the organization's performance to a lower level. Threats may be either external or internal variables that have the potential to put the organization's purpose or operations in jeopardy. Organizations are able to spot internal dangers among individuals and teams and direct appropriate training and development on defusing such threats. This training and development may include, but is not limited to, training and development of their workforce in the abilities of the 4Cs.

Strategies Based on SWOT Analysis

The following is a list of the four methods in which we utilized the data gathered from the SWOT analysis that were carried out with people, teams, or groups in order to come up with plans for implementing changes:

■ SO: Using strengths to take advantage of opportunities.
■ ST: Using strengths to avoid threats.
■ WO: Overcoming weaknesses by using opportunities.
■ WT: Minimizing weaknesses to avoid threats.

According to the facts shown above, no group, team, or organization can achieve strengths and possibilities to grow and become productive without the efforts and impacts of individual members of the group. Individuals can also significantly affect developing vulnerabilities and threats for the company, which is something to keep in mind. In light of the aforementioned, it is very necessary for any company to seriously consider offering training and development for their personnel to equip them with crucial 4Cs skills for the 21st century.

What Is Next?

Chapter 8, "Evaluating and Supporting Students and Workforce on Their Progress," is about supporting and evaluating students before entering the labor market and for the existing workforce to determine their readiness and acquisition of competencies skills.

References

Burchell, Michael. & Robin, Jennifer. (2011). *The Great Workplace: How to Build It, How to Keep It, and Why It Matters*. San Francisco, CA: Jossey-Bass.

Gupta, K., Sleezer, C. M., & Russ-Eft, D. F. (2014). *A Practical Guide to Needs Assessment* (3rd ed.). San Francisco, CA: John Wiley.

Harrison, Michael I. (2005). *Diagnosing Organizations: Methods, Models, and Processes* (3rd ed.). Thousand Oaks, CA: Sage Publisher, Inc.

Rothwell, William J. (2015). *Organization Development Fundamentals: Managing Strategic Change*. Alexandria, WV: ATD Press.

Rothwell, William J., Imroz, Sohel M., & Bakhshandeh, Behnam. (2021). *Organization-Development Interventions: Executing Effective Organizational Chang*. New York, NY: Taylor & Francis Group. CRC Press.

SWOT Analysis. (2009). *Encyclopedia of Management* (6th ed., pp. 915–918). Detroit MI. Retrieved from http://link.galegroup.com/apps/doc/CX3273100290/GVRL?u=psucic&sid=GVRL&xid=1e641eb3.

Chapter 8

Evaluating and Supporting Students and Workforce on Their Progress

Introduction

Organizations are requesting new talents throughout their employment processes due to the fundamental variations in the domestic and international economies. Employers are searching for workers who can handle a variety of duties, use creativity in their work, and effectively collaborate in teams (Soulé & Warrick, 2015).

The top two talents that have received increased attention in schools over the past few years, according to Ahmadi and Besançon (2017), are creativity and critical thinking. Spies and Xu (2018) identified teamwork and communication as two other crucial skills required for 21st-century learning at the same time. Spies and Xu (2018) claim that in order to fulfill this national demand, the national requirements for speaking and listening have been raised to a higher level across schools.

The ACT WorkKeys Assessment, the Strada Education Network, and other reputable reports, studies, and methodologies are available to support and evaluate students before they enter the workforce as well as the existing workforce to determine their level of readiness and possession of competencies skills. Additionally, these models assist learners, working adults, and the workforce in acquiring professional competencies and abilities that will benefit them in their present and future employment.

This chapter covers the following elements related to supporting students and workforce during their progress of developing 4Cs skills:

- Models to Use in Evaluating Students and Workforce.
- The Changing Nature of Working and Employment.
- High Demand for New Skills.
- 21st-Century Employment Demands 21st-Century Skilled Workforce.

DOI: 10.4324/9781003462316-10

Models to Use in Evaluating Students and Workforce

In order to help and assess students before they enter the profession and for the present workforce to assess their degree of preparation and possession of competency skills, a number of credible studies, research, and methodologies are available. Additionally, these models aid in the development of professional competencies and abilities that will benefit students, existing workers, and the workforce in their present and future professional endeavors.

SCANS Report—2000

Given the importance of teaching the 4Cs to the younger generation before they enter the workforce, this research examines the comprehensive skills, competencies, and training report SCANS Report—2000, which was created in 1999. The Commission on Achieving Necessary Skills (SCANS), which reports to the Labor Secretary, was asked to look at the demands of the American workplace and analyze whether or not the younger generation is capable of achieving them. The Commission was specifically tasked to provide the Labor Secretary with information on the employment prospects and skill levels required for high school graduates to enter the labor market (SCANS, 2000, p. 10).

Workplace Know-How

According to the SCANS assessment, strong work performance requires what they named "Workplace Know-How," which is made up of a mix of three aspects of skills and personality traits and five competencies in total. Included is workplace know-how (SCANS, 2000).

Competencies. A workforce that is successful is able to employ the following in their job in an effective and productive manner:

- **Resources.** The capability of making effective use of resources provided by organizations, such as money, time, and materials, as well as physical space and a suitable number of staff members.
- **Interpersonal Skills.** Ability to work successfully with individuals from various cultural and societal backgrounds, as well as create and educate others on how to perform their duties and responsibilities, serve customers, manage teams, negotiate positions or contracts, and work effectively with people from groups and teams.
- **Information.** Capability to gather and assess data and information, organize and manage documents and files, effectively interpret information and interact with others, and utilize computers and other electronic devices to successfully process information.
- **Systems.** Capability to comprehend organizational, technical, and social systems in order to analyze, assess, and improve one's own performance as well as that of others or to make system improvements.
- **Technology.** Capability to choose and use appropriate tools and equipment, as well as accurately apply technology to a variety of activities, all while maintaining and fixing issues with tools and technologies.

The Foundation. The following are some of the foundations that are necessary for these competencies:

- **Basic Skills.** Things like reading, writing, mathematics, and arithmetic, as well as being able to talk well and listen attentively, are examples.
- **Thinking Skills.** For example, being able to think critically, being creative, being able to make decisions, being able to solve problems, having foresight, being able to reason, working together, and understanding how to learn.
- **Personal Qualities.** Such as personal responsibility, integrity, self-esteem, the ability to self-regulate, and the capacity for socialization.

It is crucial to emphasize that the SCANS abilities and skills are not designed for distinct educational paths denoted as "general," "career," or "vocational." All educators across all subject areas are required to include them in their lessons (SCANS, 2000, p. 18). Teaching high school students the knowledge they need to know as a crucial component of learning across the curriculum, including the five core courses, is a difficult task. Using the five competencies in relation to the three foundations (Figure 8.1), SCANS (2000) claims that students will find the learning content to be more relevant and challenging, teachers will find that their classes are more attentive and interested, and workers and college administrators will be pleased with the results because the teaching curriculum will be woven with sets of real issues in the real world.

Furthermore, SCANS (2000) emphasized that it is every teacher's duty to define the know-how in every subject area, both academic and extracurricular. These abilities and talents should be cultivated, according to the SCANS study, in "the five core courses, in art and music, in foreign languages, in vocational education, in the school newspaper, or on athletic teams" (p. 18). It is clear that by developing these competencies and abilities, high school students will have the chance to learn more about the 4Cs, begin developing them while still in high school, and to be ready to use them in their future workplaces.

The link between occupational knowledge and what is expected in schools is seen in Figure 8.1.

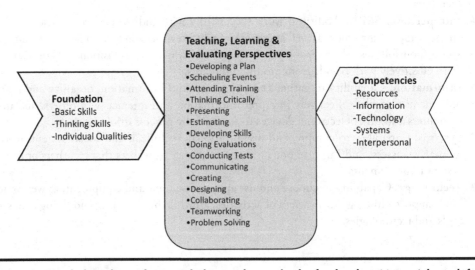

Figure 8.1 Workplace know-how and the work required of schools. Note. Adapted from SCANS Report (2000, p. 18).

The ACT WorkKeys Assessment

The issue of college and job preparedness is still relevant and at the forefront of those interested in increasing productivity in today's corporate and educational environments. As this research shows throughout this chapter, employers are very concerned with and demanding of the fundamental academic and educational skills for any entry-level workforce. As a result, organizations are holding educators and educational systems accountable for student progress and readiness achievement in educational and academic areas (Schultz & Stern, 2013).

Schultz and Stern (2013) highlighted the use of WorkKeys in relation to this concern, "In this environment, WorkKeys has emerged as a set of assessments that could respond to the needs of both employers and educators and signal to test takers their readiness for further education or a career" (p. 157). The term "Person–Occupation Fit" is currently most commonly used in the field of career and vocational counseling. When individuals are found to fit into specific occupations, this approach to developing career readiness triggers the rationality of the majority of assessments used by educators and academics for career planning, which would help career development professionals focus on relevancy and manage a set of personality options (Swaney et al., 2012).

The ACT WorkKeys Assessment System is a comprehensive method for identifying, expressing, and enhancing the abilities necessary for a person to succeed in the workplace. The ACT WorkKeys measures a person's aptitude in addition to certain employment criteria. A thorough link between the necessary and required fundamental abilities for a successful operation in any position, job, or profession would be applied by appropriately using and executing a well-suited fit (Williams, 2015). According to Williams (2015, p. 28), "Nationwide, all 50 states are currently using the ACT WorkKeys Assessment" and offer evaluation in the following ten areas:

1) Reading for Information.
2) Applied Mathematics.
3) Locating Information.
4) Applied Technology.
5) Business Writing.
6) Writing.
7) Observation.
8) Teamwork.
9) Listening.
10) Listening for Understanding.

The majority of research on WorkKeys has been done to verify the reliability of its tests and evaluations, or more simply, to ensure that it measures what it is meant to measure. There aren't many independent studies demonstrating the relationship between students' test results and their likelihood of success in certain activities, occupations, or employment in the future (Sawchuk, 2018).

As it has been displayed in Figure 8.2, the Center for Energy Workforce Development's website listed four elements of ACT WorkKeys:

1) Job profiling.
2) Assessment.
3) Training.
4) Research.

(Center for Energy Workforce Development, n.d.)

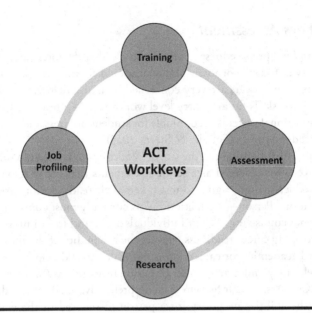

Figure 8.2 Main elements of the ACT WorkKeys system. Note. Adapted from "Center for Energy Workforce Development" (n.d., n.p.).

Job Profiling

This is a definition of the basic abilities that persons need in order to be able to do their professions and pursue their careers.

Assessment

This is a test to determine whether or not individuals already possess the fundamental abilities that are relevant to working settings.

Training

This is a curriculum standard that was developed by the publisher of the ACT Level 1 and is meant to strengthen the abilities that individuals already possess so that they can be successful in the careers that they choose.

Research

This is the result of extensive research and authentication efforts conducted by the ACT, which produced a tool that could be used with a high degree of dependability and certainty in a wide variety of educational and occupational settings, in addition to those that focus on workforce development.

Strada Education Network

Research, investments, philanthropy, policymaker involvement, and resolutions to help and support people connect their education to desirable, meaningful, and fit careers are just a few of the ways that the Strada Education Network influences and directs education and employment pathways. It has been said on the Strada Education Network that it won't be simple or straightforward to develop an "education-to-employment" system that empowers and supports all Americans (Stradaeducation.org, 2020). According to "Stradaeducation.org" (2020, n.p.), "Our mission is to improve lives by forging clearer and more purposeful pathways between education and employment."

In order to help governors and other policymakers create a skilled and qualified workforce that is in line with their states' commitments to providing career pathways for their citizens, Strada Education Network directly contacts and engages state governors and other policymakers. The Lifelong Learning Cycle is the framework through which Strada carries out its mission and commitment (see Figure 8.3) by using the following approaches for helping students and the workforce to come to *completion with a purpose*:

1) Education and career planning.
2) Student success and support.
3) Career and workforce transition.

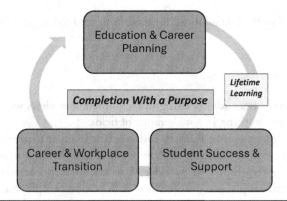

Figure 8.3   Lifelong education cycle. Note. Adapted from "Stradaeducation.org" (2020, n.p.).

Although mergers and acquisitions are common strategic actions for businesses in the private sector, they seldom have a significant impact on the public sector. Through strategic philanthropy, research, studies, and mission-aligned partners, such as the following seven organizations that operate together and as extensions of the Strada Education Network, Strada Education Network focuses on important college-to-career difficulties (Forbes, 2020).

CAEL

Services like adult career counseling and guiding growth are made available through the Council for Adult and Experiential Learning (CAEL).

College Confidential

This group fosters debates, discussions, and online forums and tools that educate and counsel individuals on their college and employment alternatives.

Dxtera

A conglomerate that focuses on improving students' and organizations' academic and professional outcomes in the higher education sector.

Education at Work

An organization that offers assistance to college students by making paid employment opportunities available to them, assisting them in graduating with less debt, and assisting them in the development of necessary skills for finding careers after graduation.

Emsi

This firm delivers extensive labor market analytics with the purpose of enlightening individuals who are on the lookout for employment that is suitable for them.

Inside Track

An organization that offers flexible solutions for mentoring and coaching to postsecondary institutions and foundations.

Roadtrip Nation

In order to provide useful career advice, this group conducts interviews with members of the student body as well as those working in a wide range of fields.

In order to leverage competencies, abilities, and expertise in order to provide a curriculum based on developing skills, mentoring students and the workforce, providing professional networking, and opening doors for internships that would end in employment, Strada Education Network research and investments emphasize partnerships with various employers, organizations, community supporters, local politicians, and educators. To help them as they organize and prepare for employment in high-demand professional routes, they concentrate especially on marginalized groups, adult learners, low-income individuals, and first-generation college students (Forbes, 2020).

The Changing Nature of Working and Employment

The top two talents that have received increased attention in schools over the past several years, according to Ahmadi and Besançon (2017), are creativity and critical thinking. The authors credit this focus to the need for greater knowledge and innovation in communication and information technologies. In addition, Spies and Xu (2018) highlighted teamwork and communication as two more crucial skills required for learning in the 21st century. Spies and Xu (2018) claim that in order to fulfill this national demand, the national requirements for speaking and listening have been raised to a higher level across schools. These fundamental abilities are the cornerstone of oral communication, the basis for interaction and teamwork, and they are crucial for students' academic success (Spies & Xu, 2018; Ahmadi & Besançon, 2017).

Simply put, without effective communication abilities, it is impossible to cooperate, express creativity, or engage in critical thought (Jones, 2015). In addition to verbal and written communication abilities, today's students need to learn how to successfully use symbols, pictures, and other digital tools (Jones, 2015). As a result, efficient digital communication is becoming more and more crucial for cooperation and collaboration.

According to a recent administration of the Program for International Student Assessment (PISA) and some other international evaluations, American students' academic performance is subpar compared to that of students in other countries, according to Soulé and Warrick (2015). Additionally, the P21 program uses Sandford University research to demonstrate how important these comparisons and findings are for education and the economy (Soulé & Warrick, 2015). Soulé and Warrick (2015) went on to mention that countries that did well on the PISA, which directly assesses 21st-century skills like problem-solving and critical thinking, have shown higher rates of Gross Domestic Product (GDP) compared to countries that have not taken part in the PISA. The efforts of these nations to integrate 21st-century skills into their current educational systems as crucial skills development for their future workforce in order to compete in a global economy are highlighted by current scholarships (Soulé & Warrick, 2015; Moore, 2013). These countries are interested in succeeding in standard and traditional measures against test scores.

In relation to the aforementioned issue, Soulé and Warrick (2015) focused our attention on an economic issue. The following realities confront the US:

1) Other countries are investing more in education and the development of 21st-century skills.
2) American businesses are facing increased competition in a world market that is expanding quickly.
3) Businesses are shifting the US economy from manufacturing to information technology.

The manufacturing-based industrial economy in the USA has transitioned over the last few decades to a service economy, especially with the rise of well-paying information technology jobs that are driven by information, creativity, innovation, and knowledge (Soulé & Warrick, 2015).

In America, where more than 80% of employment is in the service sector, these variables have rebuilt and remade US businesses as well as the fabric of work (Soulé & Warrick, 2015). With employment in well-paid information technology services, the work sector is transitioning from manufacturing to services (2015). According to a 2009 assessment from the US Department of Labor and Bureau of Labor Statistics, "The employment of professionals and related occupations is expected to increase by nearly 16.8%, growing by over 5.2 million jobs" (p. 179). As published by the US Bureau of Labor Statistics (2012), according to Soulé and Warrick (2015), these forecasts proved accurate in 2012, with the service sector making the most advancements and hiring for manufacturing positions.

To highlight this development, the US Bureau of Labor Statistics reports that the national unemployment rate for professionals and closely associated occupations fell to 1.9 in March 2019 from 2.1 in March 2018 (2019). At the same time, more affluent professions are in great demand for job opportunities in the service sector, which is seeing considerably more steady development, including engineers, doctors, lawyers, and marketing consultants (2015).

A high demand exists around the world for knowledgeable technicians with a wide range of skills and education, including technical and 4Cs training. This demand for skilled technicians is happening in conjunction with the brutal fact that the baby boomers, the most skilled generation, people with knowledge and ambition, are leaving the labor market in large numbers due to their retirement age (2015). In this regard, Tulgan (2015) reported that the post-baby-boomer generation shift is another element of the soft skills gap. The older and more experienced workforce is retiring, making more room for the new generation to fit in.

The new generation is known for lacking patience, interpersonal skills, and maturity (Tulgan, 2015). This creates conflict between the youthful energy and excitement of the younger generation and the more informal and less obvious soft skills of the older generation (Tulgan, 2015). Furthermore, Tulgan (2015) said that by 2020, post-baby boomers will make up over 80% of the labor market, with Generations X, Y, and Z subjecting them to facts, social norms, and public standards and values.

High Demand of New Skills

Organizations are requesting new talents throughout their employment processes due to the fundamental variations in the domestic and international economies. Employers are searching for workers who can handle a variety of duties, use creativity in their work, and effectively collaborate with others in a team setting (Soulé & Warrick, 2015). In the United States, routine cognitive work and physical labor began to decline from the start of the 1970s, making way for an increase in non-routine, diagnostic, and collaborative trades, according to Autor, Levy, and Murnane (2003). Organizations started replacing manual laborers who were doing regular jobs with technology, automation, and computer systems (Autor et al., 2003).

They started encouraging workers who had the skills to complete non-routine activities and apply problem-solving methods. The significant transition to a computerized workplace necessitated the development of more extensive critical thinking, problem-solving, and communication skills. These tasks included using inconsistencies, improving production systems and processes, and supervising, managing, and coordinating the tasks, activities, and performances of other people (Soulé & Warrick, 2015; Moore, 2013).

Additionally, in the job market today, companies are placing much more value on soft skills like professionalism, interpersonal abilities, and social and people skills. These are the talents that companies frequently cite as being deficient among their staff (Hurrell, 2015). In this context, Hurrell (2015) drew attention to the "blame game," in which people are frequently held accountable for lack of soft skills on behalf of themselves, their families, the school system, and the government. Meanwhile, there is some worry that employees' animosity and discontent with their bosses may be a factor in why they aren't using their soft skills (Hurrell, 2015). Hurrell (2015) also cited the companies themselves in the aforementioned "blame game" for failing to include training and development of soft skills consistently and systematically for their staff.

In a study on the subject of the value of soft skills at work, done by Robles (2012) on 57 executives, 100% of those executives named integrity and communication as their top two needed soft skills for their work as well as key competencies for today's workforce. Additionally, 84.2% of executives said that civility is an incredibly important quality to have in the job, followed by responsibility (71.9%) and interpersonal skills (61.4%) (Robles, 2012). The results of these studies and research confirm the value of early training and development in the 4Cs and soft skills for students, professors, and instructors.

21st-Century Employment Demands 21st-Century Skilled Workforce

Without a doubt, corporations are in need of a workforce that can use a certain set of functional abilities. The phrase "survival skills of the new economy" is used by workforce development experts to underline the significance of these abilities. The deeper degree of information technology expertise is no longer an extravagance for a person or an organization, as these professionals have comprehended and acknowledged (Soulé & Warrick, 2015). Unexpectedly, this is not the case (2015). It would seem straightforward to make adjustments in technology techniques in order to generate possibilities for young professionals to outperform their older counterparts or the general work population in the firm.

In his book *Winning the Global Talent Showdown*, Edward E. Gordon (2009) discussed the presence of what he called a key technical contradiction. Although the younger generation of employees tends to be what we think of as computer nerds, they lack the skills, knowledge, enthusiasm, or curiosity necessary for professions in IT, creating, building, maintaining, or managing a variety of 21st-century gear and technology (Gordon, 2009). Boyles (2012) added to this context by stating that a wake-up call has been sounded for educational systems, educators, and teachers in order to address this disparity in the workforce's interest and knowledge and to ensure the US workforce's ability to compete for its share of the global economy.

To ensure the development of 21st-century skills and competencies in American students, such as self-direction, flexibility, innovation, collaboration, communication, creativity, problem-solving, and critical thinking, it is necessary to acknowledge this challenge and to make space in the current educational programs. To be prepared for occupations in 21st-century workplaces, American students must receive an education and be equipped with 21st-century abilities (Boyles, 2012).

The development of American students' 21st-century skills and competencies, such as self-direction, flexibility, innovation, collaboration, communication, creativity, problem-solving, and critical thinking, must be ensured by acknowledging this challenge and making room in the existing educational programs for these skills (Boyles, 2012). American students must receive an education and be equipped with 21st-century abilities in order to be prepared for professions in 21st-century companies (2012).

Levasseur (2013) discussed the significance of soft skills and how they are present and used across a variety of different sectors and disciplines, including operational systems, management systems, accounting, finance, leadership, project management, and more. Stewart, Wall, and Marciniec (2016) made note of college students' exaggerated confidence in their soft skill capabilities. According to a 2016 soft skills survey (standard, Likert 1–5 scale rating) conducted by Stewart et al. on a group of students using "the NACE, Hart Research Associates, and SHRM studies" (2016, p. 280), college graduates reported having confidence in their problem-solving skills at an average of 87.9%, written communication at 84.1%, teamwork at 83.6%, and verbal communication at 72.4%. Why do businesses continue to worry about the absence of soft skills in their newly hired college graduates when these graduates have such a high degree of confidence in their ability to possess them?

Figure 8.4 depicts the aspects of hard skills, soft skills, 4Cs skills, and educational abilities in producing a 21st-century workforce to be a part of the success and growth of a 21st-century business based on the aforementioned literature review method and findings.

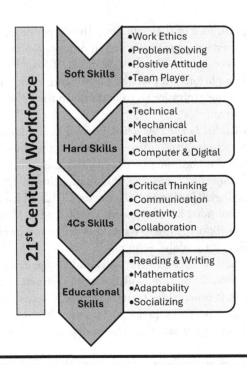

Figure 8.4 Model for developing 21st-century skilled workforce for 21st-century organizations. © Bakhshandeh 2024.

What Is Next?

We are about to start Part III of this book, reviewing what the research finds and identifying what is real and present in organizations. In Chapter 9, "Values Placed on 4Cs Skills by Organizations," we will present our research findings on what level of values organizations place on the 4Cs skills among their workforces.

References

Ahmadi, N. & Besançon, M. (2017). Creativity as a steppingstone towards developing other competencies in classrooms. *Education Research International, 2017*, 1–9, https://doi.org/10.1155/2017/1357456.

Autor, D., Levy, F., & Murnane, R. (2003). The skill content of recent technological change: An empirical exploration. *The Quarterly Journal of Economics, 118* (4), 1279–1333. https://doi.org/10.1162/003355303322552801.

Boyles, T. (2012). 21st century knowledge, skills, and abilities and entrepreneurial competencies: A model for undergraduate entrepreneurship education. *Journal of Entrepreneurship Education, 15*, 41–55. Retrieved from https://www.abacademies.org/articles/jeevol152012.pdf#page=47.

Center for Energy and Workforce Development. (n.d.). *WorkKeys Overview*. Washington, DC. Retrieved from www.cewd.org/media/doc/WorkKeysEmploymentSystem.doc.

Forbes Website. (2020). How strada education network is promoting pathways to good jobs. Retrieved from https://www.forbes.com/sites/tomvanderark/2019/05/20/how-strada-education-network-is-promoting-pathways-to-good-jobs/#285585dc2ff4.

Gordon, E. E. (2009). The future of jobs and careers. *Techniques: Connecting Education and Careers, 84*(6), 28–31. Retrieved from https://eric.ed.gov/?id=EJ858227.

Hurrell, S. (2015). Rethinking the soft skills deficit blame game: Employers, skills withdrawal and the reporting of soft skills gaps. *Human Relations, 69*(3), 605–628. https://doi.org/10.1177/0018726715591636.

Jones, V. R. (2015). 21st century skills: Communication. *Children's Technology and Engineering, 20*(2), 28–29. Retrieved from https://www.iteea.org/Publications/Journals/ESCJournal/CTEDecember2015.aspx?source.

Levasseur, R. (2013). People skills: developing soft skills - A change management perspective. *Interfaces, 43*(6), 566–571. https://doi.org/10.1287/inte.2013.0703.

Moore, T. (2013). Critical thinking: Seven definitions in search of a concept. *Studies in Higher Education, 38*(4), 506–522. https://doi.org/10.1080/03075079.2011.586995.

Robles, M. M. (2012). Executive perceptions of the top 10 soft skills needed in today's workplace. *Business Communication Quarterly, 75*(4), 453–465. https://doi.org/10.1177/1080569912460400.

Sawchuk, S. (2018). WorkKeys exam gauges literacy for work. *Education Week, 38*(6). Retrieved from http://ezaccess.libraries.psu.edu/login?url=https://www-proquest-com.ezaccess.libraries.psu.edu/docview/2116844928?accountid=13158.

SCANS Report. (2000). Employment & training administration. United States Department of Labor. Retrieved from https://wdr.doleta.gov/SCANS/whatwork/.

Schultz, Deanna & Stern, Sam. (2013). College and career ready? Perceptions of high school students related to WorkKeys assessments. *Career and Technical Education Research, 38*(2), 157–169. https://doi.org/10.5328/cter38.2.157.

Soulé, H. & Warrick, T. (2015). Defining 21st century readiness for all students: What we know and how to get there. *Psychology of Aesthetics, Creativity, and the Arts, 9*(2), 178–186. https://doi.org/10.1037/aca0000017.

Spies, T. G. & Xu, Y. (2018). Scaffolded academic conversations: Access to 21st-century collaboration and communication skills. *Intervention in School and Clinic, 54*(1), 22–30. https://doi.org/10.1177/1053451218762478.

Stewart, C., Wall, A., & Marciniec, S. (2016). Mixed signals: Do college graduates have the soft skills that employers want? *Competition Forum, 14*(2), 276–281. Retrieved from https://search.proquest.com/openview/fa7c5369a44d3fc071a43203a1ef6d5e/1?pq-origsite=gscholarcbl=39801.

Strada Education Network Website. (2020). Our Network. Retrieved from www.stradaeducation.org.

Swaney, Kyle B., Allen, J., Casillas, A., Hanson, M. A., & Robbins, S. B. (2012). Interests, work values, and occupations: Predicting work outcomes with the workkeys fit assessment. *Journal of Career Assessment, 20*(4), 359–374. https://doi.org/10.1177/1069072712448730.

Tulgan, B. (2015). *Bridging the Soft Skills Gap: How to Teach the Missing Basics to Today's Young Talent.* Hoboken, NJ: John Wiley & Sons, Inc. https://doi.org/10.1002/9781119171409.

US Bureau of Labor Statistics. (2012). *Employment Data.* Washington, DC: US Department of Labor.

US Bureau of Labor Statistics. (2019). *Economic News Releases.* Washington, DC: US Department of Labor. Retrieved from https://www.bls.gov/web/empsit/cpseea30.htm.

Williams, L. K. (2015). *ACT WorkKeys as an Indicator of Academic Success.* (Published doctoral dissertation). Mississippi State University. PreQuest.

IDENTIFYING WHAT IS REAL AND PRESENT IN ORGANIZATIONS

In this part, this book presents the actual research findings by reviewing the quantitative data, which have revealed themselves as a series of themes and sub-themes as the outcome of interviewing business professional contributors (senior managers, middle- and lower-tier managers, supervisors, and line managers). This part identifies what the real scenarios are and what is actually present in organizations and among their workforces relative to the 21st-century 4Cs skills.

Chapter 9: Values Placed on 4Cs Skills by Organizations

This chapter presents the research findings on what level of values organizations place on the 4Cs skills among their workforces.

Chapter 10: Impact of 4Cs Skills Gap on Team Performance

In this chapter we look at the perspectives of business professionals about the influence of the 4Cs skills gap on organizations regarding team performance.

Chapter 11: Effective 4Cs Skills Training and Development

This chapter examines business professionals' perspectives of what is good and effective training for developing 4Cs skills among their workforces.

DOI: 10.4324/9781003462316-11

Chapter 12: Essence of Cohesiveness and Workability

This chapter reveals the additional information gathered from business professionals about their experience of having or lacking 4Cs skills in their organization or among their workforce that they would like to share or add to the interview.

Chapter 9

Values Placed on 4Cs
Skills by Organizations

Introduction

In this chapter, we address what we have gleaned from the views of business professionals working inside organizations, such as senior managers, middle managers, line managers, and production supervisors or foremen, related to the *first intention* of this research, the "Values Placed on 4Cs Skills by Organizations" among their employees in the following three areas:

1. Their *expectations* or aspirations about the appearance of the 4Cs skills among their personnel in the context of reflecting a competent workforce. The findings indicate that the professionals working for the organizations have demonstrated the value they place on and the characteristics they seek in their desired skilled personnel.
2. What is the *current skills gap* among their personnel related to the 4Cs skills, in the present situation and real-time data? According to the findings, the business professionals working for the organizations exhibited the opinion that there is a gap in existence related to the 4Cs skills. It sheds light on what has to be done, what training needs to be provided, and how the firms are placing a value on their desired competent personnel.
3. What is the *degree of values* the organization's business professionals are placing on any of the 4Cs skills among their employees directly in the form of a quantifiable figure, with zero being the lowest value placed on these abilities and ten representing the most value placed on these skills?

Please note that these collected materials in the domain of *Themes* arose as common perspectives of their understanding during our interviews from 45 contributors within the 17 participating organizations, without any bias, input, or additions by the researcher.

In this chapter, we look at the researcher's findings, theses, and perceptions organized in the following categories:

- Organizations' Expectations of 4Cs among Their Workforces.
- The Current Skills Gap from the Organizations' Viewpoints.
- Contrast among Organizations' Expectations of 4Cs and the Current Skills Gap.
- Degree of Values Put on Any of 4Cs Skills by Organizations.

DOI: 10.4324/9781003462316-12

Organizations' Expectations of 4Cs among Their Workforces

The following section presents the themes that highlight the characteristics of what the 4Cs skills (critical thinking, communication, creativity, and collaboration) are perceived as for business professionals who represent their organizations. These themes represent the contributors' expectations of 4Cs skills for their employees. Given that the primary objective of this study is to determine how organizations' workforces feel about possessing the 4Cs capabilities, this aspect of the study constitutes the greatest portion of it. The following findings are organized by all the 4Cs skills.

Critical Thinking

The four skills that make up the 4Cs are deeply intertwined but cannot exist independently of each other. The following elements represent the organizations' professionals' expectations from their workers regarding using critical thinking.

Problem-Solving Mentality

Most interviews revealed that a critical thinking trait that business professionals expect and want in their workers is a problem-solving mentality and aptitude. Within the "Problem-solving mentality" theme, three sub-themes arose and demonstrated more related features of the theme as follows:

- **Decisiveness.** This subject highlights the managers' desire for their staff to be proactive and take charge of problem-solving in their divisions or as a team by being decisive and trusting in their decisions.
- **Patience.** Before tackling the issue, express concern and understanding for those who report to their managers, taking the time to comprehend the circumstance and related difficulties they may be communicating.
- **Broader View.** Looking at the larger picture demonstrates what businesses want their staff to do while making plans or choices.

Constant Novice

Another issue that emerged was the importance of continuous learning as a trait of the workforce that applies critical thinking and as something that business professionals anticipate and look for in their employees. The "constant novice" topic was broken down into three different sub-themes as follows:

- **Accumulating Knowledge.** This theme demonstrates the enthusiasm of the employees to continue to study and use their acquired knowledge in their profession.
- **Pay Attention.** Paying attention and learning from mistakes shows that a person is interested in and capable of attending to their job and responsibilities and avoiding repeating the same mistakes.
- **Study Tested Ideas.** This topic shows employees' eagerness to study and use tried-and-true procedures, concepts, and work disciplines rather than attempting to introduce novel ideas.

Get It Done

Another frequent theme that emerged as a quality of the workforce that applies the critical-thinking notion of thinking as something that business professionals are expecting and seeking in their workers was getting the job done. The following sub-themes evolved and provided further information on the "Get it Done" theme:

- **Learn from Others.** This researcher frequently heard businesspeople talk about the desire for their employees to be open to learning from others.
- **Think before Acting.** The desire of business professionals to have a key employee trade in their company is demonstrated by this subject. Business professionals expect their employees to think deeper and look at all corners before acting on something.
- **Do Your Best.** The majority of business professionals are particularly interested in incorporating this concept into their workforces; if you do your best, you are always ahead of the game.

You can see the summary of links between themes and sub-themes gleaned from organizations' expectations for critical thinking among their workforce in Figure 9.1.

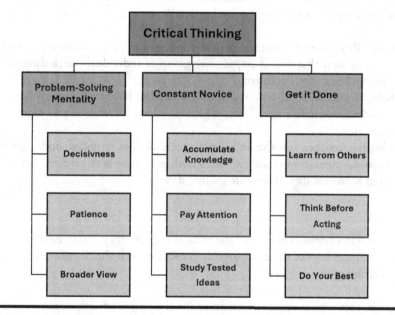

Figure 9.1 Links between organizations' expectations for critical thinking among their workforce. © Bakhshandeh, 2024.

Communication

There is a pertinent relationship between how the 4Cs skills are related and functioning hand in hand, as this researcher has previously said. The research's emergent topics related to communication are discussed in the section below.

Relatedness

The business professionals who were questioned throughout the data-collection procedure demonstrated relatedness and interpersonal relationships as the capacity to foster a welcoming workplace. The subsequent three sub-themes revealed further information on the "Relatedness" topic:

- **Connection.** This topic emerged from the interviews for this research's 4Cs skills section as a strong trait of a great communicator. The ability to connect to others is the first step to getting related to them.
- **Listening.** Another effective communication tool is listening, a common topic among effective communicators. Business professionals expect their employees to listen to them and be responsible for recognizing filters that block their listening for what the speaker is saying or pointing out.
- **Generation Gap.** Business professionals expect various generations working together in the same workplace to relate to, comprehend, and support one another.

Role Precision

Role precision and clarity, which helps individuals understand their positions in their work and jobs, is a crucial component of a well-functioning business. Under the "Role Precision" theme, three sub-themes appeared and provided further details:

- **Efficiency.** This theme became apparent due to the normal, clear, and to-the-point communication expression that would impact any group of individuals, including teams, departments, groups, or a whole company.
- **Specificity.** Businesspeople who spoke on the need to have clear and explicit communication tended to emphasize specificity, which will lead to removing any gray areas in the communication.
- **Workability.** Another sub-theme of role precision that surfaced under communication skills is commitment to workability. When both parties on both sides of communication are committed to workability, things are getting done.

Transparency

Many professional interviewees expressed the issue of transparency and stressed its significance in relation to the management of their employees. These three sub-themes provide further information on the "Transparency" subject:

- **Openness.** This subject demonstrates an essential aspect of efficient communication between workers and management and a readiness to be receptive to new information and solutions.
- **Flexibility.** Because of its capacity to adapt, this topic emphasizes the necessity to be adaptable and adopt new methods of communication to get things done.
- **Reliability.** In order to support teams' and departments' ongoing productivity and trouble-free operation, this subject evolved as a crucial component of realistic and practical communication.

You can see the summary of links between themes and sub-themes gleaned from organizations' expectations for communication among their workforce in Figure 9.2.

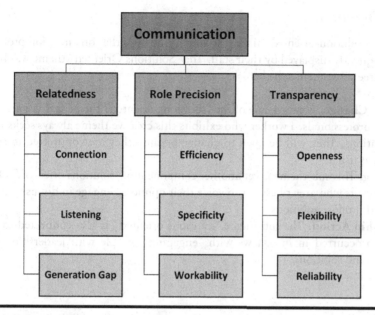

Figure 9.2 Links between organizations' expectations for communication among their work-force. © Bakhshandeh, 2024.

Creativity

There is evidence of relevance and connection between how employees and business professionals regard the 4Cs skills as the study consistently uncovers themes connected to them. The research's developing topics related to creativity are discussed in the following section.

Thinking Outside the Box

The subject of thinking outside the box surfaced, and several interviewees emphasized it as a crucial aspect of creativity that employers value in their staff. The "Thinking Outside the Box" theme had three sub-themes that showed additional information. They are as follows:

- **New Possibilities.** One of the sub-themes of "thinking outside the box" has become this one. Management desires their employees to think about new possibilities for themselves, their team, and the organization as a whole. These new possibilities will motivate and create opportunities for everyone.
- **Creative Thinking.** This subject is a sub-theme of "thinking outside the box," which came up frequently in interviews about the qualities that business executives look for in the work-force by trusting themselves to apply creative thinking to come up with a better solution for problems they are facing in performance and productivity.
- **Creative Leadership.** "Creative thinking," "creative leadership," and "creative thinker" came hand in hand and emerged as sub-themes of "thinking outside the box." One of the essences of leadership is to be creative and come up with innovative approaches and find solutions.

Solutions Oriented

The subject of a solution-oriented mindset is among the ones that organization professionals like to see most frequently displayed by their staff. The "Solutions Oriented" theme was further developed in the three subsequent sub-themes.

- **Open to Change.** A sub-theme of the "solutions-oriented" theme is this one. According to business professionals, a worker who exhibits this creative theme always seeks the necessary modifications. They will be open to change because they are committed to solutions, not business as usual.
- **Engaging.** This sub-theme is yet another component of "solutions oriented." Organizations value workers who aren't hesitant to voice their opinions, engage in discussions about problems, and propose solutions.
- **Leadership Action.** The sub-theme "solutions oriented" is also connected to this subject, which co-occurred in interviews with "engaging." People with leadership qualities take action to find solutions.

Innovative

Being innovative always goes hand in hand with exercising creativity. Business professionals' interest in and desire to see their workers use creativity in their work, job performance, and job production led to the emergence of this subject. The "Innovative" theme was further developed into three sub-themes.

- **Performing.** This subject is a sub-theme of "innovative" and occurs when people apply their imagination when they are performing their duties to accomplish their work and jobs better and more effectively.
- **Productive.** Another aspect of being innovative that arose concurrently with performance is the idea that people may utilize their creativity to become better and more effective workers by paying more attention to what they are doing, intending to remove any potential flaws in the process.
- **Merging Skills.** This subject shows how the workforce may use creativity in conjunction with other 4Cs skills like critical thinking, communication, and teamwork to improve their work and jobs.

You can see the summary of links between themes and sub-themes gathered from organizations' expectation for creativity among their workforce in Figure 9.3.

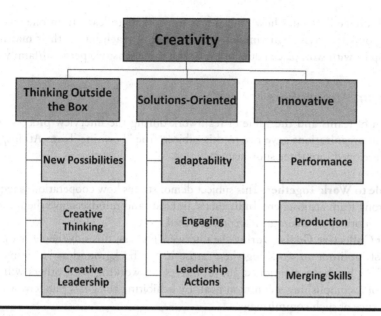

Figure 9.3   Links between organizations' expectations for creativity among their workforce. © Bakhshandeh, 2024.

Collaboration

There is a pertinent relationship between how the 4Cs skills are related, supporting one another, and cooperating together, just like there is with the other 4Cs skills. The research's emergent issues related to collaboration are discussed in the following section.

Learning from Others

During the data collection process and participant interviews, the idea of learning from others came to light as one of the qualities of collaboration from a business professional's perspective. The three sub-themes that follow revealed further specifics of the main topic of "Learning from Others."

■ **Fostering a Culture.** This topic, one of the "Learning from Others" sub-themes, emphasizes the value of developing a culture where employees support and learn from one another to work together effectively.

■ **Sharing Knowledge.** This one is another sub-theme of "Learning from Others" that highlights the value of information exchange and dissemination among coworkers. This significant subject assists firms in raising the knowledge, skills, and ability (KSB) of their workforces without using excessive time and resources to do so. Business professionals are very interested to see their workforce sharing knowledge and teaching each other.

■ **Reaching Out.** Reaching out to one's superiors, supervisors, and coworkers is a requirement for this sub-theme, which is an addition to "learning from others and sharing knowledge."

This sub-theme illustrates how crucial it is for workers to learn from one another. Besides learning opportunities, sometimes a worker needs to reach out to their managers for help and support with workplace issues or even with some sensitive personal/family matters.

Forming Team Atmosphere

The discussion of teams and the value of teamwork during the interview process with business professionals in organizations gave rise to this subject. The "Forming Team Atmosphere" theme was further developed into three sub-themes.

- **Aptitude to Work Together.** This subject demonstrates how cooperation is required to create a strong team atmosphere. Individuals' interests and mindsets give them the aptitude to work with others to accomplish a common goal.
- **Exhibit Collective Goals**. During the interview process, this sub-theme as well as the sub-theme of "aptitude to work together," arose in the background as "forming team atmosphere." As has been mentioned above, interest in working with others will increase the chance of accomplishing a common goal. By exhibiting the goals publicly, we can increase the presence of such commitment.
- **Team Approach to Issues.** This subject arose as a third sub-theme to the main theme of "forming a team atmosphere," demonstrating the importance of cooperation abilities in creating a solid and effective team environment. Nothing against the individual approach to resolving issues, but collective minds will work better than an individual due to team members' knowledge, skills, and abilities. In the end, the team will win.

Developing Relationships

This topic became apparent against the backdrop of "forming a team environment" and "aptitude to work together" as a crucial component. Constructing a functional and comprehensive team atmosphere and culture will be challenging without developing relationships. The "Developing Relationships" subject was further developed in the three subsequent sub-themes:

- **Understanding Diversity.** This sub-theme surfaced in interviews and discussions regarding building a working relationship between managers and supervisors on the one side and employees on the other. Understanding and respecting individual differences are necessary for fostering connections.
- **Drop the Ego.** One of the sub-themes that emerged as being crucial to developing connections among coworkers in a company is this one. Individuals' egos always cause friction and unworkability. One person's desire to be the shining star and get all the credit always messes up the teamwork culture.
- **Customer Relations.** Another sub-theme of this subject emphasizes the significance of establishing customer relations that are practical and acceptable for the most crucial elements of organizational development. The well-being of the organization, including job opportunities, depends on their happy and satisfied customers.

You can see the summary of links between themes and sub-themes extracted from organizations' expectation for collaboration among their workforce in Figure 9.4.

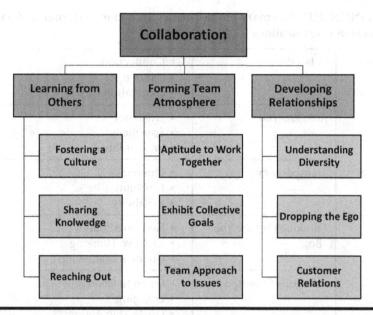

Figure 9.4 Links between organizations' expectation for collaboration among their workforce. © Bakhshandeh, 2024.

Summary of Organization's 4Cs Skills Expectations for Employees

The themes that emerged from questioning business professionals in response to the interview question concerning the organization's expectation of 4Cs skills among their workforces are summarized in Table 9.1.

Table 9.1 Summary of the Themes That Emerged from an Analysis of the 4Cs Expectations of Organizations

4Cs Skills	Themes	Sub-Themes
Critical Thinking	Problem-Solving Mentality	• Decisiveness • Patience • Broader View
	Constant Novice	• Accumulating Knowledge • Paying Attention • Studying Tested Ideas
	Get It Done	• Learn from Others • Think before Acting • Do Your Best

(Continued)

Table 9.1 (CONTINUED) Summary of the Themes That Emerged from an Analysis of the 4Cs Expectations of Organizations

Communication	Relatedness	• Connection • Listening • Generation Gap
	Role Precision	• Efficiency • Specificity • Workability
	Transparency	• Openness • Flexibility • Reliability
Creativity	Thinking Outside the Box	• New Possibilities • Creative Thinking • Creative Leadership
	Solutions Oriented	• Open to Change • Engaging • Leadership Actions
	Innovative	• Performing • Productive • Merging Skills
Collaboration	Learning from Others	• Fostering a Culture • Sharing Knowledge • Reaching Out
	Forming Team Atmosphere	• Aptitude to Work Together • Exhibit Collective Goals • Team Approach to Issues
	Developing Relationships	• Understanding Diversity • Dropping the Ego • Customer Relations

Note. © Bakhshandeh, 2024.

The business professionals who took part in this study on behalf of their companies shared their general impressions of what a workforce with the 21st-century 4Cs skills looks like. These perspectives and ideal points of view reflect the importance that business and non-profit companies place on the 4Cs skills and competencies. This research presents the business professionals' perspectives on the current gap in 4Cs abilities among their workforces in the next part.

The Current Skills Gap from Organizations' Professionals Viewpoints

The gaps in the 4Cs skills (critical thinking, communication, creativity, and collaboration) that exist in the workforces of business professionals' organizations are summarized in the following topics. The second part of their discussion discusses how businesses value the four 21st-century skills. The topics connected to how organizations view the 4Cs, how they consider the 4Cs skills to be in their evaluation, and how they wish to see it among their workforces were revealed by this research. This section discusses the disparity between what they would want to see and the actual 4Cs skills gap in their workforce.

Critical Thinking

The following topics have developed in relation to the lack of critical thinking skills within organizational workforces.

Lack of Forming Decisions

When organizations' professionals were questioned about the appearance and existing 4Cs skills gap among their workforces, the "Lack of Forming Decisions" topic arose. This section demonstrates the lack of critical thinking abilities and "Lack of Forming Decisions." Three sub-themes that provided further specifics on this main subject are as follows:

- **Absence of Autonomy.** Business professionals pointed out the absence of autonomy among their employees. They claim employees are in constant need of receiving directions and supervision. However, some of the reasons behind the lack of autonomy are due to some federal and union laws and regulations.
- **Anxiety of Making Errors.** At the same time, business professionals underlined the presence of fear and anxiety among their employees for making a decision and potentially facing the consequences of making a mistake. According to some of the interviews, they like seeing their employees swing, step out of their comfort zone, and play bigger.
- **Lack of Empowerment.** According to the interview data, there is a lack of empowerment by managers to empower employees to be expressive and to make decisions due to a lack of autonomy and fear of making mistakes.

Deficiency of Training and Development

When asking organizations' professionals about the emergence and present 4Cs skills gap among their workforces, the subject "Deficiency of Training and Development" also came up. This section demonstrates the skills gap caused by a lack of training and development. The three sub-themes that follow show additional specifics within this topic:

- **Not Obtaining Solutions.** In some cases, the workforce can see the problem, but they don't have sufficient or relevant training to fix it; therefore, the issue remains.
- **Difficult to Quantify.** Business professionals express their frustration about quantifying the need for critical thinking training for their people. They are concerned that what employees are asking for training is not needed for further development.
- **Insufficient Evaluation.** According to business professionals who were interviewed, there is no sufficient way to evaluate and assess employees' level of critical thinking. Some of these concerns arose from the need for critical thinking depending on different industries and relevant local and federal laws.

Absence of Commitment

When business professionals were questioned about the appearance and existing 4Cs skills gap among their workforces, the topic "Absence of Commitment" also came up. This section demonstrates the lack of knowledge in the area relating to the absence of commitment. The three sub-themes that follow show additional specifics within this topic.

- **Lack of Employee Commitment.** Business professionals believe that for employees to employ critical thinking, they need to have their commitment both to the organization and to their career, and they must put their mind into doing it.
- **Absence of Organizational Commitment.** On the other hand, according to some of the data collected, not all business professionals believe that organizations display an absolute commitment to their employees either. Therefore, organizations' expectations of employee commitment are unrealistic.
- **Running Business as Usual.** This theme arose from businesses that are just conducting their business as usual without any intention to use critical thinking to make a difference for their employees; therefore, employees are also just running their work as usual without using any critical thinking to improve their effectiveness or efficiency.

You can see the summary of links between emerged themes and sub-themes from organizations' professionals' viewpoint on the current skills gap in the area of critical thinking among their workforce in Figure 9.5.

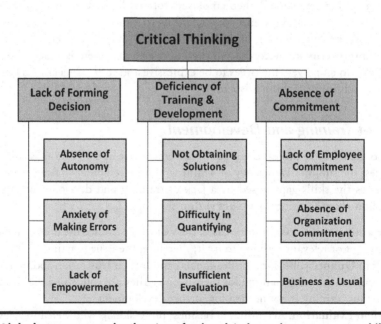

Figure 9.5   Links between organizations' professionals' viewpoints on current skills gap in the area of critical thinking among their workforce. © Bakhshandeh, 2024.

Communication

The following topics have evolved in relation to the lack of communication skills in the workforces of organizations.

The Missing Base

When business professionals were questioned about the appearance and presence of the 4Cs skills gap among their workforces, the concept of "The Missing Base" arose. The skills gap linked to the missing base in communication skills is shown in this section. Three sub-themes that provided further specifics on this main subject are as follows:

- **Working in a Silo.** When individuals, for any reason, work in a silo, there will not be any effective communication channels between them and their related team members. This issue mostly appears on a top-to-bottom communication from management to their lower tiers without managers being completely aware of the issue at hand.
- **Lost in Transmission.** Sometimes the meaning of communication or intentions of the person who is communicating is lost during the transmission of the message. Different cultural backgrounds, different languages, or email/text messages add to the possibility of losing the message intent during the transmission.
- **Missing Relatedness; Missing Communication.** Without a background of relatedness and understanding, the chance of having effective communication decreases. Just telling people what to do is not effective communication; there is always a need for some form of relatedness.

Vague Communication

When business professionals were questioned about the appearance and existing 4Cs skills gap among their workforces, the subject of "Vague Communication" also came to light. This section demonstrates the vague and unclear communication gap in communication skills. Three sub-themes that provided further specifics on this main subject are as follows:

- **Confusion by Technology.** Not completely aware and understanding new communication technology is a big issue in clear and precise communication among managers and employees, especially older generations. Given the fast and broad availability of communication platforms, it is natural for people to get confused about how to use and merge them.
- **Inadequate Tasks.** Not completing tasks and leaving them half-baked is another issue that might have been caused by lack of communication. This is the time for both sides of the transmission to communicate clear expectations, standards, and regulations for completing tasks.
- **Making Assumptions.** According to business professionals, many individuals make assumptions about what they have been told to do or how they need to complete a task. In some cases, these assumptions arise from the background of language barriers and translations.

Inadequate Quality

When business professionals were questioned about the appearance and existing 4Cs skills gap among their workforces, the issue of "Inadequate Quality" also surfaced. This section demonstrates the inadequate and poor quality of the communication skills gap. Three sub-themes that provided further specifics on this main subject are as follows:

- **Not Listening.** Business professionals complain that some people just don't listen. They say 'yes, sure,' but do whatever they want. According to interviews, people have many filters in their listening, making transmitting messages or the intended outcome of communication very hard.
- **Ineffective Communication.** Missing pieces, confused intent, and plotted filters or intentions make effective communication very hard. These issues cause such poor and inadequate communication.
- **Needs for Regularity.** There is a need for more frequent communication on a regular basis, whether it is daily at some particular time of the day or weekly at the end of the week for debriefing and/or at the beginning of a week for planning.

You can see the summary of links between emerged themes and sub-themes from organizations' professionals' viewpoints on the current skills gap in the area of communication among their workforce in Figure 9.6.

Figure 9.6 Links between organizations' professionals' viewpoints on current skills gap in the area of communication among their workforce. © Bakhshandeh, 2024.

Creativity

The following topics have surfaced in relation to the lack of creativity in the workforce of organizations.

Absence of Imagination

When asking business professionals about the appearance and existing 4Cs skills gap among their workforces, the phrase "Absence of Imagination" came up often. This section highlights the absence of an imagination gap in creativity skills. This topic was further divided into the following three sub-themes:

- **Trapped in Habitual Rut.** It is not unusual when an individual or a team gets used to certain practices and continues repeating them routinely as a habit. This way of working is a big barrier to imagination and creativity.
- **Not Thinking Contrarily.** Mixing critical thinking and creativity will guide individuals to start thinking differently. They will question the status quo and look into what else they can do? Or how else this can be done differently.
- **It Is Always Done This Way.** The good old saying "we always did it this way" is a barrier to creativity and innovation. There is a need for people to step outside this repetitive thinking so they can create something new.

Ought to Be Creative

When asking business professionals about the appearance and existing 4Cs skills gap among their workforces, the phrase "Ought to Be Creative" came up often. This section demonstrates the "ought" for a creative-related skills gap. This topic was further developed in the following three sub-themes:

- **Fearful of Expressing.** Most individuals are timid to come forward and express their ideas because they might think their opinion is not good enough, or just because they are not a manager, they should just put their heads down and work. Every contribution counts.
- **Essential to Survival.** Creativity is the way to grow and to be nimbler with the work. Creativity is a big part of surviving in any fierce market competition. Adding creativity to collaboration will make better productivity and faster progress.
- **Lack of Development.** Unfortunately, the younger generation doesn't practice creativity as much as expected at the workplace, especially in entry-level or production-line positions. Organizations must establish developmental programs encouraging new hires to express their creativity.

Think Partnership

When business professionals were questioned about the appearance and present 4Cs skills gap among their workforces, the phrase "Think Partnership" also came up frequently. This section demonstrates the think partnership creativity skills gap. This subject was further developed into three sub-themes:

- ■ **Collaboration with Organization.** Individuals who are committed to working with the organization come to managers and express their ideas. The ones who are not happy with their job stay distant and just do their hours. This is a partnership mentality, which is missing in establishing strong partnership among employees and the organization.
- ■ **Leadership Needs Creativity.** Creativity is an element of leadership. If employees know that their creativity plus the other 4Cs skills are the pathway to career development and future leadership, then they would express more and contribute more to the organization.
- ■ **Not Being Attached.** Managers and supervisors should let go of what they know or are attached to in order to build a safe environment for the new generation to express their creativity. At the same time, employees with new ideas need to learn that not all new ideas are feasible to implement, so they should not be attached to their ideas either.

You can see the summary of links between merged themes and sub-themes from organizations' professionals' viewpoint on the current skills gap in the area of creativity among their workforce in Figure 9.7.

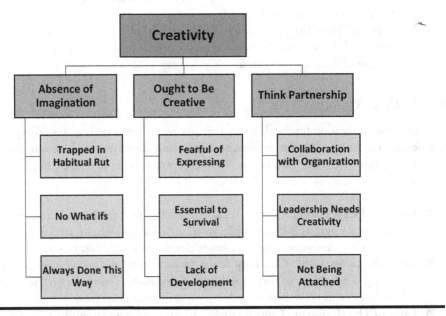

Figure 9.7 Links between organizations' professionals' viewpoints on current skills gap in the area of creativity among their workforce. © Bakhshandeh, 2024.

Collaboration

The following topics emerged while interviewing business professionals in participating organizations concerning the lack of collaboration skills across organizational workforces.

Working in Silos

When asking business professionals about the appearance and existing 4Cs skills gap among their workforces, the phrase "Working in Silos" came up often. This section highlights the lack of teamwork skills related to working in silos. This topic was further developed in the three following sub-themes:

- **Missing Teamwork.** The biggest negative impact of working alone is that working as a team enables learning from each other. There are always individuals with certain personality traits who want to work in a silo. Teamwork is one of the essential elements of collaboration skills.
- **Lost Opportunities.** Working in silos is a pathway to losing opportunities to expand knowledge, learn new skills, and grow personally and professionally. Many individuals expand their 4Cs skills just by working with and learning from a team of professionals.
- **Lack of Connections.** The other negative aspect of working in a silo is the lack of connection and building interpersonal relationships at the workplace. Unfortunately, some of the distancing issues are exacerbated because of the expansion of modern communication technology.

Defiance to Collaborate

When asked about the appearance and existing 4Cs skills gap among their workforces, business professionals' "Defiance to Collaborate" surfaced as a theme. This section demonstrates the lack of defiance to collaborate or cooperate. This topic was further developed in the following three sub-themes:

- **Competing vs. Collaborating.** Unfortunately, some individuals have a competitive personality that prevents them from collaborating with others. Being competitive is a good personality character, but it will be beneficial when used side by side with collaboration for the benefit of a team, a division, and an organization.
- **Clash of Personalities.** This is another barrier to collaboration: people's personalities clash, especially when they are attached to their ideas and want to be the one who gets all the credit. Because of this, many individuals are marked as "hard to work with" at their workplace.
- **Absence of Skills Building.** Anyone interested in building skills needs to be collaborative and work with others who walked on that pathway before they arrived. Lack of collaboration ends with a lack of skills building, which is not serving anyone.

Employ 4Cs to Collaborate

When asking business professionals about the appearance and present 4Cs skills gap among their workforces, the phrase "Employ 4Cs" began to emerge as a trend. This section demonstrates the lack of employing 4Cs in collaboration skills. This topic was further developed in the following three sub-themes:

- **Using Critical Thinking.** Critical thinking is a skill that anyone can use and mix with any other skills they are trying to develop. Regardless of professional positions, mixing critical thinking and collaboration will help people in their lives in general.

- **Utilize Communication.** To collaborate effectively, there is a need to communicate effectively and actively listen for values from others. Developing communication skills is essential to personal or professional development.
- **Express Creativity.** Creativity is a good way to collaborate with others. Brainstorming for new ideas is one of the effective ways that teams work together. Creativity allows people to express their ideas and get empowered by their managers.

You can see the summary of links between emerged themes and sub-themes from organizations' professionals' viewpoints on the current skills gap in the area of collaboration among their workforce in Figure 9.8.

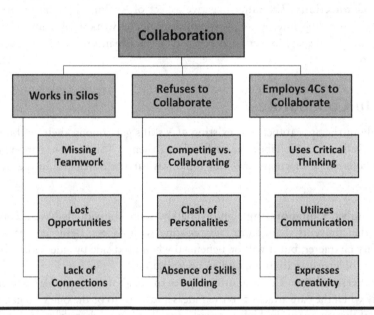

Figure 9.8   Links between organizations' professionals' viewpoints on current skills gap in the area of collaboration among their workforce. © Bakhshandeh, 2024.

Summary of Observation on Current 4Cs Skills Gap by Organizations' Management

Table 9.2 summarizes themes that arose from interviewing business professionals as outcomes of the interview question about business professionals' observations regarding the present 4Cs skills gap among their workforces.

Table 9.2 Summary of Observations on Current 4Cs Skills Gap by Organizations' Management

4Cs Skills	Themes	Sub-Themes
Critical Thinking	Lack of Forming Decisions	• Absence of Autonomy • Anxiety of Making Errors • Lack of Empowerment
	Deficiency of Training and Development	• Not Obtaining Solutions • Difficult to Quantify • Insufficient Evaluation
	Absence of Commitment	• Lack of Employee Commitment • Absence of Organization Commitment • Running Business as Usual
Communication	The Missing Base	• Working in Silo • Lost in Transmission • No Relatedness; No Communication
	Vague Communication	• Confused by Technology • Inadequate Tasks • Making Assumptions
	Inadequate Quality	• Not Listening • Ineffective Communication • Needs for Regularity
Creativity	Absence of Imagination	• Trapped in Habitual Rut • No What Ifs • It Is Always Done This Way
	Ought to Be Creative	• Fearful of Expressing • Essential to Survival • Lack of Development
	Think Partnership	• Collaboration with Organization • Leadership Needs Creativity • Not Being Attached
Collaboration	Works in Silos	• Missing Teamwork • Lost Opportunities • Lack of Connections
	Refuses to Collaborate	• Competing vs. Collaborating • Clash of Personalities • Absence of Skills Building
	Employs 4Cs to Collaborate	• Uses Critical Thinking • Utilizes on Communication • Expresses Creativity

Note. © Bakhshandeh, 2024.

Contrast among Organizations' Expectations of 4Cs and the Current Skills Gap

The topics shown in Table 9.3 are not intended to immediately correspond to one another across the columns; nonetheless, they do demonstrate a connection between the overall businesses' objectives and the current and present 4Cs skills gap among the organizations' workforces.

Table 9.3 Contrast among Organizations' Expectations of 4Cs and the Current Skills Gap

4Cs Skills	Expectation of 4Cs	Current 4Cs Gap
Critical Thinking	Problem-Solving Mentality	Lack of Forming Decisions
	Constant Novice	Deficiency of Training and Development
	Get It Done	Absence of Communication
Communication	Relatedness	The Missing Base
	Role Precision	Vague Communication
	Transparency	Inadequate Quality
Creativity	Thinking Outside the Box	Absence of Imagination
	Solutions Oriented	Ought to Be Creative
	Innovative	Think Partnership
Collaboration	Learning from Others	Working in Silos
	Forming Team Atmosphere	Refusing to Collaborate
	Developing Relationships	Employing 4Cs to Collaborate

Note. © Bakhshandeh, 2024.

Degree of Values Put on Any of the 4Cs Skills by Organizations

In general, the business experts who took part in this research on behalf of their companies shared their opinions about the existence and impact of the 4Cs skills gap in their workforces. These insights and points of view show how important 4Cs talents are to both for-profit and private-sector firms, and they are closely connected. This research exposes the business professionals' perceptions of the value they place on 21st-century 4Cs abilities by applying a quantitative grading on how much they value these talents in the next section (Degree of Values).

A discussion about the value that business professionals place on the 4Cs skills of the 21st century emerged after this researcher solicited information and collected data from them regarding their expectations of a workforce with those skills as well as their perception of the presence of a 4Cs skills gap among their current workforces. Before assigning a numerical value (ranging from zero to ten) to their selections and chosen values, the participants had the opportunity to express their overall perspective on how much they valued certain talents.

The total and average participant ratings of how much value firms place on 4Cs capabilities among their workforces are shown in the following figure (Figure 9.9). The 4Cs skills—critical thinking, communication, creativity, and collaboration—are rated on a scale of zero to ten, with ten representing the highest ranking. The researcher's goals in doing this rating task were to:

1) Observe how highly participants appreciate the 4Cs abilities in their workforce, and
2) Ask participants to consider how highly they value the 4Cs talents in their workforce.

The 17 organizations and the 45 contributors, who represented all levels of management (executives, senior management, middle managers, supervisors, and line managers), were asked to rank, in order from most valuable to least valuable, the degree to which they place importance on the following four skills: (1) *Communication*, (2) *Collaboration*, (3) *Critical Thinking*, and (4) *Creativity*.

It is crucial to note that the nature of these firms' goods has a big influence on their selection of values for each of these 4Cs skills, and that this decision is determined by what they are doing and what they are creating. Given that these organizations do not all conduct their businesses in the same industry is an important point to keep in mind. For instance, manufacturing businesses' interest in the 4Cs abilities is very different from the interest that an organization which focuses on higher education would have in the 4Cs skills among its workforce and the value that it would place on those talents. Nevertheless, in any scenario, this brief rating would assist the participants and their respective businesses in planning their method to where they should focus their training energies and what they should pay attention to in the future growth among their employees.

The closeness of the ratings and average on the top two ratings of communication (91.67) and collaboration (91.33) may be read as the most important values these firms place among skills for their workers (see Figure 9.9).

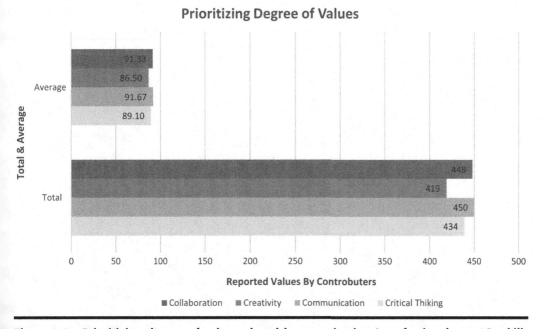

Figure 9.9 Prioritizing degree of values placed by organizations' professionals on 4Cs skills among their employees. © Bakhshandeh 2024

What Is Next?

The next chapter in Part III is titled "Impact of 4Cs Skills Gap on Team Performance" and is the second intention of the research. In Chapter 10, we talk about the perspectives of business professionals (senior managers, middle managers, and line managers) about the influence of the 4Cs skills gap on organizations regarding team performance.

Chapter 10

Impact of 4Cs Skills Gap on Team Performance

Introduction

In this chapter, we address what we have gleaned from the view of business professionals working inside organizations, such as senior managers, middle managers, line managers, and production supervisors or foremen, related to the *second intention* of this research, the "Impact of 4Cs Skills Gap on Team Performance" and the positive effects of using 4Cs skills or negative effect of not utilizing them as connected to organizations' team performance by their employees in the following two areas:

a) Assigning a numerical value to each of the 4Cs and *ranking* them in order of relevance for *improving team performance*, with the most significant 4C skills appearing at the top and the least significant one appearing at the bottom. It is interesting to note that not all of these 17 organizations operate in their sector; rather, the ranking skills of each organization are pertinent to the nature of their respective sectors.

b) Talking about a time when an employee demonstrated either *positive effects* due to any of the 4Cs skills they possessed or *negative effects* due to a lack of any of the 4Cs skills that negatively impacted the team's performance using the critical incident approach (a critical incident emphasizes a precise occurrence and captures significant information associated with an event). They discussed the circumstances, the actions they saw, and the impact or outcome.

Basically, this chapter explores the following:

- Rating the 4Cs Skills Positive Effect on Team Performance.
- Effects of Utilizing or Lacking 4Cs Skills on Team Performance.
    - Positive Effects of Utilizing 4Cs Skills on Team Performance.
    - Negative Effects of Absence of 4Cs Skills on Team Performance.

DOI: 10.4324/9781003462316-13

Rating the 4Cs Skills' Positive Effects on Team Performance

Research contributors were asked to rank the importance of any of the 4Cs skills from number one being the most essential and vital to the team performance to the fourth being the least important skill for their team performance (see Figure 10.1). The impact of the 4Cs' abilities on the team performance of the 17 organizations and the 45 contributors from all levels of management and business professionals was expressed as in Figure 10.1, from top to bottom:

1) **Communication.** 51.90% of contributors ranked communication as the *first* and most influential skill for team performance.
2) **Collaboration.** 40.70% of contributors ranked collaboration as the *second* most valuable skill for team performance.
3) **Critical Thinking.** 51.90% of contributors ranked critical thinking as the *third* most important skill for team performance.
4) **Creativity.** 59.30% of contributors ranked creativity as the *fourth* most valuable skill for team performance.

Interestingly, the percentages and the order of ranking among the 4Cs skills occurred in the same order as the order of assigning values on any of these 4Cs skills covered in the previous chapter (see Figure 9.9). It is crucial to note that the nature of these companies' businesses greatly influences the choice of the ranking of 4Cs skills on their team performance. This is because these companies do not all conduct their businesses in the same industry, which means that the nature of their products has a considerable impact. This is very dependent on what they are working on and the products that they are making. On the other hand, regardless of the circumstances, this brief rating would be helpful to the contributors and their organizations in planning their approach to where they should focus their training efforts and what they should pay attention to in the future development of their workforces.

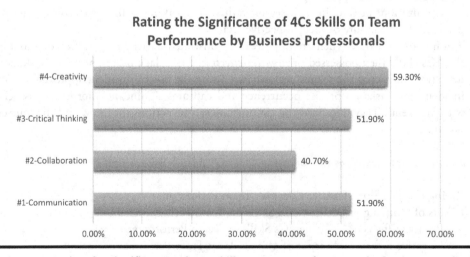

Figure 10.1   Rating the significance of 4Cs skills on team performance by business professionals. © Bakhshandeh 2024.

Effects of Utilizing or Lacking 4Cs Skills on Team Performance

The following themes arose from the contributors' descriptions of what they have seen as positive and negative consequences from their workforces' use or lack of use of the 4Cs skills when working with their teams, which therefore influenced their teams' performance. The contributors' comments were based on what they have witnessed as positive and negative effects from their workforce's use or lack of use of the skills.

Positive Effects of Utilizing 4Cs Skills on Team Performance

When business professionals were questioned about what positive effects and outcomes they have witnessed because their employees applied one or all of the 4Cs skills and produced a successful result during their team performance, the following themes came to light. Please note that the following themes result from collecting many stories and witness observations and have nothing to do with the researcher's personal bias or point of view. Given the relatively large amount of data collection in this section, we just represented several incidents for each of the following themes.

Functioning During Emergency

- "During the Covid pandemic, we saw how well-coordinated and *creatively* our team *collaborated* to transition the company to a fully online approach, which needed a brand-new operational strategy and set of protocols."
- "Our team is reworking the production plan, which would include reorganizing more than 200 personnel, employing *creativity*, *communication*, and *collaboration*, as a result of a significant equipment failure in our manufacturing line."
- "After finding a significant problem in the student financial assistance system, we had to deal with angry people and their families who were demanding quick fixes. In order to work with the federal financial aid office and develop a strategy that would address the emergency until a long-term solution and be *communicated* to the students, we employed *critical thinking* and *creativity*."

Enjoying Teamwork

- "I can state that both *collaboration* and *communication* played a part in the appreciation and happiness I witnessed among the staff as a result of the prompt completion of the crucial choices that needed to be taken."
- "It was remarkable to see our team come together, organize everything, and prepare our conference room for our crucial presentation. The degree of *communication*, excitement, and *collaboration* they showed was what made it so outstanding."
- "I let him resolve it on his own. He really thought of a few ideas for what he was doing with this central phone system that I hadn't considered. The consumer is delighted since he solved the problem through trial and error and intense determination. He exercised *creativity* and *critical thinking*."

Focusing on Dedication to Workability

- "*Critical thinking* and *communication* skills were essential because I was in charge of an institution's satellite sites. I had to transmit student-related difficulties to a location two to three hours away and work with them to fix the issues even though they weren't there since I wasn't at the home institution."

- "I told them I wanted to chat with them about something they both shared. Because, once more, you'll develop that relationship, he'll be more inclined to work with you, *communicate*, and soon you'll collaborate on a project. He did and added, 'I could use your advice on this whole project I've been working on.' I thought, *Perfect, that'll make him feel great.* It will strengthen that connection, and I believe the subsequent encounter will go more smoothly. And everything turned out as planned."
- "We implemented that handout at all seven site locations to make everyone's job a little bit easier and to give everyone a better understanding of how to assist our students and all the stakeholders. That was one of the scenarios that resulted from *collaboration*, clear *communication* methods, and *creative* problem-solving."

Initiating Newfound Ideas

- "He displayed creativity since he had never presented that thought with that idea for years on end. So, it was fairly *creative*, and the *collaborative* aspect was that he enlisted the help of others to talk about whether his suggestion would make sense and whether we are on the same page moving ahead."
- "We relocated them to a new place because, I suppose, they had various ideas that would be helpful; they suggested *critical thinking* and *creativity*. We were able to gauge their abilities by doing that, and we ultimately elevated them to a supervisor role."
- "Her *creativity* and *critical thinking* are unquestionably present. She used her *creativity* and originality to consider what would work best. She utilized what she had already learned and what she already knew about the folks she was helping, making a crucial judgment on what would benefit them the most."

Working on the Problem, Not the Emotions

- "When dealing with intense emotions, it's important to speak properly, identify the issues, and then resolve them rationally and effectively utilizing good *communication* and *critical thinking* skills. That is certainly effective, but you must keep in mind that not all issues can be resolved in a single meeting. Thus, in time, we will arrive at the point when we must utilize all 4Cs."
- "A lot of anger was present, and it had been building for a long time. *Communications* had been conducted via email, and it wasn't until we twice gathered in a large room that we attempted to come up with *creative* solutions to our problems and express our points of view. When we finally started *communicating*, setting clear guidelines for *communication*, and listening to one another, we both ended up coming out much stronger as teams than we had been before."
- "We got off to real *communication* and enthusiasm [during] *collaboration*, which boosted organizational commitment to the workers. However, the second factor connected with 'fiction versus reality' is 'plan versus where do I fit on this team?' Is that it enhanced the personal connection between the corporation and the individual rather than person to person."

Pressing the Limits

- "Since we couldn't do the task on our own, we had to break it up, use our *creativity*, and *collaborate* with others on our team. And we had to take on challenges that were uncomfortable for us."
- "As a result, the process began with *creativity* and *critical thinking*, and as it progressed, it introduced our design engineers at our headquarters to the 4Cs of *communication* and *collaboration*, enabling them to work together on the design adjustments. Because it is relatively typical for design engineers to lack significant manufacturing knowledge, they frequently create unnecessarily complex designs to build."
- "One of my employees was successful in helping a faculty member comprehend why something needed to be done. In addition, much of it involves *creativity* and *critical thinking*; to put it another way, perspective-taking, so that they may point out that you might not be able to complete the task this way."

Helping Career Development

- "She was so excited to learn how these 4Cs skills will assist her in her career development. She was someone who *communicated* well and always promoted *collaboration* as the way to get things done."
- "I was witnessing his abilities to employ *critical thinking* and effective *communication* to de-escalate the upsetting situation. He was very creative in displaying the facts and taking away interpretations and drama that were dominating the situation. I could see the bright future in his career path to higher management positions."
- "There was this supervisor who was so calm and collected when people were complaining about [his] work and demand[s]. He was using *critical thinking* and *creativity* by designing his questions so that they were not aggressive to the listener, so they were thinking about what they were saying and then questioning the validity of their complaints. This is essential to effective management and leadership positions."

Negative Effects of Lacking 4Cs Skills on Team Performance

When business professionals were questioned about what negative effects they have witnessed because of their workforce not using or employing one or all of the 4Cs skills and producing a negative outcome result during their team performance, the following themes came to light. Please note that the following themes resulted from collecting many stories and witness observations and have nothing to do with the researcher's personal bias or point of view. Given the relatively large amount of data collected in this section, we just represented several incidents for each of the following themes.

Acting First, Thinking Second

- "They didn't consider the consequences before acting, and when the issue arose, it ultimately turned out to be extremely easy. The maintenance was unable to resolve it, so one of the maintenance managers was contacted, but he was unable to resolve it either. I argued that insufficient *communication* and *critical thinking* occurred during the shift to identify the issue. Just an absolute meltdown."

■ "They didn't converse; one man received instructions from a client but didn't relay them to the man in charge of the shop floor. Additionally, the item was off by four inches. We had to create an additional bracket to allow the attachment to go straight on so that it could reach. We had to manufacture all those brackets, which cost us nearly $20,000 since the measurement was wrong by four inches. There was a severe lack of *collaboration* and *communication*."

■ "As a result, they made certain modifications up there on their own without consulting a manager or supervisor, *collaborating* with anybody in control, or using the normal channels of *communication*. Everything else was a waste of time and energy."

Reacting to Heated Emotions

■ "I believe that all of these problematic circumstances featured a lack of *communication*, most likely with managers being unable to interact with their teams. This is especially true when human resources had to become involved. And things swiftly spiral downward and out of control. It all came down to *communication* and getting individuals together in a room to discuss and share perspectives and how they're feeling, so HR had to come in."

■ "One of our employees struggles to *collaborate* with others and *communicate* effectively with his boss. He was explicitly instructed to put down his phone and to stop using it by his supervisor. And one employee had a complete meltdown, approaching HR and claiming, 'I wouldn't be treated like this.'"

■ "My staff ought to have handled it and spoken to the consumer differently. He should have utilized his *creativity* and *communication* skills to diffuse the situation when he noticed the customer's fever rising steadily or even phoned the supervisor to have someone else dispatched. But once more, a lack of *critical thinking*."

Lacking Autonomy and Creativity

■ "In the end, everything was done exactly as it should have been in black and white. However, we could have accomplished more if some of our *critical thinking* and *creativity* to work around the issue hadn't been curtailed."

■ "What had occurred differed slightly from what had normally occurred. It generated chaos because individuals were unable to *think critically* before making decisions, making alternate choices, thinking just a little differently, or being *creative* enough to picture what may happen in an alternative scenario. As a result, there is a lot of back and forth, which results in a *communication* breakdown and a worse problem. Then, certain negative emotions cause the partnership to break down. I believe that if individuals can think and envision in new ways, *communication* will also improve, which will lead to greater *collaboration*."

■ "In the past, a higher-ranking leader would essentially act arbitrarily. No *communication* or *collaboration*. If that did happen, it most likely didn't happen with the workers. Knowing who you must *collaborate* with and with whom you must *communicate* is another crucial component."

Lacking Cross-Functioning Plan

■ "That is regrettably something that results from the pace at which business is conducted, unintended repercussions because individuals may be so motivated to serve that they neglect their first team, which is an internal rather than an external one. It is cross-functional, and our most common failure and lack of *communication* and *collaboration* have an impact on everything else. This is the sort of internal contracting and commitment we make before making an outward commitment."

■ "There is a lack of preparation across departments, as well as maybe a lack of *critical thinking* and *communication*, which leads to these types of crises and breakdowns. Maybe there isn't enough of that."

■ "Recently, there was an instance when there was a complete lack of departmental coordination and *communication*, and we effectively squandered an entire day of work."

Lacking Self-Awareness

■ "He just lacked *collaboration*, awareness of how his actions affect others, and the ability to *think critically* about the effects on our business by constantly checking his phone while working on the floor during work hours."

■ "One employee was quite challenging to work with because he thought he was the new best and would criticize other workers for not focusing on the priorities he thought needed to be worked on. This employee would *communicate* internally, which caused issues with other workers. Because of his pride and conceit, he just alienated everyone and was a poor *communicator*."

■ "They were capable of doing the essential duties, but they were careless when it came to interacting with the staff and comprehending how their actions would affect B and C if they took A. I can confirm that I demoted a supervisor whose *collaboration, communication,* and *critical thinking* abilities were appalling. He was completely ignorant of his demeanor and how he was acting on the floor."

Possessing Ineffective Communication

■ "The program manager phoned me two weeks later and informed me that this and that were inside budget. Since I had failed, I took it personally and blamed my boys, inquiring as to their lack of compliance. They claimed that I never recorded it and provided us with a mechanism to do so. In order to alter the code, I created a spreadsheet with all of the tracking numbers. Thus, the failure to clearly *communicate* and *collaborate* with them had a detrimental effect."

■ "Therefore, it frequently occurs that the engineering team will declare something to be ready, but when it is passed over to production, it is a disaster, and we are unable to complete it since there was no *communication* and no *collaboration* with the people on the floor."

■ "She wasn't entirely off base when you would chat with her one-on-one. She had recognized a few things since that was what she was supposed to do, but she lacked the *creativity* to engage those around her or the *communication* skills to do so. So, what actually transpired was somewhat like a downward spiral."

Lacking Foresight

■ "I believe there is a lack of critical thinking because when you apply *critical thinking*, you must consider the current problem and the consequences of your advice. They didn't even begin to think about all the implications in this case. They didn't *communicate* and *collaborate* with the appropriate persons; therefore, they were unaware of the consequences."

■ "Our problem is that because we have so many employees who have been with us for a long time, they may just be familiar with our business and not have a comprehensive understanding of the best practice for us in the current industry. Because of this, we frequently hear 'we have always done it that way' rather than taking a step back, applying *critical thinking*, and examining why we are doing it that way and whether it is the best practice rather than just continuing to do what we have always done. Instead, they could *collaborate*, which eventually renders them obsolete if you look at it from a business perspective."

■ "*Communication* is the key to strengthening relationships because when you build relationships through *communication*, people are more likely to *collaborate*, which encourages *creativity* and encourages people to consider issues more critically."

Going through the above reports and witnesses' testimonials, we can conclude the following fact: Incorporating 4Cs skills would positively affect individuals and team performance. At the same time, not using the 4Cs skills would have a negative effect on individual and team performances (see Figure 10.2).

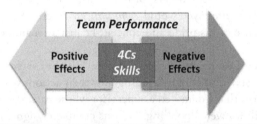

Figure 10.2   Effects of utilizing or lacking 4Cs skills on team performance. © Bakhshandeh 2024.

Summary of 4Cs' Positive and Negative Effects on Team Performance

The themes that surfaced throughout the process of gathering the data are presented in Table 10.1. These themes concern the positive influence that utilizing the 4Cs abilities has on team performance and the negative impact that not utilizing and missing them has on team performance. The themes are not intended to connect to one another across the columns in a direct manner; nevertheless, they demonstrate a relationship between the total workforce utilizing or not using the 4Cs skills and the influence it has on team performance.

Table 10.1 Summary of the Themes Centered on Positive and Negative Effects on Team Performance by Utilizing or Not Utilizing the 4Cs Skills

Positive Effects	Negative Effects
Functioning During Emergency	Acting First, Thinking Second
Enjoying Teamwork	Reacting to Heated Emotions
Focusing on Dedication to Workability	Lacking Autonomy and Creativity
Initiating Newfound Ideas	Lacking Cross-Functioning Plan
Working on the Problem, Not the Emotions	Lacking Self-Awareness
Pressing the Limits	Possessing Ineffective Communication
Helping Career Development	Lacking Foresight

© Bakhshandeh 2024.

What Is Next?

The next chapter included in Part III is titled "Effective 4Cs Skills Training and Development," as part of the third intention of the research. In Chapter 11, we discuss the business professionals" (senior managers, middle managers, and line managers) perspectives of what is good and effective training for developing 4Cs skills among their workforces.

Chapter 11

Effective 4Cs Skills Training and Development

In this chapter, we address what we have gleaned from the view of business professionals working inside organizations, such as senior managers, middle managers, line managers, and production supervisors or foremen, related to the *third intention* of this research, the "Effective 4Cs Skills Training and Development" regarding some elements of training and development that would assist managers and have a positive impact on the growth of the 21st century 4Cs skills among workforces:

a) How would your workers benefit from practical 4Cs training, and what should be covered in this training?
b) What competitive advantage does the workforce's acquisition of the 4Cs skills give organizations?
c) How will the 4Cs skills development affect the attitudes and behaviors of the workforce?
d) How will the development of 4Cs skills affect worker training and the development of leadership abilities?

In this chapter, we review the contributors' views on the following four areas of effective 4Cs skills training and development related to the above inquiries.

- Practical Training.
- Competitive Advantage.
- Attitude and Behavior.
- Leadership Proficiencies.

What Do You Consider to Be an Effective 4Cs Skills T&D for Your Workforce?

The following themes and sub-themes arose from the contributors' views and interest on how they think effective training and development would increase the 4Cs skills effectiveness among their

DOI: 10.4324/9781003462316-14

workforces. The contributors' comments were based on their observations, their experience, and what they believe would make a difference for their workforces.

Please note that the following themes result from collecting many inputs by contributors as business professionals related to their experience and desired outcome and have nothing to do with the researcher's personal bias or point of view. Given the relatively large amount of data collected for this section, we just represented the most common ideas for each of the following selected themes (see Figure 11.1).

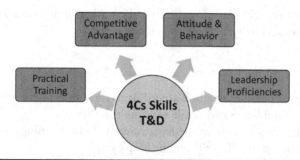

Figure 11.1   Elements of effective 4Cs skills training and development. © Bakhshandeh 2024.

Practical Training

The following topics about practical training for the 4Cs skills (critical thinking, communication, creativity, and collaboration) and what they would want to see included in such a program arose from the interviews with business professionals (see Figure 11.2).

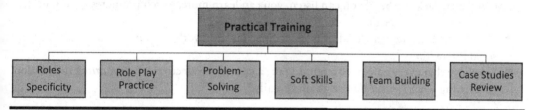

Figure 11.2   Subthemes related to "Practical Training" regarding 4Cs development by business professionals. © Bakhshandeh 2024.

Roles Specificity

- "As part of their orientation process after being employed, new employees would engage in *critical thinking* and *communication* exercises to help them understand their roles and responsibilities."
- "Yes, since I've seen someone with expertise showing beginners how to operate a machine; perhaps they might improve their *communication* and *critical thinking* skills at that time. Yes, be inventive, but consider your options carefully before acting and consult someone before making a change. Hard skill training ought to be required so that new hires are aware of what to do."
- "I think you would receive a good result from training with clearly specifying their roles on the jobs and their direct responsibilities on that production."

Role Play Practice

- "I believe that a training scenario should be developed in which the steps necessary for something to be successfully completed are created. That can only happen if everyone participates."
- "Maybe the employees should be shown examples of *critical thinking* techniques and provided scenarios they could encounter throughout the training time. Ask them, "What would you do if …?"
- "I really believe that role plays function the best when individuals are moving around, engaging in physical activity, and facing real-life events."

Problem-Solving

- "Consider grouping the staff members according to their areas of expertise so they may learn how to *collaborate* and be creative while working together."
- "Therefore, a really creative activity, perhaps a creative brainstorming session, would be quite beneficial for fostering the *4Cs skills* among employees."
- "When we discuss a development mindset, we mean questioning why we are doing things the way we are instead of just doing them the way we have always done them."

Soft Skills

- "There are several soft skills training programs available on it. Therefore, I was attempting to set up a training program here that would begin with *communication*. Listening was the aspect of *communication* that we started with since, in my opinion, it is a talent that is completely lacking. So, if you can listen, you can learn more, which promotes greater understanding and conversation."
- "It would be highly beneficial to take a course on teamwork, *communication*, and interpersonal interactions."
- "I believe that every employee ought to take a course on effective *communication* in addition to learning what *critical thinking* alone entails."

Team Building

- "I would say something really effective around team building and building trust even if you don't consider yourself an extrovert and reinforcing, really reinforcing, how they are all interconnected. But it sort of begins and ends with *communication* and *collaboration*. I would probably put a lot of emphasis, especially in the front of the training, on effective *communication* and team building."
- "I think effective training for roles would be an interactive one. You could really be interactive with those. So, that's how I would see it, you know, a lot of team building; I think all of the *4Cs* that you are looking at is about team building. So, I think you could, you know, really evolve team-building skills that we see so much in different training."
- "So, if we can talk about *creativity* and *critical thinking* and being able to work with each other, employees that have the ability to say, here is what I do well and here is what I don't do well and not use what they don't do well as an excuse, and we all have strengths, we all have

weaknesses, do we know what our strengths are, do we know what our weaknesses are, and we don't use our weaknesses as our excuses. I think that just strengthens the team."

Case Studies Review

- "I'd suggest case studies may be an example if you were intending to do training on one or all four of the *4Cs skills*. When you publish anything and state, "Here is what happened," have them then elaborate on what went wrong and what went well for me. It ought to be discussed in groups, in my opinion."
- "We all had those experiences, and since I don't want you to go through what I did, case studies are an excellent approach to train others. We engage in role-playing and case study activities with my subordinates, during which I present them with a hypothetical problem. What approach would you take? We then discussed a variety of potential remedies or concepts."
- "Bring in various research-based training materials for people. So, from the beginning, we've conducted studies to encourage individuals to think creatively and to be a little more imaginative. We concentrate on research-based training that focuses solely on the people's essential abilities."

Competitive Advantage

The following topics about educating employees in 4Cs skills and how they would provide their organization a competitive edge in their markets and industries came from the interviews with business professionals (see Figure 11.3).

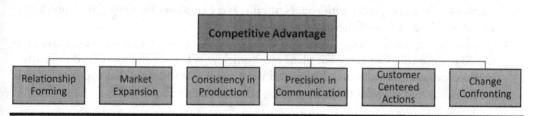

Figure 11.3 Sub-themes related to "Competitive Advantage" regarding 4Cs development by business professionals. © Bakhshandeh 2024.

Relationship Forming

- "It will help with connection development, which is important for staff retention. As a result of *communication* and *collaboration*, it fosters trust among employees. You experience a feeling of identity. You stick to your goals. From every employee, you are acquiring a vast range of information. Because of the vast range of opinions and knowledge and the mutual brainstorming, you get an overall better team."
- "As long as we're all talking to one another and *collaborating* on campus, I'm just confident that *communication* and *collaboration* are key to developing good teams and solid connections."
- "I really believe that the *4Cs skills* are what bind everything together and give people the feeling that they are safe and that we are all in this together. I may contact them since I am

aware that we are friendly and that we enjoy working together. I just believe that we are stronger when we work together, and it might be difficult for me to believe otherwise. But I believe that the more we can reinforce it, the better off the company will be."

Market Expansion

■ "I believe you rapidly get stale and out of date without the *4Cs skills*. You stop being creative, you stop being on the cutting edge, and you have to cope with many rivals overtaking you and maybe going out of business."

■ "Certainly, you can enter the market more quickly; you can save expenses, enhance the product, and raise the standard of the product."

■ "If you have employees with these *4Cs skills*, I believe there is a way to build a more supportive workplace where everyone feels like a member of the team. Everyone feels somewhat gratified once they have a sense of where they belong, what their mission is, and how they can contribute. An organization can engage actively in its competitive market with the support of this environment."

Consistency in Production

■ "Economic variables that need *collaboration* and a lot of *critical thinking* for consistent production."

■ "By putting *4Cs skills* into practice, you can decrease turnover, increase productivity naturally as a result of your people's increased experience, and have more confidence in their ability to make wise decisions as a result of their knowledge and exposure gained over the course of their employment with you. Naturally, every employee becomes more knowledgeable about the company if there is less turnover."

■ "I think having enough employees who exhibit the *4Cs skills* gives a business a competitive edge since they can carry out plans more quickly. Whatever the strategy, if the parties involved can *communicate*, *collaborate*, and work effectively together, that degree of trust is the lubricant that prevents them from being reluctant to hold back."

Precision in Communication

■ "We would be able to accomplish our goals if we could effectively convey them to management, particularly through our lower-level staff."

■ "We sometimes mistakenly believe that more *communication* would result in greater *communication*, and I believe this is why it often falls short. Better *communication* is being able to state your needs and having those needs understood by others."

■ "It's necessary to *communicate* sometimes. However, it's crucial to *communicate* strategically. As a result, I stressed earlier how crucial it is to *communicate* openly. Transparency, however, doesn't always entail telling everyone everything all the time; it also requires being able to articulate justifications for decisions and strategies that make sense."

Customer-Centered Actions

- "That, in my opinion, is a great benefit. It will take significantly less time for a team to enhance their organization or reach the market if each member of the team possesses the *4Cs skills.*"
- "Things operate more smoothly when departments connect with one another, *collaborate*, and *communicate* with one another. In the end, these only benefit customers and the business as a whole."
- "I believe that the key to maintaining a competitive advantage is to demonstrate to customers how the organization's offerings add value to their desired goods and services."

Change Confronting

- "Again, in my opinion, properly implementing the *4Cs skills* would enable a business to be adaptable when a change occurs. One day, in order to alter what we had known for so long, we had to employ *creativity* and *critical thinking.*"
- "We need to *critically* and strategically consider not just what sort of business we are today, but also what kind of business we want to be in the future. In order to be more *creative* and strategic about where certain trends are headed and what is actually needed in the workforce, you must think more deeply and strategically."
- "We must be forward-thinking, which requires a great deal of critical analysis and appreciation of the context of the environment as well as the cultural, economic, political, and social-economic developments."

Attitude and Behavior

The following topics came out of the conversations with business professionals regarding their opinions on how training in and developing 4Cs skills might help employees have a positive attitude and behave more effectively (see Figure 11.4).

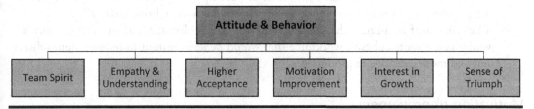

Figure 11.4 Sub-themes related to "Attitude and Behavior" regarding 4Cs development by business professionals. © Bakhshandeh 2024.

Team Spirit

- "All of these are significant, but I believe that, in particular, *collaboration* and *communication* are key to creating a sense of teamwork and shared responsibility. Feeling involved, in my opinion, helps drive things like attendance because ... it fosters engagement."
- "Because of poor *communication*, a lack of a passionate core, or a lack of team spirit, a lot of time is wasted. The use and application of team *collaboration* will foster a sense of unity."

■ "Even when there is bad news, people feel better about what they do when there is strong *communication* because they feel like they are not being left out of things. Even when there is bad news, at least they know what it is and it is not kind of hidden and makes people feel bad. Because when all four of those *4Cs skills* are functioning or doing well, morale is substantially higher."

Empathy and Understanding

■ "It's not only *communication* when it comes to communication, there is a need for being a good communicator, being kind, having empathy, and being adaptable."
■ "We frequently hear that new hires or entry-level employees lack the *4Cs skills* that they really ought to have when they first enter the profession. I believe that if management can focus on these abilities, successful *4Cs skills* training will transform attitudes and behaviors and minimize animosity toward the newer workers."
■ "Because I believe there is a psychological component to how the workforce functions, I believe that people's conduct has a significant impact on how people behave. They all come from various backgrounds and represent various cultures. Some of them think differently and react to events in various ways. I believe that developing and enhancing *4Cs skills* may significantly improve how well individuals can *communicate* with one another and *collaborate*."

Higher Acceptance

■ "The *4Cs skills* can influence how well individuals accept one another. They can work together productively, in my opinion, as long as the attitudes and actions of the younger generation alter a little bit and the elder generation learns to comprehend the younger generation. They must be receptive to that. It will take some time for that mindset and that habit to alter."
■ "There will always be one or two people who are unwilling to alter anything and are confined to their offices. However, adopting *4Cs skills* training would benefit the majority of our workforce, who would appreciate that level of participation. This would reduce resistance and perhaps lead to more acceptance among those who were fighting change."
■ "I believe that if we all have the *4Cs skills* and had them cultivated in the proper manner, we would have a more cohesive workforce that would be less resistant to management's direction and more receptive to production."

Motivation Improvement

■ "It would, in my opinion, raise spirits. It would … increase motivation and involvement among individuals. Ultimately, this will lead to an improvement in the organization's bottom line."
■ "Some individuals may say, 'I don't care about everything, and it doesn't matter anyhow.' Consequently, being able to elaborate on it and say things like 'You are a part of this, but this part is essential in those specific areas, and this is how' might help the individual comprehend what is expected of them in a wider perspective. I can be perceived as more than I am, but I can also take even more delight in stating, 'Oh because I contribute here and here and here,' etc."

- "I believe that receiving *4Cs skills* training makes students more aware of the results. They're more on board, a part of it, and understand it, and I believe they're even more inclined to think creatively, more willing to share an idea or talk about something, and be more self-assured."

Interest in Growth

- "The development of *4Cs skills* can only have a good impact if the individual is prepared to acknowledge that no matter who you are, you will never know everything. You can always learn new things and get better, even if you're 100 years old. The *4Cs skills* might thus only be beneficial for everyone as long as we take into account that time of lifelong learning."
- "Acquiring a development attitude and realizing that if we don't evolve, we won't be around in 125 years. Therefore, having the proper growth mentality, attitude, and conduct goes along with that when we are looking at onboarding new workers and upgrading and growing those that are with us."
- "I want to go into greater detail on behavioral competencies since there is a lot more to agile learning, interpersonal skills, and being a successful leader than just *collaboration*, teamwork, *communication*, *creativity*, or *critical thinking*."

Sense of Triumph

- "We have a management team here, so I believe that when we start to operate more coherently and are better in our thinking, talking, and working together, they want to attain their objectives … want to feel successful."
- "I believe it improves your capacity for original thought and simple learning, and you become more aware of what other co-workers in your organization are doing to support the success of the company. I consider that to be really significant."
- "In my team, we have been employing the 4Cs—*collaboration, creativity, communication, and critical thinking*—a lot over the past 10 years, and it has virtually quadrupled the value of what we do as a vehicle."

Leadership Proficiencies

The following themes came out of the conversations with business professionals about how they envision building leadership abilities to teach their staff in relationship to the 4Cs skills (see Figure 11.5).

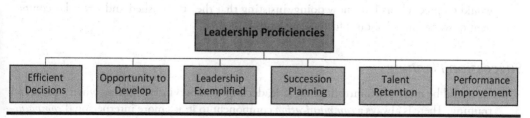

Figure 11.5   Sub-themes related to "Leadership Proficiencies" regarding 4Cs development by business professionals. © Bakhshandeh 2024.

Efficient Decisions

■ "They can strive to make excellent judgments by applying critical thinking, in my opinion, and the next step is to *collaborate* and *communicate* those conclusions."

■ "We wish to encourage innovation in our workforce. As a result, I believe that by doing that, we will become a better company overall. It will enable our workers to make decisions in a more original way."

■ "As a result, they are mutually exclusive; you cannot be a good leader if you do not comprehend the *4Cs skills* and make every effort to apply them while making choices or expressing your objectives. You must also realize that while mistakes are common, you don't always use them in the best way. To navigate these waters requires a significant amount of leadership, an art, and a significant amount of social ability. The *4Cs skills* fit right in there, so to speak."

Opportunity to Develop

■ "We are compelled to *communicate* and be *creative* while making the greatest use of the resources we have to use as much creativity as we can to position each candidate where they will fit best given their history. Sometimes, all we have to go on is what people say on their resumes and a cursory interview, and you have to decide whether or not this individual would fit in anywhere. The greatest strategy is to make an investment in their leadership skills development and shape them to what you require."

■ "We are utilizing *critical thinking* to develop better strategies for educating our employees in competencies, controlling the time it would take them to learn those abilities, and determining if they are learning them at the right pace."

■ "I believe that all of these skills—*critical thinking, collaboration,* and *communication*—help our staff develop their leadership abilities. As we move forward, there are always chances to improve their leadership abilities."

Exemplify Leadership

■ "I believe that a lot of the time, poor *communication* skills or a *communication* style that might be viewed as inappropriate or ineffective are the reasons why leaders fail."

■ "You would need to establish a culture of learning if you were creating leadership in this. Thus, you are setting an example for the rest of the organization by taking these talents and teaching them to the staff."

■ "I believe that if you master the *4Cs skills,* you will be more valuable because you will be able to impact the organization more quickly and significantly than you would otherwise. I would go precisely as I am now doing, insisting that they be finished and a regular component of work, since it would foster leadership."

Succession Planning

■ "It would be more of an introduction to leadership or supervisory training when you attend training. There is always a *communication* component to it; it's more interpersonal *communications,* coaching, and counseling, if you will, followed by more strategic *communications* to get more respect at work and convey uncompromising messages."

- ▪ "Therefore, I believe that the *4Cs skills* would assist managers and supervisors develop some of the skills that they might not currently have, or that they already have but might improve upon."
- ▪ "You want employees to take on leadership roles in your business in the future. These four terms, or the *4Cs skills*, should be a component of their strategy since they are crucial to them."

Talent Retention

- ▪ "However, if you had that internally, you could have employees with organizational expertise, organizational history, and the crucial abilities to advance since it would be far more beneficial to your company."
- ▪ "But I believe that the thought that truly entered my head was perhaps finding someone whom I would have missed since it wasn't the position for which they were employed."
- ▪ "It could also help me identify new leaders in this place that I might have missed. I believe it would make the existing leaders here stronger."

Performance Improvement

- ▪ "The staff would perform better, it would help them discover areas where they need to improve and places where they are already performing well, and I believe it would have an impact on their EPAs and performance evaluations."
- ▪ "The performance of both our existing personnel and the new hires we are bringing in, in my opinion, would benefit from training in the *4Cs skills*."
- ▪ "You can undoubtedly determine whether you truly carried things to that level, in my opinion. If you were to drive the company in this direction, you would be able to identify the performance-level deficiencies in your primary employees as well as the competences that are required for them."

Summary of Elements of Effective 4Cs Skills Training and Development

The topics that surfaced throughout the course of the data collection process in this section of the research are displayed in Table 11.1, and they pertain to the beneficial influence that utilizing the 4Cs in skills training and development for the workforce may have.

The interview questions that were asked elicited these emerging themes on the sort of successful 4Cs skills for the training and development of the workforce.

It is not the intention of these topics to immediately correlate to one another across the columns; nevertheless, they do demonstrate a connection between the training and development of the 4Cs and the development of leadership abilities among the workforce with the assistance of the organization's leadership and management.

Table 11.1 Summary of Elements of Effective 4Cs Skills Training and Development

Themes	*Sub-Themes*
Practical Training	Roles Specificity
	Role Play
	Problem-Solving
	Soft Skills
	Team Building
	Case Studies Review
Competitive Advantage	Relationship Forming
	Market Expansion
	Consistency in Production
	Precision in Communication
	Customer-Centered Actions
	Change Confronting
Attitude and Behavior	Team Spirit
	Empathy and Understanding
	Higher Acceptance
	Motivation Improvement
	Interest in Growth
	Sense of Triumph
Leadership Proficiencies	Efficient Decisions
	Opportunity to Develop
	Exemplify Leadership
	Succession Planning
	Talent Retention
	Performance Improvement

© Bakhshandeh 2024.

What Is Next?

Chapter 12 explores the "Essence of Cohesiveness and Workability" as part of the third objective of the investigation. In this chapter, we will reveal the additional information that was gathered when the researcher asked the contributors as business professionals (senior managers, middle managers, and line managers) if they had any additional information and if there was any experience about having or lacking 4Cs skills in their organization or among their workforce that they would like to share or add to the interview.

Chapter 12

Essence of Cohesiveness and Workability

Introduction

The following themes occurred throughout the data collection process and during the interviews with business professionals; however, they were unrelated to the 4Cs elements and themes that had already been identified in relation to the three primary study objectives.

These themes came up at the end of the interviews when the researcher asked the participants if they had any extra information and if there was anything they would want to share or add to the interview regarding the 4Cs skills present or absent in their businesses or among their workforces.

Additionally, participants' answers to interview questions when they described how the 4Cs skills were used in their teams' operations and organizations' production during the COVID-19 viral pandemic and crisis were excellent, given the significance of how businesses continued to operate in the face of such significant impediments.

This chapter categorized additional themes as follows:

- Empowerment.
- Connections.
- Vision and Values.
- 4Cs and Pandemic.
- Merged and Final Themes.

Additional Themes Raised Out of Interviews

Please note that the following themes result from collecting many inputs by contributors as business professionals related to their experience and desired outcome and have nothing to do with the researcher's personal bias or point of view. Given the relatively large amount of data collection in this section, we just represented several ideas for each of the following themes (see Figure 12.1).

DOI: 10.4324/9781003462316-15

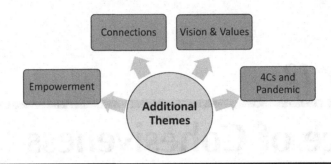

Figure 12.1 Additional elements of 4Cs skills impact on organizations and their workforces. © Bakhshandeh 2024.

Empowerment

- "Back in the day, I had a supervisor who only ever spoke to me when he had anything bad to say about me. Yes, and even now, decades later, I still recall that. I emphasize that I never want to be that boss because of this. If I approach a worker in manufacturing, I could just be interested in learning about how their day is going. I may not be angry with anything, and I don't necessarily need anything. I might be complimenting them. Everything appears to be a nail if your only tool is a hammer."
- "Give them the freedom to decide for themselves. That brings up what you may and cannot do at work, in my opinion. I believe that many individuals have relied on and continue to depend on others to simply tell them what to do."
- "I believe that feeling empowered and appreciated makes getting out of bed every morning to go to work much simpler. Therefore, I firmly believe that a business may appreciate those *4Cs skills* by empowering people, expressing gratitude, and supporting the growth of its employees in these areas."

The following three sub-themes were raised about "empowerment" during interviews with business professionals (see Figure 12.2).

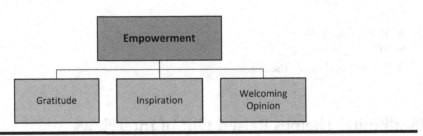

Figure 12.2 Themes raised about "Empowerment" by business professionals. © Bakhshandeh 2024.

Gratitude

- "They would likely feel more valued since they would receive better training, in my opinion. They would feel more valued and wouldn't want to go."

■ "In our company, we're so far spaced out; we're all so separated by departments. It's important sometimes to bring us all into some type of togetherness. Those are times that I have to kind of show that we appreciate them."

■ "This particular supervisor then began working in the tooling section, which he had previously criticized, after being given control over both departments, claiming that 'oh, he sees the other side of the fence.' And then he begins working with the workers directly, operating the machinery and observing what they deal with, and all of a sudden, his perspective completely changes. And now he is aware of both perspectives. He can collaborate with the machine operators on the production side and the machine operators on the side that supplies the tooling because he has open eyes. He begins to understand what it takes on both sides to complete the task. He may now make changes that are advantageous to both parties."

Inspiration

■ "The workforce would, in my opinion, feel more appreciated if they had the *4Cs skills*. More workers might be kept on board."

■ "The most crucial element, in my opinion, is to empower and encourage staff members to be able to apply these skills."

■ "If they choose poorly, they worry that they will be criticized. They are concerned about making an error. They need to be motivated by management to take action."

Welcoming Opinion

■ "Employees would likely see this positively since they would feel like they have a voice in what happens inside the company, in my opinion. They would gain respect as a result of being heard. Their willingness to express their thoughts would increase."

■ "Nobody likes to put in more effort than necessary, so if people feel heard, I mean, it really … transforms the culture."

■ "Without a doubt, I would state that there is a lack of communication at the top as well as a lack of interest in learning about the employees' lives and the problems that are plaguing them."

Connections

■ "Consequently, I was a member of a group where we were discussing skills. Three employers were present, and although they weren't senior executives and weren't quite ready to retire, they said that this generation lacked a strong work ethic. They aren't allowed to do this, they're not allowed to do that, etc. Have you ever spoken to them, I asked? Have you ever tried to understand why they think this way or learn from them in order to help them become more like us as employers? And I said, 'This generation doesn't see it that way.' They consider it to be romantic. As a result, you must have the ability to shape or adjust them to a standard."

■ "The most crucial thing, in my opinion, would be to establish a relationship. letting everyone know how important they are to the company, from the newest employee to someone who has been here for twenty years."

■ "I believe that some firms' propensity to operate in silos is caused by a lack of communication across departments. Because they don't have a relationship, one department does what it does without really thinking about how it will influence another department."

The following three sub-themes were raised about "connections" during interviews with business professionals (see Figure 12.3).

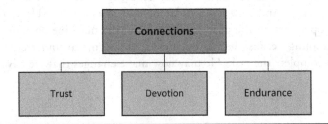

Figure 12.3 Themes raised about "Connections" by business professionals. © Bakhshandeh 2024.

Trust

■ "And this is where I reiterate how I believe that some of these things may be stifled by leadership. Trusting management is undoubtedly being negatively impacted by this."
■ "It's comparable in that employees who lack these talents typically don't have good relationships with the company and don't trust their bosses or the organization. Leadership can help close this gap."
■ "Building relationships and get[ting] connected is facilitated by mastering the 4Cs skills, and relationships are essential for employee retention. Because you are talking to each other, it fosters trust among the staff. You experience a feeling of identity."

Devotion

■ "I believe that there would be some level of enthusiasm to come to work every day if an employee knew that they would have the opportunity to exercise their critical thinking skill every day and that they would be helpful to us every day."
■ "People that are committed to our business and their jobs are what we are seeking for. Our business could benefit from *4Cs skills* training if it wants to foster such loyalty."
■ "It would, in my opinion, boost employee morale. They would likely feel more valued since they would receive better training, in my opinion. They would feel more valued and wouldn't want to go. I believe it would have a favorable effect on their outlook and method of operation."

Endurance

■ "People who are interested in a long-term career are what we're seeking … Therefore, teaching them the 4Cs skills could encourage them to remain longer."
■ "I think the *4Cs skills* would make the workforce feel more appreciated. More staff might be kept on board."

■ "They don't consider endurance or longevity in terms of five or ten years. And regrettably, it is the mentality in this region. And I doubt it's limited to our county."

Vision and Values

■ "Yes, and I believe that all four of the *4Cs skills* significantly advance a mission in fresh ways."
■ "It's everything … Whether it's the organization's grand overall vision, specific team objectives, or department missions, I believe that when people aren't *communicating* and there isn't that sense that we're all in this together, everything suffers."
■ "The most crucial benefit … would be increased employee dedication to the firm, combined with a shared sense of purpose, vision, and values."

The following three sub-themes were raised about "Vision and Values" during interviews with business professionals (see Figure 12.4).

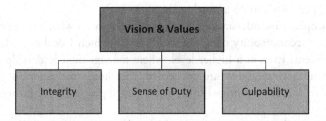

Figure 12.4   Themes raised about "Vision and Values" by business professionals. © Bakhshandeh 2024.

Integrity

■ "Since their job is to safeguard the lives and safety of other people, I would assume that the more they have the skills but are hesitant to use them out of a fear of doing anything incorrectly."
■ "Because it involves thinking outside the box and innovation, I do believe *critical thinking* is sometimes misunderstood as a bad thing. Organizational executives sometimes may not want to challenge the paradigm. This … is one of the moral dilemmas facing executives in corporations."
■ "We want to encourage *critical thinking, collaboration*, and all four of the *4Cs skills* since they support what we value and you can see results when you stand up for your ethics and the ethical ideals of the organization, like ownership."

Sense of Duty

■ "In essence … even the collaborative aspect of it would require a knowledge of responsibilities. So I believe it's a significant component in any business that is accountable. That falls under your role's responsibilities as well. People may not always be aware of their duties or what they are accountable for at work, and … this contributes to the breakdown of teamwork."
■ "Because of the federal and state laws that we have and are accountable for, I would argue that we lack originality and innovation. What we can and cannot do is extremely strictly

regulated by them. Therefore, there is a constant worry that you'll breach a rule and get in trouble with the law. Funding is lost. Therefore, these kinds of tasks are hindering *creativity*."

■ "Perhaps things would go more smoothly if we were in charge of helping our staff improve their *critical thinking*, decision-making, and *collaboration* abilities."

Culpability

■ "Then, due to their lack of accountability, those same people will claim, 'Oh no, I never heard about it.' Therefore, even when we give out information by email or newsletter, for some reason, individuals aren't receiving it. Therefore, there is a vacuum and a lack of accountability for their work. There certainly appears to be a need that needs to be addressed."

■ "Performance is impacted and made more frustrating by the absence of the *4Cs skills*. Because no matter what you are doing, if it's unclear what the expectations of what you can and cannot accomplish are, they are unsure of what is expected of them or how far they can go. It is the management's obligation and accountability to ensure that everyone is aware of what they are permitted to do and what they are not."

■ "Because of people's misunderstandings and lack of clarity on what has to be done, I genuinely believe that the accountability component of it, with which I deal on a daily basis, is pretty much non-existent. Even at a higher level, where management leadership responsibility and union leadership accountability are concerned, that keeps me quite busy. The issue is frequently a dearth of *communication* skills that prevent[s] people from hearing and being heard."

4Cs and Pandemic

Participants' replies to interview questions revealed the following themes: how the 4Cs skills were used in their teamwork and organizational production during the COVID-19 viral pandemic and emergency. This researcher chose to shed some light on this topic since it is crucial to understand how companies manage to function in the face of such significant challenges.

During interviews with business professionals, the following three sub-themes were raised about "4Cs and Pandemic" (see Figure 12.5).

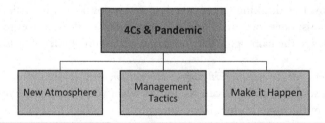

Figure 12.5 Themes raised about "4Cs and Pandemic" by business professionals. © Bakhshandeh 2024.

New Atmosphere

The topic "New Atmosphere" was developed to illustrate how an organization may utilize the 4Cs skills to establish a new working environment for its employees in the event of a pandemic or other emergency that might disrupt regular working conditions.

- "We can say we were successful in creating a new environment because this year's incoming class was the largest we've ever had, despite COVID. Nobody really believed it was possible, but it only happened because we were able to work together because we all think very differently and have different ideas about how to go about it. And yet, somehow, we got to the conclusion that, you know, we need to work together. And as I've already mentioned, although this autumn has been unique, it has been incredibly successful."
- "*Collaboration* and *communication* are two things that are worth investing in, even if COVID hasn't taught us anything else. It's just that much harder for individuals in this setting, therefore I think we should try a few various approaches. ... There are currently two attitudes among individuals. With preparations in place, masking and distance, people are ... at ease and feel safe. Or perhaps they want to be at home, which is the exact opposite. Even while they may not necessarily have the aptitude to accomplish things well, this is all they want to do. How do you *communicate* and work together between those two realms, and how significant is some of this?"
- "Employees who are working under stress, such as during the epidemic, would benefit from having someone who can explain a vision who is open-minded, honest, and *communicative*. Even during the COVID-19, managers may establish a new working environment by employing the 4Cs skills."

Management Tactics

The theme "Management Tactics" also emerged as a demonstration of the need for organizations to use the 4Cs skills to modify their management's approaches and policies in order to permit their staff to work during emergencies like pandemics or any other emergencies that would affect regular and established working policies.

- "Therefore, I believe that using the *4Cs skills* to leadership development would undoubtedly have a good effect on how management strategies are changed throughout the pandemic globally. It exists not just in my company but everywhere people work."
- "I believe I can speak for many groups, but if I were to only speak for ours, we would not have been able to withstand the past. I've lost track of the time. We've been in this scenario for, I don't know, eight or nine months, but it feels like a lot longer. Regardless, we could not have survived without employing the *4Cs skills* to change and improve our management strategies. You know, without ... some of the *4Cs skills* that we were talking about, and I could say it with certainty."
- "Just taking a step back and observing how this is actually altering how individuals interact or choose not to *communicate* is so fascinating. Similar to how you would use the *4Cs skills* to adjust to a new setting if you were a skilled communicator prior to COVID. I believe that despite COVID, you are still an excellent communicator. However, you may be becoming angry with others since some of them may have been bad communicators prior to COVID and are now just unable to respond appropriately. Some people could be obliged to study now, even if they don't want to."

Make It Happen

The theme "Make It Happen" also evolved as a demonstration of how businesses and their workforces employed the 4Cs competencies to work and function through crises and emergencies, including the pandemic and any other events that would disrupt normal working settings.

■ "Since these things like the *4Cs skills* are tested when major events like COVID occur, how can they remain strong throughout a crisis if they aren't excellent and strong beforehand? Organizations should thus focus on consistently modeling and acting in a manner that is constructive at times of crisis."

■ "The governor declared us to be essential employees, thus the entire state was put under lockdown. We carried on. We didn't stop working, but we did need a day to plan how the new installation procedure would work without entering your house. Over 2000 new accounts were added in the most recent quarter. So, we had to come up with a solution quickly. Without a doubt, we exercised *creativity* and *critical thinking.*"

■ "So, for instance, at the moment, the Corona Virus prevents us from engaging in the same activities with others as we formerly did. In terms of health, they are a vulnerable group. Therefore, we created activities for my director's monthly activity schedule. To make it happen, we *collaborated* and used our imagination."

Summary of Additional Themes Raised Out of Interviews

Table 12.1 represents the themes that emerged naturally from participants' responses to the interview questions in regard to their experiences of how the 4Cs skills were being used in their team operation and organization production. As we have mentioned before, these themes are not directly related to the three main intentions of the research, but they are significant to the cohesiveness and workability among workforces and the impact of 4Cs skills in such progress.

Table 12.1 Summary of Additional Themes Raised Out of Interviews

Themes	*Sub-Themes*
Empowerment	Gratitude
	Inspiration
	Welcoming Opinion
Connections	Trust
	Devotion
	Endurance
Vision & Values	Integrity
	Sense of Duty
	Culpability
4Cs & Pandemic	New Atmosphere
	Management Tactics
	Make It Happen

Note. © Bakhshandeh 2024.

Merged and Final Themes

During the process of data collection, including reviewing human resources and historical events documentation, observation meetings and production lines, interviewing executives and senior managers, and conducting focus groups, this researcher noticed 46 themes and 108 sub-themes related to the three main study intentions plus the additional themes.

After organizing the findings, this researcher decided to combine the finding themes and sub-themes and come up with a much shorter list, for two primary reasons:

1) Obviously bringing in all these themes and sub-themes for designing a training and development approach would be a massive undertaking, which would not serve the purpose of an effective approach to resolving the 21st-century 4Cs skills gap among workforces
2) Because of the proximity of descriptions and meanings of many themes and sub-themes, combining them became a much better and effective approach and thus arriving with a shorter list that would help design a training program based on emotional intelligence.

As a result of combining and merging, considering and reviewing 46 themes and 108 sub-themes, this researcher whittled them down to 18 combined and main themes out of all themes from Part III (Chapters 9, 10, 11, and 12). The combined themes from analyzing all the 21st-century 4Cs skills' emerging themes in relation to the three research questions are shown in Table 12.2.

Table 12.2 Summary of Merged Themes Cross Data Set and Their Explanations

Study Intention #1:	
Values Placed on 4Cs Skills by Organizations	
Merged Themes	*Explanations*
Problem-Solving Mentality	• A proactive and effective attitude to problems is made possible by having a problem-solving mindset, which involves seeking solutions rather than concentrating on the problems themselves. • People with a problem-solving mindset always consider the broader picture, are patient but determined, and are open to new opportunities.
Transparent and Prompt Communication	• Transparent communication is the act of sharing information upstream, downward, and laterally in a way that enables all parties to understand the motivations behind the statements. Advantages of open communication increases teamwork, increases trust, spurs further creativity. • Utilizing transparent communication is a method to obtain links and commitment for viability, to avoid assuming before asking, and to obtain clarification.
Generating Team Environment	• Teams are expected to create results, but when team members do not get along, performance suffers. The success of the team depends on having a collaborative team atmosphere. • When a team has shared objectives and is ready to involve others, the team environment aids in resolving team problems.
Welcoming Innovations	• In business, innovation is frequently linked to the development of new goods or services. However, it may also include altering your company practices. • People exhibit their abilities and bring fresh ideas to an inventive atmosphere. This setting is becoming more flexible.
Performance Through Emergencies	• Life's inevitable emergencies affect all types of communities and enterprises. However, things would go as well as they possibly could if companies had emergency plans and prepared for emergencies. • People who have a plan demonstrate strength, intentionality, and the ability to remain composed under pressure. They could distinguish between feelings, emotions, and the reality of the situation.
Constant Learning and Learners	• The idea of always advancing your knowledge to acquire new skills and competence is known as continuous learning, sometimes known as continual learning. Businesses that practice continuous learning encourage their staff to learn continuously by giving them access to the resources that make learning easier. • Because they are engaged in learning, constant learners are willing to learn from their mistakes, pay attention to their environment, and pick up knowledge from others.

(Continued)

Table 12.2 (CONTINUED) Summary of Merged Themes Cross Data Set and Their Explanations

Study Intention #2: Impact of 4Cs Skills Gap on Team Performance	
Merged Themes	**Explanations**
Lack of Imagination	• A small amount of imagination may greatly enhance how a business operates on a daily basis, as creative business people are aware of. Creative employees figure out how to get more done with less. Entrepreneurs might recognize opportunities for development and expansion by using their imagination. • Because they are not scared to make errors, they think differently and do not engage in regular tasks.
Working in Silos	• An organizational phenomenon known as "working in silos" refers to when a team (or set of teams) purposefully isolates itself from other teams or the entire organization. Practice often entails withholding information, poor teamwork, or just completing work that is not in line with organizational objectives. • They don't connect with one another while they operate in isolation, which prevents them from cooperating as a team and from taking advantage of numerous chances.
Absence of Motivation	• When you are unmotivated to act or just don't care about what is going on around you, you are apathetic (lack of motivation). You might not want to undertake anything that requires thought or emotion. • In business, lack of motivation might be caused by an employee's lack of commitment to the business, or not having any personal vision, personal goals, and dreams.
Lack of Communication	• Lack of communication occurs when you don't properly express yourself or leave out important details. Additionally, it may impact things like worker productivity, interpersonal connections at work, and mental wellness. Understanding the consequences of poor communication might help you recognize the warning signals and improve your communication. • Lack of communication can also be caused by a lack of detail, a fear of or confusion about new communication technologies, or plain old generational differences and resistance.
Absence of Self-Awareness	• Lack of self-awareness frequently manifests in a person's unwillingness to hear what others have to say about their actions at work, in relationships, or at home. Particularly if they are insecure, have poor self-esteem, or believe they are above reproach, they frequently interpret input as criticism. • People with no self-awareness reject change and novel concepts. They are promoting division, being negative, and spreading rumors. They are not compassionate toward others.

(Continued)

Table 12.2 (CONTINUED) Summary of Merged Themes Cross Data Set and Their Explanations

No Self-Regulation	• An adult with poor self-regulation skills may lack self-confidence and self-esteem and have trouble handling stress and frustration. Often, this might result in anger or anxiety. • They have a bad attitude, show little awareness of their own actions, and are arrogant and demeaning.

Study Intention #3:

Effective 4Cs Skills Training and Development

Merged Themes	*Explanations*
Emotional Intelligence Workshops	• Organizational resilience, talent retention, leadership, and job happiness will all increase as a result of attending emotional intelligence workshops. Employees can learn more about the practical applications of emotional intelligence at work. • Participants can learn about elements of self-awareness and self-regulation while learning about the impact of their emotions on themselves and others.
Soft Skills Training	• Unlike hard skills training, which focuses on an employee's technical aptitude, soft skills training focuses on the development of talents like communication, teamwork, and problem-solving. Emotional intelligence, a positive outlook, and initiative are further soft skills. • During the soft skills training, employees will learn about their interpersonal skills, intrapersonal skills, and relatedness skills, which directly have a positive impact on their individual and team performance.
Effective and Efficient Communication	• When a speaker effectively communicates, he or she is concerned with making sure the audience completely understands the point being made. In order to communicate efficiently, the speaker must do it in the fewest words feasible. • People with these skills, are speaking in precise and clear manners. They are practicing elements of active listening, and bridging misunderstandings and miscommunication.
Team and Trust Building	• When team members show concern, respect, and appreciation for one another's feelings and viewpoints, trust is fostered. Organizations want high-performing teams now more than ever to achieve outcomes and establish enduring bonds. • They demonstrate the ability to work together and understand their differences by learning about diversity and displaying sensitivity.
Career and Organizational Commitment	• Job performance and organizational commitment are directly related. According to the principle of organizational commitment, when workers are committed or loyal to their organization, they will work harder and more productively, increasing total job performance. • Without organizational commitment and career commitment, there will be no motivation for personal and professional growth.

(Continued)

Table 12.2   (CONTINUED) Summary of Merged Themes Cross Data Set and Their Explanations

Problem-Solving Techniques	• There are several methods for fixing problems. Examples include working backwards, brainstorming, means–ends analysis, cause and effect analysis, difference reduction, trial and error, and analogies. • By organizations' investment in problem-solving techniques, they are investing in capable employees who are willing to think and resolve their issues. This is a valuable skill that not only supports individuals and teams in their productivity and performance but also supports them on organizations' succession planning.

Note. © Bakhshandeh 2024.

What Is Next?

At this point in the last four chapters of Part III, we have expressed all the contributors' input, ideas, experiences, and what they had on their minds about the expectations of their workforce in regard to (a) values they are placing on 4Cs skills by organizations, (b) impact of 4Cs skills gap on team performance, (c) what they want as an effective 4Cs skills training and development, and (d) additional themes that arose during the data-collection process.

In Part IV "Use Emotional Intelligence to Create Competency-Based Training," Chapter 13, "Emotional Intelligence: The Key to Personal and Professional Success," explores how organizations can use clusters of emotional intelligence to train and develop their workforces in 21st-century 4Cs skills.

USE EMOTIONAL INTELLIGENCE TO CREATE COMPETENCY-BASED TRAINING

IV

In this part, the book looks at the emotional intelligence (EI) clusters and related competencies and correspondence qualities and attributes, as well as how they are related to 4Cs skills. This part also covers applying EI coaching for individuals and teams, including introducing verities of competency-based training for developing 4Cs skills among workforces. This part also looks at the necessary actions for implementing and managing such training and development undertaking. In conclusion, we look at who is an EI coach and what competencies and requirements they should have.

Chapter 13: Emotional Intelligence: The Key to Personal and Professional Success

This chapter breaks down the EI clusters and all corresponding competencies. Understanding and controlling our own and others' emotions improves relationships, mental health, communication, and overall success.

Chapter 14: Application of Emotional Intelligence Coaching

Emotional intelligence coaching involves self-awareness, goal setting, strategy development, self-evaluation, and skill practice in close collaboration with a coach. This chapter looks at elements of the EI-coaching process and the competencies of an EI coach.

DOI: 10.4324/9781003462316-16

Chapter 15: 4Cs Skills Competency-Based Training and Development Via EI

Emotional intelligence is individuals' capacity and capability to recognize, evaluate, and positively influence their emotions and others around them. This chapter covers several competency-based training and development approaches to increase 4Cs skills among individuals and teams.

Chapter 16: Implementation and Management of Training and Development

Like any other management and leadership program approach, implementing EI training and development requires implementation and management systems to ensure the quality of design and presentation and manage the well-progress process.

Chapter 17: Emotional Intelligence Coach

EI coaches are experienced specialists who improve people's emotional intelligence, a key to personal and professional success. EI coaching helps people understand and regulate their own and others' emotions, unlike traditional coaching, which focuses on skills or goals.

Chapter 13

Emotional Intelligence: The Key to Personal and Professional Success

Introduction

Emotional intelligence (EI), often referred to as emotional quotient (EQ), has emerged as a vital factor in determining an individual's success in both their personal and professional lives. Unlike traditional intelligence, which focuses on cognitive abilities, EI delves into a person's capacity to recognize, understand, manage, and effectively use their emotions, as well as the emotions of others. The good news is that EI is not a fixed trait; it can be developed and enhanced over time. Strategies for improving EI include self-reflection, mindfulness practices, seeking feedback from others, and actively working on self-regulation and empathy skills. Coaching and training programs are also available to help individuals boost their emotional intelligence.

Emotional intelligence is a powerful and transformative quality that influences our personal and professional lives in myriad ways. It involves understanding and managing our own emotions and those of others, and it contributes to improved relationships, mental health, communication, and success in various spheres of life. As we continue to recognize the significance of EI, investing in its development becomes an essential step toward personal growth and achieving our full potential.

This chapter explores all elements of EI, its clusters, and all the related qualities and competencies of someone with access to and practicing EI. More specifically, this chapter paves the way for the chapters of Part IV, which are about using special emotional intelligence training to positively impact the workforce's access to understand, possess, and use EI in developing their 4Cs skills at the workplace.

This chapter will cover the following elements related to Emotional Intelligence:

- What is Emotional Intelligence (EI)?
- Fundamental Distinctions and Comparisons between EQ and IQ.
- Importance of Emotional Intelligence and Its Effects.
- Role of EI and Its Competencies in Organizations.
- Competencies Generated from Emotional Intelligence.

DOI: 10.4324/9781003462316-17

What Is Emotional Intelligence (EI)?

Emotional intelligence, sometimes referred to as emotional quotient or EQ, encompasses the capacity to comprehend, employ, and regulate one's own emotions constructively, hence facilitating stress reduction, efficient communication, empathy toward others, resilience in the face of adversity, and resolution of conflicts. The cultivation of emotional intelligence facilitates the establishment of more robust interpersonal connections, enhances academic and occupational accomplishments, and facilitates the attainment of both professional and personal aspirations. Additionally, it can facilitate emotional connectivity, translate purpose into tangible outcomes, and enable educated decision-making regarding one's priorities (Connors, 2020; Goleman, 2019).

EI Clusters and Definitions

Emotional intelligence is generally outlined by the following four clusters: (1) self-awareness, (2) self-regulation, (3) social awareness, and (4) relationship management. Furthermore, we have added some definitions and descriptions of these clusters by some scholars and experts in the field of EI (see Figure 13.1).

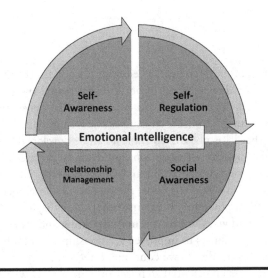

Figure 13.1 Emotional intelligence clusters. © Bakhshandeh 2024.

Emotional Intelligence

The capacity to recognize, utilize, and regulate one's own emotions in order to reduce stress, communicate clearly, sympathize with others, overcome obstacles, and diffuse conflict is known as emotional intelligence (Bakhshandeh, Rothwell, & Imroz, 2023).

- Emotional intelligence is about regulating relationships well, detecting emotions in others, finding self-motivation elements, and understanding and regulating your own emotions (Goleman, 2020).
- Emotional intelligence recognizes, controls, and fosters enduring relationships (Johnson, 2022).

Self-Awareness

Ability to be aware of your own feelings and how they influence your attitudes and actions. You are confident in yourself and aware of your advantages and disadvantages (Bakhshandeh et al., 2023).

- This is the capacity to keep track of how one's thoughts, actions, and emotions align with one's core beliefs. Self-aware people are adept at evaluating themselves, controlling their emotions, and modifying their conduct in response (Duval & Wuckland, 1972).
- Self-awareness is about personal growth and being aware of one's state of being. It is about growth that never stops, enabling a dynamic and ever-evolving process (Rasheed, Younas, & Sundus, 2019).

Self-Regulation

You can restrain impulsive thoughts and actions, regulate your emotions in healthy ways, exercise initiative, keep your word when you commit, and adjust to changing conditions (Bakhshandeh et al., 2023).

- Self-regulated individuals are adept at setting reasonable goals and selecting appropriate actions to reach them, utilizing resources that complement their own limitations (Sahranavard, Miri, & Salehiniya, 2018).
- Over time, self-regulation has expanded to include the ability to control our thoughts, behaviors, and emotions (Bauer & Baumeister, 2011).

Social Awareness

You're empathetic and are able to detect emotional indicators, feel at ease in social situations, and comprehend the needs, wants, and worries of others. You can also identify the power relationships within a group or organization (Bakhshandeh et al., 2023).

- Being socially aware entails evaluating differences among people, appreciating other points of view, and showing compassion, sensitivity, empathy, and concern for others (Beamish & Bryer, 2015).
- The capacity to adopt the viewpoint of and feel empathy for others from different origins and cultures, to comprehend social and moral standards of conduct, and to identify resources and supports from the community, school, and family (CASEL, 2015).

Relationship Management

You are skilled at building and sustaining positive connections, communicating clearly, motivating and influencing people, functioning well in a group, and handling conflict (Bakhshandeh et al., 2023).

- Relationship management aims to establish interactions with other individuals that bring value (Hudson, 2023).

■ Interpersonal communication skills, the ability to help others reach their maximum potential, and inspiring, influencing, connecting, and trusting others are all considered aspects of relationship management. It also includes helping individuals adjust to changing circumstances and deal with setbacks (Zimmerman, 2013).

Difference between IQ and EQ

It is well acknowledged that those with high intelligence do not necessarily achieve the highest levels of success or have the greatest fulfillment in their lives. It is likely that individuals within your acquaintances possess exceptional intellectual abilities yet have deficiencies in social aptitude, resulting in professional and interpersonal difficulties. The possession of intellectual capacity or intelligence quotient (IQ) alone is insufficient in and of itself to attain success in life.

Indeed, an individual's intelligence quotient (IQ) may contribute to their admission to higher education. However, their emotional quotient (EQ) plays a pivotal role in effectively navigating and regulating the many stressors and emotional challenges encountered throughout the culmination of their academic endeavors, namely during the final examination period. The coexistence of intelligence quotient (IQ) and emotional quotient (EQ) is crucial, as their synergy enhances their overall effectiveness (see Figure 13.2) (Wall, 2007).

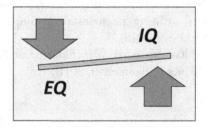

Figure 13.2   Intellectual quotient and emotional quotient. © Bakhshandeh 2024.

Definition of IQ

The intelligence quotient (IQ) is a measure of intellect derived from a standardized exam that assesses individuals' mental age relative to their chronological age, with the result multiplied by 100. The purpose of the exam is to evaluate an individual's cognitive ability in terms of their thinking and reasoning skills. William Stern initially developed the term (Goleman, 2015; Wall, 2007).

The intelligence quotient (IQ) is a metric used to assess an individual's intellectual capacity, as shown by their performance on an intelligence test relative to the scores achieved by others of the same age who took the same exam (Wall, 2007).

Definition of EQ

The term emotional quotient (EQ) refers to an individual's capacity to recognize and understand both their own emotions and those of others. The degree of emotional intelligence of an individual is assessed by their ability to differentiate between various emotions and utilize this intelligence to inform their cognitive processes and actions (Goleman, 2015; Wall, 2007).

The concept was initially introduced in 1995 by Daniel Goleman, a psychologist, in his emotional intelligence publication. Cognitive and emotional intelligence includes individuals' capacities to discern, articulate, and regulate their ideas and behaviors, comprehend the perspectives of others, accurately assess their circumstances, make sound and efficient judgments, and effectively manage stress and adversity, among other factors. Extensive study has demonstrated a positive correlation between individuals with high emotional intelligence (EQ) and several aspects of their mental well-being, work performance, and overall quality of life (Goleman, 2015; Wall, 2007).

Fundamental Distinctions and Comparisons between IQ and EQ

The present discourse provides a comprehensive analysis of the primary distinctions between intelligence quotient (IQ) and emotional quotient (EQ) through a detailed exposition of the following key aspects (Goleman, 2015) (see Table 13.1).

Table 13.1 Fundamental Distinctions and Comparisons between EQ and IQ

Emotional Quotient (EQ)	*Intelligence Quotient (IQ)*
As measured by standardized tests, emotional intelligence is commonly referred to as emotional quotient (EQ).	The intelligence quotient (IQ) is a numerical value derived from a standardized intelligence test that measures an individual's capacity for logical thinking.
Individuals' success in practical life is indicative of their emotional quotient (EQ).	The academic achievement of individuals is contingent upon their intelligence quotient (IQ).
The EQ assessment evaluates the individuals' social and emotional abilities, specifically their capacity to perceive and understand their and others' emotional expressions.	On the other hand, IQ assesses individuals' aptitudes in intellectual pursuits and capacity for logical thinking.
The acquisition and enhancement of emotional quotient (EQ) can be observed.	Unlike intelligence quotient, which is an innate capacity, emotional intelligence is a trait that individuals possess from birth.
Individuals who possess high emotional intelligence (EQ) demonstrate the ability to effectively identify, regulate, and articulate their own emotions and accurately understand and evaluate the emotions of others.	An individual with a high intelligence quotient (IQ) can acquire, comprehend, and apply information while also demonstrating proficiency in logical reasoning and abstract thinking.
High levels of emotional intelligence are evident in those who hold leadership positions, such as leaders, captains, and managers, as well as those who face social difficulties.	The intelligence quotient (IQ), which is used to assess individuals with high intellectual abilities, common sense, mental problems, and other related factors, is taken into consideration.

Source: Goleman (2015); Wall (2007).

Importance of Emotional Intelligence and Its Effects

The concept of emotional intelligence (EI) exerts a significant influence on several facets of human existence:

School and Work Performance

Possessing a high level of emotional intelligence can facilitate the effective navigation of the intricate social dynamics within the professional environment. Furthermore, it can enable individuals to successfully assume leadership roles, encourage their peers, and perform exceptionally in their chosen career paths. Indeed, in the context of evaluating significant job applicants, several organizations already assign equal importance to emotional intelligence as they do to technical proficiency and thus administer emotional intelligence assessments as part of their recruiting process (Kite & Kay, 2012).

Professional Triumphs

Emotional intelligence (EI) has emerged as a transformative factor in the modern workplace. Leaders who possess a high level of emotional intelligence (EI) have the ability to inspire and encourage their colleagues, resulting in enhanced levels of productivity and work satisfaction. Additionally, they have exceptional proficiency in dispute resolution and decision-making, both of which are of utmost importance in managerial positions (Rothwell & Bakhshandeh, 2022).

Physical Well-Being

Individuals who experience difficulty in regulating their emotions may also encounter challenges in effectively managing their stress levels. This phenomenon has the potential to result in significant health complications. Unmitigated stress has been found to elevate blood pressure, hinder immune system functioning, heighten susceptibility to cardiovascular events such as heart attacks and strokes, contribute to infertility, and accelerate the aging process. The initial stage in enhancing emotional intelligence is acquiring the skills necessary to manage stress effectively (Bakhshandeh et al., 2023).

Mental Well-Being

Unregulated emotions and stress can also influence an individual's mental well-being, rendering them susceptible to the development of anxiety and depression. Individuals who possess an inability to comprehend, acclimate to, or regulate their emotions may encounter difficulties in establishing robust interpersonal connections. Consequently, this might engender feelings of loneliness and seclusion, intensifying preexisting mental health issues (Bakhshandeh et al., 2023).

Personal Relationships

By acquiring knowledge about one's emotions and developing the ability to regulate them, individuals can enhance their capacity to effectively communicate their emotional states and gain insight into the emotional experiences of others. This enables individuals to enhance their communication skills and cultivate more robust interpersonal connections within professional contexts and in their personal spheres (Lindberg, 2023).

Social Connections

The ability to effectively recognize and regulate one's emotions holds significant societal value as it facilitates interpersonal connections and fosters a sense of interconnectedness with others and the surrounding environment. Social intelligence encompasses the ability to discern between amicable vs. adversarial individuals, gauge the level of another person's investment in one's own well-being, alleviate anxiety, achieve equilibrium within one's neurological system through interpersonal interaction, and experience sentiments of affection and contentment (Neal, Spencer-Arnell, & Liz, 2009).

Communication Quality

The foundation of emotional intelligence (EI) is predicated on the significance of proficient communication. Individuals who possess a high level of emotional intelligence (EI) are adept at effectively expressing their thoughts and emotions, resulting in a reduced occurrence of misinterpretations and improved results in interpersonal and occupational engagements (Neal et al., 2009).

Conflict Resolution

Emotional intelligence (EI) provides individuals with the necessary skills to manage and resolve disputes positively and effectively. Individuals possess the capacity to demonstrate empathy for their peers' viewpoints, establish shared understanding, and collaborate toward outcomes that are advantageous to all parties involved. This ability serves to mitigate conflicts within the workplace and enhance the overall functioning of teams (Rothwell & Bakhshandeh, 2022).

Role of EI and Its Competencies in Organizations

Irrespective of personal preferences, it is imperative for organizational leaders to effectively manage the emotional climate inside their respective firms, including the diverse range of emotional expressions exhibited by their workforce, spanning from upper-level managers to frontline staff. According to a *Harvard Business Review* (HBR) article from 2017, successful organizational leaders employ a unique blend of psychological abilities referred to as emotional intelligence (EI) to accomplish their tasks effectively.

The *Harvard Business Review* said of these company executives who are aware of EI abilities, "They're self-aware and empathetic. They can read and regulate their own emotions while intuitively grasping how others feel and gauging their organization's emotional state" (HBR, 2017, p. 4). Boyatzis and Sala (2004) define EI and its related competencies as "an ability to recognize, understand, and use emotional information about oneself or others that leads to or causes effective or superior performance" (p. 5).

Among both organization development literature (HBR, 2017; Rothwell et al., 2016; Rothwell, 2015; Cummings & Worley, 2015) and literature by emotional intelligence experts (Wayne, 2019;

Goleman, 2015, 2014; Stevens, 2009; Clarke, 2006; Goleman, 1998), it is evident that both genetic factors and environmental influences shape emotional intelligence. According to a study published in the *Harvard Business Review* (HBR, 2017), emotional intelligence is a multifaceted construct influenced by several factors listed below:

a) Genetic predisposition.
b) General personality traits.
c) Professional life experience.
d) Traditional training methods.

According to HBR (2017), the deliberate and empathetic use of emotional intelligence has the potential to drive extraordinary performance among firms, their leaders, and their workforce.

The impact of emotions on our mentality is significant and pervasive, exerting a substantial influence on our everyday life (Bakhshandeh, 2015; Hockenbury & Hockenbury, 2007). Our immediate emotional states, including sadness, anger, happiness, frustration, or boredom, often influence decisions. Consequently, our reactions are unconsciously shaped by the emotions we are experiencing (Bakhshandeh, 2015; Hockenbury & Hockenbury, 2007).

Handley (2017) has conducted a study on emotional intelligence, exploring two distinct approaches: the mental ability model and the mixed model. The mental ability model focuses on cognitive aspects, while the mixed model encompasses several abilities, including motivation, trait, and skills. The study suggests pertaining to the training and development of a workforce to acquire 4Cs skills are derived using a mixed model approach. "Boyatzis, Goleman, and Rhee (2000) empirically analyzed competencies for emotional intelligence and determined four competency clusters: self-awareness, self-management, social awareness, and social skills" (Handley, 2017, p. 142).

Competencies Generated from Emotional Intelligence

Business managers and organizational leaders must offer training and development opportunities to their workforce in the domain of emotional intelligence. This encompasses a range of knowledge, skills, and competencies that can enhance both individual professional growth and managerial capabilities. By cultivating emotional intelligence, managers can directly influence the behavior and attitudes of their teams, groups, departments, and the entire workforce, fostering a more positive and productive work environment. Several qualities and attributes are associated with individuals who grasp and actively engage in the various clusters and competences of emotional intelligence. This study presents at least three favorable characteristics and attributes exhibited by individuals possessing these skills.

In the subsequent section, we provide the four clusters of emotional intelligence and their corresponding abilities that may aid organizational leaders in implementing crucial and pragmatic emotional intelligence practices which are highly beneficial for the training and development of workforces.

Self-Awareness Cluster

According to Bakhshandeh (2015), our perception of ourselves and of others has a significant role in shaping our level of consciousness. This heightened consciousness subsequently influences our perception of reality, ultimately influencing our behavioral responses. According to Goleman (2014), individuals who exhibit self-awareness possess the ability to acknowledge the impact of their emotions on their professional performance. They also understand when it is appropriate to seek assistance and possess the skill to concentrate on enhancing their strengths rather than fixating on their weaknesses. Self-awareness may be defined as the cognitive ability of humans to recognize and comprehend their own emotions, temperaments, and intentions, as well as to acknowledge the influence of their emotions on others (Rothwell, 2015). The acquisition of self-awareness enables individuals to discern and comprehend the emotions and mental states of others, as well as their perceptions of our demeanor and conduct, and our subsequent reactions toward them (Goleman, 2015).

Competencies pertaining to the self-awareness cluster encompass a wide range of skills and abilities, with the understanding that this list is not exhaustive (see Figure 13.3).

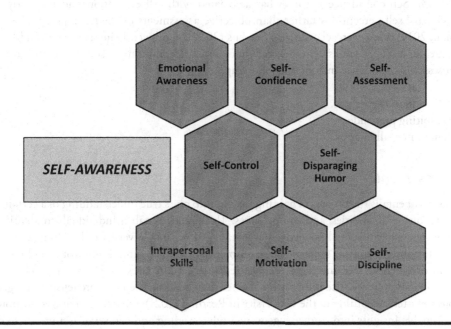

Figure 13.3   Competencies related to self-awareness cluster. © Bakhshandeh 2024.

Emotional Awareness

This pertains to the comprehension and awareness of persons regarding the essence of their emotions and the specific types of emotions they experience in any particular instant. As per the definition provided by the *Merriam-Webster Dictionary*, emotion refers to a conscious cognitive response, such as wrath or fear, which is subjectively seen as a powerful sensation directed toward a particular entity. Physiological and behavioral alterations inside the body commonly accompany this experience (Bakhshandeh et al., 2023). According to the *Oxford Dictionary*, emotion may be a potent sentiment arising from an individual's surroundings, mood, or interpersonal connections. As seen in the definitions provided by dictionaries, these concepts are linked to an individual's emotions in a certain manner. Several characteristics can be associated with those who possess emotional awareness as follows:

- Showing concern for others' feelings.
- Recognizing misunderstandings.
- Displaying a trust-based function.

Self-Confidence

The concept of self-confidence refers to the individuals' beliefs in their own abilities and skills. The perception and interpersonal connection individuals have with themselves constitute a significant component of emotional intelligence. Nevertheless, it is important to include the perspective of Stevens (2009) who emphasizes that the trait test should not be oversimplified by assuming that high scores are always indicative of positive traits, while low scores are always indicative of negative traits. In contrast, it might be argued that every score is contingent upon its specific environment (p. 53). Self-confidence is somewhat associated with self-evaluation and is mostly based on individuals' self-perceptions rather than objective assessments of their competence or talents (Goleman, 2014). However, according to Stevens (2009), good well-being is influenced by factors such as greater levels of self-esteem. Several characteristics commonly associated with individuals who possess self-confidence include the following:

- Believing in their skills.
- Exhibiting gratitude.
- Being internally happy.

Self-Assessment

Self-assessment entails the process of gaining insight into one's true understanding of a certain body of information, set of abilities, and competences. This practice enables individuals to identify deficiencies in their expertise and knowledge (Goleman, 2015). The University of Reading (2021) made an insightful observation on student self-assessment within the same framework, highlighting a significant divergence. The university emphasized that certain assessment systems solely evaluate students' capacity to reproduce information, rather than gauging their comprehension and grasp of the subject matter. According to the University of Reading (2021), self-assessment has the potential to offer valuable insights into students' genuine understanding and can serve as a means to detect any deficiencies in their knowledge. In the process of developing a viable and all-encompassing self-assessment, certain companies may permit a certain level of individual involvement in the formulation, modification, and advancement of assessment criteria. Utilizing this methodology results in developing a more inclusive and pertinent self-evaluation, exhibiting a greater degree of credibility and pertinence (Goleman, 2015; Cummings & Worley, 2015). Several characteristics may be observed in those who engage in the practice of self-assessment, which are as follows:

- Examining their learning.
- Monitoring goals' advancement.
- Performing self-efficacy.

Self-Control

The concept of self-control refers to individuals' abilities to regulate their thoughts and emotions. An essential skill necessary for possessing and utilizing emotional intelligence is their ability to effectively manage their emotions rather than suppressing or expressing them forcefully. A common misconception individuals hold is the belief that emotions are subject to control. However, it is important to recognize that emotions cannot be effectively controlled. Within this particular context, the term "controlling" one's emotions refers to acquiring mastery over them and knowledge of the most optimal methods of responding to them (Wayne, 2019). Emotions are a significant component of the human psyche, serving as a mechanism to alert individuals to the presence of salient stimuli requiring attention. The manner in which individuals respond to the subject matter that elicits their emotions is crucial in determining the significance of said subject matter and then selecting a suitable and pertinent course of action to effectively engage with it (Goleman, 1998). Emotions cannot be categorized as inherently good or evil. Instead, the distinction is in the responses individuals have toward their feelings. In this manner, individuals' responses to their emotions are characterized by a lack of impulsivity. Moreover, Stevens (2009) highlighted that self-control serves to enhance the cognitive process of logical reasoning in high-stress situations and is intended to promote and amplify constructive behaviors. Several characteristics are associated with those who possess self-control:

- Making no impulse decisions.
- Being in control of their behaviors.
- Retaining conscientiousness.

Self-Deprecating Humor

Self-deprecating humor is among the diverse array of comedic techniques humans employ during interpersonal exchanges. Similar to possessing and employing conventional humor, the manifestation of humor can occur at any point during a discussion, taking the form of a concise and straightforward remark or a more elaborate tale. Self-deprecating humor enables individuals to share amusing anecdotes about themselves in a manner that portrays themselves in a negative, humorous, or unsuccessful light (Prigo-Valverde, n.d.). Essentially, individuals possess the capacity to engage in self-deprecating humor, demonstrating a lack of preoccupation with external perceptions and judgments. Several characteristics such as those listed below may be observed in individuals who possess self-deprecating humor:

- Acknowledging their faults.
- Being at ease to laugh at themselves.
- Not being up to an immaculate image.

Intrapersonal Skills

This refers to individuals' capacity to discern and comprehend their cognitive processes, affective states, and subjective experiences. The ability to effectively strategize and manage one's personal and professional endeavors is seen as a valuable competency (Rothwell, 2015; Cummings & Worley, 2015). Individuals who possess intrapersonal abilities have a high level of proficiency in introspection, self-inquiry, and self-reflection, enabling them to effectively understand and articulate their own emotions, motives, and goals. Individuals of this kind exhibit distinct traits of introspection and cogitation as they engage in the process of self-analysis intending to attain a deeper comprehension of their own being. Individuals with intrapersonal talents tend to have intuitive tendencies and typically display introverted characteristics. The primary learning mode for individuals is predominantly autonomous and reflective in nature (Sheck & Lin, 2015). According to Sheck and Lin (2015), intrapersonal abilities serve as the underlying basis for personal growth and are essential attributes within the realm of leadership competencies. Several characteristics associated with individuals who possess intrapersonal skills include the following:

- Appreciating themselves.
- Being aware of their agenda.
- Reducing interruptions.

Self-Motivation

The desire to engage in labor is driven by personal and internal motivations rather than being solely influenced by financial considerations, which are categorized as external incentives. This phenomenon encompasses the proclivity of individuals to pursue their personal objectives with a notable degree of purposefulness, vigor, and resolve (Bakhshandeh et al., 2023). Certain characteristics exhibited by individuals who possess self-motivation are listed below:

- Displaying interest in success.
- Encouraging forward motion actions.
- Exhibiting interest in productivity.

Self-Discipline

This pertains to the inherent capacity of humans to exercise self-control and motivate themselves to exert greater effort above the bare requirements, thereby doing tasks autonomously without the need for continual monitoring or reminders. The acquisition of self-discipline is contingent upon the cultivation of self-control and self-motivation (Bakhshandeh et al., 2023). Several characteristics commonly associated with those who possess self-discipline include the following:

- Avoiding instant gratification.
- Excluding interferences.
- Not needing a constant reminder.

Self-Regulation Cluster

The term "self-regulation" pertains to the cognitive capacity to identify, comprehend, and effectively manage one's own disruptive impulses, unsuitable responses, and disposition. Individuals have a tendency to postpone making instant evaluations and instead engage in a process of deliberation and reflection prior to taking action against individuals or ideas (Goleman, 2014). According to Goleman (2014), the emotional intelligence cluster being discussed refers to leaders who possess the ability to maintain a composed and rational mindset when faced with challenging circumstances. Developing self-regulation competencies enables leaders to progress beyond being conscious of their emotions to effectively controlling their emotional impulses. This includes cultivating a positive mindset that is essential for taking initiative, establishing trustworthiness, and promoting productivity (Goleman, 2014, 1998).

Competencies pertaining to the self-regulation cluster encompass a wide range of skills and abilities, which may include but are not necessarily restricted to those in Figure 13.4.

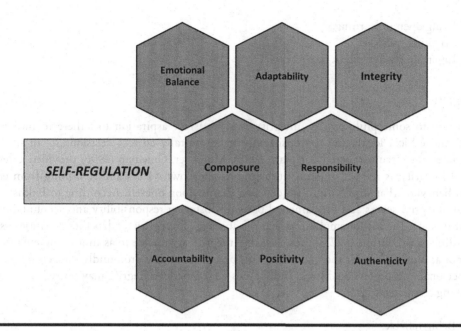

Figure 13.4 Competencies related to the self-regulation cluster. © Bakhshandeh 2024.

Emotional Balance

Emotional balance refers to an individual's ability to be cognizant of their emotions and effectively manage them rationally and compassionately. The state of emotional imbalance can be attributed to two factors: the failure to acknowledge and process one's emotions as they arise, leading to their subsequent dismissal and suppression; or the excessive attachment to these emotions, resulting in their overwhelming dominance (Goleman, 2015, 1998). The attainment of emotional balance is facilitated by individuals allowing themselves to experience their surface emotions without feeling constrained or overpowered by them. Emotional equilibrium is acquiring knowledge about one's emotions, accepting them without prejudice, and engaging in appropriate actions based on this understanding. Several characteristics mentioned below are commonly associated with individuals who possess emotional balance:

■ Correctly recognizing their emotions.
■ Being mindful of their emotions.
■ Handling impulse emotions.

Adaptability

Adaptability pertains to the extent of rigidity and severity in people's behaviors, attitudes, and methodologies, as well as their effectiveness in accommodating novel concepts, circumstances, or contexts. Stevens (2009) emphasized the significance of adaptability, asserting that the enhancement of collaboration relies on establishing a cohesive team that demonstrates a readiness to embrace change. This quality is essential for effective leadership. Several characteristics commonly associated with individuals who possess adaptability include:

- Being open to learning.
- Adapting quickly.
- Entertaining new ideas.

Integrity

According to some philosophers, integrity is a persistent aspiration to adhere to individuals' moral and ethical ideals and to consistently make morally correct decisions in all situations and under any circumstances (Goleman, 1998). Moreover, Goleman (1998) provided a description of integrity as the act of being authentic to one's own values and refraining from engaging in behaviors that would diminish or bring shame upon oneself. According to Bakhshandeh (2015), integrity serves as a fundamental basis for fostering responsibility and accountability in the workplace. The author emphasizes that the absence of integrity renders these qualities useless. According to the author (p. 27), those lacking integrity are unable to assume complete responsibility or accountability for their conduct. This potent capability profoundly impacts all facets of our personal and professional lives. Individuals who practice integrity may possess some of the following characteristics:

- Being reliable.
- Being truthful.
- Being trustworthy.

Calm Manners

Calm manners, often known as composure, refer to the capacity to regulate spontaneous behaviors even in situations of significant pressure. Individuals who possess calmness exhibit a tendency to refrain from quick reactions. Individuals may respond to situations after thoughtful analysis and evaluation, even if the outcome is not aligned with their desires or preferences. This approach reflects a deliberate endeavor to maintain composure and rationality, exemplifying a measured and composed response. According to Wayne (2019), when faced with conflicts, the objective should not be to engage in arguments but rather to achieve a resolution. This resolution serves as an opportunity to cultivate the ability to direct one's actions, thoughts, and emotions toward the common goal of resolving the dispute. Several characteristics commonly associated with those who possess composure include the following:

- Exerting confidence.
- Being calm.
- Being insightful.

Responsibility

According to Vincent E. Barry, a scholar specializing in business history, the concept of responsibility within the business realm may be defined as "a domain of duty or obligation that is assigned to an individual based on the nature of their position, function, or work" (Fitzpatrick & Bronstein, 2006). As per the definition provided by the *Merriam-Webster Dictionary* (2024b), responsibility may be understood as the condition or actuality of being obligated to address a matter or exert authority over an individual (n.p.). According to Bakhshandeh (2015), individuals demonstrate a sense of accountability from a mindfulness perspective by actively recognizing and accepting their thoughts and taking responsibility for their actions, regardless of their moral implications, without offering any explanations. Several characteristics may be attributed to those who exhibit a sense of responsibility:

- Not presenting excuses.
- Not complaining.
- Being sensible.

Accountability

According to the *Merriam-Webster Dictionary* (2024a), accountability is defined as the attribute or condition of being responsible, particularly referring to the duty or readiness to acknowledge responsibility or provide an explanation for one's conduct. Individuals who embody responsibility refrain from assigning blame and evading their own obligations by attributing fault to others for the occurrence and manner of events. The individuals in question do not assume the role of victims of external factors, so they absolve themselves of personal accountability. According to Rothwell et al. (2016), individuals demonstrate a lack of procrastination in fulfilling their obligations and responsibilities. The concepts of accountability and responsibility are closely interconnected. Engaging in responsible behavior inherently entails assuming accountability and upholding integrity. Bakhshandeh (2015) states this is the fundamental element of the three-force combination. Several characteristics of individuals that exhibit accountability include the following:

- Assuming responsibility.
- Not assigning blames.
- Being transparent.

Positivity

A positive and optimistic mindset significantly and beneficially influences workplace dynamics. The aforementioned study conducted by *Harvard Business Review* (HBR, 2017) highlights the significant importance of positive impact on individuals in many contexts, including their interactions with peers, the leadership styles used by managers, and the strategies employed by firms to engage with their clients and consumers. According to a study conducted by HBR (2017), possessing a good disposition toward others fosters an atmosphere conducive to cultivating connections, establishing trust, and fostering loyalty throughout the workforce, regardless of the hierarchical level within the firm. Conversely, in instances when individuals fail to demonstrate their concern and dedication toward fostering workability and harmony, a sense of mistrust will emerge, leading to significant disruptions in interpersonal connections, both within domestic and professional settings (Goleman, 2015). Several characteristics may be observed in those who actively engage in the practice of positivity.

- Being optimistic.
- Being resilient.
- Being grateful.

Authenticity

Cultivating authenticity involves acknowledging one's past actions and experiences in navigating various difficulties, assuming ownership of these actions, and then assuming responsibility for the outcomes (Bakhshandeh, 2015). When confronted with our own selves, we undergo a profound condition of existence that holds immense significance for every individual. According to Bakhshandeh (2015), authenticity is a significant characteristic that imbues strength, solidity, and fulfillment. One often-cited definition of authenticity is individuals' capacity to engage in introspection and align their actions with their personal ideals and aspirations rather than conforming to external expectations or societal norms ("Mind Tools," n.d.). "The flip side of authenticity is pretense" (Bakhshandeh, 2015, p. 34). Some qualities of authentic people are found below:

- Applying self-reflection.
- Being sincere.
- Not being disparaging.

Social Awareness Cluster

The development of social awareness necessitates the acquisition and utilization of social skills. Despite a business leader's capacity to demonstrate comprehension, empathy, compassion, and emotional regulation, these qualities alone may be insufficient in effectively addressing challenging and contradictory circumstances stemming from a deficiency in social awareness and associated factors (Stevens, 2009). This set of competencies is applicable not only to the workforce, but also to the clientele and consumers of the firm. According to Stevens (2009), individuals are able to do this through acquiring and sustaining a significant level of emotional intelligence. Moreover, corporate leaders who comprehend social awareness factors, such as workplace diversity and the recognition of individual differences without relying on preconceptions and generalizations, can exhibit social awareness outcomes within the context of organizational awareness (Handley, 2017). Handley (2017), as cited from Goleman (2014), stated that "Goleman describes this competency cluster with empathic listening, ability to grasp the others' perspectives, political understanding, organizational awareness, and service to others" (p. 146).

Competencies pertaining to the social awareness cluster encompass a wide range of skills and abilities with the following being among the notable examples (see Figure 13.5).

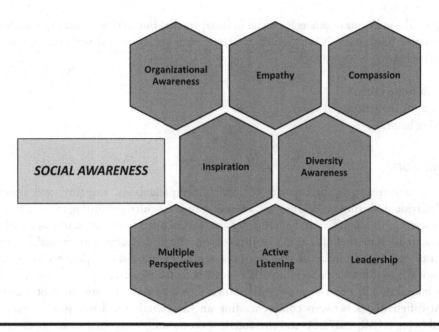

Figure 13.5   Competencies related to the social awareness cluster. © Bakhshandeh 2024.

Organizational Awareness

Organizational awareness refers to the capacity to actively observe and comprehend a group or team's prevailing emotional states, identify individuals who exert positive or negative impacts, and discern the existing dynamics within the workforce and the organization (Cummings & Worley, 2015). Organizational awareness is widely recognized as a crucial element in proactive corporate management. Organizational awareness plays a crucial role in assisting business managers in designing and planning change initiatives for their workforce. It encompasses various aspects such as team building, enhancing staffing policies, implementing efficient communication channels, fostering a productive culture, and cultivating effective leadership across all levels of the organizational hierarchy (Rothwell, Imroz, & Bakhshandeh, 2021). Several characteristics of organizational awareness include:

- Making defensible choices.
- Formulating a practical plan.
- Establishing a support coalition.

Empathy

The aforementioned capability pertains to directing attention toward others, serving as a foundation for empathy, and cultivating interpersonal connections in personal, social, and professional contexts. According to a HBR (2017), business leaders who can direct their attention toward others are more likely to establish shared interests and perspectives. Consequently, their viewpoints and contributions are regarded with greater esteem and approval by their subordinates. Individuals who emerge as natural leaders in society and organizations, regardless of their organizational hierarchy or social rank, are the ones being referred to. Individuals' inclination to recognize and value the emotional conditions of others is crucial in interpersonal interactions concerning their current affective states (Goleman, 2015). Several characteristics are associated with those who possess empathy, such as:

- Identifying talent.
- Recognizing emotional states.
- Being helpful.

Compassion

Displaying compassion is the capacity to exhibit comprehension, empathy, and benevolence toward individuals during periods of grief, adversity, and difficulty. According to Goleman (2015), empathy refers to the cognitive and emotional awareness of others' sufferings, sorrows, desires, and ambitions, to alleviate their anguish. Compassion may be understood as an extension and intensification of empathy. Individuals who possess a sense of compassion experience emotional and psychological anguish when observing other individuals facing adversity and misery, prompting them to take action in order to provide assistance. Compassion is a constituent of social awareness that differentiates between comprehending an individual and demonstrating concern for their well-being (HBR, 2017). Several characteristics commonly associated with those who exhibit compassion include:

- Putting themselves in others' places.
- Exercising active listening.
- Being fine with failures.

Inspiration

Individuals who align their visions, beliefs, and ideals with endeavors that elicit enthusiasm and fervor in others might be considered a source of inspiration. According to Cummings and Worley (2015), business leaders who possess exceptional competency and exhibit exemplary behavior have the ability to inspire their workforce to engage in actions that foster personal, professional, and organizational development. Individuals with a strong sense of inspiration often choose to engage in work motivated by causes that extend beyond personal benefit. These causes tend to resonate with individuals who have similar passions and interests. Several characteristics of individuals that inspire others include the following:

- Aspiring to make a difference.
- Being brave.
- Always supporting others' dreams.

Diversity Awareness

Organizations and individuals may achieve diversity awareness via the cultivation of appreciation and comprehension of the benefits associated with cultural variety and the variations that exist among individuals. An organization can foster a culture of dignity, mutual respect, and acceptance of diversity by cultivating awareness among its workforce. This entails recognizing and valuing individual differences, irrespective of cultural background, ethnicity, age, sexual orientation, gender, religion, socioeconomic status, and physical abilities (Rothwell, Imroz, & Bakhshandeh, 2021; Goleman, 2015). Below are some characteristics of individuals who possess diversity awareness:

■ Accepting uniqueness.
■ Exhibiting mutual respect.
■ Displaying universal treatment.

Multiple Perspectives

According to Park et al. (2000), the concept of many viewpoints encompasses various perspectives, claims, and roles that can be assumed within both collaborative and non-collaborative frameworks. In order to comprehensively understand an issue, it is crucial to examine many viewpoints. This approach enables a more holistic view, enhancing the likelihood of identifying the underlying causes and developing a solution that takes into account the preferences and emotions of all involved parties (Park et al., 2000). Several characteristics may be attributed to individuals who possess numerous views:

■ Seeing a bigger picture.
■ Looking for the root cause.
■ Obtaining mutually settled solutions.

Active Listening

Active listening is a highly significant component of effective communication, and it is a talent that can be honed by deliberate practice. Active listening is the total concentration of an individual on the speaker and the content of the conversation, as opposed to a passive hearing of the speakers and their message (Rothwell et al., 2016). Engaging in active listening facilitates the establishment of trust and respect between the listener and speaker, as it demonstrates the listener's understanding and empathy toward the speaker's circumstances. The concept of active listening involves the listener's intention to comprehend and provide assistance and empathy toward the speaker. Active listening is a conceptual framework for engaging in the process of hearing and responding to others in a manner that promotes the development of mutual appreciation and comprehension. The initial stage in effectively addressing a challenging issue and seeking viable resolutions to possible crises is to neutralize the circumstances (Cummings & Worley, 2015). Several characteristics found below are commonly associated with individuals who possess active listening skills:

■ Focusing on the speaker.
■ Responding properly.
■ Giving feedback.

Leadership

Being a leader does not necessarily imply a want to hold the position of CEO in a Fortune 500 firm, although it is a possibility. According to Donahue (2018), the statement does not imply that one is obligated to assume the role of president inside an organization. Assuming leadership roles within businesses include several positions, such as supervisors, managers, team leaders, faculty chairs, and other similar leadership positions. The act of providing leadership is not inherently tied to managerial roles, as it may encompass individuals who exhibit great qualities as employees. These individuals demonstrate initiative, serve as sources of inspiration, and serve as good role models for their respective teams (Donahue, 2018). Leadership is widely recognized as a highly studied and extensively discussed competency within the realms of business and employment. Several characteristics associated with effective leadership include those found below:

- Paying attention to the team's interest.
- Using encouraging language.
- Possessing positive attitudes.

Relationship Management Cluster

The quality of life is intricately linked to and impacted by the interpersonal interactions individuals cultivate with others, exerting both positive and negative effects. From both a personal and professional standpoint, it is unnecessary to maintain partnerships that lack any form of contribution or value. Individuals who possess knowledge of the concept of emotional intelligence are cognizant of its inherent value (Wayne, 2019; Stevens, 2009). In order to cultivate a high-quality relationship, individuals must not only prioritize shared values and personal growth but also dedicate effort toward sustaining the connection and actively seeking opportunities for its enhancement. "Emotional intelligence provides you the cognizance you need to maintain your valuable relationships and do away with the toxic ones" (Wayne, 2019, p. 119).

In a professional context, akin to interpersonal relationships, business leaders must ascertain the optimal utilization of their cognitive abilities to effectively discern and seize opportunities, proficiently communicate, endeavor to resolve challenges and foster successful collaboration with their employees and clientele (Goleman, 2015). "This ability to integrate is a crucial steppingstone to becoming a strong business leader. To be more specific, managerial positions have found that emotional intelligence is a critical part of relationship building and the development of dynamic leadership" (Stevens, 2009, p. 31).

Competencies pertaining to relationship management cluster encompass a wide range of skills and abilities, which may include but are not restricted to those listed in Figure 13.6.

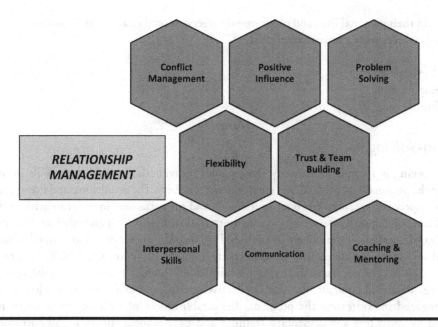

Figure 13.6 Competencies related to relationship management cluster. © Bakhshandeh 2024.

Conflict Management

This pertains to the capacity to utilize strategies for resolving conflicts in a manner that is both equitable and rational. By effectively implementing conflict management strategies, business professionals have the ability to prevent the escalation of disputes. Individual disagreements are inherent in collaborative endeavors within every organizational setting. Nevertheless, when effectively managed by applying emotional intelligence competencies and conflict management abilities, these divergences can foster organizational creativity, generate novel solutions, and cultivate cohesive professional alliances (Cummings & Worley, 2015). Several characteristics of individuals with conflict management abilities include:

- Being unbiased.
- Being patient.
- Preventing the blame game.

Positive Influence

This aptitude aims to exert an effect on another individual's thinking, conduct, character formation, and personal and professional growth. In the context of fostering relationships, positive influence refers to the ability of individuals to have a favorable impact on themselves or others by highlighting their strengths and emphasizing their good attributes, thereby empowering and motivating them. The impact exerted by individuals becomes an inherent aspect of their character, serving as a reflection of their identity, actions, and cognitive processes (Longmore et al., 2018; Martz et al., 2016). Positive reinforcement may serve as a powerful mechanism for empowering individuals, fostering their personal growth, and guiding them toward achieving favorable outcomes in their personal lives and professional careers. Several characteristics are associated with individuals who possess a favorable influence:

- Being appealing.
- Being modest.
- Wanting to help.

Problem-Solving

Problem-solving is a cognitive capacity that enables individuals to apply their skills in order to influence the personal and professional environment of others. The acquisition and use of problem-solving competency is crucial for both individuals and organizations in order to achieve success. The problem-solving skill offers business managers a valuable approach and efficient procedure for identifying the underlying problem (while avoiding fixation on symptomatic issues), generating potential solutions, and determining a constructive course of action to address these problems (Donahue, 2018). The necessary mentality for individuals to engage in the issue-solving approach within organizational contexts includes a collective openness to exploring novel ideas among all parties engaged in addressing the problem. The establishment of such an environment may be facilitated by providing supplementary training and development, providing opportunities for further education, and implementing specialized training programs focusing on conflict resolution (Soulé & Warrick, 2015). Several characteristics can be associated with those who possess problem-solving ability.

- Identifying the perceptions.
- Redefining the problem.
- Not being attached.

Flexibility

Based on the findings of behavioral science, it is posited that mental flexibility should not be regarded just as a fixed mentality or inherent personality feature but rather as a composite of behaviors that have the potential to be modified or enhanced (Coatley, 2012). Individuals have the capacity to exhibit flexibility in certain domains while demonstrating inflexibility in others. Individuals have the capacity to establish an effective and efficient setting within their personal or professional domains by adopting a perspective of flexibility as an action rather than an inherent trait. This marks the initial stage of utilizing this capacity to generate enduring effects and favorable consequences (Coatley, 2012). In order to effectively adapt to changing circumstances, it is advisable to refrain from adhering rigidly to a solid strategy, precise timetable, and meticulously crafted plan of activities. Instead, it is recommended to cultivate suitable flexibility by embracing alternative ideas and novel perspectives (Coatley, 2012). Several characteristics of individuals with the capacity to demonstrate flexibility include:

- Being open to the unexpected.
- Preventing reactions.
- Remaining unattached to one's ways.

Trust and Team Building

This skill pertains to the capacity to establish trust with individuals, perhaps aligning with other personality traits and self-concept qualities (Handley, 2017). Establishing a solid basis of trust is paramount in constructing a proficient team since the presence of trust among team members engenders a perception of security. The absence of trust within teams and organizations hinders collaboration, stifles creativity and invention, and diminishes productivity as individuals are compelled to focus on self-preservation and safeguarding their own interests (Handley, 2017). Rothwell (2015) asserts that team building is a prevalent kind of organizational growth. Business experts widely recognize the significance of interpersonal interactions among team members as a crucial element in establishing trust. This is due to the fact that team cohesion and mutual comprehension play a pivotal role in fostering trust and facilitating the process of team-building. Several characteristics of individuals who possess the capacity to establish trust and foster effective teamwork are listed below:

- Being approachable.
- Being respectful.
- Being fair and impartial.

Interpersonal Skills

These talents encompass the capacity to engage in interpersonal interactions, establish connections, comprehend others' perspectives, and collaborate efficiently with individuals in both personal and professional settings. Interpersonal skills are highly valuable competencies that facilitate the development of connections and cultivating collaboration with individuals (Spencer & Spencer, 1993). Proficiency in hard skills is crucial for individuals to carry out their work-related responsibilities in professional roles effectively. However, the ability to effectively exhibit interpersonal skills, such as collaborating with others, communicating clearly, and demonstrating self-confidence, holds equal significance. These interpersonal skills can significantly impact an individual's professional growth and advancement. Several characteristics of individuals with strong interpersonal skills include the following:

- Being conscious of everyone.
- Being cooperative.
- Showing compassion about relationships.

Communication

The concept referred to is the capacity to effectively execute the process of disseminating information from a given source, whether a specific location, individual, or team, to various recipients situated in different locations or contexts. According to Jones (2015), all modes of communication consist of at least one message, one sender, and one recipient. According to Steinfatt (2009), communication plays a crucial role in fostering human connectivity through the interchange of mutually understood symbols. While Steinfatt's perspective on communication may not be universally acknowledged as a comprehensive definition, it provides valuable insights into this fundamental talent's significance. In a broader sense, the term "communication" often denotes the process of transmitting information between individuals, encompassing both personal and professional contexts (Steinfatt, 2009). The idea of communication has been extensively studied and remains a prominent subject of theoretical and empirical research concerning human interaction (Jones, 2015). In essence, it may be stated that the absence of communication renders workability and cooperation unattainable. Effective communication leads to synchronization across teams. Moreover, communication gives rise to peace, harmony, and contentment (Lindberg, 2023). The absence of good communication hinders the establishment of meaningful connections and reduces productivity in both domestic and professional settings (Bakhshandeh, 2015). Several characteristics associated with individuals who possess strong communication abilities are listed below:

■ Being conscious of non-verbal communication.
■ Distributing clear and concise messages.
■ Exhibiting keen listening.

Coaching and Mentoring

The professional coaching process revolves around improving one's performance and is specifically meant to boost and elevate on-the-job performance (Bakhshandeh & Rothwell, 2024). Professional coaches often undergo specialized training to effectively support individuals in their respective professions to help them achieve their objectives and aims (Rothwell et al., 2016). Various professional organizations provide varying definitions of coaching. According to Arneson, Rothwell, and Naughton (2013), the International Coach Federation (ICF) defines coaching as the utilization of an interactive process to facilitate the quick development and achievement of outcomes in individuals, enhancing their capacity to establish objectives, take decisive actions, make improved judgments, and effectively leverage their inherent abilities (p. 45).

In contrast to coaching, mentoring primarily focuses on the developmental aspects, encompassing the enhancement of professional performance and attainment of goals and the broader scope of career advancement (Bakhshandeh & Rothwell, 2024). Mentoring is generally characterized by the absence of specific or structured instruction, rendering it less extensive than coaching (Rothwell et al., 2016). As a broad notion, mentoring entails a connection centered on individuals' personal growth and advancement. It involves mentors imparting their expertise, wisdom, and abilities to a mentee. Several characteristics of individuals with coaching and mentoring talents include the following:

■ Being encouraging.
■ Being empowering.
■ Being knowledgeable.

Summary of Emotional Intelligence Cluster and Competencies

Based on recommendations, evaluations, and deliberations regarding the implementation of emotional intelligence as a training method to enhance the development of 4Cs skills within the workforce, Table 13.2 presents the outcomes pertaining to emotional intelligence clusters, associated competencies, attributions, and qualities exhibited by individuals possessing such competencies and capabilities. Furthermore, the table highlights the relevance of at least two of these competencies to the four components of 21st-century 4Cs skills, namely critical thinking, communication, creativity, and collaboration.

Irrespective of the pairing of at least two of the four 4Cs skills with any of the emotional intelligence competencies outlined in Table 13.2, it is worth noting that these competencies, capabilities, attributes, and qualities positively influence all the 21st-century 4Cs skills. Furthermore, they aid organizations in effectively training and developing their workforces in order to enhance the quality and utility of the 4Cs skills. In essence, the competencies above and attributes can serve as focal points for enhancing worker capabilities concerning their 4Cs talents.

Table 13.2 Summary of Emotional Intelligence Clusters, Competencies, and Qualities and Corresponding 4Cs Skills

Self-Awareness Cluster		
Competencies	*Qualities*	*4Cs Skills*
Emotional Awareness	• Showing concern for others' feelings • Recognizing misunderstandings • Displaying a trust-based function	- Critical thinking - Communication
Self-Confidence	• Believing in their skills • Exhibiting gratitude • Being internally happy	- Communication - Collaboration
Self-Assessment	• Examining their learning • Monitoring goals' advancement • Performing self-efficacy	- Critical thinking - Communication
Self-Control	• Making no impulse decisions • Being in control of their behaviors • Retaining conscientiousness	- Critical thinking - Collaboration
Self-Deprecating Humor	• Acknowledging their faults • Being at ease to laugh at themselves • Not being up to an immaculate image	- Communication - Creativity
Intrapersonal Skills	• Appreciating themselves • Being aware of their agenda • Reducing interruptions	- Creativity - Collaboration
Self-Motivated	• Displaying interest in success • Encouraging forward motion actions • Exhibiting interest in productivity	- Critical thinking - Collaboration
Self-Discipline	• Avoiding instant gratification • Excluding interferences • Not needing a constant reminder	- Critical thinking - Creativity
Self-Regulation Cluster		
Competencies	*Qualities*	*4Cs Skills*
Emotional Balance	• Correctly recognizing their emotions • Being mindful of their emotions • Handling impulse emotions	- Critical thinking - Collaboration

(Continued)

Table 13.2   (CONTINUED) Summary of Emotional Intelligence Clusters, Competencies, and Qualities and Correspondence 4Cs Skills

Adaptability	• Being open to learning • Adapting quickly • Entertaining new ideas	- Collaboration - Creativity
Integrity	• Being reliable • Being truthful • Being trustworthy	- Critical thinking - Communication
Calm Manners	• Exerting confidence • Being calm • Being insightful	- Critical thinking - Creativity
Responsibility	• Not presenting excuses • Not complaining • Being sensible	- Creativity - Collaboration
Accountability	• Assuming responsibility • Not assigning blames • Being transparent	- Communication - Collaboration
Positivity	• Being optimistic • Being resilient • Being grateful	- Communication - Collaboration
Authenticity	• Applying self-reflection • Being sincere • Not being disparaging	- Critical thinking - Communication
Social Awareness Cluster		
Competencies	*Qualities*	*4Cs Skills*
Organizational Awareness	• Making defensible choices • Formulating a practical plan • Establishing support coalition	- Critical thinking - Creativity
Empathy	• Identifying talent • Recognizing emotional states • Being helpful	- Communication - Collaboration
Compassion	• Putting themselves in others' places • Exercising active listening • Being fine with failures	- Critical thinking - Communication
Inspiration	• Aspiring to make a difference • Being brave • Always supporting others' dreams	- Communication - Collaboration
Diversity Awareness	• Accepting uniqueness • Exhibiting mutual respect • Displaying universal treatment	- Critical thinking - Collaboration

(Continued)

Table 13.2 (CONTINUED) Summary of Emotional Intelligence Clusters, Competencies, and Qualities and Correspondence 4Cs Skills

Multiple Perspectives	• Seeing a bigger picture • Looking for the root cause • Obtaining mutually settled solutions	- Critical thinking - Creativity
Active Listening	• Focusing on the speaker • Responding properly • Giving feedback	- Communication - Creativity
Leadership	• Paying attention to the team's interest • Using encouraging language • Possessing positive attitudes	- Critical thinking - Communication
Relationship Management Cluster		
Competencies	*Qualities*	*4Cs Skills*
Conflict Management	• Being unbiased • Being patient • Preventing blame game	- Critical thinking - Collaboration
Positive Influence	• Being appealing • Being modest • Showing determination to help	- Creativity - Collaboration
Problem-Solving	• Identifying the perceptions • Redefining the problem • Not being attached	- Critical thinking - Creativity
Flexibility	• Staying open to the unexpected • Preventing reactions • Remaining unattached to one's ways	- Creativity - Collaboration
Trust and Team Building	• Being approachable • Being respectful • Being fair and impartial	- Communication - Collaboration
Interpersonal Skills	• Being conscious of everyone • Being cooperative • Showing compassion about relationships	- Communication - Collaboration
Communication	• Being conscious of non-verbal communication • Distributing clear and concise messages • Exhibiting keen listening	- Communication - Creativity
Coaching and Mentoring	• Being encouraging • Being empowering • Being knowledgeable	- Critical thinking - Communication

Source: Adapted from Bakhshandeh (2021).

What Is Next?

Chapter 14, "Application of Emotional Intelligence Coaching," will explain the essential role of emotional intelligence coaching and its effect as a platform for establishing training and development of workforces considering 21st-century 4Cs skills and all the related competencies and qualities mentioned in Chapter 13.

References

Arneson, J., Rothwell, W., & Naughton, J. (2013). Training and development competencies redefined to create competitive advantage. *T+D*, *67*(1), 42–47. Retrieved from https://www.proquest.com/docview /1270282908?accountid=13158&parentSessionId=9XS4yoQK9i61roVdrnDCTZj5BSgICZLEgt2 T2kwY40A%3D&pq-origsite=summon.

Bakhshandeh, B. (2015). *Anatomy of Upset: Restoring Harmony*. Carbondale, PA: Primeco Education, Inc.

Bakhshandeh, B. (2021). *Perception of 21st Century 4CS (Critical Thinking, Communication, Creativity & Collaboration) Skill Gap in Private-Sector Employers in Lackawanna County, NE PA* (Order No. 28841654). Available from Dissertations & Thesis @ CIC Institutions; ProQuest Dissertations & Thesis A&I. (2577123614). Retrieved from https://ezaccess.libraries.psu.edu/login?qurl=https%3A %2F%2Fwww.proquest.com%2Fdissertations-theses%2Fperception-21st-century-4cs-critical -thinking%2Fdocview%2F2577123614%2Fse-2%3Faccountid%3D13158.

Bakhshandeh, B. & Rothwell, William J. (Eds.) (2024). *Building an Organizational Coaching Culture*. Oxfordshire, UK: UK Limited Trading, Taylor & Francis Group. Routledge.

Bakhshandeh, B., Rothwell, William J., & Imroz, Sohel M. (2023). *Transformational Coaching for Effective Leadership. Creating Sustainable Change Through Shifting Paradigms*. New York, NY: Taylor & Francis Group. Routledge.

Bauer, I. M. & Baumeister, R. F. (2011). Self-Regulatory strength. In K. Vohs & R. Baumeister (Eds.), *Handbook of Self-Regulation* (pp. 64–82). New York, NY: Guilford Press.

Beamish, Wendi & Bryer, Fiona. (2015). Social and emotional learning. In S. Garvis & D. Pendergast (Eds.), *Health and Well-being in Childhood*. Melbourne, Australia: Cambridge University Press.

Boyatzis, R. E., Goleman, D. & Rhee, K. (2000). Clustering competence in emotional intelligence: Insights from the Emotional Competence Inventory (ECI). *Handbook of Emotional Intelligence*, *99*(6), 343–362. Retrieved from https://www.amazon.com/exec/obidos/ASIN/0787949841/consortiuforrese.

Boyatzis, R. E. & Sala, F. (2004). Assessing emotional intelligence competencies. In Glenn Geher (Ed.), *The Measurement of Emotional Intelligence*. New York, NY: Nova Science Publishers. https://doi.org /10.1016/S0160-2896(01)00084-8.

CASEL (Collaborative for Academic, Social, and Emotional Learning). (2015). *Guide: Effective Social and Emotional Learning Programs—Middle and High School Edition*. Retrieved from https://static1.square-space.com/static/5532b947e4b0edee99477d27/t/5d0948b6a78e0100015f652f/1560889545559/ CASEL+Secondary+Guide+2015.pdf.

Clarke, N. (2006). Emotional intelligence training: A case of caveat emptor. *Human Resource Development Review*, *5*(4), 422–441. https://doi.org/10.1177/1534484306293844.

Coatley, Megan. (2012). Spark people website. 6 ways to maintain your mental flexibility. Retrieved from https://www.sparkpeople.com/resource/wellness_articles.asp?id=1724.

Connors, Christopher D. (2020). *Emotional Intelligence for the Modern Leader*. Emeryville, CA; Rockridge Press.

Cummings, T. G. & Worley C. G. (2015). *Organization Development & Change* (10th ed.). Stamford, CT: Cengage Learning.

Donahue, Wesley E. (2018). *Building Leadership Competence. A Competency-Based Approach to Building Leadership Ability*. State College, PA: Centerstar Learning.

Duval, Shelley & Wicklund, Robert A. (1972). *A Theory of Objective Self Awareness*. Cambridge, MA: Academic Press.

Fitzpatrick, K. R. & Bronstein, C. (2006). Responsibility and accountability. In Kathy Fitzpatrick, K. Fitzpatrick, Carolyn Bronstein, & C. Bronstein (Eds.), *Ethics in Public Relations* (p. 19). Thousand Oaks, CA: SAGE Publications, Incorporated. https://doi.org/10.4135/9781452204208.n2

Goleman, Brandon. (2019). *Emotional Intelligence; For a Better Life, Success at Work, and Happier Relationships.* Middletown, DE: A Self-Published Title.

Goleman, Daniel. (1998). *Working with Emotional Intelligence.* New York, NY: Random House.

Goleman, Daniel. (2014). What it takes to achieve managerial success. *TD: Talent Development, 68*(11), 48–52. Alexandria, VA: Talent Development.

Goleman, Daniel. (2015). *Emotional Intelligence; Why It Can Matter More Than IQ.* New York, NY: Bantam Books.

Goleman, Daniel. (2020). *Emotional Intelligence: Why It Can Matter More Than IQ.* London, UK: Bloomsbury Publishing.

Handley, M. (2017). *An Interpersonal Behavioral Framework for Early-Career Engineers Demonstrating Engineering Leadership Characteristics across Three Engineering Companies.* (Unpublished doctoral dissertation). Pennsylvania: The Pennsylvania State University.

HBR. (2017). *Harvard Business Review Guide to Emotional Intelligence.* Boston, MA: Harvard Business Review Press.

Hockenbury, D. H. & Hockenbury, S. E. (2007). *Discovering Psychology.* New York, NY: Worth Publishers.

Hudson, Zack. (2023). Emotional intelligence: Relationship management. Retrieved from https://www.passingthebatonpodcast.com/relationship-management.

ICF (International Coaching Federation). 2011. Coached core competencies. Retrieved from: https://coach-federation.org/app/uploads/2017/12/CoreCompetencies.pdf.

Johnson, Morten. (2022). *Emotional Intelligence for the Modern Workplace: A Guide to Developing Emotional Intelligence and Ensuring Psychological Safety.* Chicago, IL: Johnson Publishing.

Jones, V. R. (2015). 21st century skills: Communication. *Children's Technology and Engineering, 20*(2), 28–29. Retrieved from https://www.iteea.org/Publications/Journals/ESCJournal/CTEDecember2015.aspx?source=generalSearch.

Kite, Neilson and Kay, Frances. (2012). *Understanding Emotional Intelligence. Strategies for Boosting Your EQ and Using It in the Workplace.* Philadelphia, PA; Kogan Page.

Lindberg, Carl. (2023). *Interpersonal Communication; Understand and Develop Your Inner Dialogue.* New Heaven, CT: A Self-Published Title.

Longmore, A.-L., Grant, G., & Golnaraghi, G. (2018). Closing the 21st-century knowledge gap: Reconceptualizing teaching and learning to transform business education. *Journal of Transformative Education, 16*(3), 197–219. https://doi.org/10.1177/1541344617738514.

Martz, B., Hughes, J., & Braun, F. (2016). Creativity and problem-solving: Closing the skills gap. *The Journal of Computer Information Systems, 57*(1), 39–48. https://doi.org/10.1080/08874417.2016.118149.

Merriam-Webster Dictionary. (2024a). Retrieved from https://www.merriam-webster.com/dictionary/accountability.

Merriam-Webster Dictionary. (2024b). Retrieved from https://www.merriam-webster.com/dictionary/responsibility.

Mind Tools. (n.d.). Authenticity. How to be true to yourself. Retrieved from https://www.mindtools.com/pages/article/authenticity.htm.

Neal, Stephen, Spencer-Arnell, Lisa, & Wilson, Liz. (2009). *Emotional Intelligence Coaching. Improving Performance for Leaders, Coaching and the Individual.* Philadelphia, PA: KoganPage.

Park, K., Kapoor, A., Scharver, C., & Leigh, J. (2000). *Exploiting Multiple Perspectives in Tele-Immersion in the Proceedings of IPT. Ames*, IA: CDROM.

Priego-Valverde, B. (n.d.). *Self-disparaging Humor in Conversations: A Brief Survey of a Complex Phenomenon Usually Considered as Obvious.* (Informally published manuscript, Université de Provence). Retrieved from www.lpl.univaix.fr/~fulltext/3421.pdf.

Rasheed, S. P., Younas, A., & Sundus, A. (2019). Self-awareness in nursing: A scoping review. *Journal of Clinical Nursing, 28*(5–6), 762–774. https://doi.org/10.1111/jocn.14708.

Rothwell, William J. (2015). *Organization Development Fundamentals: Managing Strategic Change.* Alexandria, WV: ATD Press.

Rothwell, Willian J. & Bakhshandeh, Behnam. (2022). *High-Performance Coaching for Managers. Step-by-Step Approach to Increase Employees' Performance and Productivity.* New York, NY: Taylor & Francis Group. Routledge.

Rothwell, William. J., Imroz, Sohel. M., & Bakhshandeh, Behnam. (2021). *Organization-Development Interventions: Executing Effective Organizational Chang.* New York, NY: Taylor & Francis Group. CRC Press.

Rothwell, William J., Stavros, Jacqueline M., & Sullivan, Roland L. (2016). *Practicing Organization Development: Leading Transformation and Change* (4th ed.). Hoboken, NJ: John Wiley & Sons, Inc.

Sahranavard, Sara, Miri, Mohamad Reza, & Salenhiniya, Hamid. (2018). The relationship between self-regulation and educational performance in students. *Journal of Education and Health Promotion*, (7), 154. https://doi.org/10.4103/jehp.jehp_93_18.

Sheck, Daniel T. L. & Lin, L. (2015). Intrapersonal competencies and service leadership. *International Journal of Disability Human Development*, 14(3), 255–263. https://doi.org/10.1515/ijdhd-2015–0406.

Soulé, H. & Warrick, T. (2015). Defining 21st century readiness for all students: What we know and how to get there. *Psychology of Aesthetics, Creativity, and the Arts*, 9(2), 178–186. https://doi.org/10.1037/aca0000017.

Spencer, L. M. & Spencer, S. M. (1993). *Competence at Work. Models for Superior Performance.* New York, NY: John Wiley and Sons, Ed.

Steinfatt, T. (2009). *Definitions of Communication.* In S. W. Littlejohn & K. A. Foss (Eds.), *Encyclopedia of Communication Theory* (Vol. 1, pp. 295–299). Thousand Oaks, CA: Sage Publication, Inc. https://doi.org/10.4135/9781412959384.n108.

Stevens, R. (2009). *Emotional Intelligence in Business: EQ, The Essential Ingredient to Survive and Thrive as a Modern Workplace Leader.* Middletown, DE: Self-published.

University of Reading. (2021). Engage in assessment. Retrieved from https://www.reading.ac.uk/engagein-assessment/peer-and-self-assessment/self-assessment/eia-why-use-self-assessment.aspx.

Wall, Bob. (2007). *Coaching For Emotional Intelligence. The Secret to Developing the Star Potential in Your Employees.* New York, NY: AMACOM.

Wayne, Jenny. (2019). *Emotional Intelligence 2.0. A Guide to Manage Anger, Overcome Negativity ad Master Your Emotions.* Middletown, DE: Self-published.

Zimmerman, Alan. (2013). Relationship management: The fourth pillar of emotional intelligence. Retrieved from https://www.drzimmerman.com/balance-stress-change/developing-relationship-management-skills-for-success.

Chapter 14

Application of Emotional Intelligence Coaching

Introduction

What is the correlation between coaching and emotional intelligence? The significance and potency of that link are of utmost importance. What are the reasons for managers' motivations to assist employees in enhancing their talents and skills to utilize them effectively? A singular motive exists for managers to be inclined toward facilitating the enhancement of their employees' emotional intelligence. Emotions serve as the driving force that establishes a profound connection between individuals and the objects of their concern. In the absence of emotional influence, individuals are able to articulate the significance of a given entity objectively, elucidate the reasons behind its value, and determine the appropriate allocation of time and effort in pursuing or avoiding it (Wall, 2007).

This chapter is about emotional intelligence (EI) coaching and all related elements that would directly influence workforces to better understand how and why they are not open to developing their skills, such as 4Cs skills. EI coaching provides an opening for individuals to better understand their self-awareness, self-regulation, social awareness, and relationship management.

As discussed in the preceding chapter, emotional intelligence, sometimes referred to as EI or EQ (emotional quotient), encompasses an individual's aptitude and proficiency in seeing, assessing, and effectively impacting their own emotions as well as those of others in their vicinity. Consequently, those who engage in the practice of emotional intelligence (EI) are capable of managing their stress in a manner that promotes well-being, successfully engaging in communication, surmounting obstacles encountered in life, and mitigating disputes.

As the understanding and significance of emotional intelligence have grown, supervisors have encountered heightened difficulties in teaching their subordinates. In the past, the discussion about performance requirements alone was seen as sufficient. Annual performance metrics were implemented, prioritizing clear and measurable targets that facilitated the evaluation of employees' work performance. The allocation of resources throughout the year was contingent upon individuals' abilities to satisfy their performance requirements effectively.

However, given the rise of emotional intelligence and its influence on professional achievement, it is imperative to go beyond mere discussion of employees' actions. Performance objectives and targets undoubtedly retain their significance. However, it is imperative for business leaders to

DOI: 10.4324/9781003462316-18

now focus on addressing several factors pertaining to individuals' work practices, including their interpersonal dynamics with colleagues. This entails discussing the correlation between actions and attributes like character, personality, and interpersonal dynamics in the context of individuals' professional performance.

This chapter will cover the following elements of EI coaching:

■ Differences between Feelings and Emotions.
■ What Is Coaching?
■ Key Factors for Creating a Coaching Culture.
■ Coaching Providing Methods.
■ What Is Emotional Intelligence Coaching?
■ Significant Advantages of EI Coaching.
■ Various Approaches to Utilize on EI Coaching.
■ The Power of Emotional Intelligence Coaching Questions.
■ Role of mindset, attitude, and Behavior in the EI Coaching.

Differences between Feelings and Emotions

Given that all human beings relate to their feelings and emotions as a real-life experience, and as it is proven that people's resistance to instructions or applying skills is directly related to how they feel about the instructions or the person who is delivering it, let's briefly discuss the differences between feelings and emotions.

One notable distinction between feelings and emotions is in their conscious experience since feelings are explicitly experienced, whereas emotions can develop either consciously or unconsciously. Certain individuals may dedicate a significant portion of their lives, or perhaps their whole lifespan, to grappling with the intricacies and complexities of their emotional experiences (Ekman, 1973).

Emotions and feelings are distinct entities despite their frequent use as interchangeable terms. Emotions can be understood as immediate sensory responses experienced within the body. Emotions have the potential to exhibit a greater degree of bias, as they can be influenced by cognitive distortions (Ekman, 1973). The cultivation of emotional awareness has the potential to mitigate reactivity and the formation of erroneous ideas. As Ekman (1999) gives a good example, our emotions show in our bodies while our feelings appear in our mind.

When an individual experiences physical and neurological alterations, specific chemical substances are produced inside the brain, prompting the onset of a psychological state commonly referred to as emotion (Ekman, 1999). Upon undergoing metabolic transformations inside the human organism, these chemical substances elicit a subjective emotional and sensory perception state. The perception of emotion might manifest as either a bodily feeling or as a subjective encounter (Ekman, 1999). For example, when you are happy, you are feeling *happiness*, but the *joy* of that moment is an emotion, or when you are resentful, the experience of *resentment* is a feeling, but when you are getting *angry* because of that resentment, that is emotion.

The Six Basic Emotions

According to the generally acknowledged hypothesis proposed by Paul Ekman (1973), there exist a set of six fundamental emotions together with their corresponding manifestations. Different emotions are expressed through specific feelings, traits, and experiences. Table 14.1 offers these related characteristics and expressions of the six basic emotions.

Table 14.1   The Six Basic Emotions, Their Corresponding Feelings and Expressions

#	*Basic Emotion*	*Corresponding Feelings*	*Expressions*
1	Sadness	Anguish, sorrow, hopelessness	No eye contact, tears, frown
2	Happiness	Joy, satisfaction, ease	Eye contact, laughter, smile
3	Fear	Defensiveness, "fight or flight"	Wide eyes, tense lips, speechless
4	Anger	Frustration, hostility	Glare, pulled eyebrows, tight lips
5	Surprise	Positively or negatively surprised	Gasp, open mouth, raised eyebrows
6	Disgust	Repulsed, revolted, rejected	No eye contact, crumpled nose, gagging

Note. Adapted from Paul Ekman (1973).

Distinct Levels of Emotional Intelligence

According to Goleman (2007), there are two distinct levels of emotional intelligence that classify people's abilities and behaviors.

Low EI

This level of emotional intelligence suggests a deficiency in individuals' capacity to effectively discern and differentiate their own feelings as well as those of others. Individuals with low emotional intelligence (EI) may lack the necessary competence to effectively utilize their emotional experiences in guiding their cognitive processes. Consequently, individuals are unable to effectively regulate their behaviors and responses to these emotional states across many domains of their existence.

High EI

This degree of emotional intelligence suggests that individuals possess the capacity to regulate and oversee their engagements with those who exhibit negative attitudes and poisonous mentalities. Individuals with high emotional intelligence (EI) demonstrate the ability to regulate and manage their cognitive processes and emotional states effectively. When confronted with the necessity of managing individuals who exhibit toxic and bad behavior, individuals should adopt a sensible attitude and take suitable actions. Individuals possess the capacity to see and acknowledge their own emotional states, thereby preventing the exacerbation of already untenable circumstances by refraining from succumbing to intense and volatile emotions, such as wrath or impatience.

Table 14.2 presents a comparative analysis of the main four EI clusters, examples whereby individuals demonstrate their capacity, or lack thereof, to effectively regulate their emotions and behaviors in different contexts, both in terms of themselves and others.

Table 14.2   Examples for Low and High Levels of Four EI Clusters

Clusters	People with Low EI	People with High EI
Self-Awareness	Because of their lack of self-awareness, they have strong opinions and are closed off to new knowledge.	They have a high level of self-awareness, making them conscious of their ignorance and eager to learn more to have an educated conversation.
Self-Regulation	They are emotionally unstable and unable to control their emotional outbursts due to their extremely low self-regulation.	They are quite self-reliant, able to take ownership of their errors, learn from them, and go on to the next task without fuss.
Social Awareness	They lack effective interpersonal skills, which prevents them from having solid personal or professional connections.	Their strong social abilities enable them to address problems by taking into account all relevant viewpoints.
Relationship Management	They usually have an extremely self-centered and self-serving mindset; everything revolves around them and their interests.	They are giving and involved when it comes to endeavors that help others and advance society or the community.

Note. Adapted from Goleman (2007); Goleman (1995).

What Is Coaching?

Before delving into the differentiation and discourse around EI coaching, it is imperative to provide a concise overview of the notion of coaching within the realm of business and organizations. In recent years, there has been a surge in the popularity of coaching. Despite the widespread popularity of coaching, there is a noticeable dearth of research articles pertaining to this field, particularly in relation to performance coaching. However, some business authors advocate for the use of coaching as a means to enhance organizational efficiency and elevate individual work performance.

Coaching is widely recognized as a highly effective method of communication. When utilized with efficacy and appropriateness, it enhances one's consciousness, akin to a laser that penetrates any tendencies of procrastination and directly focuses on the core issue. It is posited that coaching entails facilitating progress and enhancing individual performance, hence generating a ripple effect on team and organizational performance. In essence, coaching entails serving as a catalyst for facilitating constructive transformation in a manner that is suitable for individuals, assisting them in reaching their utmost potential.

Numerous definitions of coaching are provided by diverse professional coaches and consultants. The following examples are only a few of many:

- "Unlocking people's potential to maximize their performance. It is helping them to learn rather than teaching them" (Whitmore, 2017, p. 13).
- Clutterbuck, Megginson, and Bajer (2016) described coaching as "a human development process that involves structured, focused interaction and the use of appropriate strategies, tools, and techniques to promote desirable and sustainable change for the benefit of the coachee and potentially for other stakeholders" (p. 1).
- "A highly effective tool for individuals and organizations who choose to have their future realized now instead of someday. It is a systematic but non-linear inquiry into one's authenticity; it is for healthy, ambitious, brave, and open-minded people who strive for excellence" (Bakhshandeh, 2009, p. 35).
- "The process of challenging and supporting a person or a team to develop ways of thinking, ways of being and ways of learning. The purpose is to achieve personal and/or organizational goals" (Berg & Karlsen, p. 4).

Coaching Differentiation with Other Approaches

Regrettably, the term "coaching" has been employed to include a wide range of concepts and practices. Hence, it is imperative to discern the boundaries of coaching since it has seemingly emerged as a panacea for all matters pertaining to transformation, consultation, and the onboarding of novices. It is important to clarify that coaching should not be seen as a universal solution for all challenges (Bakhshandeh, Rothwell, & Imroz, 2023). The act of coaching does not involve the act of instructing an individual on what actions to take, nor does it encompass the act of offering guidance or presenting resolutions. Distinguishing itself from mentorship, counseling, training, or consultation, this phenomenon exhibits notable differences. Nevertheless, it is our strong conviction that coaching possesses significant efficacy when administered by proficient coaches who possess emotional intelligence within suitable contexts (Bakhshandeh et al., 2023).

Although there are certain resemblances to other treatments like mentorship, consultation and training, it is also important to acknowledge the existence of significant distinctions. Consider a hypothetical scenario where you are in the process of preparing a cake and you seek the assistance and insights of another individual. In what ways may a coach, mentor, consultant, or trainer provide assistance to individuals? (Neal, Spencer-Arnell, & Wilson, 2009). Both Rothwell, Stavros, and Sullivan (2016) and Cummings and Worley (2015) clearly defined the three concepts which are mixed up with the general public's understanding of what coaching is.

Mentoring

The fundamental distinction between coaching and mentoring is in the mentors' ability to impart their extensive skill, knowledge, and experience to the mentee as deemed suitable. When senior management mentors a junior individual inside the business, they effectively demonstrate and impart their own experiences pertaining to the position, hence providing insight into the organizational culture and practices.

Consulting

Consultants play a multifaceted role inside businesses, wherein they identify problem areas and inefficiencies and provide guidance and recommendations for developing effective solutions. Professionals possess a wealth of knowledge and specialized skills within their respective fields, which they utilize to provide guidance and counsel to their clients. Coaching does not primarily include dispensing advice; nonetheless, facilitating coachees to tap into their expertise is a fundamental aspect of the coaching process.

Training

Effective training programs aim to provide individuals with the necessary tools, skills, and information to enhance their personal and/or professional growth. The proficient instructors will impart the pertinent new knowledge and, ideally (but regrettably infrequently based on our observations), attend to all four dimensions of KASH (a performance coaching tool introduced by David Herdlinger that stands for knowledge, attitudes, skills, and habits) within their own domain (Neal et al., 2009). Coaching entails providing assistance for teaching or training endeavors, rather than focusing on instructing individuals in entirely novel skills. This approach has been substantiated by the subsequent study, which underscores its efficacy in facilitating the integration of acquired knowledge.

Contrast between Performance Consulting and Performance Coaching

There is a certain level of ambiguity among the general public, businesses, and organizations regarding the nature and functions of performance coaching and performance consultants, owing to their proximity and shared qualities. The distinction between coaching and consulting is rooted in the fundamental conceptual framework and divergent terminology associated with each practice. Most dictionaries do not differentiate significantly between the words "consulting" and "coaching." According to Strosinski (2003), the term "consultation" refers to providing advice, whether professional or otherwise, and teaching to those engaged in a certain profession. Both consultants and coaches focus on aiding participants in resolving their business issues. However, the key contrast lies in their respective approaches. The distinction between consulting and coaching can often become unclear, resulting in unproductive circumstances that fail to meet the client's goals and offer suitable answers (Forbes, 2018).

Different experts have identified a variety of contrasts between coaching and consulting (Bakhshandeh et al., 2023) (see Figure 14.1).

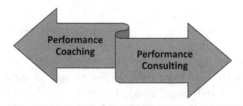

Figure 14.1 Performance coaching and performance consulting are not the same.
© Bakhshandeh 2024.

- "Coaching is 'done with you' and consulting is 'done for you'" (ValueProp, 2021, n.p.).
- Coaching encompasses the process of enhancing the competencies and capabilities of individuals, commonly referred to as coachees, via the utilization of various tools and approaches. This approach empowers coachees to address and handle any challenges they may encounter independently. Consulting involves aiding clients in comprehensively addressing their difficulties through consulting services, training programs, and various seminars and exercises (Indeed.com, 2021).
- "Coaching can help turn an entrepreneur into a great leader. Consulting, on the other hand, provides that much-needed expertise and assistance" (Forbes, 2018, np).
- The distinction between coaches and consultants lies in the manner in which they impart information and provide guidance to their clientele. "As a consultant, your role is to enhance leadership and organizational capacity. A coach helps individual leaders develop clarity on what they need to focus on and create action plans to achieve those goals" (Jordyn, 2020, n.p.).

The statements below delineate many differentiations between performance coaching and performance consulting (Bakhshandeh et al., 2023).

Performance Consulting

According to Strosinski (2003), a performance consultant analyzes and evaluates an organization's performance inconsistencies and disparities in the work environment concerning production outputs and results. The role of performance consultants is to provide support to organizational management in devising strategies and developing appropriate methodologies, processes, methods, and tools to improve the performance of teams, groups, and departments within the company or workplace as a whole.

- "The intended result often results in increased productivity, decreased costs, efficient and effective work practices and a safer working environment" (Strosinski, 2003, p. 1).
- Performance consulting involves the identification and clarification of an organization's requirements, followed by the provision of training methodologies and models that have the capacity to address those unique demands. Nevertheless, it is important to acknowledge that training may not always be sufficient to address all organizational challenges. However, it is crucial to acknowledge that determining whether training would be a viable option is essential in carrying out a performance consultation (Training Industry, 2018).
- Performance consulting is the comprehensive review and assessment of an organization's current operational performance. This endeavor's scope is identifying and proposing novel approaches, processes, and procedures that may be used to augment productivity and efficacy (Berg & Karlsen, 2012).

Performance Coaching

According to Strosinski (2003), performance coaches collaborate with individuals in order to enhance their performance. The primary objective of coaching is to optimize the performance of individuals by emphasizing their future potential while also prioritizing the preservation of their learning and retention. This approach diverges from traditional teaching methods, as it places greater emphasis on the coachees' development and growth rather than just imparting knowledge.

- Performance coaching is commonly implemented and administered by managers who also serve as coaches. This technique is recognized as a significant instrument for improving the capabilities and job performance of the individuals being coached, as well as the overall performance of employees (Strosinski, 2003).
- Within the framework of the relationship between managers/supervisors and employees/workforce, performance coaching can be defined as the assistance that managers/supervisors offer to their subordinates in evaluating their job performance, encompassing their behavior and attitude, with the aim of enhancing productivity and optimizing performance efficacy in their respective roles and associated responsibilities (Pfeiffer, 1990).
- The utilization of performance coaching as a method of coaching and mentoring is gaining popularity among companies and enterprises, which are rapidly demonstrating a greater inclination toward enhancing the capabilities and competencies of their workforce in terms of knowledge, skills, and abilities (KSAs) (Mcleod, 2004).

Coaching Culture

A coaching culture refers to a professional setting where individuals within an organization freely engage in coaching practices with one another. When a coaching culture is present, it is not an independent endeavor; instead, it serves as a pervasive element that permeates the whole organization. The presence of a coaching culture influences the manner in which individuals within an organization engage in interpersonal interactions. The utilization of coaching in interactions is not solely perceived as a dyadic (one-on-one) kind of engagement. According to Milner, Milner, and McCarthy (2020), the phenomenon under consideration is commonly perceived as the widespread adoption of a coaching approach in initiatives aimed at enhancing employee engagement, which in turn influences the dynamics of relationships between people and teams.

According to Bakhshandeh and Rothwell (2024), Vesso (2014) claims, "in a coaching culture, coaching flows in all directions from all parties, making a networked web across the organization consisting of many connections between people in the same departments, across departments, between teams, and up and down and across the hierarchy" (112).

Definition of Coaching Culture

As it has been pointed out by Bakhshandeh and Rothwell (2024), Milner et al. (2020) conducted a study that provides insights into the concept of coaching culture, offering a set of terminology that aids in comprehending this phenomenon:

- "The principles, beliefs, and mindsets driving people's behavior in the workplace are deeply rooted in the discipline of coaching" (Clutterbuck et al., 2016, p. 9).
- "It is an organizational development model that provides the structure that defines how the organization's members can best interact with their working environment and how the best results are obtained and measured" (Vesso & Alas, 2016, p. 308).
- "Where [Coaching culture] people are empowered and where coaching happens at every level. And not only does it happen at every level, but it adds to bottom-line performance. The recognized development tool touches every part of the employee lifecycle" (Jones & Gorell, 2014, p. 16).
- "When a coaching approach is a key aspect of how the leaders, managers, and staff engage and develop all their people and engage their stakeholders in ways that create increased

individual, team, and organizational performance and share value for all stakeholders" (Hawkins, 2012, p. 21).

Key Factors for Creating a Coaching Culture

In order to establish a robust framework for fostering a coaching culture, Hawkins (2012) said that leaders should prioritize the cultivation of skills and competencies, "a sustainable and meaningful coaching strategy and culture" (Gormley & Van Nieuwerburgh, 2014, p. 90). The endeavor should encompass the integration of a coaching approach developed via collaborative efforts with workers and clearly articulated within the organization's vision, purpose, and strategy.

According to Gormley and Van Nieuwerburgh (2014), extensive examination of several publications indicates that the following components are crucial for the establishment of coaching cultures:

■ It is imperative for senior executives to actively endorse and foster a coaching culture across the whole firm.
■ The implementation of a coaching framework should be directed at the endeavors made by top executives throughout all organizational departments.
■ It is important for both managers and workers to engage in effective communication and behavior that promotes the practice of coaching.
■ In order to effectively demonstrate their commitment to the organization, leaders must engage in role-playing exercises and actively cultivate their coaching abilities as a means of exemplifying workability.

Potential Efficiency of Establishing a Coaching Culture

Numerous studies (Milner et al., 2020; Whitmore, 2017; Gormley and Van Nieuwerburgh, 2014) conducted on the efficacy of coaching have identified a range of advantageous outcomes (Bakhshandeh & Rothwell, 2024):

■ A notable surge in the level of attention surrounding the concepts of goal-setting, commitment, and accomplishment mindset.
■ The implementation of strategies to improve both individual and team performance and productivity has resulted in notable enhancements.
■ Facilitated the development of enhanced critical-thinking skills and a problem-solving mindset.
■ The heightened conducive atmosphere for fostering creativity and innovation.
■ The cultivation of resilience and self-efficacy contributing to an increased sense of optimism and hope for a more favorable existence.
■ Resulted in heightened cognitive endurance, as well as improvements in both mental and physical well-being among individuals.
■ Resulted in reduced opposition and increased flexibility in managing workloads and schedules.
■ The use of strategies aimed at mitigating workplace anxiety, stress, burnout, and turnover resulting in a notable reduction in these negative outcomes.

■ An enhanced capacity to embrace and adapt to change and transformations.
■ Enhanced the development of transformational leadership skills among managers at an advanced level.

Possible Obstacles to Establishing a Coaching Culture

On the other hand, some studies (Rothwell et al., 2016; Whitmore, 2009) have highlighted many obstacles that may impede the establishment and maintenance of coaching cultures (Bakhshandeh & Rothwell, 2024):

■ The prevailing culture inside the company.
■ The lack of a comprehensive understanding of the mechanics and underlying principles of coaching and its associated ideals.
■ The apparent lack of recognition of a coaching culture's significance inside the organization.
■ The reluctance from senior management in implementing a coaching culture is both expensive and useless.
■ The managers within the organization exhibit a general lack of experience, abilities, and competencies at a lower level.
■ A lack of adequate time, financial resources, or other necessary resources to support the endeavor.

Coaching Providing Methods

According to Bakhshandeh and Rothwell (2023), there exist two primary methodologies for coaching delivery, namely *directive coaching* and *non-directive coaching*. The purpose of this section is not to discuss the superiority or effectiveness of one strategy over the other. Instead, it aims to provide a comparative analysis of the two delivery approaches and identify the more suitable approach for use by an emotional intelligence coach.

There exist divergent perspectives about the nature of coaching, specifically pertaining to the extent of directiveness or non-directiveness involved. It is widely acknowledged that non-directive coaching holds significant efficacy, mostly due to the recognition that individuals own expertise in their own lives and are more inclined to implement their own ideas rather than comply with external directives (Neal et al., 2009). Although coaching is often described as non-directive, it is important to acknowledge that it does possess a certain level of directionality. This is because coaching facilitates progress and ensures that the coachee's objectives are effectively pursued and maintained. Primarily, coaching entails tailoring the approach to suit the specific needs and characteristics of the individuals. In the role of coaches, their influence on the coaching session is significant since individuals possess a distinct combination of values, attitudes, and beliefs that shape their approach to active listening and the formulation of pertinent inquiries. The focus of the counseling relationship lies not in their state of being an empty vessel but rather in the individuals' ability to bring forth their authentic self, rather than relying solely on the material they possess (Neal et al., 2009).

Directive Coaching

The directive coaching technique entails a more active involvement of coaches in the coaching process, wherein they use their expertise, experience, and professional guidance as subject-matter experts. The relationship between coaches and coachees in this approach bears resemblance to athletic coaching, wherein coaches employ questioning techniques to gain insight into the coachees' mindset or identify areas of resistance or obstacles. Subsequently, coaches offer their guidance and may even demonstrate practical strategies to the coachees (Wilson, 2020; Whitmore, 2017; Bakhshandeh, 2009). As a result, directional coaching has gained popularity among professionals in technical and performance-related fields (see Figure 14.2).

- **Advantage.** One of the primary advantages of employing the directed coaching style is its use in situations when coachees may lack awareness of the underlying issue or are uncertain about alternative courses of action. This deficiency might potentially arise from a dearth of experience, expertise, or an inadequate degree of performance necessary for the specific job, task, or role.
- **Disadvantage.** One potential limitation associated with directive coaching is the potential for coachees to lack independent comprehension of the underlying concepts and procedures, hence requiring additional time and effort to effectively practice and develop their skills. Nevertheless, with diligent learning, the provision of assistance from their managers or supervisors, the implementation of tests, and the assessment of efficacy and performance, individuals will acquire and retain information, enabling them to effectively recall and apply what they have learned.

Non-Directive Coaching

This coaching style entails the coaches actively promoting the clients' development of their own perspectives on the matter under consideration, hence fostering the growth of the coaching relationship. In contrast, this methodology entails coaches actively engaging in the process of attentively listening to clients' narratives, experiences, and the obstacles they encounter. Concurrently, coaches employ inquiries to facilitate opportunities for clients to develop self-awareness and make autonomous decisions as they progress on their personal growth journey. The effectiveness of a non-directive approach becomes evident when coachees are able to identify solutions that align with their individual personal and professional aspirations and requirements. Hence, considering their active participation, it is more likely for the individuals being coached to adopt and apply the identified improvements within their personal or professional contexts (Wilson, 2020; Whitmore, 2017; Bakhshandeh, 2009).

- **Advantage.** In this style, it is not important for the coach to possess specialized knowledge in the subject area. The primary responsibility of the coach is to pose pragmatic and pertinent inquiries, while also creating an environment that encourages contemplation and exploration. Additionally, the coach must consistently emphasize the need to maintain a non-judgmental, open-minded, and non-resistant mindset, as seen in Figure 14.2. Non-directive coaching is a widely recognized approach that demonstrates efficacy in non-technical and non-performance contexts.
- **Disadvantage**. One potential drawback associated with non-directive coaching is the extended duration required for achieving desired outcomes and for coachees to independently arrive at their own judgments. In certain instances, individuals may fail to arrive at any definitive judgments independently.

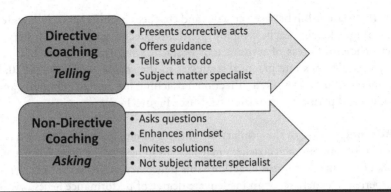

Figure 14.2 Contrast of non-directive and directive coaching style. © Bakhshandeh 2024.

What Is Emotional Intelligence Coaching?

Emotional intelligence coaching is a form of coaching that centers on the enhancement of an individual's emotional intelligence. Emotional intelligence pertains to an individual's capacity to identify, comprehend, and regulate their own emotions, alongside the emotions exhibited by others. Individuals engage in emotional intelligence coaching for a multitude of purposes. There are those who aspire to enhance their communication skills in order to enhance their interpersonal interactions. There is a desire among individuals to enhance their self-awareness and empathy as a means of cultivating greater effectiveness in their leadership roles within the workplace (Bakhshandeh, Rothwell, & Imroz, 2023; Neal et al., 2009).

Basic Operational Process of EI Coaching

At the individual level, the individualized approach to emotional intelligence coaching entails close collaboration with an emotional intelligence coach to ascertain objectives, formulate strategies, and engage in skill-building exercises. Furthermore, this process necessitates that clients engage in sincere introspection, both individually and in conjunction with their coaches. The coaching process at the group level is contingent upon the size of the group or organization and may be structured as seminars or workshops.

In order to foster these techniques, every coaching engagement incorporates regular weekly or bi-weekly meetings, unrestricted access to supplementary materials, and activities designed to prompt clients to engage in profound reflection. During these interactions, an emotional intelligence coach directs their attention toward subjects like self-awareness, self-regulation, communication, attitudes, behavioral indicators, and other abilities associated with emotional intelligence. The emotional intelligence coach collaborates with the client in order to discern potential instances where the client might engage in skill-building exercises, while concurrently offering constructive feedback and assistance throughout the process (Bakhshandeh et al., 2023; Neal et al., 2009).

(Important note: We will introduce all the elements, skills, and competencies of an EI Coach in Chapter 16 of this book as part of implementation, and management of training and development sessions.)

Significant Advantages of EI Coaching

Given the individualized nature of coaching, it is probable that one will derive distinct advantages from embarking on a personalized coaching journey. Typically, those seeking to enhance their emotional intelligence may anticipate several advantages pertaining to interpersonal connections, professional endeavors, and personal satisfaction.

Increasing Level of Self-Awareness

Self-awareness is commonly defined by psychologists as the cognitive ability to possess a comprehensive understanding and perception of one's own personality, encompassing many attributes such as shortcomings, strengths, attitudes, motivation, beliefs, and emotions. The acquisition of self-awareness enables individuals to gain insight into the perspectives of others, including their perceptions of our demeanor and our reactions toward them. This understanding facilitates recognition and comprehension of interpersonal dynamics (Rothwell, Imroz, & Bakhshandeh, 2021).

The emphasis on self-awareness is crucial in the context of individual intervention and coaching. Through this approach, coaches can gain insight into the lack of self-awareness exhibited by individuals regarding their self-motivation, actions, attitude, and underlying thought processes that shape their mentality. The amount and depth of individuals' self-awareness is contingent upon their recognition of their own being, as well as the extent to which they purposefully conceal it from others (Bakhshandeh et al., 2023).

Enhancing Personal and Professional Relationships

The utilization of emotional intelligence coaching has the potential to provide enhancements in interpersonal connections via the cultivation of essential emotional intelligence competencies, hence fostering constructive and beneficial interactions. This encompasses the acquisition of skills related to those below (Neal et al., 2009):

■ Articulate personal preferences, requirements, aspirations, and affective states, hence enhancing interpersonal communication efficacy.
■ Foster the cultivation of empathy toward individuals, hence facilitating the development of heightened levels of compassion, understanding, and tolerance toward others.
■ Enhance proficiency in conflict management and resolution, resulting in improved abilities to achieve productive compromises and foster collaboration.
■ Engage in partnerships with emotional intelligence to cultivate the requisite competencies for fostering heightened emotional closeness and more robust connections with their social circles, including friends, family members, and acquaintances, resulting in personal interactions that are more enriching and gratifying.

Developing Skills for Career Improvement

By cultivating a heightened sense of self-awareness of their emotions and acquiring the necessary skills to properly regulate them, individuals may enhance their capacity to cope with stress, adeptly navigate complex circumstances, and make judicious choices. These competencies are invaluable in the realm of business. EI coaching assists individuals in enhancing their ability to demonstrate empathy and cultivate a deeper understanding of social dynamics. These results facilitate the enhancement of one's capacity to collaborate efficiently with others, foster the formation of robust teams, and enhance communication proficiency. Furthermore, the role of an emotional intelligence coach includes the facilitation of clients' growth in conflict resolution abilities, which are of paramount importance in fostering successful leadership and cooperation. This particular form of professional development ultimately results in enhanced career achievement and progression for individuals seeking coaching services (Bakhshandeh & Rothwell, 2024).

Enriched Experience of Contentment and Satisfaction

Emotional intelligence coaching centers its attention on the cultivation of self-awareness, self-management, and self-care, with the potential to significantly enhance an individual's overall life experience. The potential advantages of emotional intelligence coaching mostly manifest in the context of the individuals' daily experiences. Coaching is intended to enhance several aspects of their well-being, such as their stress management skills, emotional regulation abilities, and overall positive mindset. It is tailored to accommodate individuals at their current stage in life and facilitate their progression to a higher degree of personal development (Bakhshandeh & Rothwell, 2024).

(Important note: We will continue distinguishing these significant advantages of participating in EI coaching in more detail in Chapter 15 and directions for developing related skills to the above elements.)

Some Reported General Benefits of EI Coaching

Several benefits of emotional intelligence coaching have been observed by experienced coaches and researchers (Connors, 2020; Goleman, 2015; Hockenbury and Hockenbury, 2007) who have undergone transformational coaching with people and teams. These benefits include the following:

1. Alleviates the tension that is brought on by both personal and professional obligations.
2. Helps individuals become receptive to receiving critical feedback in a positive manner.
3. Helps willing individuals overcome their fears and self-doubt by providing them with support and guidance.
4. Enhances both one's ability to communicate and to listen actively.
5. Strengthens connections, as well as social awareness and the ability to interact with others.
6. Contributes to the creation of a pleasant atmosphere in both the home and the office.
7. Increases one's ability to be patient in the face of discontent.
8. Assists people and teams in coping with the unpredictability produced by changes in the environment.
9. Raises the bar for one's own level of personal and professional responsibility as well as accountability.
10. Strengthens the ties inside the team as well as its cohesion.

Various Approaches to Utilize on EI Coaching

Given the exponential global expansion of emotional intelligence training and literature, it is unsurprising that a multitude of views have arisen on the essence and applicability of EI (Bakhshandeh & Rothwell, 2024; Rothwell & Bakhshandeh, 2023; Neal et al., 2009).

Nature of Personality

Personality traits tend to have a rather stable nature, although all dimensions of emotional intelligence possess the potential for modification. Emotional intelligence pertains to the manner in which individuals opt to regulate their inherent personalities. For instance, individuals who exhibit extroverted or introverted tendencies may both exhibit diminished levels of personal behavior, frequently assuming the position of a victim and attributing responsibility to external factors. It would be advantageous for individuals belonging to both of these personality types to cultivate and enhance their personal strength. The primary emphasis lies in modifying attitudes and behaviors rather than altering one's inherent personality traits.

Learned Competencies

Certain theories of emotional intelligence argue that it is a collection of skills that may be acquired via training. Nevertheless, the concept of emotional intelligence is perceived as a complex amalgamation of attitudes that may significantly influence an individual's skills. An illustrative instance is the utilization of a training course as a means to acquire enhanced listening skills. When taught in isolation, active listening skills can be viewed as a form of behavior training.

Nevertheless, without examining one's views pertaining to their consideration and understanding of others, acquiring the ability to engage in active listening may not necessarily translate into its actual implementation. Enhanced listening skills are expected to arise from the cultivation of empathy and mindfulness toward others. However, it should be noted that just instructing individuals on the necessary abilities may not provide enduring modifications in behavior. Emotional intelligence examines the fundamental factors that serve as the foundation for our conduct rather than only focusing on the observable behaviors that manifest externally.

Source of Motivation

Emotional intelligence exhibits a strong correlation with motivation. The term "motivation" may be understood as the process of stimulating and directing emotions in order to initiate action. Individuals with a high level of emotional intelligence possess a heightened comprehension of the factors that motivate them and elicit both good and negative emotions. Positive emotions can be associated with several factors such as values, attitudes, beliefs, wants, desires, preferences, and aversions.

As an illustration, consider an individual who possesses a genuine affinity for mountain climbing, driven by both the intrinsic enjoyment derived from the exercise and the conviction that engaging in this pursuit will provide positive health benefits. When a buddy extends an invitation to engage in a weekend climbing excursion, the mere contemplation of mountain climbing is expected to elicit favorable emotions. An alternative manner of articulating this concept is to assert that one possesses a strong inclination to engage in the activity of climbing. In a similar vein, those who have encountered a severe mountain climbing mishap and afterwards adopted a perception that this activity is inherently perilous may encounter adverse emotions, thus leading to a diminished drive to partake in the sport alongside their companion.

The Power of Emotional Intelligence Coaching Questions

In the ever-evolving landscape of personal and professional development, coaching has emerged as a transformative force, guiding individuals toward their fullest potential. Central to the coaching process is the art of questioning. Traditionally, questions have been seen as simple inquiries seeking specific answers. However, the nature of questions in coaching has undergone a profound transformation, reshaping the very essence of this practice and yielding unprecedented results.

Historically, coaching questions were often closed-ended, aiming for precise responses. These questions, while functional, limited the scope of exploration and understanding. However, contemporary coaching approaches recognize the inherent power of open-ended and empowering questions. By shifting the focus from "what" and "why" to "how" and "what if," coaches delve deeper into the psyche of their clients; and this approach does not differ from EI coaching. Open-ended questions invite introspection, enabling individuals to explore their thoughts, feelings, and aspirations in a more profound way.

The impact of this shift is monumental. Open-ended questions encourage participants to tap into their inner wisdom, fostering self-awareness and self-discovery. As individuals articulate their thoughts and emotions in response to open-ended questions, they often stumble upon hidden insights, enabling them to unravel the complexities of their challenges. Consequently, participants become active in their own growth, leading to more meaningful and sustainable personal and professional transformations.

Moreover, the evolution of coaching questions has also ushered in a new era of empathy and rapport building. Thoughtfully crafted questions, rooted in empathy, create a safe space for clients to express their vulnerabilities. Coaches skilled in the art of empathetic questioning create an environment where clients feel heard, valued, and understood. This emotional connection forms the cornerstone of trust, which is pivotal for any coaching relationship. As trust deepens, clients are more likely to embrace change, confront their fears, and take bold steps toward their goals.

Beyond the realms of empathy, the nature of questions in coaching has also embraced a strengths-based approach. Traditional coaching often fixated on identifying weaknesses and devising strategies to overcome them. However, contemporary and emotional intelligence coaching transcends this approach by leveraging questions to illuminate strengths and untapped potential. Strength-based questions not only boost confidence but also empower individuals to leverage their unique abilities to overcome challenges. By emphasizing strengths, clients are encouraged to adopt a positive mindset, enhancing their resilience in the face of adversities.

In addition to individual coaching sessions, the impact of transformative questioning related to self-awareness is also evident in group- and team-coaching scenarios. Open-ended, empathetic, and strength-based questions foster a sense of camaraderie and mutual respect among team members. By encouraging individuals to recognize and appreciate each other's strengths, team dynamics are enhanced, leading to improved collaboration, communication, and problem-solving skills.

In Chapters 15 and 16 of this book, we will offer additional insights into EI-coaching inquiries and introduce a more comprehensive questioning methodology. However, we present in Table 14.3 a selection of empowering questions that are pertinent to emotional intelligence coaching. These questions are commonly employed by emotional intelligence or transformational coaches during their coaching sessions.

Table 14.3 Some Examples of Emotional Intelligence Coaching Questions

Questions	Motives	Advantages
Are you aware of how your emotions and moods affect the way you behave?	Being conscious of how their feelings influence their actions.	Reducing the tendency to make poor decisions based on feelings and developing self-control.
Do you recognize the unsettling emotional blind spots you have?	Realizing the impact of their blind spots on other people.	Identifying the disparity and raising one's consciousness.
Do you know what sets off your happy or sad feelings?	Understanding the spectrum of emotions is essential to learning how to manage them.	Improving relationship management and learning how to regulate emotions and associated possible behaviors.
Do you know when your temper is getting the better of you and when you are about to act badly?	Recognizing the extent of control over intense feelings and the resulting temper outbursts.	Identifying, responding to, and restraining oneself from intense feelings; stopping harmful habits; and developing self-awareness.
Do you have empathy for other people?	Recognizing the level of emotional awareness of others.	Focusing more on interpersonal interactions and social awareness in both personal and professional contexts.
How do other people feel about your feelings?	Taking ownership of the way that other people represent themselves.	Helping with social awareness and self-control.
When your emotions are set to blow out, what social cues are you sending out?	Being aware of social cues and signals might assist in managing them.	Fostering positive interpersonal interactions both at work and at home.
Do you express your emotions via your facial expressions and body language?	Being conscious of the way one expresses emotions and, by extension, a particular message.	Comprehending and regulating our nonverbal cues and facial emotions contribute to a mature persona, aiding in social awareness and interpersonal interaction.
Do you regularly write in your journal about the feelings you feel?	Recording both happy and sad feelings and comprehending the expressions that go along with them.	It would be possible to predict how and when certain emotions will arise by identifying the patterns and consistency of those feelings, supporting self-control and self-awareness.
Do you regularly speak in a positive manner?	Recognizing the language that is being utilized on a frequent basis.	Assisting with social awareness, relationship management, and interpersonal interactions.

Note. Adapted from Bakhshandeh et al., 2023; Bakhshandeh & Rothwell, 2024.

Role of Mindset, Attitude, and Behavior in the EI Coaching

In this section we look at the role of mindset, attitude, and behavior on developing emotional intelligence and their impact on individual and team performance.

Self-awareness is sparked and participants' habits and attitudes are brought to light by EI coaches. The first step toward participants realizing how much they don't know and the need to implement corrective measures in their behavior and attitude is to guide them from a state of unconscious incompetence to a state of conscious incompetence. This will directly and positively influence the organization's strategy for achieving the desired productivity (Vidal-Salazar et al., 2012).

Effect of EI Coaching on Productivity and Individuals' Attitudes

We may briefly examine how EI coaching affects many aspects of the workforce and how those aspects relate to career and productivity. We will look deeper into this concept in Chapters 15 and 16.

Career Commitment

Those who participate in EI coaching are more likely to go further in their occupations and careers overall as a result of the experience. The workers' levels of commitment to their jobs are measured by how motivated they are to persevere in their career trajectory as well as how they feel about their profession. The types of connections that individuals are exposed to while on the job are an important factor in career commitment. According to Kim et al. (2013), there is a correlation between workers' perceptions about the organization and employee personalities and career commitment.

Organization Commitment

EI coaching may have an effect on organization commitment, which can be defined as the psychological and emotional attachment that workers have for the company that they work for. According to Kim et al. (2013), a significant number of organizational leaders place a significant focus on this connection since it is crucial to guarantee low turnover rates.

Job Performance

EI coaching has an effect on the efficacy of the workers on the job and is directly tied to individual productivity. According to Kim et al. (2013), coaching is therefore linked to performance on the job.

Increasing Sales

When EI coaching is employed, there is a possibility that the organization's sales will go up. According to Pousa, Mathieu, and Trépanier (2017), a coaching intervention in sales is a high-quality interaction that takes place between sales managers and their sales teams. During this interaction, sales managers raise their employees' awareness of many potentially critical aspects of their attitude and the impact of attitude on their sales productivity improvement.

Link between Mindset, Attitude, Behavior, and Performance

Minor occurrences have the potential to significantly influence the formation of mindsets, attitudes, behaviors, and the attainment of performance outcomes. In order for individuals to gain awareness of their thoughts and attitudes, it is necessary for them to engage in introspection and self-reflection. This concept diverges from regular, everyday cognition, since it entails profound reflection and purposeful investigations into one's mental condition. One fundamental differentiation between humans and other species is in the cognitive abilities possessed by humans, enabling them to engage in thought processes, exercise choice, and direct their mental faculties toward the pursuit of certain goals they perceive as attainable.

> To be able to think does not wholly depend on our will and wish, though much does depend on whether we prepare ourselves to hear that call to think when it comes and respond to it appropriately. Thinking is determined by that which is to be thought as well as by he who thinks.

> **(Heidegger, 1968, p. xi)**

The classification of a person's attitude as either positive or negative has a significant impact on their individual performance. This straightforward yet impactful phenomenon pertaining to attitudes enables individuals to regard themselves as either successful or unsuccessful and may also be employed to perceive others. Based on the perspective of the general populace, the amalgamation of a constructive mental outlook and a dynamic demeanor is seen as one of the most advantageous dispositions an individual may possess (Snyder and Tanke, 1976). Attitude, in a concise explication, covers an individual's cognitive framework, subjective interpretations, and personal convictions. According to Yashasvi (2019), these foundational elements contribute to the development of persons and shape their abilities and actions in the face of actual or imagined difficulties.

This is a straightforward illustration from the Buddhist faith and practice taken from Tsai Chin Chung's book *Zen Speaks*, which explains how a person's frame of mind and attitude may have a significant bearing on their actions and the results they achieve. In the Middle Ages, there is the tale of three men who worked as stonemasons. These stonemasons utilized stone chisels and hammers to chip away at enormous blocks of stone in preparation for use in a construction project. The chipped stone was then hammered into smaller pieces. They were putting in a lot of effort when a stranger who was just passing by stopped and asked each of them individually what they were working on. The first mason, who was putting in a lot of effort and was dripping with perspiration as he spoke, grumbled something. "I am chipping away at this stone." The second mason, who appeared to be experiencing far less anxiety than the first mason, exhaled deeply before responding, "I am building a road." The third mason, who was engaged in the same laborious stonework as the other masons, said with a smile on his face, "I am building a beautiful cathedral" (Chung 1994). The moral of this short tale is that although those three guys were performing the same activity, they did so from three different viewpoints, each of which altered the quality of their work. Because of the three various ways that they conducted themselves throughout the day, they would each have a unique experience of their job, their day, and their performance. Figure 14.3 displays the connection between mindset, attitude, behavior, and performance.

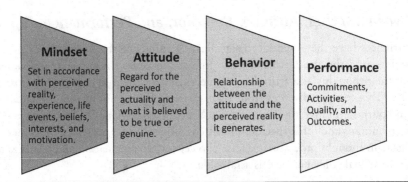

Figure 14.3   Connection among mindset, attitude, behavior, and individual and team performance. Note. Adapted from Bakhshandeh & Rothwell (2024); Rothwell et al., (2021).

Mindset

Renowned physicist Albert Einstein (1879–1955) expressed the notion that the concept of reality might be perceived as an illusory construct, but one that exhibits remarkable durability. Both you and I were brought into a preexisting realm with a multitude of ideas, practices, beliefs, customs, and regulations. The formation of our thoughts is influenced by several factors, including personal experiences, familial relationships, social interactions, media exposure, and occupational engagements. The future experienced thus far may be understood as the outcome of a young child's prospects, which have been influenced and constrained by the circumstances predetermined by preceding events. The dynamic nature of the universe and evolving realities necessitate the continual adaptation and refinement of individual and societal behaviors. The aforementioned techniques and concepts align more closely with a traditional rather than a contemporary objective. Both individuals are responsible for their own life and the outcomes they achieve.

How might we enhance our cognitive processes to better meet the demands of our current and future existence? By acknowledging and differentiating the origins of our convictions. By becoming aware of the extent to which our perception of reality is constructed by our own subjective interpretations. Indeed, we have fabricated it. I am referring to phenomena that pertain to the realm of physical reality, such as the spherical shape of the planet Earth, the presence of gravitational forces, the anatomical structure of human beings, and other scientifically established principles in the fields of physics, biology, chemistry, and related disciplines. This discourse pertains to the constructed realities that individuals have formulated regarding their own identities, as well as those concerning their colleagues within the professional environment and society as a whole. I perceive myself as lacking the necessary qualities to fulfill certain expectations or tasks, leading to self-doubt and a belief that I am incapable of achieving success. Additionally, I perceive certain personal attributes as hindrances, further reinforcing my belief that I am ill-equipped to undertake specific endeavors. Many individuals possess restrictive attitudes and mindsets, which pertain not just to their own capabilities but also to their perceptions of others.

What actions have the collective human race undertaken that have challenged prevailing perspectives? The aforementioned examples encompass significant milestones in human history, including the creation of the light bulb, the acquisition of literacy and communication skills by those with visual and auditory impairments, and the momentous achievement of mankind's initial lunar landing. What similarities may be identified among these events? Beliefs and cognitive frameworks. However, what specific kind of attitudes and mindsets are being referred to? The creation of new inventions. There exist some cognitive frameworks that have motivated numerous individuals to conceive, innovate, and fabricate realities that were previously inconceivable under the prevailing cognitive frameworks of their respective eras. "History is full of those invented realities. There are no limits, there is no difficulty, and there is no 'I can't' until we say, 'It is,' or we listen to others saying, 'It is!' What is this amazing phenomenon that some people have created a mastery of and for so many others it is still a mystery" (Bakhshandeh 2009, p. 19)?

Cherry (2020) posits that an individual's mentality encompasses their ideas on personal traits, such as talents and intellect, as well as their assessment of others' attitudes and behaviors. The mindsets in question may exhibit a degree of permanence, persisting inside individuals over an extended period of time. Alternatively, they may be subject to change, contingent upon perceptions of others or modified circumstances. According to Dweck (2016), individuals typically acquire these two mindsets throughout their formative years, mostly from their parenting and educational and life experiences. A *fixed mindset* refers to the belief held by individuals that talents and intellect are innate, unchangeable, and fixed in nature. The concept of *growth mindset* pertains to those who hold the belief that talents and intellect may be cultivated, enhanced, and strengthened by factors such as interest, motivation, and dedication (Dweck, 2016).

Attitude

Attitudes encompass the cognitive, emotional, and behavioral expressions of individuals toward other persons, events, and subjects, reflecting their thoughts, emotions, and inclinations to act in positive, negative, or indifferent ways. In general, those who possess a positive attitude exhibit optimistic self-perceptions, have pleasant sentiments toward others, experience emotional well-being in response to various circumstances, and hold constructive belief systems. Individuals who exhibit negative behavior toward themselves and others, along with a gloomy outlook on events or social collectives, can be characterized as possessing a negative attitude.

Attitude encompasses the cognitive inclination of the mind toward specific individuals, concepts, institutions, values, or societal structures. On the other hand, behavior pertains to the concrete expression of emotions through various forms of action or inaction, such as communication and body language (Bainbridge Frymier & Keeshan Nadler, 2017). One perspective posits potential shifts in an individual's mindset, although in a gradual manner. Numerous firms have endeavored to modify the attitudes of their challenging workers and establish a functional and fruitful working environment by using diverse change interventions, training programs, and development initiatives (Yashasvi, 2019).

Behavior

The conduct of individuals is influenced by their thinking and attitude toward their perceived world. Behavior refers to the observable actions or activities that occur subsequent to the expression or perception of individuals' attitudes. The order in which we address the individuals' actions or attitudes does not significantly impact our ability to exert influence over them or a given situation. According to Bainbridge Frymier and Keeshan Nadler (2017), it is advised to prioritize the examination and modification of their behavior as it is comparatively easier to identify and address observable changes. Conversely, addressing their attitudes is a more complex and time-consuming endeavor, potentially hindered by deeply ingrained beliefs that may persist for an extended period.

It is noteworthy to acknowledge that there exists a significant disparity among experts regarding the "attitude–intention–behavior" framework, since some hold the belief that attitudes do not consistently translate into corresponding behaviors. Occasionally, individuals may lack awareness of their shown attitudes, which, akin to implicit attitudes, might influence specific behaviors, regardless of alignment with explicit attitudes (Yashasvi, 2019).

Performance

By actively observing the mental states of individuals and uncovering their cognitive frameworks through a series of dialogues and exchanges inside a secure and unrestricted setting, managers may discern the correlation between participants' attitudes and behaviors and their performance. This endeavor is not devoid of challenges, and it is plausible that a substantial number of coaching sessions may be required to get the desired outcome. Nevertheless, when coaches or managers prioritize the participants' level of dedication and aspirations for their work, they have the potential to influence their performance by refraining from opposing their attitudes and behaviors. Instead, they should continue coaching them toward the understanding that they are solely responsible for their own perceptions, attitudes, and actions.

What Is Next?

Chapter 15, "4Cs Skills Competency-Based Training and Development via EI," explores variations of competency-based training approaches for developing deeper 4Cs skills by applying elements of emotional intelligence. To do this, we will be using Table 13.2, "Summary of Emotional Intelligence Clusters, Competencies and Qualities and Correspondence 4Cs Skills," from Chapter 13 to guide us.

References

Bainbridge Frymier Ann & Nadler Keeshan, Marjorie. (2017). *Persuasion: Integrating Theory, Research, and Practices* (4th ed.). Dubuque, IA: Kendall Hunt Publishing.

Bakhshandeh, Behnam. (2009). *Conspiracy for Greatness: Mastery on Love Within*. San Diego, CA: Primeco Education, Inc.

Bakhshandeh, Behnam & Rothwell, William J. (Eds.) (2024). *Building an Organizational Coaching Culture*. Oxfordshire, UK: UK Limited Trading, Taylor & Francis Group. Routledge.

Bakhshandeh, Behnam, Rothwell, William J., & Imroz, Sohel M. (2023). *Transformational Coaching for Effective Leadership. Creating Sustainable Change through Shifting Paradigms*. New York, NY: Taylor & Francis Group. Routledge.

Berg, Morten Emil & Terje Karlsen, Jan. (2012). An evaluation of management training and coaching. *Journal of Workplace Learning*, *24*(3), 177–199.

Cherry, Kendra. (2020). Why mindset matters for your success. Very Well Mind website. Retrieved from https://www.verywellmind.com/what-is-a-mindset-2795025.

Chung, Tsai Chin. (1994). *Zen Speaks*. Translated by Brian Bruya. New York, NY: Anchor Books Doubleday.

Clutterbuck, David, Megginson, David, & Bajer, Agnieszka. (2016). *Building and Sustaining a Coaching Culture*. London, UK: Kogan Page Publishers.

Connors, Christopher D. (2020). *Emotional Intelligence for the Modern Leader.* Emeryville, CA: Rockridge Press.

Cummings, T. G. & Worley, C. G. (2015). *Organization Development & Change* (10th ed.). Stamford, CT: Cengage Learning.

Dweck, Carol S. (2016). *Mindset; The New Psychology of Success* (updated ed.). New York, NY: Ballantine Books.

Ekman, P. (1973). Universal facial expressions in emotion. *Studia Psychologica, 15*(2), 140–147.

Ekman, P. (1999). Basic emotions. *Handbook of Cognition and Emotion, 98*(45–60), 16.

Forbes. (2018). Forbes Coaches Council. Key differences between coaching and consulting (And how to decide what your business needs). Retrieved from https://www.forbes.com/sites/forbescoachescouncil /2018/06/14/key-differences-between-coaching-and-consulting-and-how-to-decide-what-your-busi-ness-needs/?sh=51e9cd13d712.

Goleman, Daniel. (1995). *Emotional Intelligence: Why It Can Matter More Than IQ.* New York, NY: Bantam Books.

Goleman, Daniel. (2007). *Social Intelligence.* New York, NY: Bantam Books.

Goleman, Daniel. (2015). *Emotional Intelligence; Why It Can Matter More Than IQ.* New York, NY: Bantam Books.

Gormley, Helen & Van Nieuwerburgh, Christian. (2014). Developing coaching cultures: A review of the literature. *Coaching: An International Journal of Theory, Research and Practice, 7*(2), 90–101. https:// doi.org/10.1080/17521882.2014.915863.

Hawkins, P. (2012). *Creating a Coaching Culture (Coaching in Practice Series).* Maidenhead, Berkshire: Open University Press.

Heidegger, Martin. (1968). *What Is Called Thinking? Translated by J. Glenn Gray.* New York, NY: Harper Perennial.

Hockenbury, Don H. & Hockenbury, Sandra E. (2007). *Discovering Psychology.* New York, NY: Worth Publishers.

Indeed.com. (2021). Coaching vs. consulting: Overview, differences and similarities. Career Development. Indeed Editorial Team. Retrieved from https://www.indeed.com/career-advice/career-development/ coaching-vs-consulting.

Jones, Gillian & Gorell, Ro. (2014). *How To Create a Coaching Culture* (Vol. 3). London, UK: Kogan Page Publishers.

Jordyn, Betsy. (2020). Consulting vs. coaching. Retrieved from https://www.betsyjordyn.com/blog/con-sulting-vs-coaching.

Kim, Sewon, Egan, Toby M., Kim, Woosung, & Kim, Jaekyum. (2013). The impact of managerial coaching behavior on employee work-related reactions. *Journal of Business and Psychology, 28*(3), 315–330. https://doi.org/10.1007/s 10869-013-9286-9.

McLeod, Angus. (2004). Performance coaching & mentoring in organizations. *Resource Magazine, 1*(1), 28–31.

Milner, Julia, Milner, Trenton, & McCarthy, Grace (2020). A coaching culture definition: An industry-based perspective from managers as coaches. *The Journal of Applied Behavioral Science, 56*(2), 237–254.

Neal, Stephen, Spencer-Arnell, Lisa, & Wilson, Liz. (2009). *Emotional Intelligence Coaching. Improving Performance for Leaders, Coaching and the Individual.* Philadelphia, PA: KoganPgae.

Pfeiffer, William J. (1990). *Developing Human Resources.* San Diego, CA: Pfeiffer & Company.

Pousa, Claudio, Mathieu, Anne, & Trépanier, Carole. (2017). Managing frontline employee performance through coaching: Does selling experience matter? *International Journal of Bank Marketing, 35*(2), 220–240. https://doi.org/10.1108/IJBM-01-2016-0005.

Rothwell, William J., Imroz, Sohel M., & Bakhshandeh, Behnam. (2021). *Organization-Development Interventions: Executing Effective Organizational Chang.* New York, NY: Taylor & Francis Group. CRC Press.

Rothwell, William J., Stavros, Jacqueline M., & Sullivan, Roland L. (2016). *Practicing Organization Development: Leading Transformation and Change* (4th ed.). Hoboken, NJ: John Wiley & Sons, Inc.

Snyder, Mark. & Tanke, Elizabeth D. (1976). Behavior and attitude: Some people are more consistent than others. *Journal of Personality, 44*(3), 501–517. https://doi.org/10.1111/j.1467-6494.1976.tb00135.x.

Strosinski, Jean. (2003). Performance consulting versus performance coaching. (First article of six in the series: Coaching for Performance. Constructive Choices, Inc.) Retrieved from https://www.constructivechoices.com/articles/Art1_Performance%20Coaching.pdf.

Training Industry. (2018). What is performance consulting? Retrieved from https://trainingindustry.com/wiki/professional-development/performance-consulting/.

ValueProp. (2021). The difference between a business coach and a consultant: Which do I need? Retrieved from https://www.valueprop.com/blog/the-difference-between-a-business-coach-and-a-consultant-which-do-i-need.

Vesso, Signe. (2014). Coaching culture characteristics in Estonian companies. *Journal of Management and Change, 32/33*(12), 109–131.

Vesso, Signe & Alas, Ruth. (2016). Characteristics of a coaching culture in leadership style the leader's impact on culture. *Problems and Perspectives in Management, 14*, 306–318. https://doi.org/10.21511/ppm.14(2-2).2016.06.

Vidal-Salazar, Dolores, María, Ferrón-Vílchez, Vera, & Cordón-Pozo, Eulogio. (2012). Coaching: An effective practice for business competitiveness. *Competitiveness Review: An International Business Journal, 22*(5), 423–433. https://doi.org/10.1108/10595421211266302.

Wall, Bob. (2007). *Coaching For Emotional Intelligence. The Secret to Developing the Star Potential in Your Employees.* New York, NY: AMACOM.

Whitmore, John. (2009). *Coaching for Performance; GROWing Human Potential and Purpose* (4th ed.). Boston, MA: Nicholas Brealey Publishing.

Whitmore, John. (2017). *Coaching for Performance; The Principle and Practice of Coaching and Leadership* (5th ed.). Boston, MA: Nicholas Brealey Publishing.

Wilson, Carol. (2020). *Performance Coaching: A complete Guide to Best-Practice Coaching and Training* (3rd ed.). New York, NY: KoganPage.

Yashasvi, G. (2019). Styles at life.com. 4 different types of attitudes of people as per psychology. Retrieved from https://stylesatlife.com/articles/types-of-attitudes/.

Chapter 15

4Cs Skills Competency-Based Training and Development via EI

Introduction

After conducting an analysis of the identified themes and the expressed interest of professionals within organizations regarding the training and development of their employees in the 4Cs skills, this researcher has concluded that implementing emotional intelligence (EI) training can have a positive impact on organizations. This training can effectively enhance the awareness of employees while equipping them with soft skills, competencies, communication abilities, and leadership qualities. The implementation of these training programs has a significant impact on the cultivation of leadership skills among employees, especially the management teams within the respective organizations.

The training and development model for emotional intelligence encompasses all four components of the 21st-century 4Cs framework, namely critical thinking, communication, creativity, and cooperation. These elements are integrated into various parts of emotional intelligence, hence fostering leadership growth within the workforce (Bakhshandeh & Rothwell, 2024). This training program encompasses the many levels of management and workforce throughout production levels, with the aim of enhancing knowledge, comprehension, and application of the 21st-century 4Cs skillset.

In Chapter 5, "Impact of 4Cs Skills Gap on the Economy," this book briefly explained and defined skills and competencies and distinguished between them in relationship to training. In addition, in Chapter 6, "Role of Needs Assessment in Competencies and Skills Development," this book explained what *Needs Assessment* is and how it can be used for assessing the gap and the depth of it in employees' skills. In this chapter, we attempt to briefly explain what *Competency-Based Training* is and how we can introduce EI training into competency-based training.

This chapter will cover the following elements:

- Competencies and Emotional Intelligence.
- What Is Competency-Based Training?
- Include Elements of EI and Emotions in the Training.

DOI: 10.4324/9781003462316-19

- Ten Steps Competency-Based Training Process.
- Methods for Measuring Performance.
- Use of Emotional Intelligence (EI) for Training and Development in 4Cs.
- Various Forms of Incorporating EI into 4Cs Skills Training.
- Diving Deep into the Advantages of EI Coaching.

Competencies and Emotional Intelligence

According to Donahue (2018), competencies may be defined as a composite of measurable and observable knowledge, skills, attitudes, and behaviors (KSABs) that enhance individuals' performance in their professional endeavors and facilitate the attainment of their personal and career objectives. Donahue (2018) argues that the term "competency" has acquired a colloquial connotation, being frequently employed as a buzzword devoid of substantive meaning. Contrarily, contemporary organizational development endeavors place significant emphasis on competency-based growth and education as the trajectory toward the future of education/learning, team building, and organization development (see Figure 15.1). "Competencies are the measurable and observable *knowledge, skills, attitudes, and behaviors* (KSABs) critical to successful job performance" (p. 21).

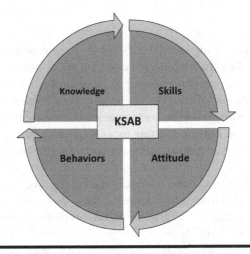

Figure 15.1   Knowledge, skills, attitudes, and behaviors (KSAB). © Bakhshandeh 2024.

Additionally, Donahue (2018) highlighted the observation that several organizations have either implemented or are now in the process of implementing formal skills assessments for their employees. Competency-based assessments are increasingly gaining popularity inside businesses as a means to evaluate the level of preparedness, effectiveness, task execution, and overall job performance of their workforce. "Thus, the level at which a person can demonstrate specific competencies will impact how valuable the person will be to an employer" (Donahue, 2018, p. 21).

Therefore, the utilization of EI competency-based evaluation and training, specifically focused on the cultivation of the 21st-century 4Cs skills, has significance and applicability in augmenting the prevalence and application of these skills within the labor force (Rothwell & Graber, 2010).

The evaluation of workers' existing 4Cs skills and their proficiency in each competence cluster is crucial in enabling organizations to develop strategic initiatives aimed at enhancing 4Cs skills in areas that require improvement. According to Donahue (2018), there is an expectation that the workforce will enhance their efficacy by operating with an elevated level of expertise, resulting in improved performance and increased productivity.

What Is Competency-Based Training?

Competency-based learning, often known as competency-based education, is a pedagogical paradigm that encompasses both teaching and assessment methodologies. It is also characterized as an educational approach centered on pre-established "competencies," emphasizing the attainment of certain objectives and practical application in real-world contexts (Rothwell & Graber, 2010). Competency-based learning is occasionally posited as a viable substitute for conventional modes of evaluation within educational and professional contexts. Within the context of a competency-based education framework, individuals, whether they are students or employees, exhibit their acquired knowledge and abilities to attain specified and particular "competencies" (Marousis, 2023).

The collection of competencies required for a certain course or within a given organization is commonly known as the competence standards. In the context of a competency-based learning paradigm, it is incumbent upon the teacher or trainer to delineate precise learning outcomes in relation to observable behaviors and performance while also establishing a suitable criteria level for assessing the attainment of these outcomes (Rothwell, Imroz, & Bakhshandeh, 2021). Experiential learning serves as a fundamental idea, whereas competency-based learning places emphasis on the student or employee and is frequently driven by the learner (Lytras et al., 2010).

The methodology of competency-based learning acknowledges that learners often encounter varying levels of difficulty when acquiring certain skills or competencies. Due to this rationale, the educational process often accommodates diverse individuals who progress at various rates within a given course. Moreover, whereas several conventional learning approaches rely on summative assessments, competency-based learning places emphasis on learners' attainment of specific learning goals. Learners and instructors possess the ability to adapt and modify instructional tactics in response to the performance of students in certain skills (Marousis, 2023; Lattuca & Stark, 2011).

According to Marousis (2023), the interpretation of competence mastery is contingent upon the specific subject matter and the criteria established by the instructor. In the domain of abstract learning, such as algebra, learners are typically expected to exhibit a certain level of proficiency in identifying suitable formulas. Conversely, in domains that have potential safety implications, such as operating a vehicle, instructors may demand a more comprehensive demonstration of mastery (Rothwell & Graber, 2010). Regardless of the comprehensiveness or thoroughness of training programs, it is unlikely that employees would retain all the facts after a single session. When it comes to the training of newly recruited personnel, it is crucial to provide them with feedback and direction that is tailored to their performance. Competency-based training plays a crucial function as a supplementary component of training, serving to address any ignored gaps and guarantee that employees have attained the requisite skills to effectively fulfill their job responsibilities (Lattuca & Stark, 2011).

Competency-Based Training Is Not Comprehensive Training

Competency-based training is an instructional methodology that centers on the assessment of employees' aptitude and expertise in order to ascertain their ability to carry out job responsibilities proficiently. The focus is placed on the cultivation of pragmatic skills and competencies, prioritizing their acquisition over the mere dissemination of theoretical information (Rothwell & Graber, 2010). A substantial component of competency-based training entails evaluating the employees' capacity to successfully execute a designated activity or achieve a predetermined aim. The primary objective is to detect deficiencies within their repertoire of abilities and offer targeted training programs to rectify these specific gaps (Sturgis & Casey, 2018).

Competency-based training is distinct from comprehensive training courses that provide a thorough overview of a particular topic or procedure from its inception to its conclusion. While it is crucial to provide thorough training, especially when introducing new employees or instructing them in a new ability from the beginning, it is acknowledged that they may not retain every aspect of the course or training session after their initial exposure (Kolb, 2014).

Include Elements of EI and Emotions in the Training

Envision a professional environment where workers have a sense of worth and stability. The individuals possess an understanding that they are integral to a broader undertaking, collaborating with others to establish an environment wherein individuals with starkly contrasting viewpoints may converge and establish agreement. If this evokes a sense of enchantment and folklore, do not lose hope. The implementation of emotional intelligence training programs for employees has the potential to facilitate the attainment of desired outcomes. This is the methodology employed (Garbarino, 2011).

Recognizing and Labeling Emotions

The use of emotional intelligence abilities is relevant across several industries. When individuals possess the capacity to identify and comprehend specific emotional stimuli and assign appropriate labels to them, they are able to gain insight into the reasons behind their reactions to various situations. In a rudimentary illustration, consider healthcare workers who are collaborating with families of individuals experiencing chronic or fatal illnesses. Employees who possess a higher level of emotional intelligence are more likely to effectively address the requirements of patients and their families compared to individuals who lack the ability to manage their emotions or engage in problem-solving during emotionally charged situations (Green & Palmer, 2019).

In many contexts, such as professional environments and workplaces, the use of emotional intelligence may assist employees in discerning the genuine underlying concerns throughout their work, thereby preventing the detrimental effects of rage, frustration, destructive behaviors, and impulsive reactions. Furthermore, this practice can prove to be particularly advantageous for educators, supervisors, and those in frontline managerial roles. Emotional intelligence, among several other soft talents, contributes to enhanced job performance and increased job satisfaction among individuals inside the workplace (Kite & Kay, 2012).

New Generation; New Workforce; New Work Environment

According to projections, it is anticipated that by the year 2025, over 75% of the labor force will consist of individuals belonging to the millennial generation. The personnel possess a strong aptitude for technology, have a preference for socially conscious organizations, and prioritize the practice of mindfulness in their professional pursuits. Millennials want employment opportunities with organizations that prioritize their worth and contributions. These individuals express a desire for their employers to possess emotional intelligence, which would facilitate their personal and professional development. As employers, it is also desirable to possess it.

According to research findings, individuals who possess high levels of emotional intelligence, although having ordinary intellectual abilities as measured by IQ, tend to outperform those with outstanding IQ scores around 70% of the time. What is the rationale behind this? Emotionally intelligent professionals possess a significant level of two crucial talents, namely personal competence, and social competence (Goleman, 2006).

Employees who possess a high level of personal competence are less likely to exhibit uncontrolled behavior in response to unsatisfactory circumstances. Individuals demonstrate resilience and a capacity to persevere in the midst of personal adversities. Certainly, these aforementioned employees also exhibit an elevated degree of social competency. Individuals possess the capacity to effectively interpret social cues and non-verbal signals in order to enhance their communication and comprehension within a given environment. They possess the ability to effectively handle this knowledge in order to engage with others from diverse backgrounds and in various emotional states. The measurement and instruction of emotional intelligence abilities pose inherent difficulties and complexities; however, they are not insurmountable (Connors, 2020).

Ten Steps Competency-Based Training Process

Competency-based training is a crucial aspect for firms, particularly within deskless sectors, as it serves to guarantee that employees possess the necessary skills and knowledge to carry out their job responsibilities with optimal effectiveness. The presence of competency gaps inside an organization can result in several negative consequences, including inefficiencies, errors, and accidents, all of which have the potential to significantly impact the company's performance and reputation (Gervais, 2016).

When employees see a pattern of repeated failure or underperformance in a task, it is likely to result in a decline in their motivation levels, which in turn negatively impacts their productivity. By promptly recognizing these deficiencies and providing assistance through competency-oriented training, both the person and the organization may maintain a competitive advantage. By proactively identifying gaps in competencies, organizations may effectively address these gaps and offer workers the requisite training and development opportunities to enhance their skills and knowledge. This phenomenon can lead to heightened levels of productivity, enhanced job quality, fewer mistakes, and heightened levels of customer pleasure (Rothwell & Graber, 2010).

Figure 15.2 illustrates the ten essential processes involved in the development and execution of a comprehensive competency-based training program for employees. This training program is specifically designed to address the skills gap pertaining to the 4Cs (communication, collaboration, critical thinking, and creativity).

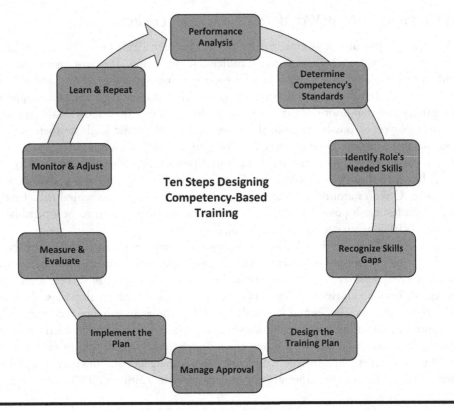

Figure 15.2   Ten key steps for establishing a competency-based training. © **Bakhshandeh 2024.**

Step 1: Performance Analysis

Determine in great detail the set of skills needed for each individual job function. This may be accomplished in a few different ways: by executing the task oneself, by examining one's work history and experience, or by utilizing the end that is wanted as a guide.

Step 2: Determine Competencies Standards

Establish standards for competency, as well as assessment criteria. Determine how the standard is going to be set, as well as how you are going to convey this information to the employee. Be sure to give some thought to how you will help them if they don't live up to your expectations.

Step 3: Identify Role's Needed Skills

Determine the kinds of abilities needed for a job in order to successfully do a specific task associated with a particular work process. To arrive at that conclusion, you can make use of something called a job performance standard (JPS), key performance indicators (KPI), or an industry skills standard.

Step 4: Recognize Skills Gaps

Evaluate the performance of personnel in comparison to the predetermined competency requirements, key performance indicators, or job performance criteria. You should see the employees accomplish the particular work when they are doing it themselves. Make notes on the areas in which they shine as well as those in which they have room for growth.

Step 5: Design the Training Plan

Create a useful training program by basing it on your observations and discoveries made while going through the processes outlined above. This program should be able to fill in any lacking skills or gaps in competencies. Make a decision on the training material, methodologies, and models that will be utilized throughout such training.

Step 6: Get Management Approval

At this point, you should present your training plan to the senior management in order to receive their buy-in and support as well as permission of the necessary time and budget, including any need for the use of external sources such as coaches, consultants, or space.

Step 7: Implement the Plan

Provide the staff with the chance for training and development so that any gaps in competency may be filled. Make sure it is inspiring, and make sure you present concrete solutions and ways forward. It is essential that they have a clear understanding of any weaknesses in a constructive light.

Step 8: Measure and Evaluate

You can determine how far along you are if you watch how well-acquired abilities and competencies are put into practice, and you should also ask direct superiors for their input. This will make it easier for you to analyze the influence that the training had on the development of skills and competencies.

Step 9: Monitor and Adjust

Maintaining a consistent system of monitoring and evaluation of employee performance is essential for sustaining growth. You can keep staff on track by providing them with ongoing opportunities to participate in reinforcement training sessions.

Step 10: Learn and Repeat

During the last two phases, you should collect and evaluate your results, examine the outcomes with the instructors, learn from what worked and what did not, and adapt your training plan for future usage based on what you discovered.

Methods for Measuring Performance

In the above section, several times we mentioned the terms job performance standards (JPS), key performance indicators (KPI), best industry practices, and criteria. Maybe it is a good idea to briefly explain and describe these terms.

Job Performance Standards (JPS)

The term "job performance standard" refers to the minimal educational qualification necessary for an employee to meet the expected level of performance in their role. A job performance standard refers to the level of production achieved by an employee who possesses average knowledge and skills or the average rate at which a person produces, as commonly referred to in colloquial language. This description expands upon McCormick's (1979) model, which is rooted in job analysis. McCormick's model posits that the standard or accepted time for a specific unit of work should be determined based on the time taken by a skilled worker, utilizing a standardized approach and working at a consistent pace, to complete a designated task (McCormick, 1979).

A work performance standard may be seen as a benchmark that represents the lowest acceptable level of performance expected from an employee. According to Cummings and Worley (2015), the job performance standard should be understood as a set of minimal performance standards or levels that workers are required to meet rather than being considered a goal, outcome, or aim.

Key Performance Indicator (KPI)

Over the past 20 years, numerous organizations have endeavored to align their organizational values, vision, mission, and strategic goals with key performance indicators (KPIs). These KPIs are measured using components of the Balanced Scorecard framework, and performance targets are established for individuals, teams, departments, and the organization as a whole (Rothwell & Bakhshandeh, 2022).

The Balanced Scorecard provides a framework for high-performance coaches, HPI practitioners, and managers to assess an organization's performance from four distinct perspectives (refer to Figure 6.3). It also addresses four fundamental questions related to the organization's performance metrics, taking into account its values, vision, mission, and strategies (Kaplan & Norton, 1996, 1992) (refer to Figure 15.3).

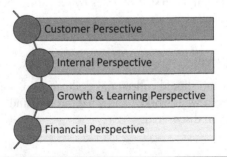

Figure 15.3 Organization's performance from four key perspectives. Note. Adapted from Kaplan and Norton (1996); Kaplan and Norton (1992).

- **Customer Perspective.** How do the clients and consumers perceive and establish a connection with your organization?
- **Internal Perspective.** This encompasses the efficiency, effectiveness, and performance level of company processes and procedures. What are the areas of expertise and distinctive qualities of your organization?
- **Growth and Learning Perspective.** The inherent capacities and advancements. Is it possible for us to sustain growth, enhance our capabilities, and generate value?
- **Financial Perspective.** How do you project yourself to the organization's shareholders? In summary, the bottom-line metrics refer to the evaluation of costs of products and revenue extremes.

(Kaplan & Norton, 1996,1992).

While this approach appears to be novel, it is important to note that the four categories of the Balanced Scorecard are linked to the conventional operational aspects and management framework of a healthcare organization. These categories include finance (pertaining to the financial bottom line), marketing (related to clients and customers), operations (encompassing processes, production, and structure), and growth and learning (focusing on human resources development) (Kaplan & Norton, 1996). Key performance indicators (KPIs) serve the purpose of translating an organization's overarching objectives into more manageable units on the performance chart, so facilitating comprehension for both managers and employees (Liraz, 2013).

Best Industry Practices

In addition to job performance standards and key performance indicators (KPIs), several businesses employ the Best Practices method as a means to provide a baseline for evaluating the performance indicators of their workforce. "A best practice is an exemplar, a practice worthy of emulation because it represents the best approach" (Rothwell, 2015, p. 118).

Many organizations engage in the process of seeking for and implementing best practices through internal benchmarking as well as using insights gained through external benchmarking. Camp (1989) defined benchmarking as "the search for industry best practices that lead to superior performance" (p. 11). The notion of Best Practices presents an alternative method for identifying the ideal course of action within an organization's interactions with both its internal and external environment, encompassing aspects such as employee performance and productivity.

Performance coaches and managers who adopt a coaching approach have the ability to conceptualize the ideal state of affairs by evaluating comparative practices within their teams, departments, and organizations. This enables them to gain insights from the exemplary practices employed by top performers and industry leaders within their own field, as well as from analogous sectors.

Criteria

Similar to key performance indicators (KPIs), the criteria that define the performance of the workforce are assessed based on the results or behaviors exhibited and are categorized as excellent (acceptable), average (moderate), or poor (unacceptable). The criteria serve as the benchmarks against which performance is evaluated. According to Cardy and Leonard (2011), it is essential that these criteria are established by a methodical evaluation of the work in question. The performance criteria must be specifically linked and oriented toward a work or task, hence facilitating the process of job or task analysis.

Concerning the significance of evaluating workers' performance against their jobs, Cardy and Leonard (2011) mentioned:

> It would not make business sense to judge someone on criteria that are unrelated to job performance. Yet, this is a common perception among employees, and charges of discrimination in the evaluation and management of performance are made on a routine basis.
>
> **(p. 43)**

Regrettably, some factors such as gender, age, and ethnicity, despite their lack of relevance to job performance, occasionally infiltrate the performance evaluations of employees by their managers or supervisors. The criteria elements in question pertain to the cognitive assessments of managers or supervisors, particularly in situations when the criteria for work or task performance is imprecise and ambiguous (Cardy & Leonard, 2011). In order to effectively employ criteria within company operations on a regular and pragmatic basis, it is imperative that those criteria possess a high degree of specificity, tangibility, and functionality. Cardy and Dobbins (1994) offer three fundamental levels of criteria, as seen in Figure 15.4.

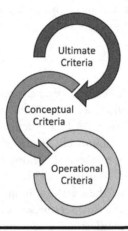

Figure 15.4   Correlation among levels of criteria. Note. Adapted from Cardy & Leonard (2011); Cardy & Dobbins (1994).

Ultimate Level. At this level, the objective of performance is elucidated, encompassing the communication of values or strategic intentions that underlie the task. The identification of definitive benchmarks can provide employees with a clear understanding of the expected objectives and goals associated with their role within a certain job. The utilization of ultimate criteria can serve as a valuable tool for a high-performance coach when constructing a justification for the preservation of one's performance and the sustained motivation required to maintain a high-performance level.

Conceptual Level. This level provides an explanation of the characteristics associated with performance. The conceptual level is situated one level below the ultimate level and serves as a potential means for attaining the ultimate requirements. When a business prioritizes "customer satisfaction" as a primary criterion, it is essential to consider factors such as product quality, manufacturing speed, adherence to specifications throughout delivery, and the provision of professional customer service at a conceptual level.

Operational Level. This level is a metric that would assess the level of performance. The operational level is responsible for converting abstract operational concepts into concrete and measurable indicators. When individuals within a company seek operational criteria, they are in search of answers to inquiries such as the following:

- What methods may be employed to assess the caliber of our products or services?
- How can the velocity of our output or the duration of our services be quantified?
- How can the monetary worth of our products or services be quantified?
- How can we effectively assess and improve the quality of experience for our consumers or clients?
- How can we determine whether our endeavors to enhance the quality of our products or services have had the desired impact?

One potential approach for comprehending the performance criteria includes conducting interviews with several managers and supervisors to inquire about the criteria that should be established for evaluating human performance inside the company, department, or group. The prompt provided in Table 15.1 can be utilized by the performance coach or the manager-as-coach in order to accomplish this objective.

Use of Emotional Intelligence (EI) for Training and Development in 4Cs

In this book, the author suggests using emotional intelligence and its related clusters as a platform for providing workforces with training and development in 4Cs skills.

Emotional Intelligence

EI has gained considerable recognition and importance in personal and professional development over the years. It is a crucial component for enhancing the 4Cs skills—communication, collaboration, critical thinking, and creativity. In this section, we will explore how the use of emotional intelligence can significantly benefit the training and development of these essential skills.

Critical Thinking

Critical thinking involves the ability to analyze information, evaluate situations, and make informed decisions. Emotionally intelligent individuals are better equipped to manage stress and maintain clarity of thought in high-pressure situations. They can also consider multiple perspectives and remain open to new ideas that are essential components of critical thinking. Training in emotional intelligence can help individuals develop resilience, adaptability, and the ability to approach problems with a calm and rational mindset.

Communication

Communication is the cornerstone of success in any field. EI plays a pivotal role in improving communication skills. Individuals with high EI are more attuned to their own emotions and those of others. This heightened awareness enables them to listen actively, empathize, and adapt their communication style to the needs and emotions of their audience. In a training context, teaching emotional intelligence can help individuals become better communicators by fostering empathy, active listening, and clear expression of thoughts and emotions.

Creativity

Creativity is about thinking outside the box, generating novel ideas, and solving problems in innovative ways. Emotional intelligence can fuel creativity by encouraging individuals to explore and express their emotions. Emotionally intelligent people often have a rich inner world that provides a wellspring of inspiration for creative endeavors. Moreover, EI can help individuals overcome self-doubt and fear of failure, which are common inhibitors of creative thinking.

Collaboration

Collaboration is essential in today's interconnected world. EI enhances collaboration by promoting better interpersonal relationships. People with high EI can navigate conflicts with finesse, understand the needs and motivations of their team members, and build trust. When individuals are trained to recognize and manage their emotions, they are better equipped to collaborate effectively, resolve conflicts, and build strong, cohesive teams.

Various Forms of Incorporating EI into 4Cs Skills Training

The following are just some of the means of incorporating EI into 4Cs skills training and development:

- **Self-awareness Exercises.** Activities that assist participants in becoming more in tune with their feelings, as well as their strengths and flaws, can be included in training programs. Emotional intelligence requires a strong basis, and this self-awareness serves as that foundation. The ability to think critically will be improved by this form of activity.
- **Empathy-building Activities.** Empathy is a vital component of good communication and cooperation abilities; exercises that enable individuals to comprehend and share the sentiments of others can help promote empathy in those who participate.
- **Stress Management Techniques.** Learning how to regulate stress and emotional reactions is essential for keeping a clear head when performing jobs that require critical thought, for cultivating a pleasant and creative atmosphere, and for improving one's ability to be creative.
- **Conflict Resolution Training.** Conflict is an inevitable byproduct of collaborative work, but people who are emotionally intelligent are better equipped to settle disagreements in a way that benefits everyone involved. Obtaining training in this area can increase one's ability to collaborate.
- **Mindfulness and Meditation.** Conflict is an unavoidable outcome of collaborative work, but individuals who are emotionally intelligent are better equipped to resolve differences in a way that is to the mutual advantage of all parties involved. A person's capacity to collaborate can be improved by the acquisition of training in this area.

Diving Deep into Advantages of EI Coaching

In the preceding chapter, the considerable benefits of employing emotional intelligence coaching were briefly alluded to. In this section, we will go further into the subject matter and provide a more comprehensive analysis of the advantages. We will also explore their significance in fostering the development of 4Cs abilities and competencies, specifically in relation to interpersonal relationships, professional pursuits, and personal fulfillment.

Increasing Level of Self-Awareness

Figure 15.5 represents a self-awareness model inspired by the Johari Window Model. The Johari Window is a conceptual tool that may be employed to enhance one's comprehension of both conscious and unconscious biases. Engaging in this practice has the potential to enhance one's self-awareness and comprehension of others. However, it may also serve as a tool for personal growth and fostering improved professional connections.

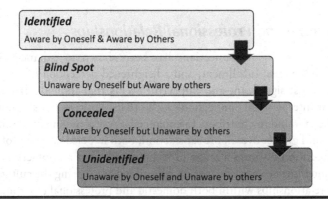

Figure 15.5   Self-awareness model.   Note. Inspired by the Johari Window and adapted from Bakhshandeh, Rothwell, & Imroz (2023).

Identified

At this level, individuals possess self-awareness regarding their emotions, thoughts, desires, attitudes, behaviors, and beliefs. These aspects of the individuals' inner world are also recognized and comprehended by others, irrespective of whether they have positive or negative, constructive or detrimental implications. The crucial aspect lies in the individuals' awareness of these aspects, as well as the recognition of them by others, within both personal and professional contexts.

Blind Spot

At this level, individuals lack self-awareness regarding their own emotions, thoughts, and actions, but those in their vicinity possess the ability to perceive and acknowledge the emotions and behaviors shown by the unaware individual. This scenario might be likened to a cognitive blind spot, when an individual lacks awareness of the perceptions and perspectives that others hold toward their own selves. These folks lack awareness of the underlying reasons behind the behaviors shown by those in their vicinity.

Concealed

At this level, individuals possess a heightened level of self-awareness regarding their emotions, thoughts, attitudes, and behaviors. However, they exhibit a remarkable ability to conceal these aspects from others, resulting in a lack of awareness among others regarding their true emotional and cognitive states. Consequently, this lack of awareness leads others to form inaccurate perceptions and beliefs about these individuals. This pertains to a rudimentary degree of self-awareness wherein an individual possesses an understanding of their own thoughts and evaluations of their emotions and activities.

Unidentified

At this level of self-consciousness, individuals lack conscious knowledge of their cognitive processes and emotional expressions while they also remain unnoticed by others. At this stage, their self-awareness remains unrecognized by both them and other observers. This phenomenon represents a profound lack of self-awareness regarding one's own actions.

Enhancing Personal and Professional Relationships

Cultivating strong interpersonal connections has been shown to enhance overall well-being, fostering a sense of happiness, fulfillment, and a heightened perception of support and connectedness. One of the most significant and impactful events that individuals might have in their life pertains to their interpersonal connections with others. Positive and supportive interpersonal connections have been found to contribute to enhanced physical and mental well-being, increased levels of happiness, and greater overall life satisfaction, both in personal and professional domains.

The following section illustrates a range of recommendations and practices derived from the field of emotional intelligence coaching, specifically aimed at fostering the cultivation of constructive and beneficial relationships within both domestic and professional environments.

Establish Rapport and Connect with Others

Rapport unites people and facilitates cooperation, communication, and most crucially, understanding. Rapport is emotional interactions with people and is the foundation for building relationships based on shared experiences or views.

Recognize, Respect, and Celebrate Diversity

We're all different, which makes partnerships difficult. We see the world in numerous ways. A desire or expectation that others think like us is a stumbling barrier while trying to form connections. This makes it simpler to generate rapport.

Acquire and Practice Communication Skills

Communication is not simply when you talk, but also when someone understands you. When it comes to communication, one of the biggest risks is assuming that the other person has grasped the point we are attempting to make.

Practice Elements of Active Listening

A person's ability to listen is a vital component of self-esteem building; it's the tacit kind of flattery that gives others a sense of worth and support. The most crucial element of a good connection is listening to and comprehending what people are saying to us.

Develop and Practice Empathy and Compassion

People connect when they have empathy and compassion for one another. It is the ability to understand and relate to the needs and feelings of another person without placing blame, offering counsel, or attempting to resolve the issue.

Be Approachable and Available to Others

Giving someone your time is also a great gift. We often lack the time to dedicate to our friends, family, and coworkers in a world where time is of the essence, and we are attempting to fit in many lifetimes.

Assist and Collaborate with Others

Offer assistance and your skills and knowledge to work together with others. Working together with others may lead to a better understanding of yourself and a stronger bond between you and them.

Be Open to Receiving and Giving Feedback

Though it might not always taste nice, feedback is the fuel of advancement and can be highly beneficial to you. Giving people constructive criticism encourages them to reach their full potential and may build enduring, mutually beneficial relationships.

Self-Rating Process. Please take some time now to browse over Table 15.1, using the supplied quality rating scale of 1 (the lowest) to 5 (the highest), and grade yourself on your level of paying attention and applying the categories of developing your personal and professional relationships. This exercise and honest self-evaluation of the process parts will improve your growth in the areas of 4Cs skills.

Table 15.1   Enhancing Personal and Professional Relationships Self-Rating Process

Instruction: (a) Using the rating scale (shown below), self-evaluate yourself as a manager, supervisor, or independent on enhancing your activities regarding personal and professional relationships, (b) then tally your rating, and (c) finally, come up with actions you will take to increase your rating on the next rating period.						
Date:		Participant:		Organization:		
Quality Rating Scale: **1** = Poor, **2** = Marginal, **3** = Acceptable, **4** = Good, **5** = Excellent						
#	*Categories*	*1*	*2*	*3*	*4*	*5*
1	Establish rapport and connect with others					
2	Recognize, respect, and celebrate diversity					

(Continued)

Table 15.1 (CONTINUED) Enhancing Personal and Professional Relationships Self-Rating Process

3	Acquire and practice communication skills					
4	Practice elements of active listening					
5	Develop and practice empathy and compassion					
6	Be approachable and available to others					
7	Assist and collaborate with others					
8	Be open to receiving and giving feedback					
Total per rating						
Total (total of above totals per ratings)						
Average (above total divided by 8)						
Three correctional and developmental actions I will take that will raise my three lowest self-ratings by at least one scale on the next rating:						
Action 1:						
Action 2:						
Action 3:						

Note. Author's original creation. © 2024 by Behnam Bakhshandeh.

Developing Skills for Career Improvement

The pursuit of career progression has significant importance for the majority of individuals, and the dearth of avenues for professional improvement stands as a primary catalyst for job transitions. A survey conducted (Longmore, Grant, & Golnaraghi, 2018) revealed that a significant majority of workers expressed their intention to remain committed to their present company in the event that they were provided with enough assistance for learning and development.

Occasionally, the responsibility is on individuals to choose training opportunities that align with their personal objectives and aspirations. This chapter aims to present a range of talents that may be cultivated through emotional intelligence coaching within the four primary clusters of self-awareness, self-regulation, social awareness, and relationship management.

These skills, whether acquired through organizational channels or pursued privately, are universally crucial for professional growth and progression.

Critical Thinking

Critical thinkers possess a set of characteristics that include skepticism, open-mindedness, a commitment to fair-mindedness, a reverence for facts and logic, an appreciation for clarity and precision, a willingness to consider other perspectives, and a readiness to revise their opinions based on rational deliberation. Possessing this talent is highly advantageous for those in managerial and leadership roles.

Self-Reflection

The initial step for individuals with ambitious aspirations in any professional capacity is the utilization of emotional intelligence to assess one's own competencies, knowledge base, and objectives for personal growth. Numerous organizations actively promote training programs that are specifically tailored to align with their corporate objectives, in order to fulfill their business planning and talent mapping requirements. It is important to cultivate the capacity to adopt a reflective stance, evaluate one's professional performance, and then pursue personal development opportunities. This frequently emphasizes the talents commonly referred to as soft skills.

Data Collection and Analysis

In the contemporary landscape, the prominence of digital information has become vital in propelling business and commerce. Consequently, possessing the capacity to gather, evaluate, and utilize data may significantly augment one's work opportunities. All individuals responsible for making decisions, ranging from high-level executives to lower-level managers, must possess the necessary skills and knowledge to handle data with confidence and in accordance with relevant regulations. In addition to facilitating company development, the ability to do forensic, real-time, and predictive analysis jobs is crucial.

Creativity and Innovative Thinking

The aforementioned field of learning and development is closely associated with the acquisition of this talent, which is vital in both job advancement and personal development. Occasionally, exceptional ideas of remarkable ingenuity may materialize overnight. However, it is frequently the case that innovation arises through a substantial amount of observation and inquiry.

Open Channels of Communication

A significant number of innovative concepts in the field of business arise from the strategic utilization of effective inquiry techniques and the promotion of open channels of communication both vertically and horizontally within a company (Rothwell, Imroz, & Bakhshandeh, 2021). Subsequently, it is vital to be prepared to allocate sufficient time toward the cultivation of practical methodologies for the purpose of expanding and substantiating the aforementioned preliminary ideas.

Managing Change with Ease

Not all modifications inside a company are met with enthusiasm, and even the most effective ones are invariably not straightforward. This is the reason why several organizations place significant importance on leaders who possess the ability to effectively lead in high-pressure situations. It is important to enhance one's capacity to effectively navigate and adapt to change while minimizing any potential resistance.

Flexibility and Agility

Being proficient in change management might be challenging if you possess a tendency to be inflexible and narrow-minded in your approach. Having a narrow perspective might also diminish one's capacity to anticipate future challenges. Developing the capacity to be more sensitive and adaptive is a skill that may need a gradual investment of time and effort.

Professional Resilience

Professional resilience implies an individual's inherent ability to flourish and succeed in challenging circumstances (Rothwell & Bakhshandeh, 2022). Resilience is exemplified by the decisions we make in navigating challenging circumstances, as well as our disposition and proactive approach toward taking action. By collaborating, we have the ability to enhance the professional resilience of both our peers and ourselves.

Collaboration Skills

Collaboration abilities encompass the ability to effectively engage in cooperative efforts with individuals and collectively attain a shared objective. However, the process extends beyond just completion of a project in collaboration with a team of individuals. Additionally, it entails cultivating interpersonal connections with one's team members, effectively addressing and resolving issues, and establishing a work milieu that fosters inclusivity and mutual respect for all individuals involved.

Problem-Solving Skills

These phenomena have been categorized collectively due to their capacity to be encapsulated by the concept of cognitive agility. Possessing an intuitive personality is advantageous (Martz, Hughes, & Braun, 2016). However, individuals may also cultivate this type of expertise to enhance their job advancement, as being the originator of pragmatic and efficient resolutions, they can further solidify their indispensability in any professional position.

Conflict Resolution Ability

The acquisition of this skill can be facilitated via the accumulation of extensive information and insightful perspectives, enabling individuals to rapidly access and use their acquired understanding. Having exceptional interpersonal and communication skills is advantageous in order to effectively integrate emotional intelligence with active listening.

Enhanced Presentation Skills

Your proficiency in the art of public speaking holds significant value across a wide range of professional positions and diverse contexts. Enhancing one's competence and confidence may be achieved via the acquisition of this skill, particularly in the context of negotiation, persuasion, and influence (Rothwell, 2013).

Digital Communication Technology

You can already perceive yourself as a proficient communicator capable of effectively engaging in meetings and networking events. Nevertheless, it is in this particular domain that there frequently exists potential for enhancement, particularly in the context of effective digital communication.

Self-Confidence

The acquisition of transferrable skills is crucial while transitioning between different professional trajectories. The possession of a positive self-perception and a true conviction in one's ability to contribute value to one's company (Goleman, 2014). The aforementioned reasons highlight the significance of investing in work skills, which can contribute to the development of a high degree of confidence.

Empathy

The cultivation of empathetic leadership abilities has the potential to positively impact one's work relationships, personal development, and professional opportunities. The measurement and simulation of empathy pose significant challenges, although its importance remains a subject of inquiry (Bakhshandeh, 2015). Empathy serves as a crucial component of emotionally intelligent leadership, including several skill sets such as change management and conflict resolution, as discussed before (Clarke, 2006).

Respect and Practice DEI

The shifting population composition in the United States and globally necessitates that enterprises take into account the requirements of an increasingly diverse and varied workforce. In addition, it is imperative for enterprises to reassess their current cultures and adopt novel structures, policies, and norms that are congruent with the values and requirements of the next workforce. This is necessary in order to effectively address matters of diversity, equality, and inclusion (DEI).

Self-Rating Process. Please take some time now to browse over Table 15.2 using the supplied quality rating scale of 1 (the lowest) to 5 (the highest), and grade yourself on your level of paying attention and applying the elements of developing skills for career improvement. This exercise and honest self-evaluation of the process parts will improve your growth in the 4Cs skills.

Table 15.2 Developing Skills for Career Improvement Self-Rating Process

Instruction: (a) Using the rating scale (shown below), self-evaluate yourself as a manager, supervisor, or independent on enhancing your activities regarding developing your skills for your career improvement, (b) then tally your rating, and (c) finally, come up with actions you will take to increase your rating on the next rating period.							
Date:		Participant:		Organization:			
*Rating Scale: **1** = Poor, **2** = Marginal, **3** = Acceptable, **4** = Good, **5** = Excellent*							
#	*Elements*			*1*	*2*	*3*	*4*	*5*
1	Critical Thinking							
2	Self-Reflection							
3	Data Collection and Analysis							
4	Creativity and Innovative Thinking							
5	Open Channels of Communication							
6	Managing Change with Ease							
7	Flexibility and Agility							
8	Professional Resilience							
9	Collaboration Skills							
10	Problem-Solving Skills							
11	Conflict Resolution Ability							
12	Enhanced Presentation Skills							
13	Digital Communication Technology							
14	Self-Confidence							
15	Empathy							
16	Respect and Practice DEI							
	Total per rating							
	Total (total of above totals per ratings)							
	Average (above total divided by 16)							
Three correctional and developmental actions I will take that will raise my three lowest self-ratings by at least one scale on the next rating:							
Action 1:							
Action 2:							
Action 3:							

Note. Author's original creation. © 2024 by Behnam Bakhshandeh.

Enriched Experience of Contentment and Satisfaction

The prevailing belief instilled in many individuals is that pleasure is intricately connected to your achievements. You would hypothesize that the attainment of marriage would engender happiness, or that a promotion in the workplace would result in increased job satisfaction. It is evident that you have the ability to cultivate a sense of satisfaction in the present moment, irrespective of external conditions (Green & Palmer, 2019).

Genuine satisfaction may be seen as a profound inner state characterized by the acceptance of one's current circumstances and personal identity. Frequently, individuals become deeply immersed in their demanding routines to the extent that they fail to perceive their present circumstances. Upon resurfacing, individuals tend to direct their attention toward their past or future circumstances rather than their present state (Garbarino, 2011). Put simply, our attention is directed toward either the preceding or forthcoming periods, as opposed to the current moment. Is that concept recognizable? However, prior to achieving satisfaction with our current state, it is imperative that we possess a comprehensive understanding of our existing circumstances.

The transitory nature of happiness derived from achievement or material possessions is evident. Even those who appear to possess many resources and achievements can struggle to attain happiness, as they continuously strive for further acquisitions and harbor dissatisfaction with their own circumstances. It is important to elucidate that the state of happiness does not negate the presence of aspiration. This does not imply a lack of desire for further resources (Garbarino, 2011). Contentment may be seen as a state of being characterized by the virtues of thankfulness, appreciation, and acceptance, which are directed toward the present circumstances. Therefore, begin the initial action toward attaining a state of contentment. Engaging in this practice will bestow upon you a perpetual benefit throughout the entirety of your existence.

Happiness Versus Contentment

The terms "happiness" and "contentment" are frequently employed synonymously, but they represent distinct states of existence. While the experience of happiness is often transitory and ephemeral, contentment may be seen as a cognitive and emotional state that permeates one's overall thought and is consistently present across many contexts and circumstances. Gaining knowledge of further distinctions will enhance one's ability to cultivate contentment in life. There exist several distinctions between satisfaction and happiness (Green & Palmer, 2019).

- The experience of happiness is subject to the impact of external stimuli, whereas contentment is shaped by a combination of both external and internal elements.
- Happiness is typically experienced on a short-term basis, but contentment tends to be more enduring in nature.
- Happiness may be classified as an emotional experience, while contentment can be characterized as a disposition and cognitive state.
- Happiness may be understood as a transient emotional response, whereas contentment refers to a sustained state of tranquility that endures over time.

The maintenance of happiness and contentment can be achieved by the deliberate selection of a sequence of conscious decisions. This section focuses on exploring beneficial exercises that facilitate the development of happiness and fulfillment in life through the utilization of the emotional intelligence coaching technique.

Be True to Yourself

Individuals possess varying perspectives on what they perceive as significant or purposeful. Hence, the maintenance of one's genuine identity is vital to sustaining a state of contentment throughout life. Why should people make an effort to portray themselves as someone they are not? (Bakhshandeh, 2009). To enhance the individuals' self-awareness and gain insight into personal passions, it is essential to cultivate a deeper understanding of themselves. This enables individuals to maintain a sense of concentration on the aspects of life that have significant value to them.

Create a Vision for Your Life

A vision refers to a comprehensive and overarching perspective. The life's vision of an individual encompasses their desired identity, the reputation they aspire to establish, and the specific array of experiences and achievements they strive to attain (Bakhshandeh, 2009). The ability to see and conceptualize a vision aids in establishing objectives by providing a structure for assessing and appraising these objectives.

Suspend Contact

When you encounter dissatisfaction with an individual or a situation, it is advisable to take a little break. Engage in a deliberate inhalation and exhalation of air, while consciously acknowledging the necessity of accepting others in their current state and appreciating their positive attributes or adopting a positive perspective when faced with challenging circumstances.

Exhibit Appreciation for Others

It is important to maintain a state of presence. Extend compassionate words and engage in benevolent activities to foster the growth of your emotional reservoir. The greater the extent to which you contribute to society, the more reciprocation you are likely to get.

Show More Gratitude

The process of cultivating thankfulness facilitates an enhanced concentration on good feelings and serves as a reminder of the significance of many aspects in one's life. One effective strategy for cultivating a sense of gratitude is to engage in the practice of journaling, wherein individuals can freely express and document their ideas using a style or voice of their choosing.

Journal Your Feelings

Although journaling is typically seen as a personal activity, it is also possible to express one's gratitude to friends or loved ones. Research has indicated that the act of sharing happy experiences with others has the effect of intensifying positive feelings and ultimately contributing to an increased sense of life satisfaction. This statement emphasizes the significance of identifying the aspects that hold personal significance in one's life and the subsequent emotional satisfaction derived from engaging with them.

Express Your Creativity

Creative expression refers to the cognitive capacity and imaginative prowess that enables individuals to generate artistic or original manifestations that serve as reflections of their unique selves. There exists a myriad of avenues via which individuals might manifest their creative inclinations, including domains such as music, visual art, crafting, writing, photography, theater, and dance.

Keep in Touch with Your Loved Ones

Maintaining tight relationships with friends and loved ones enhances one's social well-being and capacity to navigate adversities in life. Empirical evidence indicates that an individual's support system plays a crucial role in facilitating problem-solving abilities, stress management, and the enhancement of self-esteem. The individuals inside your social network provide you with unwavering support throughout both moments of success and adversity. Despite residing at a considerable distance from your cherished individuals, it is necessary to exert ourselves in maintaining frequent communication with them by various technological means, such as telephonic conversations, video conferencing, or instant messaging.

Find Joy in Simple Things

Significant dialogues, engaging in nature walks, engaging in the act of perusing a well-written literary work, an excursion to the seaside are activities that are provided at no cost and frequently yield greater satisfaction than costlier pursuits.

Live in Now

Avoid delaying the experience of happiness by refraining from waiting for a future time when your life is characterized by reduced levels of busyness or stress. The possibility of the day occurring is uncertain. Instead, you should actively seek out occasions to appreciate and get enjoyment from the simple and mundane joys that are encountered in everyday existence. It is advisable to direct one's attention toward the favorable aspects of the present moment, rather than fixating on previous events or harboring concerns about the future.

Drop the Past

Ruminating on previous experiences is not conducive to effectively engaging with the current moment. However, relinquishing attachment to previous events enables individuals to direct their attention onto the current moment and future prospects. It is essential to direct one's attention toward that which warrants appreciation. Releasing yourself from the past might be a challenging endeavor, although it is possible to gradually relinquish its hold by incremental measures. One possible approach to achieving this objective is through the practice of self-forgiveness, when individuals acknowledge their faults and recognize the ample opportunities for personal growth and development that lie ahead in their future life experiences.

Set Goals for Yourself

One's objectives are indicative of their aspirations and desires in life. Contributions to one's life are crucial in fostering a sense of fulfillment and satisfaction, thus enhancing the overall meaningfulness of one's existence. Consider employing the specific, measurable, attainable, realistic, and timely (SMART) goal-setting methodology as a means to establish purpose-driven objectives that are in accordance with your own beliefs. If individuals have difficulties in life planning, they may consider establishing short-term objectives as a means to enhance self-assurance and maintain a pragmatic list of tasks.

Stop the Clutter

When experiencing the desire to make a purchase, it is advisable to contemplate if the item in question is a necessity or a desire. When considering an item that is classified as a "want," it is important to reflect on the reasons for one's dissatisfaction with their current possessions. Ask yourself: Is it now necessary for me to possess this item? It is advisable to exercise patience for a few days and see whether the want to make the purchase diminishes.

Maintain Your Health and Vitality

The maintenance of one's physical and mental well-being extends beyond the transient experience of immediate gratification. The attainment of a long and tranquil future necessitates the cultivation of both mental and physical well-being. Begin considering mindfulness techniques that can contribute to your mental well-being, such as engaging in meditation and yoga, in order to effectively manage stress levels and maintain a positive emotional state. When considering one's physical well-being, it is advisable to contemplate strategies that promote bodily movement that elicits a sense of pleasure, as well as the consumption of nourishing meals that provide adequate sustenance.

Self-Rating Process. Please take some time now to browse over Table 15.3, using the supplied quality rating scale of 1 (the lowest) to 5 (the highest), and grade yourself on your level of paying attention and applying the elements of enriching your experience of contentment and satisfaction. This exercise and honest self-evaluation of the process parts will improve your growth in the 4Cs skills.

Table 15.3   Enriched Experience of Contentment and Satisfaction Self-Rating Process

Instruction:
(a) Using the rating scale (shown below), self-evaluate yourself as a manager, supervisor, or independent on enhancing your activities regarding enriching your experience of contentment and satisfaction, (b) then tally your rating, and (c) finally, come up with actions you will take to increase your rating on the next rating period.

Date:	Participant:				Organization:		
Rating Scale: 1 = Poor, 2 = Marginal, 3 = Acceptable, 4 = Good, 5 = Excellent							
#	*Elements*		*1*	*2*	*3*	*4*	*5*
1	Be true to yourself						
2	Create a vision for your life						
3	Suspend contact						
4	Exhibit appreciation for others						
5	Show more gratitude						
6	Journal your feelings						
7	Express your creativity						
8	Keep in touch with your loved ones						
9	Find joy in simple things						
10	Live in now						
11	Drop the past						
12	Set goals for yourself						
13	Stop the clutter						
14	Maintain your health and vitality						
	Total per rating						
	Total (total of above totals per ratings)						
	Average (above total divided by 14)						
Three correctional and developmental actions I will take that will raise my three lowest self-ratings by at least one scale on the next rating:							
Action 1:							
Action 2:							
Action 3:							

Note. Author's original creation. © 2024 by Behnam Bakhshandeh.

Revisit the Summary of Emotional Intelligence Cluster and Competencies

This is a good time to revisit Table 13.2, "Summary of Emotional Intelligence Clusters, Competencies and Qualities and Correspondence 4Cs Skills," of Chapter 13. You can include the findings represented in that table in an EI-based competency-based training and development undertaking for your workforce. The following two paragraphs are directly from Chapter 13 for the purpose of refreshing your memory.

> Based on recommendations, evaluations, and deliberations regarding the implementa-tion of emotional intelligence as a training method to enhance the development of 4Cs skills within the workforce, the subsequent Table 13.2 presents the outcomes pertaining to emotional intelligence clusters, associated competencies, attributions, and qualities exhibited by individuals possessing such competencies and capabilities. Furthermore, the table highlights the relevance of at least two of these competencies to the four components of 21st-century 4Cs skills, namely critical thinking, communica-tion, creativity, and collaboration.
>
> (Chapter 13, Table 13.2)

> Irrespective of the pairing of at least two of the four 4Cs skills with any of the emo-tional intelligence competencies outlined in Table 13.2, it is worth noting that these competencies, capabilities, attributes, and qualities positively influence all the 21st-century 4Cs skills. Furthermore, they aid organizations in effectively training and developing their workforces in order to enhance the quality and utility of the 4Cs skills. In essence, the competencies above and attributes can serve as focal points for enhancing worker capabilities concerning their 4Cs talents.
>
> (Chapter 13, Table 13.2)

What Is Next?

Chapter 16, "Implementation, and Management of Training and Development," explores key ele-ments required for delivering an effective EI coaching and the process of coaching interventions. In addition, Chapter 16 displays what it takes to be an EI coach, the role of the team leader as the change agent, and how to evaluate training and development.

References

Bakhshandeh, Behnam. (2009). *Conspiracy for Greatness: Mastery on Love Within*. San Diego, CA: Primeco Education, Inc.

Bakhshandeh, Behnam. (2015). *Anatomy of Upset: Restoring Harmony*. Carbondale, PA: Primeco Education, Inc. development. Pennsylvania State University.

Bakhshandeh, Behnam & Rothwell, William J. (Eds.) (2024). *Building an Organizational Coaching Culture*. Oxfordshire, UK: UK Limited Trading, Taylor & Francis Group. Routledge.

Bakhshandeh, Behnam, Rothwell, William J., & Imroz, Sohel M. (2023). *Transformational Coaching for Effective Leadership. Creating Sustainable Change Through Shifting Paradigms*. New York, NY: Taylor & Francis Group. Routledge.

Camp, Robert C. (1989). *Benchmarking: The Search for Industry Best Practices That Lead to Superior Performance.* Milwaukee, WL: Quality Press.

Cardy, R. L. & Dobbins, G. H. (1994). Performance appraisal: The influence of liking on cognition. *Advances in Managerial Cognition and Organizational Information Processing, 5,* 115–140.

Cardy, Robert L. & Leonard, Brian. (2011). *Performance Management. Concepts, Skills and Exercises.* Armonk, NY: Me. E. Sharp. Inc.

Clarke, N. (2006). Emotional intelligence training: A case of caveat emptor. *Human Resource Development Review, 5*(4), 422–441. https://doi.org/10.1177/1534484306293844.

Connors, Christopher D. (2020). *Emotional Intelligence for the Modern Leader.* Emeryville, CA: Rockridge Press.

Cummings, Thomas G. & Worly, Christopher G. (2015). *Organization Development & Change* (10th ed.). Stamford, CT: Cengage Learning.

Donahue, Wesley E. (2018). *Building Leadership Competence. A Competency-Based Approach to Building Leadership Ability.* State College, PA: Centerstar Learning.

Garbarino, James. (2011). *The Positive Psychology of Personal Transformation: Leveraging Resilience for Life Change.* Chicago, IL: Springer.

Gervais, J. (2016). The operational definition of competency-based education. *The Journal of Competency-Based Education, 1*(2), 98–106. https://doi.org/10.1002/cbe2.1011.

Goleman, Daniel. (2006). *Social Intelligence; The Revolutionary New Science of Human Relationships.* New York, NY: Banton Books.

Goleman, Daniel. (2014). What it takes to achieve managerial success. *TD: Talent Development, 68*(11), 48–52.

Green, Suzy & Palmer, Stephen. (Eds.) (2019). *Positive Psychology Coaching in Practice.* New York, NY: Routledge.

Kaplan, Robert S. & Norten, David P. (1992). The balanced scorecard: Measures that drive performance. *Harvard Business Review.* Retrieved from https://hbr.org/1992/01/the-balanced-scorecard-measures-that-drive-performance-2.

Kaplan, Robert S. & Norton, David P. (1996). *The Balanced Scorecard: Translating Strategy Action.* Cambridge, MA: Harvard Business Press.

Kite, Neilson & Kay, Frances. (2012). *Understanding Emotional Intelligence.* Philadelphia, PA: Koganpage.

Kolb, David A. (2014). *Experiential Learning: Experience as the Source of Learning and Development* (2nd ed.). Upper Saddle, NJ: FT Press.

Lattuca, Lisa R. & Stark, Joan S. (2011). *Shaping the College Curriculum: Academic Plans in Context.* Hoboken, NJ: John Wiley & Sons.

Liraz, Meri. (2013). *How to Implement Management by Objectives in Your Business a Step by Guide to Implementing MBO.* (No City) Liraz Publishing.

Longmore, A. -L., Grant, G., & Golnaraghi, G. (2018). Closing the 21st-century knowledge gap: Reconceptualizing teaching and learning to transform business education. *Journal of Transformative Education, 16*(3), 197–219. https://doi.org/10.1177/1541344617738514.

Lytras, Miltiadis D., Pablos, Patricia Ordonez De, Avison, David, Sipior, Janice, Jin, Qun, Filho, Walter Leal, Uden, Lorna, Thomas, Michael, & Cervai, Sara. (2010). *Technology Enhanced Learning: Quality of Teaching and Educational Reform: 1st International Conference, TECH-EDUCATION 2010, Athens, Greece, May 19–21, 2010.* Proceedings. Berlin: Springer Science & Business Media.

Marousis, Athena. (2023, April). Competency based training: definition, examples, and how to implement it step by step. *Talentcards. Learning and Development.* Retrieved from https://www.talentcards.com/blog/competency-based-training/

Martz, B., Hughes, J., & Braun, F. (2016). Creativity and problem-solving: Closing the skills gap. *The Journal of Computer Information Systems, 57*(1), 39–48. https://doi.org/10.1080/08874417.2016.118149.

McCormick, Ernest J. (1979). *Job Analysis: Methods and Applications.* New York, NY: AMACO.

Rothwell, William J. (2013). *Performance Consulting: Applying Performance Improvement in Human Resource Development.* San Francisco, CA: John Wiley & Sons.

Rothwell, William J. (2015). *Beyond Training & Development: Enhancing Human Performance Through a Measurable Focus on Business Impact (3rd ed.).* Amherst, MA: HRD Press, Inc.

Rothwell, Willian J. & Bakhshandeh, Behnam (2022). *High-Performance Coaching for Managers. Step-by-Step Approach to Increase Employees' Performance and Productivity.* New York, NY: Taylor & Francis Group. Routledge.

Rothwell, William J. & Graber, James M. (2010). *Competency-Based Training Basics.* Alexandria, VA: ASTD Press.

Rothwell, William J., Imroz, Sohel M., & Bakhshandeh, Behnam. (2021). *Organization-Development Interventions: Executing Effective Organizational Chang.* New York, NY: Taylor & Francis Group. CRC Press.

Sturgis, Chris & Casey, Katherine. (2018). *Quality Principles for Competency-Based Education (PDF).* Vienna, VA: iNACOL.

Chapter 16

Implementation and Management of Training and Development

Introduction

Executing, overseeing, and providing a training session is not as simple as some may assume, particularly when educating on a subject as delicate as emotional intelligence. Creating a conducive atmosphere for training and coaching necessitates a transformation in behavior at all levels, with a special emphasis on organizational leaders. Although mentoring others might be a time-intensive task, many leaders frequently discover that issuing directives and expecting obedience is more efficient and effortless.

This chapter covers the following elements of implementing and managing of using EI for 4Cs skills training and development:

- Organization Leadership Buy-In for EI Training.
- Role of Organization Leaders in Coaching and Training.
- Process of Emotional Intelligence Coaching and Training.
- Role of Transformational Coaching in Emotional Intelligence Coaching.
- The Fundamental Principles of Transformational Coaching.
- Fundamental Requirements for Personal Transformation.
- The Way of Being.
- Integrating Coaching Methods to Compliment Transformational Coaching.
- Tips for Successful Coaching.
- Understanding and Practicing EI Clusters and Competencies Self-Evaluation.
- Team Leader as the Change Agent.
- Training and Development Evaluation.

DOI: 10.4324/9781003462316-20

Organization Leadership Buy-In for EI Training

In order to establish a coaching culture that would welcome training, it is imperative to engage organizational leaders and leadership at all levels to exemplify the characteristics and practices of coaching. Put simply, people must lead by demonstrating their actions and expressing their words. They should be able to mentor or coach others to help them achieve their full capabilities while also being receptive to accepting mentorship themselves (Bakhshandeh & Rothwell, 2024). This will encompass tactics for cultivating coaching proficiency and benchmarks for assessing whether a leader is employing a directive and authoritative style or an empowering and inclusive one. Organizational leaders who demonstrate the desired behaviors are more likely to observe their staff doing such behaviors (Zaballero, 2024).

The role of organizational leaders in establishing a coaching culture that embraces training is crucial as they establish the atmosphere, generate commitment, exemplify coaching behaviors, offer assistance, and distribute resources (Zaballero, 2024). Through the prioritization of coaching and development, leaders can establish a culture that fosters ongoing learning, resulting in heightened employee engagement, enhanced performance, and promoted training and reduced attrition (Yukl, 2013).

To cultivate a happy and empowered workforce, it is essential to have a proactive stance toward culture development and equip leaders with the necessary skills and resources for their success. Nevertheless, certain corporate leaders lack knowledge about the principles of coaching and the concept of fostering a coaching culture and even needed training and development because they may be unaware as to what training may be needed for their organizations (Bakhshandeh & Rothwell, 2024). Assisting people in this undertaking is complex and involves a deliberate process of evaluating the issue, adapting coaching methods, defining the leadership's responsibilities, and establishing a structure for ongoing training and development (Zaballero, 2024).

Role of Organization Leaders in Coaching and Training

Effectively managing a culture of development in dynamic contexts may be extremely challenging. Nevertheless, a coaching and training culture may thrive in an environment characterized by constant change, where innovation, learning, transformation, and flexibility are the standard practices. An organizational setting must foster a culture of individual learning and critical thinking among all its members, prioritizing empowerment above strict control and direction (Vesso & Alas, 2016).

Be a Behavior Model

Organizational leaders may demonstrate coaching and training on a regular basis by integrating coaching behaviors into their everyday interactions, as well as by actively participating in both being coached and coaching others and participating in training and development programs. They may facilitate their understanding of how coaching can enhance their comprehension of the coaching process, acquire novel tactics and strategies, and polish their aptitude in communication and leadership (Zaballero, 2024). Additionally, it can aid in the cultivation of self-assurance, the construction of resilience, and the regulation of one's emotions and actions.

They may enhance their coaching skills and establish a coaching and development culture inside their organizations through self-coaching. In order to effectively mentor and coach others, it is crucial that they consistently offer constructive criticism, pose open-ended inquiries, and attentively engage with their team members. By doing this, they can establish a precedent that others can emulate. Promote coaching dialogues which are centered around goal establishments, skill enhancements, or professional advancements that facilitates the acquisition of understanding, precision, and outlook. The key behaviors that need to be exhibited include active listening, employing open-ended questions, providing feedback, and offering support and encouragement (Gormley & van Nieuwerburgh, 2014).

Determine Expectations

Establishing explicit coaching and training expectations and outcomes is essential and ensures that they align with the strategic objectives and expectations of other leaders within the organization. The strength of a coaching and training culture relies on its foundation, which may be bolstered by the presence of organizational leaders acting as pillars (Bakhshandeh & Rothwell, 2024). Expectations include adherence to confidentiality guidelines to safeguard the privacy and confidentiality of all information exchanged during coaching sessions; establishing the frequency and duration of structured coaching and training sessions; and addressing logistical details, including location, format, and timing (Zaballero, 2024).

The leaders in their business have a vital role in establishing coaching and training expectations that effectively convey the goal and advantages of coaching or training. This results in obtaining support and agreement from individuals at all levels, particularly when those in positions of authority continually demonstrate coaching behavior. Leaders need to encourage their organizational leaders to collaborate vertically and horizontally to establish and clarify overall coaching and training expectations which encompass the coach's objectives, duties, responsibilities, and the individuals being coached (Milner, McCarthy, & Milner, 2018).

Assign and Distribute Resources

The allocation of resources serves as a clear indicator of the intrinsic worth of any effort to all stakeholders. Suppose company leaders express their support for a coaching and training culture but fail to provide the necessary resources to enable it. Under those circumstances, coaching or training will be perceived as a passing trend lacking durability (Zaballero, 2024). To establish a productive coaching and training environment, it is essential to have access to exemplars, evaluation instruments, systems for receiving feedback, training opportunities, and resources. Technology can serve as a means to facilitate coaching and training. Coaching may be made more accessible and efficient through the utilization of tools such as coaching platforms, video conferencing, and online coaching materials (Bakhshandeh & Rothwell, 2024).

Promote the allocation of resources by organizational leaders towards coaching and training. This includes the provision of coaching, training and development, the availability of coaching tools, and the option to engage external coaches as necessary. Corporate leaders actively endorse coaching programs by allocating resources such as time and money, fostering a culture of participation among all individuals. This demonstrates the significance of coaching and training inside their business.

Connect the Outcome to the Organization's Goals

Well-defined coaching or training objectives are essential for effective communication among their organizational leaders. This entails establishing quantifiable and attainable objectives, pinpointing pivotal performance indicators that demonstrate advancement, and delineating the intended outcomes (Bakhshandeh & Rothwell, 2024). Coaches may enhance support and agreement across all levels by assisting their organizational leaders in establishing and harmonizing measures to gauge progress. This entails identifying specific areas where coaching exerts the most significant influence, such as enhancing employee engagement and improving staff retention (Zaballero, 2024).

Create a Coaching and Training Program

An organizational coaching program, initiated and backed by their executives, may provide comprehensive guidance to the whole business. Figure 16.1 depicts the suggested procedures. The following processes adhere to the analyze, design, develop, implement, and evaluate (ADDIE) methodology and are crucial for training purposes. The ADDIE methodology was developed during the 1970s at the Center for Educational Technology at Florida State University. The notion was originally conceived as a constituent of a United States military training endeavor (Zaballero, 2024). It is vital for both trainers and their organizational executives to contemplate how coaching and training may effectively bolster their organization's objectives. Ensure to inquire about the rationale, purpose, timing, location, individuals involved, and methodology of the coaching or training programs. By responding to these inquiries, coaches may establish the program's objective and verify that it is in accordance with their organization's objectives.

Figure 16.1   ADDIE model of creating coaching program. Note. Adapted from: Florida State University's Center for Educational Technology, 1970s.

Integrate Coaching with Performance Management

Coaches should promote the incorporation of coaching and training into performance management among their organizational leaders by establishing explicit objectives, delivering constructive criticism, and fostering occasions for enhancing skills and advancing. Additionally, this will guarantee that both their leaders and other members of the company are held responsible for establishing a coaching, training, and development culture. Support leaders in evaluating coaching programs/initiatives to ensure they align with objectives (Zaballero, 2024). This may involve soliciting input from coaches, trainers, workers, and other relevant parties and monitoring and analyzing crucial performance and growth indicators.

Table 16.1 is a valuable tool that can be shared with the trainers' organizational leaders to enhance their effectiveness in creating and sustaining a coaching and training culture. This tool is specifically developed to assist leaders in evaluating their efficacy and conducting a thoughtful evaluation of their existing coaching and training methodologies. The tool can provide valuable insights into areas for growth in maximizing their role in promoting a coaching and training culture.

Table 16.1 Role of Organization Leaders in a Coaching and Training Self-Rating Form

Role of Organization Leaders in a Coaching and Training Self-Rating Form						
Instruction: (a) Using the rating scale (shown below), self-evaluate yourself as a manager, supervisor, or independent on enhancing your activities regarding your role of organization leaders in a coaching and training, (b) then tally your rating, and (c) finally, come up with actions you will take to increase your rating on the next rating period.						
Date:	Participant:				Organization:	
Rating Scale: 1 = Poor, 2 = Marginal, 3 = Acceptable, 4 = Good, 5 = Excellent						
#	*Roles and Activities*	*1*	*2*	*3*	*4*	*5*
1	Be a Behavior Model					
2	Determine Expectations					
3	Assign and Distribute Resources					
4	Connect the Outcome to the Organization's Goals					
5	Create a Coaching and Training Program					
6	Integrate Coaching with Performance Management					
	Total per rating					
	Total (total of above totals per ratings)					
	Average (above total divided by 6)					
Three correctional and developmental actions I will take that will raise my three lowest self-ratings by at least one scale on the next rating:						
Action 1:						
Action 2:						
Action 3:						

Note. Adapted from Bakhshandeh & Rothwell (2024) and Zaballero (2024).

Process of Emotional Intelligence Coaching and Training

The sequential stages of an emotional intelligence (EI) coaching or training intervention may be observed in Figure 16.2 and Table 16.1, spanning from the first phase to its completion. Consider this process as a comprehensive approach to inspire and empower employees to change their viewpoints and behaviors in order to establish and participate in an organizational coaching culture. The essential stages in this process can be modified to accommodate the needs of certain employees and situations, as well as the type of support provided by certified coaches.

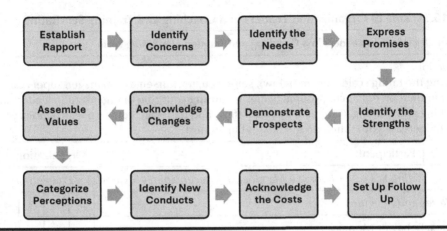

Figure 16.2   Process of emotional intelligence coaching. Note. Adapted from Rothwell and Bakhshandeh (2022).

Establish Rapport

Establishing rapport and cultivating a sense of relatedness are crucial for promoting transparent and sincere communication between a coach or trainer and coachee or participants in any coaching or training approaches.

Identify Concerns

Attentively address the coachees' or participants' anxieties, fears, or any other emotional or mental issues that may hinder their active engagement and prevent them from sharing their gifts with other team members or organizations. Coaches should recognize the presence of any worries that they may have, such as prejudice or prejudgment.

Identify the Needs

Collaborate closely with the coachees or participants to thoroughly understand the requirement for change and the importance of making the required modifications in response to the need, whether it is for personal or professional purposes.

Express Promises

The present time is the opportune time to discuss their dedication to attend to these requirements and the method of tutoring that focuses on strengths. The foundation of this revolutionary coaching or training session will be their explicit declaration of dedication and promises.

Identify the Strengths

The participants are invited to inquire about their inherent talents and identify their top three or four strengths that have consistently contributed to their achievements.

Demonstrate Prospects

Inquire about possible strategies to use their skills in order to meet their desired criteria. Provide them with illuminating elucidations about the concept of opportunity and how they may effectively utilize their skills to capitalize on such prospects.

Acknowledge Changes

Examine the necessary modifications in light of the newly identified strengths and available possibilities. Reassure them that the act of change is a voluntary decision made by themselves. Clarify to them that no alternative surpasses another; each possesses its own array of disadvantages. Motivate them to recognize the correlation between their requirements and their decisions.

Assemble Values

Which set of novel values and guiding principles would they embrace to navigate these recent transformations effectively? Ensure that individuals comprehend that their previous values are not inherently flawed and do not necessarily require abandonment. However, it is important for them to cultivate novel values and grasp the underlying reasons for the alterations if they want to effectively navigate new changes and harness their abilities to do so.

Categorize Perceptions

Possessing varying perspectives and viewpoints is typical; there is no reason for apprehension. Nevertheless, it is vital to instruct them in the process of comprehending that because of the application of their recently acquired principles and desired enhancements in their approaches, they possess the capability to generate a fresh perspective of themselves, others, productivity, and performance.

Identify New Conducts

Assist participants in comprehending how their fresh viewpoints, convictions, and self-perceptions, which prioritize the improvement of their strengths and disregard their deficiencies, benefit the formation of new behaviors or the alteration of their current habits. Observe their cognitive interpretation of their activities.

Acknowledge the Costs

Thoroughly and sensitively identify the individual and collective costs or damages inflicted on the coachees, their teams or departments, and the company as a whole. The outcomes directly result from their prior thoughts, attitudes, and actions.

Setup Follow-Up

Irrespective of the established maintenance plan, periodically initiate contact with the coachees to inquire about their development and the extent to which they are sustaining their learning and enhancing their knowledge. Offer the necessary resources or arrange a coaching session to cater to their needs.

Please review Table 16.2 and assess your degree of attention and application of emotional intelligence coaching and training using the provided quality rating scale ranging from 1 (lowest) to 5 (highest).

Engaging in this activity and doing a sincere self-assessment of the procedural components will enhance your progress in giving emotional intelligence coaching or training to enhance the development of advanced 4Cs abilities in individuals.

Table 16.2 Process of Emotional Intelligence Coaching and Training Self-Rating Form

Instruction:
(a) Using the rating scale (shown below), self-evaluate yourself as a manager, supervisor, or independent in enhancing your activities regarding the process of emotional intelligence coaching and training, (b) then tally your rating, and (c) finally, come up with actions you will take to increase your rating on the next rating period.

Date:	Participant:			Organization:		
Rating Scale: 1 = Poor, 2 = Marginal, 3 = Acceptable, 4 = Good, 5 = Excellent						
#	*Steps of the Process*	*1*	*2*	*3*	*4*	*5*
1	Establish Rapport					
2	Identify Concerns					
3	Identify the Needs					
4	Express Promises					
5	Identify the Strengths					
6	Demonstrate Prospects					
7	Acknowledge Changes					
8	Assemble Values					
9	Categorize Perceptions					
10	Identify New Conducts					
11	Acknowledge the Costs					
12	Setup Follow-Up					
Total per rating						
Total (total of above totals per ratings)						
Average (above total divided by 12)						
Three correctional and developmental actions I will take that will raise my three lowest self-ratings by at least one scale on the next rating:						
Action 1:						
Action 2:						
Action 3:						

Note. Author's original creation. © 2024 by Behnam Bakhshandeh.

Role of Transformational Coaching in Emotional Intelligence Coaching

According to expert coaches, most coaching talks, particularly those focused on emotional intelligence coaching, tend to be intellectual and abstract. Transformational coaches provide assistance to persons who possess the autonomy to articulate their thoughts, elucidate their mindsets, discuss the emotions that arise within the context of their mindsets, convey their values and beliefs, and articulate their personal and professional aspirations. This principle applies equally to collaborating with teams, departments, and organizations.

Explaining Transformational Coaching

Transformational coaching refers to a process which a coach utilizes to help individuals or groups make significant and lasting changes in their lives or organizations. It involves guiding and supporting clients in exploring their beliefs, values, and behaviors, and helping them develop new perspectives and strategies to achieve their goals.

In essence, transformational coaching focuses on empowering individuals and promoting their self-actualization. The objective is to achieve more than mere "options–strategy–action" to fulfill objectives and goals or improve performance, actions, work, or behavior (Bakhshandeh, 2009). Transformational coaching delves into the depths of the coachees' minds, focusing on their identity and aspirations for personal growth. Hence, transformational coaching may be characterized as an ontological method of facilitating change, since it emphasizes the state of being rather than mere actions. This distinction will be explored in subsequent chapters of the book (Seale, 2011).

Transformational coaching has evolved into a comprehensive coaching method that goes beyond a simple performance-focused tool (Bakhshandeh, Rothwell, & Imroz, 2023). It is traditionally used in humanistic and psychological coaching approaches. However, it now considers the mindset and behaviors of individuals as a whole, rather than just focusing on their visible attitude and behavior (Seale, 2017). "It is a reflective way of coaching that aims to explore the coachees' cognitive, emotional, sensory and relational patterns in order to create a complete understanding of their perspectives on the world" (VanderPol, 2019, p. 18).

Personal awareness enables individuals to experience profound shifts in their mindsets and perspectives, both personally and professionally. It dismantles the detrimental frameworks and patterns of negative opinions and beliefs they held about themselves and others, which hindered their progress and impacted their relationships in various spheres of life (Bakhshandeh et al., 2023). This paradigm shift in thinking has a significant influence on the performance of individuals in various contexts, such as individual, group, or organizational-level interventions for organizational development (Seale, 2017).

Transformation Coaching for Emotional Intelligence Change

The transformational coaching technique is applicable to emotional intelligence change interventions, whether for individuals, teams, or management and leadership development. The impact of transformational coaching on both productivity and employee attitudes, as well as the utilization of transformational coaching by workforce education experts in any change interventions, are visible.

Business professionals increasingly recognize that professional coaching, especially transformational coaching, may be a potent and efficient tool for enhancing worker education, self-awareness, and productivity. This information highlights the significance of the transformational coaching approach for educational and learning professionals. It emphasizes the need for these professionals to gain knowledge about transformational coaching, its approaches, and its methods (Bakhshandeh et al., 2023). By doing so, the business professionals can effectively impact their employees' attitudes and behaviors, resulting in sustainable outcomes in the development of emotional intelligence, irrespective of their positions.

The rapid dissemination of coaching in enterprises and organizations underscores the need of acquiring comprehensive knowledge about various coaching methodologies, comprehending their dynamics, and effectively leveraging them to enhance the organization's vision and objectives. With the increasing use of professional coaching by enterprises, the significance of utilizing it is becoming increasingly apparent for coaching professional groups.

Contrasting Transactional Coaching with Transformational Coaching

In order to provide clarity and comprehension about transformational coaching, this section emphasizes a significant distinction between transactional and transformational coaching methodologies based on the following essential principle.

Transactional coaching operates under the premise that individuals will uncover self-knowledge and progress in significant ways based on their current state of being. In essence, individuals should not have their states of being explored or altered in order for them to achieve their intended objectives in life (Cox, 2015). Transactional coaching refers to a dialogue or exchange between coaches and their coachees with the purpose of establishing a goal or objective. In this scenario, the coaches would adopt the roles of active listeners and questioners to aid the coachees in gaining a clear understanding of their objectives and intents (Bakhshandeh et al., 2023). Upon achieving a high level of understanding, individuals are able to explore novel concepts, cultivate fresh perspectives, construct alternative choices, devise innovative methods, and formulate a detailed plan of action that will propel their focus and objectives ahead (Egan, 2013). "It is often conducted in a more systemized or process-driven way with change happening primarily through cognitive thinking and action—by 'thinking and doing differently.' Because of this, it can be perceived as a relatively impersonal approach" (VanderPol, 2019, p. 14).

Transactional coaching differs from transformational coaching in that it places less emphasis on exploring the coaches' "internal operating system," as referred to in transformational coaching (Cox, 2015). Egan (2013) defines the "internal operating system" as an intricate and multifaceted cognitive system that encompasses several parts of human mental processes, including beliefs, assumptions, mental models, meanings related to life aspects, self-identity, and both our conscious and unconscious states of mind. VanderPol (2019) seeks to streamline the function of transactional coaching in the following manner:

> To use a computer analogy, transactional coaching is focused on upgrades to our operating system that enable us to be more effective at what we are trying to achieve; it is not concerned with understanding the nature of the operating system itself or with any redesign of it.
>
> **(p. 15)**

The method of transactional coaching involves the coaches or coachees avoiding delving into difficult memories, raw emotions, or exploring prior challenges that have influenced the coachees' current experiences and future possibilities. Simultaneously, the transactional coaching technique does not go into deeply ingrained ideas and values, despite their potential to restrict transformative outcomes in the coaches' thinking, attitude, and actions (Effingham, 2013).

"Transactional coaching remains on the surface of our human existence" (VanderPol, 2019, p. 15).

The Fundamental Principles of Transformational Coaching

The fundamental principles of transformational coaching will help coaches and participants create an environment that fosters a strong and effective connection with few obstacles. Prior to establishing an honest and trustworthy connection, the coaches might proactively communicate these fundamental principles to their participants or customers. Kindly refer to Table 16.3.

Table 16.3   The Transformational Coaching Values and Principles

#	Values	Descriptions	At the Field
1	*Practice Integrity*	The backbone of effective transformational coaching is the integrity in process, with the coach and the participants.	Without integrity, nothing will work. This powerful distinction influences every part of our day-to-day lives and what we are doing. To make necessary changes in our lives, we must first start practicing integrity in all aspects of what we do, personally and professionally. The effectiveness of transformational coaching depends on the level of integrity that the coach and participants bring to the process.
2	*Be Whole*	There is nothing lacking with people; they are whole the way they are and concurrently develop a deeper experience of themselves and their lives.	Transformational coaching is not for fixing something with people, but for providing access for them to see their potentials and practice their choices and own their state of being in the matter of their own lives. The world usually focuses on what's wrong with people or what needs to change or improve, which is accompanied by assessments and perceptions of people's brokenness. Relating to people as whole moves the concept of broken to relatedness and respect, which would allow for establishing the foundation of partnership between the coach and participants.

(Continued)

Table 16.3   (CONTINUED) The Transformational Coaching Values and Principles

#	Values	Descriptions	At the Field
3	*Honor Diversity*	The transformational coaching process will go much deeper by honoring people's diversity of experience.	Transformational coaching is honoring people's diverse experiences, including their feelings and emotions about what they have gone through and what they experience during the process of coaching. The process allows for participants to embrace the breadth of their life experiences generated from their past, their family, their culture, and every other experience that might be in their way for transforming themselves and accessing deeper self-awareness.
4	*Be Responsible*	We are free when we take responsibility for the way we have reacted to all upsetting events in our lives.	In the transformational coaching process, the coach invites participants to take responsibility for how they have reacted and responded to upsetting situations in their lives. Not as the creator of the upsetting situation, but as the ones who took the route they took. When we are responsible, we show our willingness to own every thought we have and own up to every action we take: good or bad, right or wrong, happy or sad, enough or not enough.
5	*Establish Accountability*	To get what we want in life, we must make promises and declare our intentions.	Our power and dignity are built on the background of our promises to ourselves and others. People do not clearly understand how much their actions impact the world around them. Any action, broken promise, and everything we say will influence our relationship with others.
6	*Be Creative*	People are fundamentally creative, intelligent, and resourceful.	They are trusting that participants are creative, intelligent, and resourceful enough to find their ways through the transformation process. This place for a transformational coach to stand allows expansion of self-inquiry, curiosity, and emerging participation, connecting them to new insights, realizations, and actions.

(Continued)

Table 16.3   (CONTINUED) The Transformational Coaching Values and Principles

#	Values	Descriptions	At the Field
7	*Be Authentic*	Authenticity allows for complete self-expression and freedom to be with whoever there is to face.	What will lead people to become authentic is a combination of having the integrity and courage to own what they have done and who they have been in the face of life's upsetting situations, then become responsible for what they have done and face the reality of how they have done it. That is where people are giving up on learning about themselves when they think owning their results is an admission of guilt. It is just becoming real, and that is amazingly powerful.
8	*Allow Freedom of Expression*	People have complete freedom to respond and express themselves appropriately.	Coaches are freeing themselves from judgment by allowing participants to express themselves freely and share their experiences, circumstances, shortcomings, and even expectations. Coaches shall not take responsibility for how the participants feel and how they express themselves. By coaches accepting what participants' feelings are, they allow for natural transformation of such experiences by the participants and allow for their experiences of humility and honor by their coach.
9	*Have Choices*	People always have choices. They have a variety of choices in their wants and needs.	Participants can choose any actions, and any way they want to approach their issues at work or in their personal lives. Coaches shall not interfere with the participants' choices of actions or reactions in any shape or form. The coaches' place is to remind participants about being responsible for possible consequences of their choices. The participants will be free when they own the outcome of their choices.
10	*Look for Opportunities*	Looking for opportunities is a true expression of growth and development.	When participants are free of the restraints that their past experiences have on them, and when they understand the consequences of their choices and own the outcome of where they are, they are free to select opportunities for what is next for them.

(Continued)

Table 16.3 (CONTINUED) The Transformational Coaching Values and Principles

#	Values	Descriptions	At the Field
11	Be Open to Possibilities	There are so many more possibilities available for each person on any given day of their lives.	The beauty of the transformational coaching process is in the mystery of the outcomes. Nobody can plan what might come out of this process, neither the coaches nor the participants can imagine in advance what might happen and what they might get out of the process. However, anything and everything is possible when people are open to transformation and do not resist changes in their mindset and perception of reality.

Note. The content of this table is from the book *Anatomy of Upset; Restoring Harmony* (Bakhshandeh, 2015) and used with express permission from Behnam Bakhshandeh and Primeco Education, Inc.

Fundamental Requirements for Personal Transformation

Individuals seeking personal or professional transformation in areas such as emotional intelligence, health, relationships, productivity, performance, careers, addictions, damaging behavior, or unproductive mindset must fulfill several essential prerequisites. This approach significantly increases the likelihood of achieving personal transformation (Bakhshandeh, 2015; Bakhshandeh, 2009). Refer to Table 16.4.

Table 16.4 Fundamental Requirements for Personal Transformation

#	Requirements	Descriptions
1	Have a desire to change	In order to initiate the change, it is important for them to make a firm commitment and possess a genuine willingness to change, driven by a clear recognition of the need for change.
2	Have a vision for their life	They need to possess a clear and well-defined understanding of their metamorphosis. What is the ultimate result, the culmination of this transformation?
3	Align supports	They should seek and get the support of their immediate family and close friends to help them stay on the path to change. This assistance includes psychological, behavioral, or pragmatic interventions and can be offered to prospective colleagues, superiors, or executives in a working environment.
4	Obtain external accountability	It is necessary for them to have an external accountability partner. This collaboration includes engaging a personal or executive coach to address personal matters or to implement a coaching and mentoring system with managers serving as coaches to address professional matters.

Note. Adapted from Bakhshandeh et al., (2023); Bakhshandeh (2015, 2009).

Individuals are constantly building teams (as a pair), groups (as a family), enterprises (family businesses), and organizations in all of their connections, whether they are personal or professional. This is true in both contexts. According to research (Bakhshandeh, 2015, 2009), the first step in making positive changes in the coaches' personal and professional life is to undergo a transition on an individual level.

The Way of Being

Our actions serve to strengthen and demonstrate our fundamental nature. The term "Way of Being" refers to our individual perception of the world around us and our corresponding actions or reactions to our perceived reality at each given instant. Our perception of the world is influenced by our observations of people, things, events, and circumstances (Bakhshandeh, 2015). Upon careful examination, it becomes evident that many of our relationship problems, both in the workplace and at home, or our lack of desire to obtain a higher level of skills or education, stem from our inability to distinguish between objective reality and our subjective interpretations. This includes the tendency to assign additional meanings or significance to events and the failure to act or behave in a manner that aligns with our desired outcomes (Bakhshandeh, 2015, 2009).

Being and Doing

The occurrence of individuals, teams, or organizations experiencing failure in their endeavors to implement a change initiative is not a novel occurrence. We are familiar with it, either by reading or witnessing previous occurrences. Studies have demonstrated that 75% of organizational change initiatives do not meet the anticipated expectations or plans (Rothwell, 2015). Nevertheless, the percentage of failure is quite high. Studies show that around 66% of employees in businesses experiencing transformation activities opt out of participating (Levi, 2016).

What is the reason behind this? The majority of individuals who undergo change initiatives often emerge from the process without experiencing significant transformation or profound effects. This is mostly due to the predominant focus of trainers and consultants on the practical aspects of change, neglecting the crucial aspects of personal development and self-transformation. The majority of CEOs and managers in businesses focus their planning for individual, team, and organizational achievements solely on the act of doing, neglecting the importance of both being and doing. The concept of *Doing* is determined by the individuals' state of *Being* at a specific moment, as well as their perspective on themselves, others, and the world (Bakhshandeh, 2009). Any change, whether it is personal, team-oriented, or organizational, has two aspects. "The *Doing* side is about processes, measurement, tools, structures, and procedures. This side is about management. The *Being* side is about participation, commitment, attitude, creativity, overcoming resistance to change, and self-leadership. This side is about leadership" (Primeco Education, 2023).

The majority of our time is spent on human activities. Irrespective of age, gender, nationality, ethnicity, culture, or upbringing, individuals possess the ability to perceive the emotional state of others, whether it be distressing or joyful, even in the absence of verbal communication or explicit explanation. They possess the ability to discern feelings of wrath, regret, misery, and several other emotional states in others. Conversely, they can also recognize an individual's attention, involvement, dedication, communication skills, focus on achieving outcomes, and leadership qualities.

This approach toward an organization's development, team-building endeavors, or individual interventions with executives or managers reminds the management team that practicing effective management is not enough to foster long-term viability and expansion within the organization or the team they are striving to revive and strengthen. Furthermore, it is necessary to modify an individual's state of being to guarantee a person's durability and lifespan. This is because their current state of being, whether it be resentful, regretful, or dissatisfied, directly impacts their actions, such as communication or productivity (Bakhshandeh, 2009). Martin Heidegger, a German philosopher and ontologist, articulated his perspective on the transparency of being in his book *Being and Time* (1953), "the self-evident concept. Being is used in all-knowing and predicting, in every relation to being, and in every relation to oneself, and the expression is understandable without further ado" (p. 3).

A crucial and significant aspect of organization development is the practice of organization leaders serving as role models by demonstrating good conduct that is consistent with the desired behavior for people, teams, or organization growth (Rothwell, Stavros, & Sullivan, 2016). Organizations can achieve personal growth and change by providing transformational and behavioral coaching to individuals who hold significant positions and directly impact the well-being of a team or company. Behavioral coaching has been a well-established practice in facilitating change, especially in individual interventions. Behavioral coaching involves the use of the Person-Centered Psychology model by trained transformational coaches. This model helps individuals better understand themselves by reflecting on their behavior and attitude development over time. This strategy is highly successful for individuals to enhance their self-awareness and self-realization. Through engaging in an inquiry process with the guidance and assistance of coaches, individuals are able to get deep insights into their own selves. Thus, individuals consistently retain their own process of self-actualization as they personally discover it, rather than having it imposed upon them by other forces.

Our Way of Being Determines Our Way of Doing

We possess the nature of human beings, although our actions predominantly consist of engaging in activities. By observing our own state of being, we can discern that irrespective of factors such as age, gender, nationality, race, culture, or upbringing, we possess the ability to perceive the emotional state of others, whether they are experiencing distress or joy, even in the absence of verbal communication or explicit explanation. We possess the ability to discern feelings of wrath, regret, dissatisfaction, and several other emotional states in individuals. Alternatively, we may also recognize someone who is interested, involved, dedicated, communicative, focused on achieving outcomes, and capable of taking charge (See Figure 16.3).

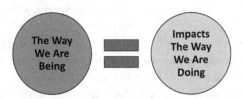

Figure 16.3   Our way of being determines our way of doing.   Note. Adapted from Bakhshandeh et al. (2023).

In his book *Being and Nothingness*, Jean-Paul Sartre, the French philosopher and ontologist, provided an explanation for this occurrence, "no being which is not the being of a certain mode of being, none which cannot be apprehended through the mode of being which manifests being and veils it at the same time" (Sartre, 1943, pp. 24–25). They are capable of recognizing those features inside themselves without the necessity for any specific action or effort on their part (Bakhshandeh, 2009). "State of being is what makes us all do what we do, or even feel what we feel. It makes us interested in what we do, and it allows us to relate to others or take ourselves away from them! It makes us succeed or fail, and it makes us love or hate ourselves and others!" (Bakhshandeh, 2009, p. 22).

Integrating Coaching Methods to Complement Transformational Coaching

Transformational coaching is not just one way and delivered in a certain way. In this section, this chapter briefly explains and describes two coaching approaches as integrated models to transformational coaching that deeply impacts its process: (1) ontological coaching, and (2) positive psychology coaching.

Ontological Coaching

The following are some available definitions for *ontology*:

- *Merriam-Webster Dictionary* describes *ontology* as: "A branch of metaphysics concerned with the nature and relations of being. *Ontology* deals with abstract entities. A particular theory about the nature of being or the kinds of things that have existence" (Merriam-Webster, 2023, n.p.).
- *Oxford University Dictionary* describes ontology as "a branch of philosophy that deals with the nature of existence," and "that shows the relationships between all the concepts and categories in a subject area" (Oxford University Dictionary, 2023, n.p.).

Contemporary ontology, under the field of analytic philosophy, focuses largely on inquiries on the existence of entities and their characteristics, including their appearance, sensation, and experiential qualities (Effingham, 2013). Some philosophers, namely those from the Platonic school, contend that all nouns, even conceptual nouns, denote the existence of persons. Certain philosophers contend that nouns do not invariably denote specific persons or entities. For instance, the term "mind" can be used as a substitute to refer to a person, including a range of mental experiences that an individual has had or is now having (Effingham, 2013).

Ontological Approach

Modern ontology has become integrated into the fields of psychology and social science, since several psychologists and social scientists have used ontological techniques in their work. Aristotle, Plato, Martine Heidegger, Friedrich Hegel, and Jean-Paul Sartre are well-known ancient and modern ontologists (Effingham, 2013).

Ontological coaching is a method of exploring and understanding one's self-awareness, reflecting on the individual's connection to their existence and their relationship with the world around them (Bakhshandeh, 2009). This coaching methodology encompasses elements of psychology, sociology, philosophy, linguistics, personal integrity, responsibility, and accountability. Ontological coaching focuses on facilitating personal development via the process of inquiry, contemplation, self-observation, and self-realization (D'Addario, 2016). It involves gaining awareness of one's state of being and how it influences behavior and attitudes. This coaching style focuses on facilitating personal and professional growth by empowering participants via effective communication, emotional intelligence, creativity, leadership abilities, and learning processes (Effingham, 2013).

Advantages of Ontological Coaching

The participants who underwent transformational coaching recognized several advantages of ontological coaching:

1. Increased personal speed.
2. Enhanced output and general prosperity.
3. Rediscovered hobbies and interests.
4. Greater progress in less time.
5. Exerted creativity and self-expression.
6. Developed and implemented personal life vision.
7. Focused, understandable, and effective communication.
8. Enhanced general efficacy and efficiency.
9. Developed stronger connection and sense of relatedness with others.
10. Rediscovered and truly enjoyed life!

(Primeco Education, 2023)

Positive Psychology Coaching

Abraham Maslow is credited with originally coining the phrase Positive Psychology. Subsequently, Martin Seligman spearheaded Positive Psychology as a psychological methodology grounded in empirical investigation and methodical frameworks. This novel method aims to investigate the factors contributing to individuals' happiness and the strategies required to maintain happiness as a central component of their life and productivity (Seligman, 2002).

After doing thorough research and comprehensive surveys, Seligman concluded that those who identified and effectively exploited their "signature strengths" were the most pleased and optimistic. These attributes encompassed qualities such as compassion, self-discipline, and tenacity. He supported his concept of happiness with the principles and moral values of Confucius, Mencius, and Aristotle and the insights from modern psychology. Drawing from motivational theories and self-awareness, Seligman concluded that personal happiness can be cultivated, nurtured, and promoted through three distinct dimensions (see Figure 16.4):

1) The pleasant life.
2) The good life.
3) The meaningful life.

(Seligman, 2002)

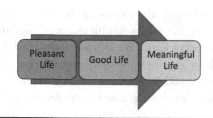

Figure 16.4   Personal happiness direction. Note. Adapted from Seligman (2002).

The influence of our sentiments and emotions on our thinking is significant, leading to subsequent behaviors. However, which one takes precedence? Do emotions give rise to our cognitive processes, or do our cognitive processes give rise to our emotions? Speaking scientifically and definitively about the causal relationship between two variables is challenging. Nevertheless, it may be asserted that both possibilities are valid and likely to occur. When experiencing sadness, distress, or bitterness, we may have pessimistic beliefs about ourselves, others, or the circumstances at hand. Occasionally, when we harbor pessimistic ideas on certain previous occurrences or relationships, we may begin to feel melancholic, agitated, or even encounter feelings of anxiousness. This approach may also be used to cultivate optimistic ideas that lead to pleasant emotions or evoke joyful emotions that trigger happy thoughts (Bakhshandeh, 2015).

By building upon the principles of positive psychology, we have the ability to consciously choose our happiness and actively cultivate it with greater frequency. Positive psychologists prioritize the examination of the favorable aspects of our lives and stress the aspects that are functioning well, as opposed to those that are not. It entails adopting a positive perspective toward the matter, or as a proverbial expression suggests, perceiving the glass as being half full rather than half empty. There is a significant movement and emerging area of study focused on this empowering approach, which greatly impacts individual and team coaching methods, resulting in direct and beneficial outcomes for individual treatments.

Positive Thinking Is Not Equal to Positive Psychology

Positive psychology and positive thinking are often confused, although they have a basic difference. As described by Seligman (2002), positive thinking refers to the cognitive process in which individuals contemplate positive aspects and ideas. Positive psychology is a branch of psychology that is backed by scientific study. Positive psychology is extensively studied and substantiated via rigorous academic research, while positive thinking is predominantly a behavior associated with popular culture.

Possessing a positive outlook and the ability to perceive goodness in both situations and individuals is an exceptional trait. However, relying solely on optimistic emotions, trusting others' words without critical evaluation, or basing plans solely on pleasant sentiments is a display of naivety. We can maintain an optimistic perspective on life, events, and other people while still taking responsibility for thoroughly investigating their claims or assertions. After carefully evaluating all relevant factors, we can reach a decision on whether to engage in a business transaction with someone, accept their proposal, or launch certain initiatives. From my perspective as someone who identifies as positive, positivity is refraining from making snap judgments and assessments of individuals at the initial encounter. I provide the benefit of the doubt to individuals by refraining from harboring initial mistrust or predetermined notions or engaging in internal dialogue about them. Maintaining a positive mindset is beneficial, but it is equally important to acknowledge and take responsibility for the constraints imposed by factors such as time, distance, and circumstances.

We are essentially cognitive beings who engage in the process of constructing meaning, both in relation to ourselves and others. We assign significance to things and hence experience frequent distress due to our numerous expectations. "We create realities, and then we forget we have created them, and then we relate to them as something that someone else put upon us. Others' responses to us reflect our expectations for and about them" (Bakhshandeh, 2016). In the wise words of Albert Einstein, *"Reality is merely an illusion, albeit a very persistent one."*

Advantages of Positive Psychology Coaching

Extensive research (Seligman and Csikszentmihalyi, 2010; Green 2014; Diener et al., 2002) has substantiated several advantages associated with applying positive psychology. The subsequent outcomes have been often documented by positive psychology practitioners who have engaged in research and have seen that those who experienced positive psychology practice:

1. They saw a significant increase in their overall happiness levels.
2. They fostered a more profound interpersonal bond.
3. They maintained a fruitful professional collaboration.
4. They enhanced their level of self-assurance.
5. They exhibited more efficacy and productivity in their field of work.
6. They had a beneficial impact on their surroundings.
7. They prioritized their well-being and adopted a more wholesome way of living.
8. They exerted a greater impact on their localities.
9. Their positivism and happiness were continuous.
10. They enhanced their energy.

Tips for Successful Coaching

I am aware that the personal and professional development industry offers a wide range of coaching models and methodologies. Nevertheless, with more than three decades of expertise in this field, I have discovered that the following suggestions are valuable in effectively directing coaching sessions of any nature.

Remember That Coaching Is a Relationship

Keep in mind that coaching entails a mutual connection between individuals. Coaches need to consistently engage in a reciprocal connection with their coachees. Developing a foundation of connection and developing a positive relationship is crucial for fostering trust and creating an effective coaching atmosphere.

Do Not Seize Control

It is customary for coaches to assume control and instruct the coachees during coaching sessions since the coaches possess the necessary knowledge and understanding. Implementing this technique will result in opposition to the coaching process, leading to a detrimental impact on the coaching relationship and undermining the coachees' trust.

Choose the Optimal Coaching Model

Coaching does not adhere to a universal strategy that suits everyone. As experienced and proficient coaches, it is necessary to choose the coaching style that aligns with the evident requirements for personal growth or the challenges pertaining to team effectiveness.

Coaching Is a Form of Inquiry

While individuals or teams may articulate their goals or aspirations for reaching a certain outcome during coaching or at the conclusion of the coaching process, it is important to note that there are no definitive endpoints in a change strategy. The essence of coaching emerges from the process of the trip.

Understanding and Practicing EI Clusters and Competencies Self-Evaluation

As you read in Chapter 13, Table 13.2 presented the outcomes pertaining to emotional intelligence clusters, associated competencies, attributions, and qualities exhibited by individuals possessing such competencies and capabilities based on recommendations, evaluations, and deliberations regarding the implementation of emotional intelligence as a training method to enhance the development of 4Cs skills within the workforce. Table 13.2 also underlined the importance of at least two of these talents in relation to the four components of 21st-century 4Cs skills, namely critical thinking, communication, creativity, and collaboration.

(Important Note: The following paragraph is directly from Chapter 13 of this book):

> Irrespective of the pairing of at least two of the four 4Cs skills with any of the emotional intelligence competencies outlined in Table 13.2, it is worth noting that these competencies, capabilities, attributes, and qualities positively influence all the 21st century 4Cs skills. Furthermore, they aid organizations in effectively training and developing their workforces in order to enhance the quality and utility of the 4Cs skills. In essence, the competencies above and attributes can serve as focal points for enhancing worker capabilities concerning their 4Cs skills.

(Chapter 13, Table, 13.2 note)

In this section, we ask you to conduct a self-evaluation as a coach, consultant, manager-as-coach, or independent on the level of enhancing your understanding and practicing the four clusters of emotional intelligence, their competencies, their related qualities, and their relevance to 4Cs skills in connection to Table 13.2.

However, we have separated the original Table 13.2 into four independent tables (16.6, 16.7, 16.8, and 16.9) based on each of the four EI clusters. This way, any coaches, consultants, or managers attempting to coach trainees in their emotional intelligence in order to develop their skills can recognize their own level of understanding and depth of their practicing EI, and their own level of competencies related to any of the competencies related to EI clusters.

Self-Rating Process

Please take some time now to browse over Tables 16.5, 16.6, 16.7, and 16.8, using the supplied quality rating scale of 1 (the lowest) to 5 (the highest), and grade yourself on your level of enhancing your understanding and practicing the four clusters of emotional intelligence, their competencies, their related qualities, and their relevance to 4Cs skills. This exercise and honest self-evaluation of the process parts will improve your growth in the areas of 4Cs skills.

Table 16.5 Self-Awareness Cluster, Competencies, Qualities, and Correspondence 4Cs Skills Self-Rating

Instruction: (a) Using the rating scale (shown below), self-evaluate yourself as a coach, consultant, manager-as-coach, or independent on enhancing your understanding and practicing self-awareness competencies and their related qualities, (b) then tally your rating, and (c) finally, come up with actions you will take to increase your rating on the next rating period.								
Date:		Participant:		Organization:				
Quality Rating Scale: **1** = Poor, **2** = Marginal, **3** = Acceptable, **4** = Good, **5** = Excellent								
#	*Competencies*	*Qualities*	*4Cs Skills*	*1*	*2*	*3*	*4*	*5*
1	Emotional Awareness	• Showing concern for others' feelings • Recognizing misunderstandings • Displaying a trust-based function	- Critical thinking - Communication					
2	Self-Confidence	• Believing in their skills • Exhibiting gratitude • Being internally happy	- Communication - Collaboration					
3	Self-Assessment	• Examining their learning • Monitoring goals' advancement • Performing self-efficacy	- Critical thinking - Communication					
4	Self-Control	• Making no impulsive decisions • Being in control of their behaviors • Retaining conscientiousness	- Critical thinking - Collaboration					
5	Self-Disparaging Humor	• Acknowledging their faults • Being at ease to laugh at themselves • Not being up to an immaculate image	- Communication - Creativity					
6	Intrapersonal Skills	• Appreciating themselves • Being aware of their agenda • Reducing interruptions	- Creativity - Collaboration					

(Continued)

Table 16.5 (CONTINUED) Self-Awareness Cluster, Competencies, Qualities, and Correspondence 4Cs Skills Self-Rating

7	Self-Motivation	• Displaying interest in success • Encouraging forward motion actions • Exhibiting interest in productivity	- Critical thinking - Collaboration					
8	Self-Discipline	• Avoiding instant gratification • Excluding interferences • Not needing a constant reminder	- Critical thinking - Creativity					
			Total per rating					
			Total (total of above totals per ratings)					
			Average (above total divided by 8)					
Three correctional and developmental actions I will take that will raise my three lowest self-ratings by at least one scale on the next rating:								
Action 1:								
Action 2:								
Action 3:								

Note. Adapted from Bakhshandeh (2021).

Table 16.6 Self-Regulation Cluster, Competencies, Qualities, and Correspondence 4Cs Skills Self-Rating

Instruction: (a) Using the rating scale (shown below), self-evaluate yourself as a coach, consultant, manager-as-coach, or independent on enhancing your understanding and practicing self-regulation competencies and their related qualities, (b) then tally your rating, and (c) finally, come up with actions you will take to increase your rating on the next rating period.								
Date:		Participant:		Organization:				
Quality Rating Scale: **1** = Poor, **2** = Marginal, **3** = Acceptable, **4** = Good, **5** = Excellent								
#	*Competencies*	*Qualities*		*4Cs Skills*	*1*	*2*	*3*	*4*	*5*
1	Emotional Balance	• Correctly recognizing their emotions • Being mindful of their emotions • Handling impulse emotions		- Critical thinking - Collaboration					

(Continued)

Table 16.6 (CONTINUED) Self-Regulation Cluster, Competencies, Qualities, and Correspondence 4Cs Skills Self-Rating

2	Adaptability	• Being open to learning • Adapting quickly • Entertaining new ideas	- Collaboration - Creativity					
3	Integrity	• Being reliable • Being truthful • Being trustworthy	- Critical thinking - Communication					
4	Calm manners	• Exerting confidence • Being calm • Being insightful	- Critical thinking - Creativity					
5	Responsibility	• Not presenting excuses • Not complaining • Being sensible	- Creativity - Collaboration					
6	Accountability	• Assuming responsibility • Not assigning blames • Being transparent	- Communication - Collaboration					
7	Positivity	• Being optimistic • Being resilient • Being grateful	- Communication - Collaboration					
8	Authenticity	• Applying self-reflection • Being sincere • Not being disparaging	- Critical thinking - Communication					
			Total per rating					
		Total (total of above totals per ratings)						
		Average (above total divided by 8)						
Three correctional and developmental actions I will take that will raise my three lowest self-ratings by at least one scale on the next rating:								
Action 1:								
Action 2:								
Action 3:								

Note. Adapted from Bakhshandeh (2021).

Table 16.7 *Social Awareness Cluster, Competencies, Qualities and Correspondence 4Cs Skills Self-Rating*

Instruction:
(a) Using the rating scale (shown below), self-evaluate yourself as a coach, consultant, manager-as-coach, or independent on enhancing your understanding and practicing social awareness competencies and their related qualities, (b) then tally your rating, and (c) finally, come up with actions you will take to increase your rating on the next rating period.

Date:	Participant:	Organization:					
Quality Rating Scale: **1** = Poor, **2** = Marginal, **3** = Acceptable, **4** = Good, **5** = Excellent							
#	Competencies	Qualities	4Cs Skills	1	2	3	4	5
1	Organizational Awareness	• Making defensible choices • Formulating a practical plan • Establishing support coalition	- Critical thinking - Creativity					
2	Empathy	• Identifying talent • Recognizing emotional states • Being helpful	- Communication - Collaboration					
3	Compassion	• Putting themselves in others' places • Exercising active listening • Being fine with failures	- Critical thinking - Communication					
4	Inspiration	• Aspiring to make a difference • Being brave • Always supporting others' dreams	- Communication - Collaboration					
5	Diversity Awareness	• Accepting uniqueness • Exhibiting mutual respect • Displaying universal treatment	- Critical thinking - Collaboration					
6	Multiple Perspectives	• Seeing a bigger picture • Looking for the root cause • Obtaining mutually settled solutions	- Critical thinking - Creativity					

(Continued)

Table 16.7 **(CONTINUED)** *Social Awareness Cluster, Competencies, Qualities and Correspondence 4Cs Skills Self-Rating*

7	Active Listening	• Focusing on the speaker • Responding properly • Giving feedback	- Communication - Creativity					
8	Leadership	• Paying attention to the team's interest • Using encouraging language • Possessing positive attitudes	- Critical thinking - Communication					
			Total per rating					
		Total (total of above totals per ratings)						
		Average (above total divided by 8)						
Three correctional and developmental actions I will take that will raise my three lowest self-ratings by at least one scale on the next rating:								
Action 1:								
Action 2:								
Action 3:								

Note. Adapted from Bakhshandeh (2021).

Table 16.8 **Relationship Management Cluster, Competencies, Qualities, and Correspondence 4Cs Skills Self-Rating**

Instruction:
(a) Using the rating scale (shown below), self-evaluate yourself as a coach, consultant, manager-as-coach, or independent on enhancing your understanding and practicing relationship management competencies and their related qualities, (b) then tally your rating, and (c) finally, come up with actions you will take to increase your rating on the next rating period.

Date:		Participant:		Organization:				
Quality Rating Scale: **1** = Poor, **2** = Marginal, **3** = Acceptable, **4** = Good, **5** = Excellent								
#	*Competencies*	*Qualities*	*4Cs Skills*	*1*	*2*	*3*	*4*	*5*
1	Conflict Management	• Being unbiased • Being patient • Preventing blame game	- Critical thinking - Collaboration					
2	Positive Influence	• Being appealing • Being modest • Showing determination to help	- Creativity - Collaboration					

(Continued)

Table 16.8 (CONTINUED) Relationship Management Cluster, Competencies, Qualities, and Correspondence 4Cs Skills Self-Rating

3	Problem-Solving	• Identifying the perceptions • Redefining the problem • Not being attached	- Critical thinking - Creativity					
4	Flexibility	• Staying open to the unexpected • Preventing reactions • Remaining unattached to one's ways	- Creativity - Collaboration					
5	Trust and Team Building	• Being approachable • Being respectful • Being fair and impartial	- Communication - Collaboration					
6	Interpersonal Skills	• Being conscious of everyone • Being cooperative • Showing compassion about relationships	- Communication - Collaboration					
7	Communication	• Being conscious of non-verbal communication • Distributing clear and concise messages • Exhibiting keen listening	- Communication - Creativity					
8	Coaching and Mentoring	• Being encouraging • Being empowering • Being knowledgeable	- Critical thinking - Communication					
			Total per rating					
			Total (total of above totals per ratings)					
			Average (above total divided by 8)					
Three correctional and developmental actions I will take that will raise my three lowest self-ratings by at least one scale on the next rating:								
Action 1:								
Action 2:								
Action 3:								

Note. Adapted from Bakhshandeh (2021).

Team Leader as the Change Agent

Regardless of whether the analysis of performance difficulties or skills-related issues is executed flawlessly, and the manager, coach, or consultant has chosen a meticulously developed and pertinent performance-improvement intervention to empower the workforce for enhanced productivity, change interventions will not provide extraordinary results unless they align with the organization's targeted outcomes for employee performance and team behavior objectives (Rothwell, Imroz, & Bakhshandeh, 2021).

It is also proven that learning change interventions information, processes, and knowledge can and will provide individuals, groups, or teams with new knowledge and skills, but the new understanding and knowledge does not guarantee that organization management or team leaders will manage and implement what they newly learned on their jobs and team productions (Rothwell & Sredl, 2014). This phenomenon is one of the most disempowering reasons for change intervention failings: Lack of follow-up and managing the change.

Organizational and team change interventions can establish a work environment that ensures the right individuals are selected and equipped with the necessary tools and equipment. These interventions also ensure that individuals and teams are appropriately rewarded within the boundaries of the reward system, based on their personal and collective efforts. However, there is no assurance that individual employees or teams possess knowledge of the most effective course of action or adhere to the desired objectives of the team or company (Rothwell et al., 2021).

Given the reasons as mentioned above, it is essential that all change interventions, whether for the entire organization or a specific team, are developed and implemented in a supportive and motivating environment that fosters learning, positive individual actions, and progress. The responsibility for this crucial approach and pivotal role will rest with a team leader and a change agent (Rothwell & Sredl, 2014). As per the ASTED models, the role of the change leader is to motivate the workforce to accept the change, establish a path for the change initiative, assist the organization's workforce in adjusting to the change, and ensure that interventions are consistently monitored and guided in accordance with the desired outcomes of stakeholders (Rothwell & Sredl, 2014, p. 241).

Team Leader Competencies

Multiple resources (Rothwell et al., 2021; Kolb, 2011; Bakhshandeh 2004, 2001) have demonstrated that there exists a set of skills and competencies that can improve the capabilities of team leaders in leading and facilitating their teams, particularly in different team settings. Hence, many more skills and competencies are related to effective and competent team leaders, but the following competencies are the ones that are most related to a team leader who will act as a team agent for managing the process of 4Cs skills development and training. Please see Figure 16.5.

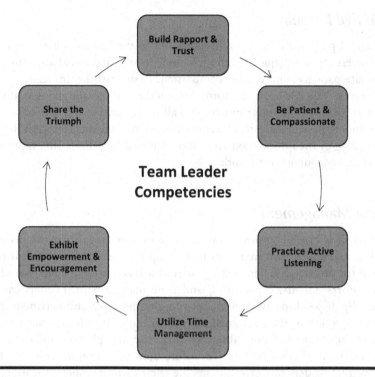

Figure 16.5   Team leader competencies. Note. Author's Original Creation. © 2024 by Behnam Bakhshandeh.

Build Rapport and Trust

Fostering trust between the team leader and team members is crucial to effectively work with and manage any team. Irrespective of the real or virtual setting, the effectiveness and efficiency of teams depend on the foundation of trust. Trust-building may be accomplished when team leaders exemplify authenticity by openly and honestly discussing their skills, faults, and personal and professional experiences with team members in a respectful manner. Another effective team building activity occurs when team leaders demonstrate their dedication to work alongside their teams as equals, offering their experience and knowledge for the teams' advantage.

Be Patient and Compassionate

It is important to acknowledge that team members may have varying approaches and productivity levels, particularly when working with individuals from various linguistic, cultural, or customary backgrounds. The disparities are especially conspicuous in virtual teams. Considering the distance and the likelihood of utilizing telephone or video communication platforms, it is quite probable that we will be unable to perceive their emotional states through their facial expressions and body language. Exercising patience, demonstrating compassion and empathy, and acknowledging and respecting others' differences are crucial for the successful development of a team and effective leadership.

Practice Active Listening

The cornerstone of good skills in active listening lies in the ability to listen without judgment, maintain awareness of one's prejudice, refrain from interpretation, avoid attachments to the findings, demonstrate patience, and exhibit compassion. A successful team leader prioritizes active listening as the most valuable form of information intake. This entails giving undivided attention to the speaker, refraining from interruptions, and allowing them to fully articulate their thoughts before responding. Repeating what team leaders have heard is a beneficial habit that demonstrates their understanding of the information and ideas conveyed by others. This approach also fosters mutual respect and encourages teamwork.

Utilize Time Management

As team leaders, it is crucial to possess a receptive mindset regarding the necessary requirements and time frame for team members to accomplish their duties or fulfill their responsibilities for a team project. Efficient team leaders possess a comprehensive understanding of their team members' talents, capabilities, and time management. Leaders can bolster their team members by dispatching them with encouraging prompts and pertinent information to expedite the completion of their assigned activity or duty. In order to execute this technique efficiently, it is important to know about all domestic and global holidays and events that might influence the project's schedule. To ensure continuous productivity within the team, it is imperative that leaders proactively schedule their team members' vacations on the team calendar ahead of time.

Exhibit Empowerment and Encouragement

Team leaders should ensure that they are cognizant and recognize their team members for their diligent labor and endeavors with a straightforward statement of "Job well done." They should additionally ensure that they consistently use the terms "please" and "thank you" in their phrases since they are intangible assets that may be utilized freely and without any reservations or expenses. Demonstrating reverence for the cultures of others and understanding their preferred methods of obtaining recognition and gratitude is a characteristic of perceptive and considerate team leaders or managers.

Share the Triumph

Adept team leaders would ensure the inclusion of all team members in the team's achievements and generously acknowledge their contributions by consistently emphasizing the collective work and collaboration that led to the team's success (Table 16.9).

Table 16.9   Team Leader Competencies Self-Rating

Instruction:
(a) Using the rating scale (shown below), self-evaluate yourself as a manager, supervisor, or independent on enhancing your understanding and activities on team leader competencies, (b) then tally your rating, and (c) finally, come up with actions you will take to increase your rating on the next rating period.

Date:	Participant:			Organization:		
	Rating Scale: 1 = Poor, 2 = Marginal, 3 = Acceptable, 4 = Good, 5 = Excellent					
#	*Steps of the Process*	*1*	*2*	*3*	*4*	*5*
1	Build Rapport and Trust					
2	Be Patient and Compassionate					
3	Practice Active Listening					
4	Utilize Time Management					
5	Exhibit Empowerment and Encouragement					
6	Share the Triumph					
	Total per rating					
	Total (total of above totals per ratings)					
	Average (above total divided by 6)					
Three correctional and developmental actions I will take that will raise my three lowest self-ratings by at least one scale on the next rating:						
Action 1:						
Action 2:						
Action 3:						

Source: Rothwell, Imrozand, Bakhshandeh (2021); Kolb, (2011); Bakhshandeh (2004, 2001).

Training and Development Evaluation

Like any other training and development process, organizations need to employ an evaluation model or method to evaluate the success or validity of such training and development. An essential approach to assess the efficacy and legitimacy of a training and development initiative, from the perspective of both the company and the trainer or facilitator, is to analyze the effectiveness and impact of the training and development programs. The evaluation methodology differs based on the program's design and the trainer or facilitator's approach to delivery and assessment. Some assessments occur at the program's conclusion, while others take place at the program's commencement, throughout, and at its conclusion.

The researcher found Dr Donald Kirkpatrick, Ph.D.'s Four Levels of Evaluation to be a very successful approach for assessing training and development programs. This model is sometimes referred to as the Kirkpatrick Evaluation Model. The original design of the training program was created and published in the 1950s in a trade magazine. It was later refined and published as a book in 1975 by Dr Kirkpatrick, titled *Evaluating Training Programs* (Kirkpatrick & Kirkpatrick, 2016). The four tiers of assessment are as follows (see Figure 16.6).

Figure 16.6   Four levels of training and development evaluation. Note. Adapted from Kirkpatrick and Kirkpatrick (2016).

Level One—Reaction

This level aims to elicit participants' perspectives on their learning experience upon completion of the program. Typically, the purpose of asking questions is to ascertain the following:

1) The level of satisfaction among participants.
2) Whether they derived value from the program.
3) Whether they felt engaged with the program.
4) If they found the training program applicable to their job.

A significant number of training and development programs—around 80%—include this level of evaluation.

Level Two—Learning

This level assesses the extent to which participants have acquired the expected skills, knowledge, and attitudes as a result of the program. This level is specifically tailored to teach leaders of companies and organizations in order to determine whether the program's intents and objectives were understood. Organizations can enact the required modifications or enhancements by clearly delineating the knowledge acquired or lacking among members. Level two can serve as both pre-event and post-event assessments, or only as a post-assessment upon completion of the training program.

Level Three—Behavior

This level quantifies the magnitude and extent to which participants' actions or attitudes have changed as a result of the training program. Essentially, the company must determine if the participants have applied the program's material, skills, and knowledge in their profession. This dimension represents the extent to which participants have acquired the knowledge and subject matter of the training program. Level three evaluation encompasses measuring the learner's attitude and conduct before and after the program.

Level Four—Results

This level aims to assess the "tangible results" of a training program, as defined by Kirkpatrick. These results include the following:

1) Decreased operational costs, improved working conditions, and enhanced effectiveness.
2) Increased productivity within the organization and improved employee retention.
3) Higher sales levels and boosted employee morale.

While quantifying these benchmarks may not be simple or inexpensive, doing such measurements is crucial and the sole means by which businesses and trainers can validate the essential return on investment (ROI) for their training and development initiatives. Level four necessitates the evaluation of both pre-program and post-program measurements to assess the expected goals and outcomes of the training.

What Is Next?

Chapter 17, "Emotional Intelligence Coach," looks at EI coaches as a key instrument of emotional intelligence and what companies and skills are needed for someone to coach individuals and teams on their EI training and development.

References

Bakhshandeh, Behnam. (2001). *What Is Making a Great Team? Unpublished workshop on team building.* San Diego, CA: Primeco Education, Inc.

Bakhshandeh, Behnam. (2004). *Effective Communication: Getting Present.* 2-Set CD. San Diego, CA: Primeco Education, Inc.

Bakhshandeh, Behnam. (2009). *Conspiracy for Greatness; Mastery of Love Within.* San Diego, CA: Primeco Education, Inc.

Bakhshandeh, Behnam. (2015). *Anatomy of Upset: Restoring Harmony.* Carbondale, PA: Primeco Education, Inc.

Bakhshandeh, Behnam. (2016). *The Power of Belief: All Realities are not Invented Equally!* Carbondale, PA: Primeco Education, Inc. Retrieved from: http://media.wix.com/ugd/4afcde_ad36a7f8a3d74202afd01966b83ffed7.pdf.

Bakhshandeh, Behnam. (2021). *Perception of 21st Century 4Cs (Critical Thinking, Communication, Creativity & Collaboration) Skill Gap in Private-Sector Employers in Lackawanna County, NE PA (Order No. 28841654).* Available from Dissertations Theses @ CIC Institutions; ProQuest Dissertations Theses AI (2577123614). Retrieved from https://ezaccess.libraries.psu.edu/login?qurl=https%3A%2F%2Fwww.proquest.com%2Fdissertations-theses%2Fperception-21st-century-4cs-critical-thinking%2Fdocview%2F2577123614%2Fse-2%3Faccountid%3D13158.

Bakhshandeh, Behnam & Rothwell, William J. (Eds.) (2024). *Building an Organizational Coaching Culture.* Oxfordshire, UK: UK Limited Trading, Taylor & Francis Group. Routledge.

Bakhshandeh, Behnam, Rothwell, William J., & Imroz, Sohel M. (2023). *Transformational Coaching for Effective Leadership. Creating Sustainable Change Through Shifting Paradigms.* New York, NY: Taylor & Francis Group. Routledge.

Cox, Elaine. (2015). Coaching and adult learning: Theory and practice. *New Directions for Adult and Continuing Education, 2015*(148), 27–38.

D'Addario, Miguel. (2016). *Ontological Coaching: Transformation and Development of Oneself* (2nd ed.). Translated by Sofia Navarro. San Bernardino, CA: European Community.

Diener, Ed, Nickerson, Carol, Lucas, Richard E., & Sandvik, Ed. (2002). Dispositional affect and job out-comes. *Social Indicators Research, 59*(3), 229–259.

Effingham, Nikk. (2013). *An Introduction to Ontology*. Malden, MA: Polity Press.

Egan, Toby. (2013). Response to Nieminen et al.'s feature article on executive coaching and facilitated multisource feedback: Toward better understanding of a growing HRD practice. *Human Resource Development Quarterly, 24*(2), 177–183.

Gormley, H. & van Nieuwerburgh, C. (2014). Developing coaching cultures: A review of the literature. *Coaching: An International Journal of Theory, Research and Practice, 7*(2), 90–101. https://doi.org/10 .1080/17521882.2014.915863.

Green, Lucy S. (2014). Positive education: An Australian perspective. In M. J. Furlong, R. Gilman, & E. S. Huebner (Eds.), *Handbook of Positive Psychology in Schools* (2nd ed., 401–415). New York, NY: Taylor & Francis.

Heidegger, Martin. (1953). *Being and Time*. Translated by Joan Stambaugh. New York, NY: State University on New York Press.

Kirkpatrick, J. D. & Kirkpatrick, W. K. (2016). *Kirkpatrick's Four Levels of Training Evaluation*. Alexandra, VA: Association for Talent Development.

Kolb, Judith A. (2011). *Small Group Facilitation: Improving Process and Performance in Groups and Teams*. Amherst, MA: HRD Press Inc.

Levi, Daniel. (2016). *Group Dynamics for Teams* (5th Ed.). Los Angeles, CA: Sage Publications.

Merriam-Webster Online Dictionary. (2023). Ontology. Retrieved from https://www.merriam-webster .com/dictionary/ontology.

Milner, J., McCarthy, G., & Milner, T. (2018). Training for the coaching leader: How organizations can support managers. *Journal of Management Development, 37*(2), 188–200. https://doi.org/10.1108/ JMD.

Oxford University Dictionary. (2023). Ontology. Retrieved from https://wwww.oxfordlearnersdictionaries .com/us/definition/english/ontology?q=Ontology.

Primeco Education Website. (2023). *Team and Organizational Training*. Retrieved from https://www .primecoeducation.com/business-consulting.

Rothwell, William, J. (2015). *Organization Development Fundamentals: Managing Strategic Change*. Alexandria, WV: ATD Press.

Rothwell, Willian J. & Bakhshandeh, Behnam. (2022). *High-Performance Coaching for Managers. Step-by-Step Approach to Increase Employees' Performance and Productivity*. New York, NY: Taylor & Francis Group. Routledge.

Rothwell, William J., Imroz, Sohel M., & Bakhshandeh, Behnam. (2021). *Organization-Development Interventions: Executing Effective Organizational Chang*. New York, NY: Taylor & Francis Group. CRC Press.

Rothwell, William J. & Sredl, Henry J. (2014). *Workplace Learning and Performance: Present and Future Roles and Competencies, Volume II* (3rd Ed.). Amherst, MA: HR Press.

Rothwell, William J., Stavros, Jacqueline M., & Sullivan, Roland L. (2016). *Practicing Organization Development: Leading Transformation and Change* (4th ed.). Hoboken, NJ: John Wiley & Sons, Inc.

Sartre, Jean-Paul. (1943). *Being and Nothingness: A Phenomenological Essay on Ontology*. Translated by Hazel E. Barnes. New York, NY: Washington Express Press.

Seale, Alan. (2011). *Create a World That Works: Toles for Personal & Global Transformation*. San Francisco, CA: Weiser Books.

Seale, Alan. (2017). *Transformational Presence: How to Make a Difference in a Rapidly Changing World*. Topsfield, MA: The Center for Transformational Presence.

Seligman, Martin E. P. (2002). *Authentic Happiness: Using the New Positive Psychology to Realize Your Potential for Lasting Fulfillment*. New York, NY: Free Press.

Seligman, Martin and Csikszentmihalyi, Mihaly. (2010). Positive psychology: An introduction. In *Flow and the Foundations of Positive Psychology* (pp. 279–298). Dordrecht: Springer.

VanderPol, Leon. (2019). *A Shift in Being: The Art and Practices of Deep Transformational Coaching*. Imaginal Light Publishing.

Vesso, S. & Alas, R. (2016). Characteristics of a coaching culture in leadership style: The leader's impact on culture. *Problems and Perspectives in Management, 14*(2), 306–318. http://dx.doi.org/10.21511/ppm .14(2-2).2016.06.

Yukl, Gary. (2013). *Leadership in Organizations*, 8th ed. Upper Saddle River, NJ; Pearson.

Zaballero, Aileen G. (2024). Working with organizational leaders. In Behnam Bakhshandeh & William J. Rothwell (Eds.), *Building an Organizational Coaching Culture*. Oxfordshire, UK: UK Limited Trading, Taylor & Francis Group. Routledge.

Chapter 17

Emotional Intelligence Coach

Introduction

Emotional intelligence (EI) coaches are skilled professionals dedicated to enhancing people's emotional intelligence, a critical aspect of personal and professional success. Unlike traditional coaching, which often focuses on specific skills or goals, EI coaching delves into the realm of emotions, helping individuals recognize, understand, and manage their own emotions, as well as the emotions of others.

At the heart of the emotional intelligence coaches' role is the understanding that emotions profoundly influence human behavior and decision-making. These coaches are experts in the field of psychology and human emotions, equipped with a deep knowledge of emotional intelligence frameworks and theories. They employ their expertise to guide individuals or teams in developing the four key components of emotional intelligence: self-awareness, self-regulation, social awareness, and relationship management. First and foremost, emotional intelligence coaches serve as a mirror, reflecting the individuals' emotional strengths and areas needing improvement. Through assessments, feedback, and open conversations, they help their participants gain self-awareness, allowing them to recognize their emotional triggers and patterns of behavior. This awareness forms the foundation for individuals to build a more robust emotional intelligence.

This chapter covers the following topics:

- The EI Coach and the Coaching Relationship.
- Emotional Intelligence Coach Key Competencies.
- Ethics, Core Values and Standards in Coaching.
- Using Self-Reflection and Self-Evaluation to Enhance Coaching Skills.

The EI Coach and the Coaching Relationship

EI coaches are adept at teaching emotional regulation techniques. They help clients and training participants manage stress, anxiety, and other negative emotions, enabling them to navigate challenging situations with composure and grace. These professionals introduce mindfulness practices, relaxation techniques, and cognitive behavioral strategies tailored to an individual's specific needs. Moreover, emotional intelligence coaches act as a supportive guide in developing motivation. They assist participants in identifying their intrinsic motivators and aligning personal and professional goals with their core values. By fostering a strong sense of purpose and determination, individuals become more resilient, facing setbacks with a positive mindset and the determination to overcome obstacles.

DOI: 10.4324/9781003462316-21

Empathy, a cornerstone of emotional intelligence, is another area where these coaches excel. They help individuals understand the perspectives and emotions of others, fostering healthier relationships both personally and professionally. Through active listening and perspective-taking exercises, clients learn to connect on a deeper level with colleagues, family, and friends, improving communication and understanding. In the realm of social skills, emotional intelligence coaches provide valuable insights and practical guidance. They assist clients in enhancing their interpersonal communication, conflict resolution, and teamwork abilities. By honing these skills, individuals can build strong, harmonious relationships in the workplace, social circles, or intimate partnerships.

Importantly, emotional intelligence coaches tailor their approach to meet each client's unique needs or the core purpose of EI training. They are skilled communicators, empathetic listeners, and motivators who inspire positive change. Whether working one-on-one with executives, teams within a corporate setting, or individuals seeking personal growth, these coaches create a safe and non-judgmental space for clients to explore and enhance their emotional intelligence.

The Relationship between EI Coaches and Participants

The relationship and rapport between EI coaches and coachees are crucial for building a robust working connection, which is essential for achieving the goals specified for the participants' coaching process. Many training and development experts have emphasized that a strong connection is crucial for coaching effectiveness and attaining desired goals (Bakhshandeh, 2009). Unfortunately, while extensive research and investigation have been conducted on the interaction between therapists and clients, there has been less focus on the relationship between coaches and coachees (Baron & Morin, 2009). However, we may consult the *Oxford Dictionary*'s definition of coaching, which characterizes it as a verb used to "tutor, train, give hints to, prime with facts."

However, this definition fails to accurately delineate the relationship between a coach and coachee, as the activities of instructing, training, providing clues, and imparting factual knowledge can occur in various contexts without necessarily constituting a coaching relationship. However, coaching encompasses not only how these distinctions are conveyed but also pertains to the content conveyed, the information concealed, and the knowledge revealed (Rothwell, Imroz, & Bakhshandeh, 2021).

The coaching technique enables the coachee to achieve exceptional outcomes due to the close, compassionate, and supporting relationship between the coaches and coachees. The technique, kind, and style of communication between them are crucial elements for building a successful partnership. The essence and effectiveness of this partnership lie in the coaches' refusal to provide answers or fix challenges for the coachees. Instead, the coachees acquire answers by self-inquiry and generating solutions (Whitmore, 2009).

Establishing Rapport and Relationship for
Effective EI Coaching Relationships

Developing a connection and understanding of the commonalities between the coaches and the participants, persons, or teams is essential for creating a robust, efficient, and successful partnership in emotional intelligence coaching. Undoubtedly, you have likely encountered somebody, or perhaps you are acquainted with someone who can effortlessly establish connections with others. These individuals can establish connections and harmonious relationships with others, regardless of their background or professional field, fostering a sense of trust and ease within a very short period.

Through the establishment of rapport, creating a connection, and cultivating connections, coaches provide the groundwork for efficacy and functionality in the coaching relationship (refer to Figure 17.1) and ensure success in the process of EI coaching. Establishing rapport and relationships with others, particularly their participants, involves creating a partnership between the coaches and coachees. This partnership is based on mutual interest in the success of the coaching endeavor, as the coachees experience a sense of connection and comfort with the coach.

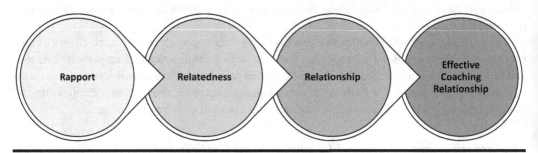

Figure 17.1   Rapport, relatedness, and relationship for an effective coaching relationship. Note. Adapted from Rothwell and Bakhshandeh (2023).

Rapport

Rapport serves as the foundation for establishing a significant relationship between two individuals or a collective group. Below are concise explanations about rapport and the process of cultivating a favorable relationship with people.

- "Rapport is a positive connection with another person, one that involves caring and understanding" (Angelo, 2012, p. 11).
- "Rapport is one's capability to establish a background of relatedness and connect with others" (Bakhshandeh, 2002, n. p.).
- "I like to define rapport as a deep emotional connection and understanding between two people" (Gilmore, 2019, p. 2).
- "Colloquially, rapport is the emotional experience of high-quality interactions. While the emotional experience of a high-quality interaction may often be associated with objective measures of high-quality interactions, this will not always be the case" (Baker, Watlington, & Knee, 2020, p. 330).

Tickle-Degnen and Rosenthal (1990) suggested that when we are building rapport with someone, we engage in the following forms of interaction:

- **Attention.** Each of us will concentrate on the other person's actions while demonstrating genuine attention in their words.
- **Positivity.** Both exhibit amicability and satisfaction while demonstrating attentiveness and regard for one another.
- **Coordination.** Both individuals sense synchrony and a common understanding. The user's energy levels, tone, and body language exhibit striking similarities.

Rather than viewing rapport only as a tool for building connections, coaches should consider it a potent practice and a pathway to success. As they cultivate rapport, coaches are establishing a relationship and trust with other individuals, creating the possibility for beneficial impact and mutual learning. Rapport is employed in several contexts, such as work possibilities, job interviews, social relationships, or as a means to enhance social skills (Tickle-Degnen & Rosenthal, 1990). Occasionally, individuals are able to build rapport immediately, but in other cases, it may take a longer period to cultivate the essential connection required to generate the trust needed to establish rapport. The success of managers or any others in leadership roles relies heavily on establishing a solid rapport and trust between managers and their employees (Rothwell and Bakhshandeh, 2023), as well as between transformational coaches and their participants in this context.

Rapport encompasses more than mere displays of social skills, friendship, or casual connections. It entails demonstrating emotional awareness, including compassion, empathy, and understanding of others' feelings (Gilmore, 2019). Gilmore (2019) emphasized that this link facilitates cooperation, communication, and, most significantly, a more profound understanding among individuals. Rapport, once created and nurtured, becomes deeply ingrained in both parties and has the ability to last for an extended duration (Angelo, 2012). In this regard, Travelbee (1963) mentioned:

> Rapport is a particular way in which we perceive and relate to our fellow human beings; it is composed of a cluster of inter-related thoughts and feelings, an interest in, and a concern for others, empathy, compassion, and sympathy, a non-judgmental attitude, and respect for the individual as a unique human being.
>
> **(p. 70)**

Relatedness

The second stage in developing effectiveness in a coaching relationship involves establishing a sense of connection based on the foundation built by establishing rapport (see Figure 17.1). Below are many concise explanations and descriptions of the concept of relatedness:

- "The state or fact of being related or connected" (Lexico, 2023, n.p.)
- "The social nature of human beings and the connectedness with others. Both can be considered as being part of the panhuman psychology, and both are intrinsically intertwined" (Keller, 2016, p. 1).

In his work, Keller (2016) proposed the integration of relatedness and autonomy as two essential human wants. He said that the concept of self and others may encompass the aspects of autonomy and relatedness. Autonomy and relatedness are fundamental human needs and cultural constructions that coexist. Although they may have distinct definitions, they both retain equal significance. The concept of autonomy and relatedness is instilled in individuals via their socialization process, which occurs through the everyday events and routines of life starting from infancy onward (Hofstede, 1980). The conceptualizations of relatedness and autonomy and their interaction have been the subject of many perspectives across time (Triandis, 1995).

Aristotelous (2019) highlighted the persuasive evidence from literature reviews and research that strongly indicates that fostering a sense of connection among individuals by cultivating stronger human relationships leads to increased optimism in workplaces and organizations. Simultaneously, Aristotelous (2019) continued by underlining, "at the same time, preserving our humanity and our sense of relatedness with one another at such times of unprecedented technological development seems a daunting task" (p. 53).

Relationship

A relationship is the result of developing a connection and shared understanding with another individual or a collective. A relationship refers to the emotional and behavioral dynamics between two individuals or groups. There are many ways people use to describe their good relationships with others. We are all familiar with them in informal discussions or when someone is discussing their connections (McMahon, 2019):

- We possess a strong mutual comprehension.
- We have established a positive and harmonious relationship.
- Our acquaintance spans a significant duration.
- We have a close and amicable friendship.
- They are my trusted companions.
- We maintain a harmonious and congenial relationship.
- We share several common ideals and interests.

To ensure the effectiveness, feasibility, and success of EI coaching with the participants, it is crucial for the EI coaches to create rapport, relatedness, and cultivate a connection with the individuals.

The Three Main Gears of Coaching Relationship Effectiveness

The coaching connection in emotional intelligence (EI) is indistinguishable from any other coaching or mentoring relationship. As previously stated, the first degree of effectiveness and functionality between the coaches and participants involves building rapport and relatedness. This serves as the basis for a functional connection between both parties. The second tier of efficacy and practicality, referred to as the cogwheels of coaching, has three elements:

1) Respect.
2) Trust.
3) The framework of the relationship (refer to Figure 17.2).

In the following part, we will provide a concise explanation of the three gears and their significance in terms of their impact on the effectiveness of a coaching relationship.

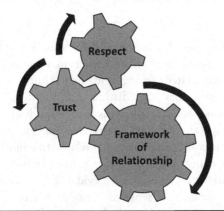

Figure 17.2 The three main gears of coaching relationship effectiveness. Note. Adapted from Behnam Bakhshandeh, Rothwell, and Imroz (2023).

Respect

The initial gear represents the concept of respect. Transformational coaches demonstrate their reverence for their trainees by wholeheartedly dedicating themselves, fully committing, and refraining from withholding anything. The individuals will demonstrate their admiration by refraining from compromising their principles at challenging times and by refusing to tolerate participants who limit their potential. They will persist by asking probing questions and insisting that participants delve into profound aspects of themselves. Dedicated coaches will demonstrate their appreciation for the investments made by their participants, including time, effort, and financial resources (either provided directly by the clients or sponsors), by persisting and resisting feelings of resignation and despair resulting from years of disappointment, lack of understanding, or being ignored (Bakhshandeh, 2009) (refer to Figure 17.2).

Occasionally, participants may harbor dislike toward their coaches or the coaching process. They may see their trainers as lacking understanding, being overly demanding, or lacking empathy, which can lead to emotions of pain. Due to the coaches' admiration for them, they persist in overcoming their various sentiments and emotions, and continue to exert more effort and intensity. The other aspect of this connection involves the participants' respect for the instructors; it is a reciprocal relationship. As participants, it is important for you to show respect toward your coaches by not taking their teaching style and approach personally. This is because transformational coaching aims to help you become more aware, effective, productive, and fulfilled personally and professionally in all areas of your life (Bakhshandeh, 2009) (see Figure 17.2).

Trust

The second gear represents the concept of trust. Requesting participants to trust their coaches instantly without prior knowledge or the establishment of rapport and relationship may appear illogical. Developing trust over time and via encounters is very comprehensible. Simultaneously, participants have nothing to risk by starting the relationship with trust in their coaches, unless the coaches provide concrete proof of untrustworthiness. The transformational coach will start the connection with their participants by establishing a foundation of respect and trust. Simultaneously, they will seek the participants' trust in order to enhance their relationship and achieve workability more quickly (Bakhshandeh, 2009).

The coaches must have confidence in the participants' willingness to express their problems, demonstrate their comprehension, and consistently speak the truth. The coaches first place their faith in the participants, assuming that they would not conceal any information throughout the coaching process, and instead will be sincere, true, and genuine. The crux of the situation is that if participants withhold information and fail to fully engage, the coach is unable to provide them with crucial coaching insights, inquiries, and support. Conversely, the participants need to have confidence in their coaches, believing that they are supportive and dedicated to providing the information and facilitating the process effectively (Bakhshandeh, 2009) (see Figure 17.2).

Framework of Relationship

The third and final gear is the framework of relationship between the coach and their participants. The sole connection present in this context is the coach and coachee relationship, devoid of any other associations. We do not have any affiliations, such as being married, being siblings, being part of the same family, or having any other business partnership or therapist–patient relationship.

This occurs because it is inherent in the human mind to oppose suggestions or advice from family and friends instinctively. When transformational coaches go deeper into creating and examining possible difficulties, individuals may recall earlier instances of controlling and domineering behaviors shown by their parents, siblings, partners, or friends. Participants must recall the context of this coaching interaction at that moment. Understanding this background is crucial for developing a functional and harmonious coaching relationship, free from any assumptions or misinterpretations (Bakhshandeh, 2009).

The coaches prioritize the participants' knowledge acquisition, engagement, behaviors, and ability to handle their behaviors effectively. Transformational coaches focus on the participants' actions and are not concerned with personal conflicts, narratives, grievances, or justifications. Their primary focus is on their acquisition of knowledge and the practical application of that knowledge as they devise a strategic course of action to address these matters. Evidently, if the coaching connection deviates from the coaches' and coachees' dynamics, it will not be functional or successful. This is because, in any other type of interaction, there will be several expectations and interpretations (Bakhshandeh, 2009) (refer to Figure 17.2).

Requirements for Delivering a Successful EI Coaching

EI coaches need to exhibit the following behaviors and achieve a level of mastery in their own emotional intelligence to effectively use emotional intelligence to impact the transformation of the people they work with and help them achieve their goals. According to Bakhshandeh et al. (2023):

■ They must possess a commanding awareness of the foundations of emotional intelligence for leadership development, as well as the capacity to describe them and provide instances of how they work, and the attributes and attributions that are connected to them.
■ They must continue to make uninterrupted and ongoing progress and improvement on their own emotional intelligence and the associated traits and attributes.
■ Their vision, as well as how it relates to the values and ideals they uphold in their professional and personal lives, serves as the foundation for their vision.
■ Robust personal and professional ties with the people who make up their initial social and professional circle are crucial to their goal for mastery.
■ They must apply honesty, responsibility, and accountability not just in their professional lives but also in their personal lives as a whole.
■ Participation in transformation coaching for themselves and continuing to engage in activities will build their capabilities to provide transformational coaching.

Emotional Intelligence Coach Key Competencies

When it comes to coaching others, EI coaches must possess self-assurance in their capacity to perceive the underlying problem and possess the necessary abilities and competencies to maintain the clients' attention on the issue at hand. It is important to consider the apparent problem and the underlying causes that led to the problem manifesting in the clients' personal or professional settings. The link between the symptoms and the sickness may be likened to the issue being the symptom and the illness's source. Bakhshandeh (2015) suggests that this skill may be ascribed to possessing compassion for others, exercising patience with individuals, attentively listening, fostering personal accountability, and distinguishing between reality and interpretations. Kindly refer to the following list by Bakhshandeh (2015).

Professionalism

Professionalism refers to the state or characteristic of being skilled, courteous, and morally upright in one's professional endeavors. The way in which individuals present themselves to others is crucial in effectively conveying professionalism and guaranteeing achievement. Professionalism encompasses three essential elements: physical presentation, exemplary conduct, and professional demeanor.

Compassion

Possessing and cultivating compassion is a fundamental component of any accomplished coach. It is important to be aware of the clients' location and the challenges they are encountering, including any pain, suffering, or lack of efficacy they may be feeling. Recognizing that if they had the ability to modify that problem, they would have already done it, and there is no fault in their current position in their life or business. I ensure that they see the insignificance of what has occurred in their lives when contrasted to the profound changes taking place within their inner being.

Empathy

Empathy is the capacity to comprehend and partake in the emotions of another individual. It is an essential ability for EI coaches, as it enables them to establish rapport, trust, and connection with their clients. Empathy furthermore allows coaches to engage in active listening, pose impactful inquiries, and provide efficacious comments.

Patience

In addition to being sympathetic, exercising patience with others is a valuable asset in enabling the client to navigate the process of self-awareness and self-realization without feeling coerced. It is important to recognize that individuals vary in their ability to discover and develop their personalities, actions, and attitudes and may not be able to assume full responsibility and ownership of their own growth as quickly as their coach or others.

Collaboration

Collaboration refers to a partnership or cooperative effort in which many persons work together to accomplish shared goals or objectives. At its core, collaboration involves the exchange of ideas, the will to work together, the ability to coordinate actions, active involvement, the facilitation of communication, mutual give and take, thoughtful consideration, and active involvement.

Effective Communication

Coaches always remain cognizant and attuned to any filters that may impact their personal perspectives. They must formulate the intended message, pose inquiries that enhance lucidity and comprehension, and offer feedback to strengthen the message. Obtaining feedback by employing skillful asking allows them to assess the listeners' comprehension.

Keen Listening

They need to embrace their own grandeur and perfection while being immune to pettiness or insignificance while perceiving and analyzing the scenario. The circumstance accurately reflects the clients' descriptions or their true identity in no way whatsoever. We must ensure that interactions with them do not contribute to the multitude of excuses they generate to justify their inability to achieve their desires. Instead, coaches should provide them with one or two justifications that empower them to believe in their capabilities.

Personal Responsibility

Coaches need to advocate for the clients to assume accountability for their decisions. The root cause of misery frequently stems from either evading decision-making or lacking dedication to the coaches' chosen choices. Deciding is a simple task. The challenge lies in preserving and strengthening the decisions coaches have taken. There is a multitude of individuals in the world who consistently evade accountability for their actions. They just desire to attribute their own lack of pleasure, contentment, or effectiveness personally or professionally to something or someone. Coaches will thoroughly examine themselves and identify the responsibilities they wish to avoid. The secret to their tranquility lies within reach.

Reality Versus Interpretations

Coaches should ensure to guide them toward distinguishing between objective reality and subjective fabrication. When they take complete responsibility for their actions and the entirety of their lives, the quality of their lives is not determined or influenced by events, circumstances, or situations—the coaches determine it! They experience many events; some challenging, some sorrowful, and some unforeseen. Simultaneously, remarkable, enjoyable, and jubilant occurrences also take place. Each of these occurrences that constitute their existence serves as a reminder of their vitality!

Ethical Performance

Adhere to ethical and professional norms, including maintaining professional boundaries with coachees, avoiding excessive fees, safeguarding their confidentiality, and complying with other ethical guidelines.

True accomplishment and success are only realized when coaches are willing to develop, change, or modify their behaviors and routines. As I have consistently emphasized, attempting to achieve success without a structured and planned approach is akin to constructing a high-rise without a meticulously designed and solid foundation. In such a scenario, the building is vulnerable to external factors, and its eventual collapse is inevitable. It is not a question of possibility but rather a matter of timing. In the realm of the physical world, our ability to exert control is limited to our actions in the present now, and our commitment to carry out our plan until its completion. Upon reflection, coaches have unexpectedly constructed a future (Table 17.1).

Table 17.1 Emotional Intelligence Coach Key Competencies Self-Rating Sheet

Instruction:
(a) Using the rating scale (shown below), self-rate yourself as a manager, supervisor, coach, consultant, or independent in understanding and enhancing your key emotional intelligence competencies, (b) then tally your rating, and (c) finally, come up with actions you will take to increase your rating on the next rating period.

Date:	Participant:		Organization:			
	Rating Scale: 1 = Poor, 2 = Marginal, 3 = Acceptable, 4 = Good, 5 = Excellent					
#	*EI Competencies*	*1*	*2*	*3*	*4*	*5*
1	Professionalism					
2	Compassion					
3	Empathy					
4	Patience					
5	Collaboration					
6	Effective Communication					
7	Keen Listening					
8	Personal Responsibility					
9	Reality versus Interpretation					
10	Ethical Performance					
	Total per rating					
	Total (total of above totals per ratings)					
	Average (above total divided by 10)					

Three correctional and developmental actions I will take that will raise my three lowest self-ratings by at least one scale on the next rating:
Action 1:
Action 2:
Action 3:

Note. Author's original creation. © 2024 by Behnam Bakhshandeh.

Ethics, Core Values, and Standards in Coaching

Values are core principles that shape our attitudes, establish standards of behavior, and influence our judgments of what is morally right or wrong (Cooks-Campbell, 2022). Individuals possess inherent personal values, such as integrity, compassion, honesty, and discipline. However, these values may be significantly shaped by external factors such as the individuals' environment, beliefs, background, education, and social network (Active Social Care, 2023). Besides personal values, there are also professional values, which are the fundamental principles that govern our professional behavior, such as non-maleficence and justice. Additionally, there are organizational values, a collection of essential ideas upheld by a company, such as customer service, teamwork, and inclusion (Imroz, 2024).

Ethics may be defined as the logical basis of our moral judgments, which enables us to differentiate between what is morally correct and incorrect or what is fair and unfair. Ethical behavior refers to the implementation of moral ideals in a certain scenario. The presence of ethics is crucial in professional coaching since it establishes the fundamental basis of coach–client interaction (Imroz, 2024). Coaches are commonly known as mentors, facilitators, or guides. Coaches have the ability to observe and track the advancement of their customers using their own methods. However, their primary aim is to assist clients in achieving their specific aims, goals, or transitions (Yadav, 2021). The fundamental principles that underpin coaching, such as honesty, respect, and responsibility, form the foundation of coaches' actions and motivations. Given the personal nature of most coaching relationships, professional coaches rely on these coaching ideals as a framework and set of principles to guide their work (Yadav, 2021).

The primary objective of professional ethics is to implement the principles that regulate the moral conduct of people and groups within a corporate setting. Bond (2015) states that professional ethics is a crucial component of the individuals' professional identities, which encompasses attitudes, values, knowledge, beliefs, and abilities that are shared among members of a professional organization (Matthews, Bialocerkowski, & Molineux, 2019, p. 1). Professional ethics serve as the fundamental basis for education and application in several different fields of work (Imroz, 2024).

Ethics in the Context of Coaching

Ethical codes inherently possess constraints while they intend to establish a framework of conduct. Abstracting moral principles disregards the implicit frameworks that shape the individuals' self-perception, self-esteem, and moral conduct (Taylor, 1989). An aspect of ethical concern frequently expressed by esteemed coaches is the issue of competency. Coaches may make exaggerated claims in order to persuade clients. They may mistakenly believe that they can contribute to making significant improvements or offer valuable perspectives to customers that are above their own skill level (Brennan & Wildflower, 2010).

Within a career where the act of interaction carries emotional and moral consequences, it becomes increasingly essential and challenging to articulate appropriate ethical conduct. The most crucial aspect of an ethical practice is precisely inside this realm of nuanced moral assessment. Furthermore, it is the point at which the progression of adult growth and moral abilities intersect with ethical principles. Regrettably, it is impossible to enact legislation or impose penalties to regulate or control conduct at this level (Brennan & Wildflower, 2010).

Within any coaching scenario, it is important to rely on the coaches' instincts to avoid causing harm and diligently strive for favorable outcomes for the client. The following instances involve scenarios with coaches in which unethical conduct may go unnoticed by a code of ethics (Brennan & Wildflower, 2010):

- ◼ They deceive about their capacity to achieve a desired result in order to retain a customer or, in a more benign manner, to enhance the clients' satisfaction.
- ◼ They develop emotional attachments to the clients' problems and unintentionally influence the clients to fulfill their own personal desires.

- They maintain clients who have a strong affinity for coaching but fail to demonstrate any improvement in their coaching endeavors.

The desire to behave ethically is inherently linked to the individuals' capacities to distinguish themselves from others and possess a refined degree of moral cognition. Being coaches necessitates a steadfast dedication to ethical principles, constant mindfulness, and a commitment to continued education (Brennan & Wildflower, 2010).

Core Values of Professional Coaching

The International Coaching Federation (ICF) (a non-profit organization committed to professional coaching) presents the following core values.

Professionalism

Professionalism refers to the state of possessing competence, respect, and ethical behavior in one's professional endeavors. The way individuals present themselves to others is crucial for effectively conveying professionalism and guaranteeing achievement (Grant, 2020). According to Grant (2020), these are the three key components of professionalism:

- Appearance.
- Professional behavior.
- Professional conduct.

According to Imroz (2024), the ICF Core Values (2022) provide the following guidelines for coaches to exhibit professionalism:

- Coaches should ensure that their coaching perspective is consistent with their professional behavior. It is important for them to prioritize the importance of humanity in every encounter they have.
- Coaches must adhere to a strict standard of honesty and precision in their comments, and they should continuously engage in ongoing professional learning and growth throughout their careers. In addition, it is important for coaches to provide assistance in the continuous growth and progress of their customers, students, and other professionals affiliated with the ICF.
- Coaches must possess an understanding of ethical predicaments and possess the ability to address them in accordance with the ICF Code of Ethics. In accordance with the ICF Core Competencies, individuals should also disseminate their experience and abilities to others.
- Coaches should exhibit resilience and confidence, consistently conduct themselves with respect, and maintain transparency in all coaching-related transactions.

Collaboration

Collaboration refers to a synergistic and cooperative effort when several persons work together to accomplish shared goals or objectives (AIIM, 2023). At its core, collaboration encompasses several elements, such as awareness, motivation, self-synchronization, involvement, mediation, reciprocity, reflection, and engagement (AIIM, 2023).

Imroz (2024) states that ICF Core Values (2022) provide coaches with the subsequent suggestions for fostering collaboration:

- Coaches should cultivate ingenuity and adaptability to advance the practice of coaching and collaborate with diverse social-identity groups.
- Coaches should be aware of their personal involvement while working and collaborating with customers, sponsors, and other professionals affiliated with the ICF from other fields, associations, and coaching organizations.

Humanity

As per the *Merriam-Webster* dictionary definition, humanity refers to the characteristic or condition of being human, encompassing compassionate, empathetic, or generous behavior or disposition. For certain individuals, the concept of humanity encompasses the act of showing compassion toward others and providing assistance during their most vulnerable moments. Some individuals may perceive acts of assisting others as manifestations of altruism. The intrinsic worth of people is inherently central to all coaching vocations, which is unsurprising.

Imroz (2024) states that the ICF emphasizes the need for coaches to display humanity through the methods outlined in the ICF Core Values 2022, specifically in the section on humanity:

- Coaches ought to foster a culture characterized by transparency, introspection, and self-acceptance among their clients while recognizing their own limits and errors. In addition, individuals should demonstrate a willingness to comprehend and appreciate the perspectives of others, while embodying principles of inclusivity, dignity, self-worth, and human rights.
- Coaches should cultivate coaching relationships characterized by honesty and transparency, taking ownership of their actions, expressing their achievements with humility, and refraining from behaviors that imply superiority.

Equity

Equity may be defined as the characteristic of being equitable, which means being fair, just, and unbiased. The National Association of Colleges and Employers (NACE) clarified the distinction between the frequently misunderstood concepts of equality and equity. According to NACE (2023), equality refers to the provision of the same resources to everyone, while equity acknowledges that individuals do not all begin from the same position and necessitates recognizing and addressing existing imbalances. The principle of fairness is equally relevant in the realm of professional coaching.

Imroz (2024) suggests that coaches might show equality by following the guidelines outlined in the ICF Core Values (2022, p. 4):

- Coaches should acknowledge and honor all identity groupings and treat every individual with dignity. In addition, it is important to uphold parity and impartiality in all coaching interactions.
- Coaches must possess an understanding of their own biases, as well as biases present in others, and comprehend the impact of biases on coaching relationships. Furthermore, individuals should know about social diversity, systemic equity, and systemic oppression that may arise within the coaching profession.

Role of Coaching Industry Standards and Ethics in Coaching at Workplaces

The use of coaching in workplaces is essential for achieving organizational success and ensuring employee retention. A coaching culture is established via the principles of trust, cooperation, and responsibility. Companies that embrace a coaching culture have explicit guidelines for employee performance and standards (Tan, 2022). Funck (2023) suggests that organizational leaders should take into account three crucial criteria when implementing a coaching culture. Initially, leaders ought to exhibit the significance, advantages, and influence of coaching to employees, such as acquiring more self-assurance, developing self-sufficiency, and enhancing certain talents through coaching (Imroz, 2024). Furthermore, leaders should see coaching as a fundamental component of the organization's initiatives for developing leadership skills and managing talent. Leaders should also actively promote the development of coaching abilities and a coaching mentality among important influencers, such as HR professionals. The outcomes of implementing a coaching culture in organizations demonstrate the establishment of a high-performance work environment and a notable enhancement in employee accountability while "fostering a climate of full engagement, personal development, and mutual support" (Funck, 2023, para. Outcomes of a Coaching Culture; Imroz, 2024).

Implementing a coaching culture in the workplace assists people with many workplace concerns, including career advancement, influence and dispute resolution, employee welfare, leadership, communication, time management, productivity, and strategic planning. Kirk (2019) highlights the need to maintain professional standards in an emerging business such as coaching. He asserts that engaging with competent coaches who adhere to established coaching standards enhances the effectiveness and confidence of the coaching relationship with their customers (Imroz, 2024). The implementation of professional coaching standards and adherence to a code of ethics can provide coaches with a framework to enhance their expertise and proficiency. This framework enables coaches to navigate their responsibilities effectively, providing optimal outcomes for their clients while avoiding potential pitfalls (Imroz, 2024). Moreover, coaching standards ensure that coaches conduct themselves professionally, adhere to ethical principles, uphold client confidentiality, and demonstrate a strong dedication to personal growth (Kirk, 2019).

Standards and Code of Ethics

According to Imroz (2024), the International Coaching Community (ICC) (ICC is a non-profit organization for professional coaches with more than 15,000 certified coaches from 78 countries) presented the following coaching standards and ethics (ICC Standards and Code of Ethics, 2023):

Professional Conduct at Large. "Coaches will not knowingly make any public statement that is untrue or misleading about what they offer as coaches or make false claims in any written documents relating to the coaching profession or the coaches' credentials" (Section 1).

Conflict of Interest. "Coaches will seek to avoid conflicts of interest and potential conflicts of interest and openly disclose any such conflicts. Coaches will offer to remove themselves when such a conflict arises" (Section 2).

Professional Conduct with Clients. "Coaches will seek to avoid conflicts of interest and potential conflicts of interest and openly disclose any such conflicts. Coaches will offer to remove themselves when such a conflict arises" (Section 3).

Confidentiality and Privacy. "Coaches will maintain the strictest levels of confidentiality with all client and sponsor information. Coaches will have a clear agreement contract before releasing information to another person unless required by law" (Section 4).

Using Self-Reflection and Self-Evaluation to Enhance Coaching Skills

As professional coaches, including coaches specializing in emotional intelligence (EI), we engage with people, teams, groups, and organizations. Irrespective of the reason or objective behind the engagement or the commercial rationale for the participation, our interaction with individuals aims to positively impact their productivity, performance, and skill development. In essence, we are establishing a connection with human beings.

Engaging in self-reflection and self-evaluation will allow us to accurately assess our strengths and shortcomings that require more focus in order to strengthen the process and boost our coaching abilities and competencies. Furthermore, this strategy enhances our skills as a more proficient and capable coach, enabling us to provide a more favorable and productive assessment of our participants and the evaluation reports we provide to individuals, teams, and group supervisors or senior managers.

Self-reflection and self-evaluation, often referred to as self-assessment, are effective methods for gaining insight into our strengths and limitations and enhancing our learning, skills, and behaviors (Bakhshandeh, 2009). Thus, these genuine contemplations and sincere assessments have a crucial impact on coaching practice and on the growth of a transformative coach who works with individuals and teams.

Throughout this book, we have frequently utilized various self-rating and self-evaluation forms for coaches to engage in a personal assessment in order to develop strategies to improve their talents or better their self-directed learning endeavors. Therefore, please regard the information presented in this section as supplementary to what you have already learned from the self-ratings and self-evaluations in prior chapters.

First, we will begin by providing concise and precise explanations for important terms and concepts.

Self-Reflection

Self-reflection enables us to utilize our experiences in order to gain a more profound comprehension of ourselves and our actions. Engaging in self-reflection enables us to become more conscious and self-aware of our mental attitudes and behaviors, which in turn influence our actions and habits in life (Barbazette, 2006). This self-awareness would enable us to discern aspects of ourselves and our methods that should be abandoned, modified, improved, or further developed.

■ Oxford Languages (2023, n.p.) defines self-reflection as "meditation or serious thought about one's character, actions, and motives."
■ According to the *Merriam-Webster* (2023a, n.p.) dictionary, synonyms for *self-reflection* are "introspection, self-contemplation, self-examination, self-observation, self-questioning, self-scrutiny, self-searching, soul-searching."

Engaging in self-reflection requires deliberate effort and a specific level of self-control, which entails a genuine curiosity in understanding ourselves and exploring what is effective and ineffective (Bakhshandeh, 2018). EI coaching involves the use of self-reflection by coaches to assess their efficacy in working with participants and identify areas for improvement in their practices.

Self-Evaluation

Self-evaluation is a process of critically examining and assessing our own behaviors, habits, and performance in the workplace or other aspects of our lives. Rothwell and Kazanas (2004) defined self-evaluation as a chance for employees to assess and document their own performance, activities, and workplace experiences from their own perspectives. This strategy is a self-assessment that employees may communicate to their supervisors or higher-level management. By doing so, they can collaboratively develop an effective action plan to address any problems or improve performance.

- *Merriam-Webster* (2023b) dictionary provides the following synonyms: "self-abnegation, self-revelation, self-examination, self-absorption."

(Important Note: In this book and in this chapter, we shall use the words "self-evaluation" to encompass the concepts of self-rating, self-reflection, and self-assessment.)

The Principal Intention of Self-Evaluation

At its most basic level, the primary objective of self-assessment in businesses is for workers to assess their own performances and productivity and subsequently compare it with the appraisal provided by their supervisors at the yearly performance review (Phillips & Pulliam Phillips, 2011). At an elevated level, self-evaluations assist employees in comprehending the obstacles they face in terms of professional advancement and progress inside their respective departments and companies. By engaging in self-evaluations, employees have the opportunity to synchronize their individual and professional objectives with those of their supervisors (Thompson, 2021). Self-evaluations offer employees the autonomy to articulate their thoughts and communicate their opinions to their employers, thus fostering autonomy for them and facilitating the development of a more robust connection between employees and their superiors. Regarding this book, the self-evaluation of EI coaches aids in enhancing their coaching process and acquiring the necessary skills for development (Bakhshandeh et al., 2023).

Prerequisites for Conducting Self-Evaluation

Self-evaluation entails individuals critically examining and evaluating their own performances while reflecting on the mindsets, attitudes, and behaviors impacting their productivity and effectiveness (Whitmore, 2017). In essence, this approach ultimately improves their knowledge acquisition and sense of responsibility for the outcomes they achieve, both in their personal and professional lives. According to Bakhshandeh et al. (2023), for self-evaluation to be most effective, persons must adhere to the following:

- Exhibit honesty and authenticity by accurately reflecting the truth.
- Abandon the need to be "correct" about what is ineffective or harmful.

■ Assess their performance in comparison to established standards or criteria.
■ Maintain regular and systematic monitoring of their development at appropriate intervals (weekly, monthly, quarterly, etc.).
■ Identify and differentiate their areas of expertise and the ways in which they have cultivated them.
■ Identify and differentiate their shortcomings and determine the necessary actions to address them.
■ Establish attainable, controllable, and quantifiable objectives for areas that are not functioning well.
■ Develop a strategic plan to address areas of weakness and improve areas of strength.
■ Discuss their set of goals and action plans with their supervisors or higher-level managers for evaluation.
■ Solicit input from their superiors or higher-level executives.
■ Engage in introspection over the comments received and make appropriate modifications to their action plans.
■ Engage in introspection and assessment of their preferred methods and frameworks for acquiring knowledge.
■ Utilize external resources such as books, articles, webinars, etc., to augment their learning.

Some Examples of Self-Evaluation for EI Coaches

This section examines EI coaches' skills, abilities, disciplines, and performances in five specific areas. These areas directly influence the development of participants' skills, talent, and effectiveness, whether as individuals or as part of a team:

■ Presence of coaching culture in organizations.
■ Emotional intelligence.
■ Leadership attributes.
■ Coaching disciplines.
■ Common skills and competencies.

Presence of Coaching Culture in Organizations

Developing a coaching culture inside businesses is crucial for the successful and efficient implementation of coaching, particularly the transformational coaching method. The presence of a coaching culture allows transformative coaches to effectively implement coaching strategies to enhance performance and effectiveness in individuals and teams. This is achieved with minimal resistance and with a greater acceptance of the coaching processes and inquiries (Rothwell & Bakhshandeh, 2023). A coaching culture that fosters transformative coaching and successful leadership possesses certain and discernible attributes. Kindly utilize Table 17.2 to evaluate the unique characteristics of the organization's coaching culture. Next, provide novel suggestions for enhancing the current components in order to develop a coaching culture inside their organization.

Table 17.2   Evaluating the Presence of an Organization's Coaching Culture by EI Coach

Name	Date	Organization				

Instruction:
(a) Using the rating scale (shown below), as a manager, supervisor, coach, consultant or independent on your assessment in the presence of coaching culture in the organization, (b) then tally your rating, and (c) finally, come up with at least three suggestion you will take to increase the rating on the next rating period.

Rating Scale: *1* = Poor, *2* = Marginal, *3* = Acceptable, *4* = Good, *5* = Excellent

Areas of Coaching Culture		*1*	*2*	*3*	*4*	*5*
1	Relationships and mutual trust are the cornerstones of the organization.					
2	Self-realization and self-discovery are promoted by the organization.					
3	Transparency and openness are the foundation of the organization.					
4	Managers and supervisors encourage and facilitate self-awareness.					
5	Managers and supervisors support and foster education and personal growth.					
6	It gives workers a secure environment in which to own their strengths and weaknesses.					
7	It encourages and demonstrates deep dialogue to change people's lives.					
8	It encourages self-improvement and stimulates workers.					
9	The company exhibits a readiness to provide and accept criticism in order to grow.					
10	It is evident that managers see possibilities for everyone's growth and development.					
11	Management is committed to fulfilling its leadership role by helping its employees grow.					
12	It gives workers a secure and welcoming environment in which to discuss matters that are significant to them.					
13	The management shows that they are committed to and want a coaching culture.					
14	Regardless of level, managers and supervisors express interest in receiving guidance.					

(Continued)

Table 17.2 (CONTINUED) Evaluating the Presence of an Organization's Coaching Culture by EI Coach

15	Managers and supervisors promote understanding and active listening.					
16	In order to identify problems and develop solutions, managers encourage staff members to ask questions.					
17	Teams and groups are empowered to practice team coaching by the company.					
18	It promotes comprehension of coaching procedures, standard coaching terminology, and concepts.					
19	The company uses many methods to assess employee performance.					
20	Managers use their abilities to solve challenges for both people and teams.					
	Individual Columns' Totals					
	Total of Above Individual Columns					
	Final Average (above total divided by 20)					
What are you suggesting to this organization as corrective actions for improving their presence of coaching culture:						
Suggestion 1:						
Suggestion 2:						
Suggestion 3:						

Note. © 2024 by Behnam Bakhshandeh

Emotional Intelligence

Within this section, we extend an invitation to EI coaches to assess and assign a rating to their comprehension and implementation of the various components of emotional intelligence. Table 17.3 is intended for coaches to assess their own comprehension and use of emotional intelligence when working with their players during practice. This will serve as their inaugural endeavor and evaluation, which may be extended inside the subsequent half-year or the following year, contingent upon whether the evaluation attains a sufficient level or falls below a satisfactory threshold.

Table 17.3 Coaches' Emotional Intelligence Self-Evaluation

Name	Date	Organization

Instruction:
(a) Using the rating scale (shown below), self-rate yourself as a manager, supervisor, coach, consultant, or independent on understanding and enhancing your own emotional intelligence, (b) then tally your rating, and (c) finally, come up with actions you will take to increase your rating on the next rating period.

Rating Scale: 1 = Never, 2 = Hardly, 3 = Occasionally, 4 = Generally, 5 = Constantly

Clusters		*Areas Needing Attention*	*1*	*2*	*3*	*4*	*5*
Self-Awareness	1	Be aware of how your body language responds to what other people are saying.					
	2	Observe others' facial expressions when having a conversation.					
	3	Examine your prejudices and ideas while assessing circumstances.					
	4	Recognize your feelings before, during, and after delicate discussions.					
Self-Regulation	5	When you are angry, you control yourself and remain calm.					
	6	Avoid saying or doing something just because you have a strong need to.					
	7	Before speaking or acting, take some time to consider your feelings and ideas.					
	8	Control your emotions and attitudes; don't bring them into discussions.					
Social Awareness	9	Recognize how other people see you while we are interacting.					
	10	Identify the emotions and dispositions of people through non-verbal cues.					
	11	Show sympathy and understanding for other people in their circumstances.					
	12	Recognize the diversity of individuals and their cultural backgrounds.					

(Continued)

Table 17.3 (CONTINUED) Coaches' Emotional Intelligence Self-Evaluation

Relationship Management	13	Accept responsibility for errors promptly and make amends.					
	14	When conversing with people, use language that is supportive.					
	15	Handle emotional actions with tact and composure.					
	16	Persuade and inspire people to examine alternative viewpoints.					
Individual Columns' Totals							
Total of Above Individual Columns							
Final Average (above total divided by 16)							
Three correctional and developmental actions I will take that will raise my three lowest self-ratings by at least one scale on the next rating:							
Action 1:							
Action 2:							
Action 3:							

Note. © 2024 by Behnam Bakhshandeh

Leadership Attributes

Coaches have a direct role in creating a conducive learning environment to foster effective leadership development in individuals and teams, directly impacting the overall quality of leadership within organizations. In order to accomplish this, coaches must cultivate a profound level of leadership attributes within themselves (Bakhshandeh, 2002). Within this area, the coaches assess their leadership attributes via their engagements with individuals, teams, and organizations. Table 17.4 displays a self-assessment rating for specific leadership attributes of a coach.

Table 17.4 Leadership Attributes of Coach Self-Evaluation

Name	Date	Organization
Instruction: (a) Using the rating scale (shown below), self-rate yourself as a manager, supervisor, coach, consultant or independent on understanding and enhancing your own leadership attributions, (b) then tally your rating, and (c) finally, come up with actions you will take to increase your rating on the next rating period.		

(Continued)

Table 17.4   (CONTINUED) Leadership Attributes of Coach Self-Evaluation

Rating Scale: *1* = Poor, *2* = Marginal, *3* = Acceptable, *4* = Good, *5* = Excellent						
Attributes		**Descriptions**	*1*	*2*	*3*	*4*	*5*
1	**Respectful**	Show consideration for all individuals, irrespective of their status.					
2	**Positive**	Be a positive role model and affect others around them without provoking opposition.					
3	**Willing to Share Triumphs**	As a team, celebrate your successes and share the wins.					
4	**Solution Oriented**	To diffuse others' problem-based habits, pose inquiries with a focus on solutions.					
5	**Innovative**	Encourage learning and experimenting to foster creativity and innovation.					
6	**Communicative**	To create coalitions for action, encourage efficient communication and attentive listening.					
7	**Engaging**	Interact with others and encourage them to express their talents and passions.					
8	**Flexible**	React quickly and nimbly to shifting and unstable conditions.					
9	**Transparent**	Be genuine, promote trust, and cultivate connections with others.					
10	**Empathetic**	Be humble, empathetic, and kind to raise spirits.					
		Individual Columns' Totals					
		Total of Above Individual Columns					
		Final Average (above total divided by 10)					
Three correctional and developmental actions I will take that will raise my three lowest self-ratings by at least one scale on the next rating:							
Action 1:							
Action 2:							
Action 3:							

Note. © 2024 by Behnam Bakhshandeh

Coaching Disciplines

Similar to other professions, EI coaching, as well as other forms of coaching, must adhere to specific practices in order to advance as professional coaches and maintain a thriving practice. This section examines the essential factors that contribute to the success of coaches in their profession. Table 17.5 presents a selection of essential disciplines that can assist coaches in establishing a prosperous practice.

Table 17.5 Coaches' Disciplines Self-Evaluation

Name	Date		Organization			

Instruction:
(a) Using the rating scale (shown below), self-rate yourself as a manager, supervisor, coach, consultant or independent on understanding and enhancing your coaching disciplines, (b) then tally your rating, and (c) finally, come up with actions you will take to increase your rating on the next rating period.

Rating Scale: 1 = Never, 2 = Hardly, 3 = Occasionally, 4 = Generally, 5 = Constantly

#	*Disciplines*	*1*	*2*	*3*	*4*	*5*
1	During coaching sessions, put critical thinking skills to use.					
2	Use the solution-based methodology when you are coaching.					
3	Engage in effective communication with participants by being accurate and unambiguous.					
4	During coaching sessions, practice the components of active listening.					
5	Behave and present yourself with professionalism to the participants.					
6	Take responsibility for how they do in coaching sessions.					
7	Take accountability for their behavior and the outcomes of your coaching.					
8	Make the real problems at hand clear and distinct for the participants.					
9	Continue and maintain to have a good rapport with the participants.					
10	Correct their approach by taking lessons from their successes and mistakes.					
11	Arrange their strategy and collaborate with the participants.					
12	Set and adhere to a schedule for their work and communication.					

(Continued)

Table 17.5 (CONTINUED) Coaches' Disciplines Self-Evaluation

13	Make inquiries, pose questions, and look for clarification.					
14	Observe and put into practice what functions well and poorly.					
15	Finish the weekly and daily procedures and tasks.					
16	Maintain honest and open communication with everybody involved.					
17	Utilize and apply emotional intelligence concepts.					
18	In coaching sessions, empower participants as well as yourself.					
19	Take advice from the top producers currently working in their field.					
20	Possess a distinct career vision and aim.					
	Individual Column's Totals					
	Total of Above Individual Columns					
	Final Average (Above total divided by 20)					
Three correctional and developmental actions I will take that will raise my three lowest self-ratings by at least one scale on the next rating:						
Action 1:						
Action 2:						
Action 3:						

Note. © 2024 by Behnam Bakhshandeh

Common Skills and Competencies

Proficiency and abilities are crucial in every professional occupation and labor. The coaching profession is similar to other professions in that it depends on the expertise and abilities of its practitioners. Within this area, we want coaches to self-evaluate and assess their proficiency and expertise in their abilities and competencies. The rating system has two advantages for coaches: first, it allows them to assess their proficiency in conducting coaching sessions for individuals, teams, and organizations; second, it highlights the substantial influence of these abilities on their development as highly skilled and capable coaches. Table 17.6 presents a comprehensive set of skills and competencies that coaches can use to evaluate themselves.

Table 17.6 Coaches' Common Skills and Competencies Self-Evaluation

Name		Date		Organization				

Instruction:
(a) Using the rating scale (shown below), self-rate yourself as a manager, supervisor, coach, consultant or independent on understanding and enhancing your common skills and competencies, (b) then tally your rating, and (c) finally, come up with actions you will take to increase your rating on the next rating period.

Rating Scale: 1 = Poor, 2 = Marginal, 3 = Acceptable, 4 = Good, 5 = Excellent

Common Skills and Competencies		*1*	*2*	*3*	*4*	*5*
1	Establish precise and unambiguous expectations for both parties involved in the coaching partnership.					
2	Use both novel concepts and up-to-date coaching models and techniques.					
3	Utilize a successful coaching approach to meet each participant's unique requirements.					
4	Tailor coaching sessions to the specific requirements of individuals who want to develop.					
5	Recognize the needs and opinions of participants by using effective communication and active listening techniques.					
6	Recognize and appreciate the participants' efforts to apply the coaching techniques.					
7	Determine and address any possible causes of the participants' poor performance.					
8	Provide constructive and encouraging feedback to help participants become more confident in their performance.					
9	Determine the causes of disputes and dysfunctions in teams and groups.					
10	Determine the source of the participants' inspiration for their present and future professional endeavors.					
11	Before participants feel overburdened, give them adequate assignments and responsibilities.					
12	Communicate and set apart the mission, vision, and values of the organization.					
13	Describe the idea of a larger picture and divide it into more manageable objectives.					

(Continued)

Table 17.6 (CONTINUED) Coaches' Common Skills and Competencies Self-Evaluation

14	Recognize and describe the possible risks associated with performance and objectives.					
15	Understand the compensation, perks, incentives, and reward programs offered by the company.					
16	Give a workable description of the management organization, accountabilities, and chain of command.					
17	Explain and provide examples of how teams and individuals have contributed to the success of the company.					
18	Assist individuals in determining their objectives, priorities, and the importance of their intents.					
19	Provide a secure atmosphere for involvement and promote growth.					
20	Take responsibility for the caliber of your work and the coaching techniques you impart.					
	Individual Columns' Totals					
	Total of Above Individual Columns					
	Final Average (Above total divided by 20)					
Three correctional and developmental actions I will take that will raise my three lowest self-ratings by at least one scale on the next rating:						
Action 1:						
Action 2:						
Action 3:						

Note. © 2024 by Behnam Bakhshandeh

What Is Next?

In the last five chapters of Part IV, we have looked at the use of emotional intelligence to create competency-based training, in regard to (a) emotional intelligence and its clusters, (b) application of emotional intelligence coaching, (c) 4Cs skills competency-based training and development via EI, (d) implementation and management of training and development and (e) the emotional intelligence coach.

At the beginning of Part V, "Foresight, Summary, and Final Thoughts," Chapter 18, "Upskilling, Reskilling, and Cross-Skilling Your Workforce," reviews the positive impact and use of upskilling and reskilling workforces and preparing them for upgrading their career path.

References

Active Social Care. (2023). Personal values, attitudes and beliefs. Retrieved from https://activesocialcare .com/handbook/understanding-your-role/personal-values-attitudes-and-beliefs/.

AIIM. (2023). What is collaboration? Retrieved from https://www.aiim.org/what-is-collaboration.

Angelo, Gabriel. (2012). *Rapport; The Art of Connecting with People and Building Relationships*. Middletown, DE: SN & NS Publications.

Aristotelous, Philppos. (2019). *The Marvel of Engagement*. Middletown, DE: Self-Published.

Baker, Zachary G., Watlington, Emily M., & Knee, Raymond C. (2020). The role of rapport in satisfying one's basic psychological needs. *Motivation and Emotion, 44*(2), 329–343.

Bakhshandeh, Behnam. (2002). *Business Coaching and Managers Training*. Unpublished workshop on coaching businesses and training managers. San Diego, CA: Primeco Education, Inc.

Bakhshandeh, Behnam. (2009). *Conspiracy for Greatness; Mastery on Love Within*. San Diego, CA: Primeco Education, Inc.

Bakhshandeh, Behnam. (2015). *Anatomy of Upset: Restoring Harmony*. Carbondale, PA: Primeco Education, Inc.

Bakhshandeh, Behnam. (2018). *Team Building & Problem Solving*. Unpublished two-days' workshop on resolving team conflict and building a strong relationship among team members. Carbondale, PA: Primeco Education, Inc.

Bakhshandeh, Behnam & Rothwell, William J. (Editors) (2024). *Building an Organizational Coaching Culture*. Oxfordshire, UK: UK Limited Trading, Taylor & Francis Group. Routledge.

Bakhshandeh, Behnam, Rothwell, William J., & Imroz, Sohel M. (2023). *Transformational Coaching for Effective Leadership. Creating Sustainable Change Through Shifting Paradigms*. New York, NY: Taylor & Francis Group. Routledge.

Barbazette, Jane. (2006). *Training Needs Assessment: Methods, Tools and Techniques*. San Francisco, CA: Pfeiffer, an Imprint of Wiley.

Baron, L. & Morin, L. (2009). The coach–coachee relationship in executive coaching: A field study. *Human Resources Development Quarterly, 20*(1), 85–106. https://doi.org/10.1002/hrdq.20009

Bond, Tim. (2015). *Standards and Ethics for Counselling in Action* (4th ed.). London, UK: Sage Publishing.

Brennan, Diane & Wildflower, Leni. (2010). Ethics in coaching. In Elain Cox, Tatiana Bachkirova, & David Clutterbuck (Eds.), *The Complete Handbook of Coaching*. Thousand Oak, CA; Sage Publication.

Cooks-Campbell, Allaya. (2022). Belief or value? Learn the difference and set yourself free. Retrieved from https://www.betterup.com/blog/beliefs-vs-values.

Funck, F. (2023). How to instill a coaching culture. *Center for Creative Leadership: Leading Effectively*. https://www.ccl.org/articles/leading-effectively-articles/instill-coaching-culture/#:~:text=A%20c oaching%20culture%20creates%20a,length%2C%20but%20strong%20in%20impact.

Gilmore, Mike. (2019). *The Power of Rapport*. Middletown, DE: Partridge.

Grant, Jennifer. (2020). The 3 key elements to a professional image. Retrieved from https://www.linkedin .com/pulse/3-key-elements-professional-image-jennifer-grant-.

Hofstede, Geert. (1980). *Culture's Consequences. International Differences in Work Related Values*. Beverly Hills, CA: Sage.

ICC Standards and Code of Ethics. (2023). ICC standards and code of ethics. Retrieved from https://int ernationalcoachingcommunity.com/standards-and-ethics/.

ICF Core Values. (2022). Retrieved from https://coachingfederation.org/app/uploads/2022/01/ICF-Core -Values.pdf.

Imroz, Sohel M. (2024). *Professional Coaching Industry Standards and Ethics*. In Behnam Bakhshandeh & William J. Rothwell (Eds.), *Building an Organizational Coaching Culture*. Oxfordshire, UK: UK Limited Trading, Taylor & Francis Group. Routledge.

Keller, Heidi. (2016). Psychological autonomy and hierarchical relatedness as organizers of developmental pathways. *Philosophical Transactions of the Royal Society B: Biological Sciences, 371*(1686), 20150070. https://doi.org/10.1098/rstb.2015.0070.

Kirk, Dale. (2019). Why are coaching standards so important? Retrieved from https://www.linkedin.com/ pulse/why-coaching-standards-so-important-dale-kirk.

Lexico.com. (2023). Relatedness. Powered by Oxford. Retrieved from https://www.lexico.com/en/definition/relatedness.

Matthews, Jordan, Bialocerkowski, Jordan, and Molineux, Matthew. (2019). Professional identity measures for student health professionals – A systematic review of psychometric properties. *BMC Medical Education, 19*, 308. https://doi.org/10.1186/s12909-019-1660-5.

McMahon, Lindsay. (2019). All Ears English website. The English adventure. How to describe relationships in English. Retrieved from https://www.allearsenglish.com/aee-1275 who-do-you-get-along-with -how-to-describe-relationships-in-english/.

Merriam-Webster. (2023a). Self-Reflection. Retrieved from https://www.merriam-webster.com/dictionary/ self-reflection#synonyms.

Merriam-Webster. (2023b). Self-Evaluation. Retrieved from https://www.merriam-webster.com/dictionary /self-evaluation.

NACE. (2023). Five core values. Retrieved from https://www.naia.org/champions-of-character/five-core -values.

Oxford University Dictionary. (2023). Self-Reflection. Retrieved from https://languages.oup.com/google -dictionary-en/.

Phillips, Jack J. & Pulliam Phillips, Patricia. (2011). *Handbook of Training Evaluation and Measurement Methods* (4th ed.). New York, NY: Routledge. Taylor & Francis Group.

Rothwell, William J. & Bakhshandeh, Behnam. (2023). *High-Performance Coaching for Managers*. New York, NY: Routledge-Taylor and Francis.

Rothwell, William J., Imroz, Sohel M., & Bakhshandeh, Behnam. (2021). *Organization-Development Interventions: Executing Effective Organizational Chang*. New York, NY: Taylor & Francis Group. CRC Press.

Rothwell, William J. & Kazanas, H. C. (2004). *Improving on-the-Job Training*. San Francisco, CA: Pfeiffer, an Imprint of Wiley.

Tan, Anna. (2022). Four keys to establishing a coaching culture. Retrieved from https://www.forbes .com/sites/forbescoachescouncil/2022/08/10/four-keys-to-establishing-a-coaching-culture/?sh =46c5336d6f45.

Taylor, C. (1989). *Sources of the Self: The Making of Modern Identity*. Cambridge, MA: Harvard University Press.

Thompson, Megan. (2021). Why is self-evaluation important for development. Retrieved from https:// wethrive.net/performance-reviews-and-appraisals/self-evaluation-important-for-development/.

Tickle-Degnen, Linda & Rosenthal, Robert. (1990). The nature of rapport and its nonverbal correlates. *Psychological Inquiry, 1*(4), 285–293. Retrieved from https://www.jstor.org/stable/1449345.

Travelbee, Joyce. (1963). What do we mean by rapport? *The American Journal of Nursing, 63*(2), 70–72. https://doi.org/10.2307/3452595.

Triandis, Harry C. (1995). *Individualism and Collectivism*. Boulder, CO: Westview.

Whitmore, John. (2009). *Coaching for Performance: Growing Human Potential and Purpose* (4th ed.). Boston, MA: Nicholas Brealey Publishing.

Whitmore, John. (2017). *Coaching for Performance; The Principle and Practice of Coaching and Leadership* (5th ed.). Boston, MA: Nicholas Brealey Publishing.

Yadav, Amisha. (2021). Ethics in coaching for coaches. Retrieved from https://xmonks.com/ethics-in -coaching-for-a-coaches/.

FORESIGHT, SUMMARY, AND FINAL THOUGHTS

In the final part, this book looks at potential foresight for upskilling and reskilling the workforce and several implications, suggestions for use and future research, and study limitations. This part continues with the book summary, a brief conclusion, and final thoughts and briefly presents the details and demographics of the study.

Chapter 18: Upskilling, Reskilling, and Cross-Skilling Your Workforce

This chapter is about having foresight for what kind of skills an organization needs currently and in the future. Upskilling is any procedure that helps workers gain new skills or improve existing job skills. Reskilling is for employees who want to change lanes. It allows individuals to respond, "What skills do I need to switch departments?"

Chapter 19: Implications, Suggestions, and Restrictions

This chapter will briefly discuss these training proposals and their possible effects on companies, the present workforce, educational institutions, workforce education professionals, and local, state, and federal government. In addition, this chapter will discuss research limits and constraints.

Chapter 20: Summary and Final Thoughts

This chapter represents the overall summary of the book, a brief conclusion, and final thoughts by the researcher.

Chapter 21: Elements and Demographics of Study

In this chapter, we present all the related elements and demographics of our study.

DOI: 10.4324/9781003462316-22

Chapter 18

Upskilling, Reskilling, and Cross-Skilling Your Workforce

Introduction

In order to stay competitive, organizations can develop the necessary skills by reskilling and upskilling as the need for new talents increases. According to the World Economic Forum's projections, by 2025, there is a possibility that a change in the distribution of work between machines and people might result in the displacement of up to 85 million jobs (Bloom, 2023). Simultaneously, it is projected that 97 million new positions will emerge as a result of technological advancements and ongoing digital transformation. Even for individuals who are able to retain their current positions, it is anticipated that 40% of their fundamental abilities will undergo changes. This underscores the urgent requirement for acquiring new skills and enhancing existing ones in all occupations, divisions, and organizations. Given the significant transformations expected by 2025, it is imperative to start this process without delay (Talentguard, 2023).

As a business or HR executive, you may have observed that employee upskilling and reskilling are now gaining significant attention. In 2023, skills have become a prominent subject of attention, and Gartner has identified skills management as one of this year's most vital HR technologies. It is not unexpected that many CEOs prioritize skills, as organizations that focus on skills are 49% more inclined to enhance processes for optimal efficiency than their counterparts that prioritize job roles (Loughlin, 2023).

Although skill-building is a crucial element of any talent management plan that prepares individuals for the future, several upskilling plans fail to achieve their intended goals. Organization leaders will have difficulties developing skill-building efforts that effectively address knowledge gaps and generate maximum impact if they lack a complete understanding of worker capabilities. Fortunately, there are some innovative tools and strategies that CEOs may utilize to enhance their approach to upskilling and reskilling (Schriber-Shearer, 2023).

This chapter looks at the following elements related to reskilling and upskilling:

- What Is Upskilling, Reskilling, and Cross-Skilling?
- Distinctions among Upskilling, Reskilling, and Cross-Skilling.
- Establishing Business Success by Upskilling, Reskilling, and Cross-Skilling.
- Key Advantages of Upskilling, Reskilling, and Cross-Skilling Workforce.

DOI: 10.4324/9781003462316-23

- Strategies for Upskilling, Reskilling, and Cross-Skilling Your Workforce.
- Leveraging Emotional Intelligence in Upskilling, Reskilling, and Cross-Skilling for Professional Growth.

What Is Upskilling?

Upskilling refers to any systematic procedure aimed at assisting employees in acquiring new skills or enhancing existing knowledge in areas directly relevant to their present job responsibilities. Generally, when employees accumulate more experience in their specific field, their skills and expertise in their positions will also grow (Panth & Maclean, 2020). Upskilling refers to a deliberate learning process in which employees acquire profound knowledge through coursework that focuses on specific material and practical learning experiences. Upskilling encompasses the enhancement of employees' proficiency in both technical and soft skills. Frequently, a primary objective of any upskilling endeavor is to assist individuals in acquiring the necessary competencies to assume a more sophisticated position within their organization (Schriber-Shearer, 2023) (see Figure 18.1).

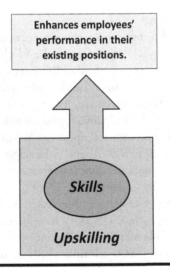

Figure 18.1   Upskilling. © 2024 by Behnam Bakhshandeh.

Hence, upskilling is an integral element of most succession planning plans. This is because employees must acquire the necessary skills and experience to fulfill their duties and provide guidance to their peers before they can transition into a leadership position. Managers and workers frequently convene to discuss upskilling options that match each individual's long-term aspirations, as well as the overall objectives of the organization (Newsome, 2023).

What Is Reskilling?

Reskilling is a process that involves acquiring new skills that are distinct from an individual's current skill set, comparable to upskilling. It can facilitate a shift to a new profession or assume supplementary duties linked to an employee's current position.

Reskilling often occurs as a result of necessity, such as when a person's work is terminated (e.g. through layoffs) or rendered obsolete by technological progress (Talentguard, 2023) (see Figure 18.2).

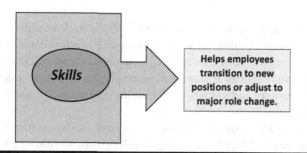

Figure 18.2 Reskilling. © 2024 by Behnam Bakhshandeh.

Occasionally, a corporation may opt to retrain its employees in order to adapt to changing market needs. Alternatively, employees have the option to freely engage in reskilling endeavors when they choose to transition into different professions, such as enrolling in a coding boot camp on weekends or returning to school in the evenings to obtain a new degree (Newsome, 2023).

What Is Cross-Skilling?

The process of gaining new abilities that may be applied across a variety of roles is referred to as cross-skilling, which is also sometimes referred to as cross-training. Cross-skilling aims to reduce the likelihood of any operational gaps occurring inside an organization by training several employees in the same activity (Li, 2022). For instance, learning the principles of software development might help a user experience designs to enhance their ability to collaborate across functional lines and increase their overall efficiency (Panopto, 2022) (see Figure 18.3).

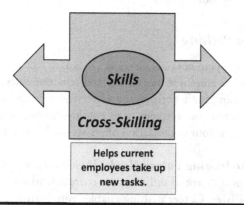

Figure 18.3 Cross-skilling. © 2024 by Behnam Bakhshandeh.

Distinctions among Upskilling, Reskilling, and Cross-Skilling

The phrases "upskilling" and "reskilling" are sometimes used interchangeably, but they really have distinct differences. Here is a method to differentiate between them, according to Schriber-Shearer (2023):

- *Upskilling* refers to any method that assists individuals in determining the additional abilities required to advance in their existing profession. It involves empowering people to expedite their advancement within conventional, sequential career trajectories.
- On the other hand, *reskilling* is intended for employees who have a desire to change their career paths. It enables individuals to determine the necessary abilities for transitioning between departments.
- Given the essential skills required in the evolving work landscape, firms must emphasize the development of *cross-skilling* abilities. Cross-skilling aims to cultivate a repertoire of talents that hold significant value across several sectors, roles, or areas of expertise.

How Career Pathing Can Help

Implementing organized career pathing is an excellent strategy for leveraging reskilling and upskilling inside your organization. A professional career path refers to the individuals' strategic approach to plan and navigate their professional growth and development (Li, 2022). Introducing both reskilling and upskilling techniques to your organization may be achieved by implementing a career pathing program (Swaminathan & TaskHuman, 2023). This program aims to link your workers' career aspirations with your organization's business goals. Effective career pathing methods are developed using a competency-based approach. This enables your organization to appraise and analyze the distinct competencies necessary for each individual function and comprehend the skill enhancement needed for personnel transitioning into new roles (Talentguard, 2023).

An individual's career path is a personalized route that outlines the necessary steps to accomplish long-term career objectives and advance professionally, either by moving horizontally or through promotion. It necessitates comprehension of the requisite information, talents, and personal attributes, aiding in the identification of specific skills and supplementary training necessary to achieve those ambitions (Waddill, 2021).

Advantages of Career Pathing

Implementing a career pathing plan not only serves as a means to recruit talented individuals to your organization but also enhances employee motivation and retention rates. Career pathing facilitates internal mobility, encompassing both horizontal and vertical transitions, and serves as a tangible indication of your organization's commitment to its employees. According to Talentguard (2023), implementing career pathing in your organization offers several benefits such as those listed below:

- **Anticipating and Addressing Future Needs.** By identifying the present capabilities, you may focus on developing essential skills in your current workforce to satisfy future demand.
- **Uncover Latent Abilities.** Career pathing enables your staff to evaluate and appraise their capabilities meticulously, unveiling possibilities the firm may not be cognizant of.

■ **Foster a Culture-Promoting Talent Mobility.** In today's job market, prospective employees seek companies that demonstrate a strong dedication to long-term career growth.

In the face of relentless digital transformation, implementing a career pathing plan that integrates reskilling and upskilling is advantageous for both the workforce and the organization. Furthermore, it is crucial for your organization to see this as a mandatory talent requirement in order to stay competitive in the evolving talent market.

Urgency for Upskilling, Reskilling, and Cross-Skilling

The significance of skill-building has always been paramount, but contemporary developments are heightening the need even further. We are currently experiencing a period commonly referred to as the *Fourth Industrial Revolution,* characterized by significant advancements in artificial intelligence (AI) and automation that fundamentally transform our work practices (Bloom, 2023). Given the increasing speed of change and the decreasing duration of abilities, it is imperative to prioritize the development of new competencies rather than seeing it as a secondary concern (Schriber-Shearer, 2023).

However, research indicates that upskilling and reskilling are necessary conditions for achieving success. According to the World Economic Forum, the growing use of technology will need almost 50% of workers to undergo reskilling by 2025. Contrary to previous concerns, the increase in automation and artificial intelligence (AI) will not result in the displacement of humans from the labor market. However, the World Economic Forum anticipates that it will generate up to 69 million new positions. While this is positive news, these professions will require new expertise, leading to a greater demand for upskilling and reskilling (Morandini et al., 2023).

New Hiring or Upskilling, Reskilling, and Cross-Skilling?

It is indisputable that upskilling and reskilling efforts necessitate a financial and temporal commitment. Superior techniques often involve incorporating high-quality information into a learning and development program and providing experience opportunities such as mentorship, projects, and jobs (Waddill, 2021).

Considering the substantial work that upskilling and reskilling demand, one can question if it would be more convenient to give higher priority to external hiring. Although it may appear to be a more straightforward approach, relying on new talent will not effectively address any worries regarding skill development (Diaz, Halkias, & Thurman, 2022). To begin with, the current labor shortage, which has reached unprecedented levels, will pose significant challenges in recruiting suitable candidates. Furthermore, even if businesses successfully hire people with the desired skills, they will still need to develop additional competencies. Given the increasing speed of change, every individual must prioritize the acquisition of new skills and the enhancement of existing ones (Morandini et al., 2023).

Hence, the sole method to equip firms for the future of work is by prioritizing talents as the focal point of a plan. There are several advantages to favoring internal mobility over external employment, such as enhanced retention and engagement (Diaz et al., 2022). According to a survey, 94% of workers expressed their intention to remain with their firm for a longer period if their employers made efforts to enhance their professional development. Additionally, 86% of CEOs said that implementing digital training and education initiatives resulted in increased employee engagement (Schriber-Shearer, 2023).

Establishing Business Success by Upskilling, Reskilling, and Cross-Skilling

Acquiring new skills is a reliable method to assist corporations in getting ready for upcoming industry fluctuations and alterations in customer requirements. Efficient talent redeployment is facilitated when teams possess a wide range of skills, and executives have full visibility into the location of knowledge. Consequently, organizations will have the ability to react more quickly, maintaining a significant advantage over the competition (Schriber-Shearer, 2023).

Furthermore, continuous upskilling programs are cost-efficient to guarantee that recruiting managers have the necessary access to the desired personnel. Given that the cost of recruiting, training, and onboarding talent from external sources is 1.7 times higher and these individuals have a 61% higher likelihood of being terminated, it is prudent for businesses to promote internal mobility. This may be achieved by enabling the existing workforce to develop new abilities (Morandini et al., 2023).

Ultimately, upskilling is associated with increased job contentment and decreased turnover hazards. Ninety-three percent of chief executive officers (CEOs) implementing upskilling initiatives observe a positive impact on employee retention and increased productivity (Schriber-Shearer, 2023).

Key Advantages of Upskilling, Reskilling, and Cross-Skilling Workforce

There are many good reasons to upskill and reskill your workforce, but according to Newsome (2023), Panopto (2022), and Lanore (2021), the following are the most apparent benefits for your organization:

Keeping Up with Fast-Paced Technology

In order for businesses to stay up with the unending progression of technology, they need to be fundamentally on a road of constant innovation. When it comes to the capabilities of their workers, companies that wish to maintain their positions at the top cannot afford to be complacent. Ensuring that the firm has the competent personnel it needs to compete in the market and avoid falling behind may be accomplished by implementing a systematic strategy for upskilling.

Constantly Engaging Employees

The expectations that workers have for their jobs have evolved significantly over the course of the last generation. People want to work in interesting occupations rather than go to the same place every day for decades performing the same tasks. Upskilling employees helps firms maintain employee engagement, contributing to increased productivity and employee retention.

Developing and Retaining Talent

Upskilling and cross-skilling outstanding individuals helps keep talent by investing in their professional progress, which is essential in such a competitive environment. Retaining top talent is essential to maintaining productivity and growth, and it is particularly important to do so in order to maintain growth. This guarantees that companies are able to retain employees who possess the appropriate mix of hard and soft talents.

Remaining Competitive in Your Market

The provision of possibilities for upskilling has the additional benefit of assisting an organization in terms of employment. In the first place, those seeking work consider it advantageous; the most qualified candidates will be looking for businesses that provide them with opportunities to enhance their careers. Second, it ensures that businesses remain on par with the most prominent employers in the sector, which have incorporated the process of upskilling as an essential component of their business strategy in order to conform to the ever-changing standards of the business world.

Promoting Innovation and Constant Learning

Even though businesses, markets, and even day-to-day business processes are always changing, the skills and expertise of employees continue to be the foundation of organizational innovation. Employees are looking for a sense of purpose and influence, and creativity flourishes when the company's aims connect with the employees' career ambitions.

Increasing Productivity

A recent study found that 79% of professionals working in the field of learning and development feel that it is more cost-effective to retrain an existing employee than it is to hire a new one. Even though there may be some expenses connected with the implementation of a reskilling and cross-skilling program, the program ultimately saves resources for the firm by increasing the abilities of the people who are already working there.

Strategies for Upskilling, Reskilling, and Cross-Skilling Your Workforce

Many good strategies are available in the human resources industry for upskilling, reskilling, and cross-skilling employees. Table 18.1 displays several valuable and practical strategies that any business manager or HR department can establish and implement for upskilling, reskilling, and cross-skilling their workforce.

Table 18.1 Strategies for Upskilling, Reskilling, and Cross-Skilling Your Workforce

#	*Strategies*	*Brief Description*
1	**Evaluate Current Skills**	Skills your team has today you may need later. When creating an upskilling and cross-skilling program, consult your team. Since your staff knows their duties and the company, start by evaluating employee competencies and growth opportunities.
2	**Set Up Definite Upskilling Goals**	Help your staff set professional objectives before determining what skills they need by doing a skills analysis to uncover gaps in technical skills.
3	**Create Upskilling Programs**	You decide how your upskilling program appears, but it must be accessible and frequent. Employees must have time to utilize the applications, and they must be done periodically and regularly.
4	**Determine the Suitable Learning Format**	Are some training program aspects in place? Some employ in-person training sessions. Asynchronous video-based learning enables flexibility and scalability throughout the training program for others. You and your team must evaluate all possibilities and choose the best one.
5	**Tailor Programs to Employees' Needs**	Upskilling must be targeted to employees' requirements, learning styles, and preferences to function and benefit the company. Managers must examine their teams and find good program fits here. Don't forget that workers recognize their weaknesses.
6	**Monitor the Progress**	Upskilling and cross-skilling work best when employees can increase their responsibilities. After training, linking people with employment that requires these new abilities shows an organization's dedication to upskilling and cross-training to give employees more options.
7	**Build a Coaching and Mentoring Culture**	Coaching and mentoring boost retention, satisfaction, and promotion rates. Coaching and mentoring help upskill by tapping into the expertise of more experienced workers and passing it on to newer ones.
8	**Promote Self-Selected Career Development**	Add upskilling and reskilling to company-led efforts by encouraging employees to pursue and pay for it independently. Online courses, certifications, conference attendance, and organization memberships that employees want can be covered or subsidized by the employer, expanding their expertise.
9	**Collaborate with External Experts**	Consult an expert when unsure. The growing demand for upskilling has led to the formation of several organizations that assist corporations in doing it, from consultants who advise on best practices to agency-style teams who handle clients' entire upskilling needs.

(Continued)

Table 18.1   (CONTINUED) Strategies for Upskilling, Reskilling, and Cross-Skilling Your Workforce

#	Strategies	Brief Description
10	**Distribute the Knowledge**	How you learn doesn't matter. Knowledge should be available in many places. We prioritize user experience. Thus, performance-based learning is the aim. This learning method incorporates knowledge management. Employees can upload knowledge material to the content platform for public access.
11	**Provide Apprenticeship Programs**	Apprenticeships bring in diverse, skilled workers from atypical backgrounds. Apprenticeships combine paid on-the-job training with classroom teaching for specialized jobs. Apprenticeships train workers for high-paying careers by teaching skills. Apprenticeships assist firms in hiring, training, and retaining talented workers.
12	**Utilize Technical Schools**	Student partnerships at vocational, technical, and business schools are another way to employ skilled individuals. Business and education complement each other. When educational institutions combine with companies for student employment, they educate students to be effective future employees by teaching life skills.

Note. Adapted from Loughlin (2023); Newsome (2023); ITA Group (2023); Panopto (2022); Waddill (2021).

Now, take time, using Table 18.2, to score your level of using these strategies for upskilling, reskilling, and cross-skilling your workforce, mentioned in Table 18.1.

Table 18.2   Evaluating Your Use of Strategies for Upskilling, Reskilling, and Cross-Skilling Your Workforce Self-Rating

Name		Date		Organization		
Instruction: (a) Using the rating scale (shown below), as a manager, supervisor, coach, or consultant on your assessment in *Evaluating Your Use of Strategies for Upskilling, Reskilling, and Cross-Skilling Your Workforce Self-Rating*, (b) then tally your rating, and (c) finally, come up with at least three suggestions you will take to increase the rating on the next rating period.						
Rating Scale: 1 = Poor, 2 = Marginal, 3 = Acceptable, 4 = Good, 5 = Excellent						
Strategies				*1*	*2*	*3*	*4*	*5*
1	Evaluate Current Skills							
2	Set Up Definite Upskilling Goals							

(Continued)

3	Create Upskilling Programs					
4	Determine the Suitable Learning Format					
5	Tailor Programs to Employees' Needs					
6	Monitor the Progress					
7	Build a Coaching and Mentoring Culture					
8	Promote Self-Selected Career Development					
9	Collaborate with External Experts					
10	Distribute the Knowledge					
11	Provide Apprenticeship Programs					
12	Utilize Technical Schools					
	Individual Columns' Totals					
	Total of Above Individual Columns					
	Final Average (above total divided by 12)					
	What are your actions on improving your strategies for upskilling, reskilling, and cross-skilling your workforce rating system to bring up your scores on the next self-rating?					
	Action 1:					
	Action 2:					
	Action 3:					

Note. © 2024 by Behnam Bakhshandeh.

Leveraging Emotional Intelligence in Upskilling, Reskilling, and Cross-Skilling for Professional Growth

In the rapidly evolving landscape of the professional world, individuals constantly need to adapt and acquire new skills to stay relevant. Upskilling, reskilling, and cross-skilling have become essential personal and career development strategies. However, the success of these endeavors goes beyond technical proficiency; emotional intelligence (EI) plays a pivotal role in navigating the complexities of learning and growth. In this section, we explore the significance of emotional intelligence in the context of upskilling, reskilling, and cross-skilling and how individuals can harness their emotional intelligence to maximize the effectiveness of these processes.

In the ever-evolving landscape of professional development, emotional intelligence emerges as a critical factor in the success of upskilling, reskilling, and cross-skilling endeavors. The ability to understand and manage one's emotions, navigate social dynamics, and build meaningful relationships enhances the effectiveness of skill acquisition and application effectiveness. By harnessing emotional intelligence, individuals acquire the technical expertise needed for their roles and develop the interpersonal skills necessary for sustained success in today's dynamic work environment. As we continue to embrace the era of lifelong learning, emotional intelligence stands as a guiding force, empowering individuals to navigate the complexities of skill development with resilience, adaptability, and a collaborative spirit.

The Intersection of Emotional Intelligence and Skill Development

- **Self-Awareness in Skill Assessment.** Before embarking on any upskilling, reskilling, or cross-skilling journey, individuals must assess their current skill set and identify areas that require development. Self-awareness enables individuals to objectively recognize their strengths and weaknesses, fostering a realistic understanding of their abilities.
- **Self-Regulation for Effective Learning.** Learning new skills can be challenging, and setbacks are inevitable. Self-regulation allows individuals to manage stress, control impulses, and persevere through difficulties. Cultivating emotional resilience is crucial in overcoming obstacles encountered during the learning process.
- **Motivation as a Driving Force.** Intrinsic motivation, driven by personal values and passion for one's chosen path, enhances the commitment to skill development. Individuals with high emotional intelligence can tap into their inner motivation, maintaining a positive outlook despite potential challenges.
- **Empathy in Collaborative Learning.** Collaboration is a cornerstone of effective learning. Empathy, the ability to understand and share the feelings of others, facilitates constructive communication and teamwork. Recognizing the challenges faced by peers and offering support creates a positive learning environment.
- **Social Skills for Networking and Collaboration.** Building a diverse skill set often involves collaboration with others. Social skills, including effective communication and conflict resolution, are essential for successful teamwork. Emotional intelligence aids in navigating social dynamics and fostering mutually beneficial relationships for skill development.

Applying Emotional Intelligence in Upskilling

- **Developing a Growth Mindset.** Individuals with a growth mindset perceive challenges as opportunities for learning and growth. Emotional intelligence supports the cultivation of this mindset, enabling individuals to embrace continuous learning.
- **Adapting to Change.** Upskilling often involves adapting to new technologies and methodologies. Emotional intelligence helps individuals navigate the uncertainties associated with change by fostering adaptability and openness.
- **Feedback and Continuous Improvement.** Receiving feedback is integral to the learning process. Emotional intelligence enables individuals to accept constructive criticism, view it as a tool for improvement, and incorporate it into their skill development journey.

Applying Emotional Intelligence in Reskilling

- **Navigating Career Transitions.** Reskilling often accompanies career transitions. Emotional intelligence assists individuals in managing the emotional aspects of change, such as fear and uncertainty, allowing for a smoother transition.
- **Building Confidence in New Roles.** Transitioning to a new role may challenge one's confidence. Emotional intelligence helps individuals build self-confidence, manage self-doubt, and approach new responsibilities positively.

Applying Emotional Intelligence in Cross-Skilling

- **Integrating Diverse Skill Sets.** Cross-skilling involves integrating knowledge from diverse domains. Emotional intelligence facilitates effective communication and collaboration between individuals with different skill sets, fostering a synergistic approach to problem-solving.
- **Cultural Intelligence in Global Contexts.** In an interconnected world, cross-skilling often involves working with individuals from diverse cultural backgrounds. Emotional intelligence, particularly empathy and cultural sensitivity, is essential for effective cross-cultural collaboration.

What Is Next?

Chapter 19, "Implications, Suggestions, and Restrictions," looks at all implications of 4Cs skills training for organizations, current workforce, educational system, workforce education professionals, developmental programs, and local and state agencies. In addition, Chapter 19 will look at some recommendations for future research and conclude with this study's limitations and restrictions.

References

Bloom, E. P. (2023). 4 ways upskilling and reskilling can fill hard-to-hire positions. *Cio*. Retrieved from https://ezaccess.libraries.psu.edu/login?url=https://www.proquest.com/trade-journals/4-ways -upskilling-reskilling-can-fill-hard-hire/docview/2766632594/se-2.

Diaz, Jordi, Halkias, Daphne, & Thurman, Paul W. (2022). *The Innovative Management Education Ecosystem; Reskilling and Upskilling the Future.* New York, NY: Routledge. https://doi-org.ezaccess .libraries.psu.edu/10.4324/9781003308652.

ITA Group. (2023). ITAGroup.com. How upskilling your workforce benefits your organization. employee experience. Retrieved from https://www.itagroup.com/insights/employee-experience/how-upskilling -your-workforce-benefits-your-organization.

Lanore, L. (2021). Upskilling and reskilling. *Independent Banker, 71*(7), 27. https://ezaccess.libraries.psu .edu/login?url=https://www.proquest.com/trade-journals/upskilling-reskilling/docview/2550299750 /se-2.

Li, L. (2022). Reskilling and upskilling the future-ready workforce for industry 4.0 and beyond. *Information Systems Frontiers*, 1–16. https://doi.org/10.1007/s10796-022-10308-y.

Loughlin, S. (2023). Upskilling and reskilling: A robust learning culture helps attract and retain top talent. *BenefitsPRO*. Retrieved from https://ezaccess.libraries.psu.edu/login?url=https://www.proquest.com/ trade-journals/upskilling-reskilling-robust-learning-culture/docview/2811045055/se-2.

Morandini, S., Fraboni, F., De Angelis, M., Puzzo, G., Giusino, D., & Pietrantoni, L. (2023). The impact of artificial intelligence on workers' skills: Upskilling and reskilling in organizations. *Informing Science, 26*, 39–68. doi: https://doi.org/10.28945/5078.

Newsome, Pete. (2023, March). 6 Strategies for Upskilling and Reskilling Your Workforce. Employee Retention. Retrieved from https://www.4cornerresources.com/blog/upskilling-and-reskilling-your -workforce/.

Panopto. (2022, September). What is upskilling and cross-skilling? Retrieved from https://www.panopto .com/blog/learning-and-development-what-is-upskilling-cross-skilling/#:~:text=Cross%2Dskilling %20(also%20known%20as,risk%20of%20lapses%20in%20operation.

Panth, B. & Maclean, R. (2020). Developing a Robust system for upskilling and reskilling the workforce: Lessons from the skills Future movement in Singapore. In *Anticipating and Preparing for Emerging Skills and Jobs*. Springer Singapore Pte. Limited.

Schriber-Shearer, Nicole. (2023, November). Gloat.com. Upskilling, reskilling, and preparing for the future. Retrieved from https://gloat.com/blog/upskilling/.

Swaminathan, R. & TaskHuman. (2023). Upskilling and reskilling: The secret to retaining talent and doing more with less. Brentwood: Newstex. Retrieved from https://ezaccess.libraries.psu.edu/login ?url=https://www.proquest.com/blogs-podcasts-websites/upskilling-reskilling-secret-retaining-talent/ docview/2799381675/se-2.

Talentguard. (2023). TalentGroup.com. Reskilling and upskilling: A strategic response to changing skill demands. Retrieved from https://www.talentguard.com/blog/reskilling-upskilling-strategic-response -changing-skill-demands.

Waddill, Debrah. (2021, December). HBR.com. 4 Strategies for upskilling and reskilling your workforce. *Harvard Business Review*. Retrieved from https://hbr.org/sponsored/2021/12/4-strategies-for-upskill-ing-and-reskilling-your-workforce.

Chapter 19

Implications, Suggestions, and Restrictions

Introduction

This chapter examines three key aspects of the study: (a) the effects of 21st-century 4Cs training and development on organizations and society, (b) suggestions for future research on factors that influence the provision of training and development in emotional intelligence and soft skills, including the 4Cs skills, and (c) the limitations and constraints faced by this research that need to be emphasized.

This chapter will cover the following elements:

- Implication of Findings.
- Recommendations for Future Exploration.
- Limitations and Restrictions.

Implications of Findings

This section examines the consequences of the study and conclusions about the significance of emotional intelligence abilities in educating the workforce. It focuses on both soft skills, such as 4Cs, and hard skills, employing emotional intelligence, and 4Cs.

In addition, this study provides concise suggestions for implementing such training and examining the prospective consequences for:

a) Organizations.
b) Present workforce.
c) Educational systems.
d) Workforce education professionals.
e) Developmental programs.
f) Local, state, and federal governments.

DOI: 10.4324/9781003462316-24

Extensive research strongly indicates the crucial correlation between emotional intelligence and soft and technical skills development (Sheck & Lin, 2015; Cherniss et al., 2010; Bartram, 2005; Lopes et al., 2004). The strong correlation between components of emotional intelligence and the enhancement of skills is crucial for these suggestions, highlighting the importance of incorporating emotional intelligence education into educational systems and technical training and development programs within organizations. Nevertheless, it is widely acknowledged that incorporating these technologies into educational curriculums or organizational changes would not be effortless and would present many problems.

Typically, it is not straightforward to observe, define, and determine the existence or absence of emotional intelligence abilities (Handley, 2017; Rothwell & Lindholm, 1999; Spitzberg & Cupach, 1989). Handley (2017) found that studying interpersonal intelligence among early-career engineers confirms the challenges of defining, identifying, and enhancing interpersonal skills. Handley (2017) said that Spencer and Spencer (1993) concluded that it is challenging to create hidden underlying traits such as purpose, trait, and self-concept (p. 153). According to industry and subject-matter experts, the educational system, educators, and organization trainers have a significant problem in discovering and developing hidden qualities (Handley, 2017; Cherniss et al., 2010; Rothwell & Lindholm, 1999).

It is crucial to note that the research findings regarding the behaviors of the workforce in relation to possessing or lacking 21st-century 4Cs skills, as well as their emotional intelligence's relevance to these behaviors, do not serve as the ultimate solution to any ongoing issues related to productivity, turnover, or general attitudes and behaviors of the workforce. Acquiring, constructing, and enhancing emotional intelligence skills is primarily a complex undertaking, particularly due to the diverse range of viewpoints, hypotheses, theories, and arguments regarding the accuracy and challenges of assessing the presence or absence of emotional intelligence skills among individuals, groups, or organizations (Cherniss et al., 2010; Murphy, 2006; Cherniss, 2000; Rothwell & Lindholm, 1999). However, as Handley (2017) stated, "Emotional intelligence research suggests a strong and positive base for school-based emotional intelligence programs" (Cherniss et al., 2010, p. 154).

Figure 19.1 presents a framework and possible structure illustrating the potential growth of a future workforce that possesses both advanced technical abilities and essential soft skills, including the 4Cs talents. This framework/structure incorporated components for applying 21st-century 4Cs abilities and emotional intelligence in both organizational and educational settings, spanning from middle schools to universities. Studies suggest (Sheck & Lin, 2015; Cherniss et al., 2010; Bartram, 2005; Lopes et al., 2004) a correlation between components of emotional intelligence clusters and their competencies and traits and the advancement of individuals in their careers during the first phases. This link aids in improving and progressing their skills, knowledge, and talents, hence facilitating their professional growth.

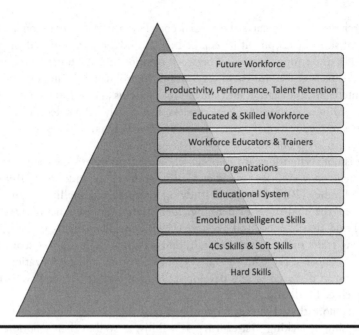

Figure 19.1 A structure for training emotional intelligence in workforce development for increased productivity, performance, and talent retention. Note. © Bakhshandeh, 2024.

Organizations

The dedication of the employees to their jobs and professions, as well as their loyalty to their company, plays a crucial role in the organization's present and future growth and general welfare. Gaining insight into employees' dedication toward the firm may assist professionals in designing training and development initiatives for their workforce. Additionally, this understanding can help professionals anticipate and address any potential resistance or lack of interest from employees toward these programs. Yousef (2017) identified three distinct kinds of organizational commitment.

Affective Commitment

Employee commitment refers to a state in which individuals possess a strong emotional attachment to the organization they work for and actively choose to work there due to their strong determination (Yousef, 2017).

Continuance Commitment

This refers to a level of dedication when a person believes that the potential losses from leaving their present work outweigh the benefits of staying with the firm. This type of commitment is rooted in apprehension and a sense of reluctance to go. Typically, these worries revolve around one's earnings, personal relationships with colleagues, the status associated with the job title, or the potential social disadvantages (Yousef, 2017).

Normative Commitment

Employee commitment refers to the sense of duty and responsibility that employees have toward remaining with the firm. The sense of duty may arise from the individuals' moral and personal ethical values, or it might be due to the organization being a charity or having invested significant resources in their training and development (Yousef, 2017).

Unlike educational institutions, firms and organizations are not constrained by numerous bureaucratic procedures, rules, and governmental directives when it comes to educating their employees and implementing training programs. Based on a thorough examination of data, it is recommended that successful emotional intelligence training and learning efforts should include the following four crucial components (see Table 19.1).

Table 19.1   Successful Emotional Intelligence Training and Learning Efforts

#	Crucial Components
1	Ascertain the driving force behind the participants' desire for change.
2	Develop enduring strategies that participants can consistently employ over an extended period.
3	Demonstrate the interventions through modeling and offer regular feedback.
4	Establish a supportive environment encouraging participants to express their concerns and reservations freely.

Note. Adapted from (Cherniss et al., 2010; Murphy, 2006; Cherniss, 2000; Rothwell & Lindholm, 1999; Dubois, 1993).

Present Workforce

In addition to the organization's dedication to training and developing its staff, the workforce's commitment, desire, and interest are the primary factors contributing to the effective implementation of these interventions. The research's introduction and subsequent chapters incorporated the perspectives of several researchers that emphasized the significance of non-technical talents, including soft skills and 4Cs, for both present and future workforces (Longmore et al., 2018; Handley, 2017; Martz et al., 2016; Boyles, 2012). Handley (2017) highlighted the significance of incorporating technical skills training and non-technical skills training in workforce education and development. This emphasis emerged primarily in the early 2000s and led to various leadership development programs encompassing non-technical skills, such as soft skills.

The acquisition of various soft skills necessitates a distinct learning methodology. Consequently, the present workforce must possess a constructive and encouraging mentality and disposition toward education, training, and advancement related to non-technical and soft skills (Charoensap-Kelly et al., 2016; Cherniss, 2000). This imperative endeavor necessitates full support from the entire workforce, including education and training. It will require a commitment from current industry leaders, professional associations, and organizations to endorse, validate, invest in, and legitimize the crucial requirements for non-technical and soft skills training (including the 4Cs). Additionally, it is important to recognize and support the diverse learning methods employed by the current and future workforce: "leaders must also be willing to model effective behaviors associated with ideas such as emotional intelligence as modeling is a key aspect of emotional learning (Cherniss, 2000)" (Handley, 2017, p. 159).

Educational System

One of the primary ways to gain knowledge about the effects of soft skills (including 4Cs) and comprehend the components of emotional intelligence is through formal education in the schooling system, as Handley (2017) quoted Dubois (1993): "The research underscores the importance of education and training programs that take into account both the cognitive and emotional domains of learning which can address the development of hidden underlying characteristics" (Dubois, 1993, p. 153). Academic and educational institutions, including high schools, colleges, and technical vocational institutes, should revise and adjust their curricula to address this urgent requirement by incorporating 21st-century abilities, such as the 4Cs and soft skills, into their education (Martz et al., 2016). The outcomes of this research can assist the educational system and instructors in formulating and developing a curriculum specifically aimed at teaching emotional intelligence abilities.

There is a well-known problem in educational institutions and among companies about the development of a competent workforce. Irrespective of whether high school graduates intend to join the workforce immediately after graduation or pursue vocational training or a college degree, they must exhibit specific skills, knowledge, and abilities in order to be productive members of an organization or even be considered for employment. In addition to possessing technical skills and cognitive abilities in subjects such as science, math, and physics (Handley, 2017), individuals must also possess strengths and soft skills that enable them to think critically, demonstrate creativity, effectively communicate, and solve problems in their professional environment (Soulé & Warrick, 2015; Martz et al., 2016).

Teaching the younger generation the fundamentals of emotional intelligence and its associated skills would yield significant benefits in developing the future workforce. Based on current research, successful communication, team building, conflict resolution, and problem-solving necessitate comprehending and using interpersonal behaviors to enhance one's presence in the environment and effectively engage with others. Hence, it is crucial to acquire knowledge about emotional intelligence and understand its many components and skills in educational settings in order to cultivate the future labor force (Longmore et al., 2018; Handley, 2017; Martz et al., 2016; Soulé & Warrick, 2015; Goleman, 2015; Boyles, 2012). The educational system should integrate diverse educational approaches to enhance students' acquisition of emotional intelligence and its associated skills. This should involve instructing and implementing modeling and experiential learning techniques while also offering feedback to students and fostering their emotional development (Handley, 2017; Cherniss et al., 2010; Cherniss, 2000).

Workforce Education Professionals

The findings of this research can be advantageous for professionals in workforce education, namely those in organizational development (OD), human resource development (HRD), and workplace learning and performance (WLP). These professionals aim to enhance leadership skills among existing employees. This study revealed the significance of acquiring emotional intelligence in the cultivation of 21st-century 4Cs skills. It suggests that training and development programs should incorporate policies and tactics that are similar to the educational system approaches mentioned in the previous section. The suggested approach should include experiential learning techniques, simulated scenarios, constructive feedback, and empowering support (Handley, 2017; Cherniss et al., 2010).

HR, HRD, OD, and WLP professionals and trainers need to use emotional intelligence principles to train and develop higher-level HR and HRD professionals in organizations. These professionals are responsible for on-the-job training, employee performance evaluations, and mentoring employees on the importance of emotional intelligence in learning and working environments. This will help build the emotional intelligence competencies identified in this study, which are essential for developing both the 4Cs skills and hard skills (Handley, 2017; Cherniss et al., 2010). In order to achieve this task, experts in organizational development (OD), human resources (HR), human resource development (HRD), and workplace learning and performance (WLP) need to collaborate with other corporate trainers and professionals. Their objective is to educate corporate leaders and get their full support in implementing emotional intelligence programs.

Furthermore, it is important to offer and educate managers in coaching skills as a vital means of fostering and nurturing an organizational climate that promotes the acquisition and cultivation of emotional intelligence. Establishing an atmosphere that fosters emotional intelligence necessitates implementing tactics to influence behavioral transformation among employees. The objective and purpose of coaching are to bring about continuous transformation in the behaviors of the workforce that have a beneficial influence on their performance (Lazar & Bergquist, 2008). This strategy is characterized by the implementation of a "manager-as-coach" concept, which involves providing positive and constructive feedback to encourage positive changes and motivate individuals to perform at their best (Joo, Sushko, & Mclean, 2012).

Developmental Programs

The findings of this research can contribute to ongoing efforts to enhance the relevance and overall efficacy of development and training programs, thereby achieving their objectives of establishing a comprehensive approach to an emotional intelligence learning environment: "Developmental programs require researching the transfer of knowledge and skill from the training program. The body of knowledge on transfer of training is broad and ultimately concludes a relationship between cognitive ability and transfer" (Blume et al., 2010; Handley, 2017, p. 158). Cherniss (2000) highlights the complexity of this study issue, noting that emotional intelligence learning involves different practices compared to cognitive learning. Furthermore, the effects of emotional intelligence learning are long-term and can be hindered or disrupted by many difficulties.

Local, State, and Federal Governments

The supply of skilled workers in the employment market is directly influenced by the policies and laws of the local, state, and federal governments, as well as their implementation and expansion. The findings of this research and the recommended training strategies can be advantageous for local and state government agencies in defining their educational systems. These recommendations can be applied to technical training schools and other institutions involved in adult education, with the aim of producing skilled labor that is prepared to enter the labor pool and contribute to the workforce in various local and state municipalities with the help of career and technical education (CTE) programs.

Providing training and development for CTE instructors in emotional intelligence competency-based programs is crucial for this endeavor, considering the scarcity of CTE teachers. Gordon's (2014) research indicates that from 1991 to 2001, there was a minimum 10% decline in the number of higher education institutions providing vocational teacher preparation programs. Moreover, several local and statewide communities are confronting a worrisome scarcity of CTE instructors, which they attribute to the absence of CTE teacher programs at colleges and institutions inside their jurisdictions (Gordon, 2014).

Recommendations for Future Exploration

The subsequent part pertains to suggestions for prospective future study on factors that influence the provision of training and growth in emotional intelligence soft skills, including the 4Cs skills within the workforce.

Training Educators and Trainers

There is a requirement for more extensive study on training educators and professional workforce education trainers who deal with high school and college students in developing their emotional intelligence abilities. A thorough investigation of the effects of emotional intelligence competency-based training on various management levels across several firms in diverse industries is needed. The impact of this training on the acquisition and enhancement of 4Cs skills and general learning abilities (both technical and interpersonal) will be assessed. The competency-based model of emotional intelligence would differentiate the workforce behaviors associated with the competencies required for building abilities in the areas of 4Cs, soft skills, and leadership.

Cognitive Education and Emotional Intelligence Capabilities

Undoubtedly, emotional intelligence necessitates the comprehension and application of emotional learning, which involves the utilization of many brain pathways, in contrast to only cognitive learning (Goleman, 2015, 1998). A good recommendation would be to conduct further study on alternative methods of acquiring emotional intelligence abilities, in addition to cognitive learning and current educational, training, and developmental methodologies. This will involve conducting more research on present techniques and patterns that require reprogramming or rethinking in order to facilitate the development of emotional intelligence in relation to the incoming generation of workers in the market. Handley (2017) pointed to this emissary need: "The emotional learning that takes place not only requires reprogramming learned responses and habits but also involves change related to core personal identity (Cherniss, 2000)" (p. 154).

In order to address these novel issues, emotional intelligence learning environments necessitate distinct and alternative methodologies compared to the typical cognitive learning environments found in educational systems or organization development businesses (Handley, 2017). Thus, it is important to do strategic research that can precisely identify the requirements for novel learning methodologies.

Developmental Programs

Research suggests that, despite the aforementioned challenges in designing development programs, there is a necessity for more extensive study on the efficacy and durability of emotional intelligence training programs (Handley, 2017). These prospective queries are essential for identifying the most successful methods of establishing emotional intelligence learning programs that would favor the workforce's acquisition and application of soft skills and 4Cs abilities, as well as general hard skills.

Manager-as-Coach

Additional study is required to examine the efficacy of coaching training and development programs on the coaching and mentoring abilities and behaviors of managers inside businesses (Joo et al., 2012). Another study on the effects of a manager-as-coach strategy in creating emotional intelligence competencies-based learning would be beneficial. The focus should be on the consequences for subordinates or mentees (Handley, 2017; Joo et al., 2012).

Limitations and Restrictions

In this section, the researcher examines the limitations of the research in order to acknowledge and address certain constraints that may impact the overall scope of the study on this issue.

Geographic Area

This investigation was conducted only inside the confines of Lackawanna County in Northeast Pennsylvania. The option to choose this specific geographical location was based on two factors:

1) Undertaking the same research on the full state of Pennsylvania or all counties in NEPA would be an extensive endeavor that would require a minimum of two to three years to accomplish. This would include working with samples from other counties in NEPA.
2) The researcher's residency is in Lackawanna County, NEPA. Nevertheless, it is feasible to explore the prospect of performing a comparable study in other NEPA counties and gathering data from a more extensive sample with the aid of the State of Pennsylvania.

Participating Organizations

Similarly, due to the expansive geographic region of the study, Lackawanna County in NEPA also hosts a substantial number of private-sector and non-profit organizations. Therefore, it was decided to choose a sample of only 17 organizations from this region. Another constraint arises when attempting to gather data from a significantly greater number of firms in order to provide a more comprehensive perspective on the perception of 4Cs skills among their employees in the NEPA region as a whole or even the labor pool of the state of Pennsylvania.

Participating Contributors

The interview participants for the research were selected from a diverse group of individuals, including executives, senior, middle, and junior managers, human resources directors or managers, and supervisors. The researcher extended invitations to four participants from each of the 17 organizations, resulting in a total of 45 people who agreed to participate in the interviews. The problem arises from the possibility that conducting interviews with a larger number of participants from each organization or from different levels of the organization's management structure might yield more meaningful data for the research.

In the future, it may be more effective to acquire data by doing research that specifically focuses on the perceptions and opinions of different management levels in isolation from other levels. For instance, each set of executives, middle managers, and supervisors is considered individually and autonomously. Implementing this strategy would need a significant investment of time and effort. However, it would yield a wealth of detailed insights from participants, which might be utilized for the purposes of management training and supervisors' professional growth.

No Floor Employees

No data was collected from any of the staff or floor personnel in this investigation. This issue in and of itself poses a constraint on this research. The research focused on gathering the perspectives of organizations regarding the 4Cs skills possessed by their employees. Consequently, the data collection was limited to individuals in managerial and supervisory positions within the organizations. However, this approach overlooked the chance for employees to share their own opinions on their colleagues' proficiency in the 4Cs skills.

What Is Next?

Chapter 20, "Summary and Final Thoughts," provides a comprehensive overview of the study and the book, encompassing my concluding reflections.

References

Bartram, D. (2005). The great eight competencies: A criterion-centric approach to validation. *The Journal of Applied Psychology*, *90*(6), 1185–203. https://doi.org/10.1037/00219010.90.6.1185.

Blume, B. D., Ford, J. K., Baldwin, T. T., & Huang, J. L. (2010). Transfer of training: A metanalytic review. *Journal of Management*, *36*(4), 1065–1105. https://doi.org/10.1177/0149206309352880.

Boyles, T. (2012). 21st century knowledge, skills, and abilities and entrepreneurial competencies: A model for undergraduate entrepreneurship education. *Journal of Entrepreneurship Education*, *15*, 41–55. Retrieved from https://www.abacademies.org/articles/jeevol152012.pdf#page=47.

Charoensap-Kelly, P., Broussard, L., Lindsly, M., & Troy, M. (2016). Evaluation of a soft skills training program. *Business and Professional Communication Quarterly*, *79*(2), 154–179. https://doi.org/10.1177/2329490615602090.

Cherniss, C. (2000). Social and emotional competence in the workplace. In B. Reuven & J. D. Parker (Eds.), *The Handbook of Emotional Intelligence*. San Francisco, CA: Jossey-Bass.

Cherniss, C., Extein, M., Goleman, D., & Weissberg, R. P. (2010). Emotional intelligence: What does the research really indicate? *Educational Psychologist*, *1520*(May 2014), 37–41. https://doi.org/10.1207/s15326985ep4104.

Dubois, D. D. (1993). *Competency-based Performance Improvement: A Strategy for Organizational Change.* Amherst, MA: Human Resource Development Press.

Goleman, Daniel. (1998). *Working with Emotional Intelligence.* New York, NY: Random House.

Goleman, Daniel. (2015). *Emotional Intelligence; Why It Can Matter More Than IQ.* New York, NY: Bantam Books.

Gordon, H. R. D. (2014). *The History and Growth of Career and Technical Education in America* (4th ed.). Long Grove, IL. Waveland Press, Inc.

Handley, M. (2017). *An Interpersonal Behavioral Framework for Early-Career Engineers Demonstrating Engineering Leadership Characteristics across Three Engineering Companies.* (Unpublished doctoral dissertation). Pennsylvania: The Pennsylvania State University, State College.

Joo, B. B., Sushko, J. S., & Mclean, G. N. (2012). Multiple faces of coaching: Manager-as-coach, executive coaching, and formal mentoring. *Organization Development Journal, 30*(1), 19–38. Retrieved from https://search.proquest.com/openview/0eb48f69c3641a7843ae5138cf46617e/1?pq-origsite=gscholar&cbl=36482.

Martz, B., Hughes, J., & Braun, F. (2016). Creativity and problem-solving: Closing the skills gap. *The Journal of Computer Information Systems, 57*(1), 39–48. https://doi.org/10.1080/08874417.2016.118149.

Murphy, K. R. (2006). *Critique of Emotional Intelligence.* Mahway, NJ: Lawrence Erlbaum Associates.

Lazar, J. & Bergquist, W. (2008). The philosophical foundations of organizational coaching. *The International Journal of Coaching in Organizations, 2*, 91–101.

Longmore, A.-L., Grant, G., & Golnaraghi, G. (2018). Closing the 21st-century knowledge gap: Reconceptualizing teaching and learning to transform business education. *Journal of Transformative Education, 16*(3), 197–219. https://doi.org/10.1177/1541344617738514.

Lopes, P. N., Brackett, M. A., Nezlek, J. B., Schütz, A., Sellin, I., & Salovey, P. (2004). Emotional intelligence and social interaction. *Personality and Social Psychology Bulletin, 30*(8), 1018–1034. https://doi.org/10.1177/0146167204264762.

Rothwell, W. J. & Lindholm, J. E. (1999). Competency identification, modelling and assessment in the USA. *International Journal of Training and Development, 3*, 90–105. https://doi.org/10.1111/1468-2419.00069.

Sheck, Daniel T. L. & Lin, Le. (2015). Intrapersonal competencies and service leadership. *International Journal of Disability Human Development, 14*(3), 255–263. https://doi.org/10.1515/ijdhd-2015-0406.

Soulé, H. & Warrick, T. (2015). Defining 21st century readiness for all students: What we know and how to get there. *Psychology of Aesthetics, Creativity, and the Arts, 9*(2), 178–186. https://doi.org/10.1037/aca0000017.

Spencer, L. M. & Spencer, S. M. (1993). *Competence at Work. Models for Superior Performance.* New York, NY: John Wiley and Sons, Ed.

Spitzberg, B. H. & Cupach, W. R. (1989). *Handbook of Interpersonal Competence Research.* New York, NY: Springer-Verlag.

Yousef, D. A. (2017). Organizational commitment, job satisfaction and attitudes toward organizational change: A study in the local government. *International Journal of Public Administration, 40*(1), 77–88. https://doi.org/10.1080/01900692.2015.1072217.

Chapter 20

Summary and Final Thoughts

Introduction

This study and book aimed to investigate the perspectives of private-sector businesses in Lackawanna County, Northeastern Pennsylvania, regarding the 21st-century 4Cs skills gap and its influence on company productivity. The study utilized qualitative methods to evaluate, explore, and characterize these perceptions.

The study started by presenting the overarching problem of the soft skills gap, encompassing the 4Cs, both in the United States and as a worldwide concern for organizations and enterprises. In the 21st century, organizations and businesses experienced significant changes in business concepts and the environment compared to previous decades. They had to embrace a completely new learning process to remain competitive and successful in this new environment (Longmore et al., 2018; Soulé & Warrick, 2015).

In this chapter we explore:

- Summary of the Research.
- The Prevalence of the 21st-Century 4Cs Skills Gap.
- Impact on Organizational Performance.
- The Competitive Landscape.
- Bridging the 21st-Century 4Cs Skills Gap.
- Different Ways to Include EI into 4Cs Skills Training.
- Final Thoughts.

Summary of the Research

This study and book elucidated the intricacy of soft talents, including the 4Cs, and their utilization by firms. Charoensap-Kelly et al. (2016) defined soft skills as being linked to emotional intelligence and categorized them as self-regulation, self-awareness, empathy, motivation, and social skills. Charoensap-Kelly et al. (2016) established a connection between soft skills and career attributes and abilities, including communication, teamwork, problem-solving, leadership, and customer service. Levasseur (2013) defined soft skills as a categorization of abilities and proficiencies, including self-awareness, communication, leadership, interpersonal skills, and teamwork, which closely resembles the description provided by Charoensap-Kelly et al. (2016).

                                                    DOI: 10.4324/9781003462316-25

The primary grievance is that the scarcity of workers with fundamental skills is attributed to the new hires rather than the current workforce. Proponents of this viewpoint ascribe this deficiency to the existing flaws and failures of the education system, particularly in relation to K–12 public education (Cappelli, 2015; Soulé & Warrick, 2015; Boyles, 2012). According to Robles (2012), soft skills have equal importance to cognitive skills. Students who have cultivated their soft skills significantly enhance their prospects of securing employment in their preferred domain. Insufficient proficiency in interpersonal skills can significantly hinder students' prospects in acquiring and using technical expertise and professional aptitude, while lacking the capacity to effectively interact with others.

This research investigated the industry's understanding and perspective on the global issue of companies missing soft skills and 21st-century 4Cs skills, using an introduction and literature review as the methodology. We thoroughly examined several factors listed below that contribute to a lack of comprehension of the issue:

a) Inadequacies in educational systems and related policies.
b) Individuals' drive and conduct.
c) Challenges with political policies at the local, state, and federal levels.
d) The impact of individuals' families and society as a whole.
e) Other relevant matters that influence the acquisition and growth of soft skills, including the 4Cs.

This study and book examined the crucial importance of 4Cs (communication, collaboration, critical thinking, and creativity) and soft skills in relation to the modern economy of the 21st century. It is noted that the 21st-century economy has experienced more rapid and robust growth compared to economies of the 20th and 19th centuries (Tindowen, Bassig, & Cagurangan, 2017; Soulé & Warrick, 2015). The rapid advancement of technology, the quick speed of the global economy, and intense rivalry both domestically and globally have significantly changed the structure of the workforce and the social and economic aspects of companies (Soulé & Warrick, 2015). Tulgan (2015) highlighted that soft talents may be less tangible and more challenging to articulate and quantify than hard abilities.

Soft skills are crucial for both personal and professional success or failure in the workplace, since they indirectly impact businesses, costs, workers' progress, and stability. Based on the aforementioned discoveries, an increasing number of businesses recognize the significance of competencies and abilities in the process of hiring, acquiring, and keeping highly capable workers, which directly influences their company development and success. Due to this recognition, educational institutions are increasingly focusing on the advancement of competency-based learning and development to meet the demands of a competency-based workforce in the current and future job market (Donahue, 2018; Rothwell, Stavros, & Sullivan, 2016; Cummings & Worley, 2015).

This study and book recommend that educators incorporate the 4Cs (critical thinking, communication, collaboration, and creativity) and soft skills into their curriculum. It suggests pedagogical ideas and strategies that teachers can use to facilitate the integration of these skills, along with problem-solving and innovation, in schools. When combined with technology, these tactics can create a more inclusive educational environment and provide opportunities for developing 21st-century skills (Levin-Goldberg, 2012). Undoubtedly, firms want a staff that possesses the capacity to utilize a range of practical talents effectively. Workforce development experts highlight the significance of these abilities by labeling them as the survival abilities of the modern economy (Soulé & Warrick, 2015). Charoensap-Kelly et al. (2016) reported that enterprises have increasingly acknowledged the need to provide soft skills training. Consequently, employers have progressively allocated more resources and time toward enhancing their employees' soft skills.

Soft skills are more difficult to measure and evaluate compared to hard talents (Charoensap-Kelly et al., 2016). Various factors, including the trainer's traits, training structure, content, and level of organizational support, might influence the results of soft skills training and development (Charoensap-Kelly et al., 2016). Multiple studies consistently demonstrate that instructors overwhelmingly assert that the most impactful learning experiences occur in a classroom environment that integrates many subjects and disciplines. By integrating 21st-century skills teaching into their class curriculums, teachers can enhance their teaching approach and establish a more productive learning environment (Urbani et al., 2017; Tindowen et al., 2017; Soulé & Warrick, 2015; Levin-Goldberg, 2012; Boyles, 2012).

Through the process of gathering data by interviewing participants, coding, and identifying emerging themes and sub-themes, this research has identified 18 themes. These themes represent:

a) The importance that organizations place on the 4Cs skills among their employees.
b) The impact of having these skills on team performance.
c) The most effective training and development approaches for equipping employees with the 4Cs skills.

Providing education and training to employees on these topics and enabling them to apply or remove them is crucial for their development and very beneficial for organizations and enterprises in cultivating competent and efficient staff.

In addition, this research suggests utilizing various organizational diagnosis models, including the Individual and Group Behavior Model, the Great Place to Work Model, and SWOT analysis. These models can help organizations identify skill gaps in the 4Cs (critical thinking, communication, collaboration, and creativity) among their workforces. Organizations can use these models to determine which employees need further training or development in specific 4Cs skills.

Ultimately, this research and book suggest that utilizing emotional intelligence training as competency-based training and development can enhance the development of 4Cs abilities among employees. This result is drawn from an analysis of emergent themes and their correlation with emotional intelligence clusters and competencies. Extensive research indicates a crucial correlation between emotional intelligence and soft and technical skills development (Sheck & Lin, 2015; Cherniss et al., 2010; Bartram, 2005; Lopes et al., 2004). The following are acknowledged clusters of emotional intelligence:

a) Self-awareness.
b) Self-regulation.
c) Social awareness.
d) Relationship management.

This research identified a total of 32 competencies and capabilities within the four clusters of emotional intelligence. These competencies and capabilities are related to the 4Cs skills and can be utilized by organizations to train and develop their workforce. In addition to enhancing the 4Cs skills, this training also focuses on improving soft skills and building the knowledge and competencies of the workforce, making it easier for them to acquire hard skills.

In conclusion, we can point out the following categories as a condensed summary of the research and book.

The Prevalence of the 21st-Century 4Cs Skills Gap

Despite the increasing importance of these skills, a significant gap exists between the demand for and the supply of the 4Cs skills in the workforce. This book covers several factors that contribute to this gap:

- **Outdated Education Systems.** Many educational institutions still prioritize rote learning and standardized testing over skills development. As a result, graduates often lack the practical skills needed in the workplace.
- **Rapid Technological Advancements.** The pace of technological change requires employees to continually adapt and learn. Those who can't keep up find themselves falling behind.
- **Demographic Shifts.** An aging workforce and a younger generation with different learning styles and expectations have created challenges in bridging the skills gap.

Impact on Organizational Performance

The 4Cs skills gap has a profound impact on organizational performance. This book covers the nature of many such impacts; however, here are some key aspects to consider:

- **Reduced Productivity.** Employees lacking 4Cs skills may struggle to communicate effectively, work well in teams, or make informed decisions. This can lead to inefficiencies, missed opportunities, and decreased productivity.
- **Hindered Innovation.** Creativity and critical thinking are at the heart of innovation. Without these skills, organizations may struggle to develop groundbreaking products and services, stifling their competitiveness in the market.
- **Employee Engagement and Retention.** Employees who feel they lack opportunities for growth and skill development are more likely to become disengaged and seek employment elsewhere. This turnover can be costly for organizations.

The Competitive Landscape

Organizations that can adapt quickly and leverage the 4Cs skills are more likely to succeed in a globalized and highly competitive business environment. Those with a skills gap may find themselves falling behind competitors. This book sheds light on many of such issues throughout the book; however, here are some ways in which the 4Cs skills gap affects an organization's competitiveness:

- **Global Market Challenges.** In the interconnected world of business, organizations often need to collaborate with partners and customers from different cultures and backgrounds. Effective communication and collaboration skills are essential in such scenarios.
- **Rapid Response to Change.** Critical thinking enables organizations to navigate uncertainty and adapt to rapidly changing market conditions. Companies with a skills gap may struggle to respond effectively to disruptions.
- **Innovation and Differentiation.** Creativity is the driving force behind innovative products and services. Organizations lacking in this skill may struggle to differentiate themselves in the market, relying on outdated offerings.

Bridging the 21st-Century 4Cs Skills Gap

To address the 4Cs skills gap, organizations must take proactive steps. In this book, the author pointed out several solutions for such proactive actions:

- **Training and Development.** Investing in training programs that focus on communication, collaboration, critical thinking, and creativity can help employees develop these skills.
- **Recruitment Strategies.** Organizations should consider hiring candidates not only for their technical knowledge but also for their 4Cs skills and potential for growth.
- **Fostering a Learning Culture.** Creating an environment that encourages continuous learning and skill development is crucial. This includes promoting a growth mindset among employees.
- **Technology Integration.** Utilizing technology and digital tools can facilitate skill development and collaboration, especially in remote or distributed work environments.

Different Ways to Include EI into 4Cs Skills Training

Here are some methods and activities to include EI in 4Cs skills training and development:

- **Self-Awareness Activities.** Include self-awareness activities in training programs to help participants understand their feelings, strengths, and weaknesses. A solid foundation for emotional intelligence is self-awareness. This practice improves critical thinking.
- **Empathy-Building Activities.** Fostering empathy via exercises that help individuals understand and share others' feelings is crucial for effective communication and cooperation.
- **Stress Management Techniques.** Regulating stress and emotions contributes to clear thinking, a positive work environment, and enhanced creativity.
- **Training in Conflict Resolution.** Emotionally intelligent individuals may resolve problems to benefit all parties involved. Training in this area improves collaboration.
- **Meditation and Mindfulness.** Working together can lead to conflict, but emotional intelligence can help overcome disagreements for mutual benefit. Collaboration skills may be strengthened with training.

Final Thoughts

Undoubtedly, the crucial significance of 4Cs and soft skills in cultivating proficient and efficient workforces cannot be questioned. According to this study, including emotional intelligence competency-based training and development is a promising method for enhancing the skills and abilities of the workforce in the future. The mentality and actions of individuals are crucial for a workforce to achieve success. Enhancing the 4Cs skills of the workforce will lead employees to do the following:

1) Develop self-awareness to shape their mindset.
2) Cultivate self-control to regulate their mindset, attitude, and behavior.
3) Gain social awareness to comprehend and connect with their work environment and colleagues.

4) Acquire the necessary knowledge and skills to effectively manage their relationships with others, which are crucial for fostering a productive, efficient, and competent workforce.

The significance of training on personal and professional growth should not be underestimated or disregarded in preference for training and enhancing the workforce's technical knowledge and hard skills. The significance of emotional intelligence abilities and the necessity for their cultivation is clearly evident in all 17 firms included in this study, as indicated by the final 18 themes that emerged from the analysis of 45 interviews.

This study and book suggest utilizing emotional intelligence competency-based training as a foundation and context for coaching employees in cultivating a good and productive mentality, conduct, and attitude. This undertaking necessitates a rigorous exploration of hypotheses and an assessment of the alignment of cognitive learning and emotional intelligence competency-based approaches in relation to the understanding of both soft and hard skills in the workforce. Therefore, based on the results, this study proposes incorporating emotional intelligence into competency-based training through a coaching curriculum. This curriculum would be designed to enhance the skills and knowledge of educators, instructors, trainers, practitioners, and managers. Educational institutions and corporate associations should prioritize the cultivation of both 4Cs (critical thinking, communication, collaboration, and creativity) and soft skills, in addition to their focus on developing hard and technical abilities in the workforce.

This leads to the development of a more robust and proficient workforce equipped with a profound understanding of productivity and effective interpersonal relationships. Implementing this approach in the educational and organizational systems is a challenging task that requires substantial support and endorsement from both state and federal governments. This includes overhauling the educational systems, providing funding for industries, and garnering public support. This undertaking is significant and will yield valuable outcomes for our nation, organizations, and workforce.

What Is Next?

In Chapter 21, "Elements and Demographics of Study," we present all the related elements of our study including all the demographics and selection criteria for organizations and contributors.

References

Bartram, D. (2005). The great eight competencies: A criterion-centric approach to validation. *The Journal of Applied Psychology, 90*(6), 1185–203. https://doi.org/10.1037/0021-9010.90.6.1185.

Boyles, T. (2012). 21st century knowledge, skills, and abilities and entrepreneurial competencies: A model for undergraduate entrepreneurship education. *Journal of Entrepreneurship Education, 15*, 41–55. Retrieved from https://www.abacademies.org/articles/jeevol152012.pdf#page=47.

Cappelli, P. H. (2015). Skill gaps, skill shortages, and skill mismatches: Evidence and arguments for the united states. *ILR Review, 68*(2), 251–290. https://doi.org/10.1177/0019793914564961.

Charoensap-Kelly, P., Broussard, L., Lindsly, M., & Troy, M. (2016). Evaluation of a soft skills training program. *Business and Professional Communication Quarterly, 79*(2), 154–179. https://doi.org/10.1177/2329490615602090.

Cherniss, C., Extein, M., Goleman, D., & Weissberg, R. P. (2010). Emotional intelligence: What does the research really indicate? *Educational Psychologist, 1520*(May 2014), 37–41. https://doi.org/10.1207/s15326985ep4104.

Cummings, T. G. & Worley C. G. (2015). *Organization Development & Change* (10th ed.). Stamford, CT: Cengage Learning.

Donahue, Wesley E. (2018). *Building Leadership Competence. A Competency-Based Approach to Building Leadership Ability.* State College, PA: Centerstar Learning.

Levasseur, R. (2013). People skills: developing soft skills—A change management perspective. *Interfaces, 43*(6), 566–571. https://doi.org/10.1287/inte.2013.0703.

Levin-Goldberg, J. (2012). Teaching generation techX with the 4Cs: Using technology to Integrate 21st century skills. *Journal of Instructional Research*, (1), 59–66. Retrieved from https://eric.ed.gov/?id=EJ1127608.

Longmore, A.-L., Grant, G., & Golnaraghi, G. (2018). Closing the 21st-century knowledge gap: Reconceptualizing teaching and learning to transform business education. *Journal of Transformative Education, 16*(3), 197–219. https://doi.org/10.1177/1541344617738514.

Lopes, P. N., Brackett, M. A., Nezlek, J. B., Schütz, A., Sellin, I., & Salovey, P. (2004). Emotional Intelligence and Social Interaction. *Personality and Social Psychology Bulletin, 30*(8), 1018–1034. https://doi.org/10.1177/0146167204264762.

Robles, M. M. (2012). Executive perceptions of the top 10 soft skills needed in today's workplace. *Business Communication Quarterly, 75*(4), 453–465. https://doi.org/10.1177/1080569912460400.

Rothwell, William, J., Stavros, Jacqueline, M., & Sullivan, Roland, L. (2016). *Practicing Organization Development: Leading Transformation and Change* (4th ed.). Hoboken, NJ: John Wiley & Sons, Inc.

Sheck, Daniel T. L. & Lin, Le. (2015). Intrapersonal competencies and service leadership. *International Journal of Disability Human Development, 14*(3), 255–263. https://doi.org/10.1515/ijdhd-2015-0406.

Soulé, H. & Warrick, T. (2015). Defining 21st century readiness for all students: What we know and how to get there. *Psychology of Aesthetics, Creativity, and the Arts, 9*(2), 178–186. https://doi.org/10.1037/aca0000017.

Tindowen, C. D. J., Bassig, J. M., & Cagurangan, J. A. (2017). Twenty-first-century skills of alternative learning system learners. *SAGE Open, 7*(3), 1–8. https://doi.org/10.1177/2158244017726116.

Tulgan, B. (2015). *Bridging the Soft Skills Gap: How to Teach the Missing Basics to Today's Young Talent.* Hoboken, NJ: John Willey & Sons, Inc. https://doi.org/10.1002/9781119171409.

Urbani, J. M., Roshandel, S., Michaels, R., & Truesdell, E. (2017). Developing and modeling 21st-century skills with preservice teachers. *Teacher Education Quarterly, 44*(4), 27–50. Retrieved from https://www.jstor.org/stable/90014088?seq=1#page_scan_tab_contents.

Chapter 21

Elements and Demographics of Study

In this chapter, we present all the related elements of our study as follows.

Organizations and Contributors

Table 21.1 displays the invitation and selection profiles criteria for organizations as well as those who took part and contributed to the data-gathering interview procedure.

Organizations. The 17 organizations included in this study were chosen based on the use of five criteria. These businesses were chosen from a pool of seven various industries. Due to the participating organizations' confidentiality agreements, this research does not specify any specific organizations or professional fields.

Contributors. Two or three business experts (executives, senior managers, middle managers, HR directors and supervisors) total of 45 individuals from each of the 17 organizations included in this study were identified according to the following criteria.

Table 21.1 The Invitation and Selection Criteria for Organizations and Contributors

#	Organizations	Contributors
1	Is a privately owned business doing business in Pennsylvania.	Hold a managerial or supervisory role at the executive, director, senior, middle, or junior levels.
2	Has at least 50 workers, or	Have held their present position for at least three years with the company.
3	Appears on a list of the "Top 50 Employers in Pennsylvania" compiled by the Pennsylvania Department of Labor & Industry.	Have lived in Pennsylvania for the previous three years.
4	Is not a new firm and has been a functioning organization in Pennsylvania for at least the past five years.	Be directly responsible for managing at least ten workers.
5	Has been operating for at least three years at their current location.	Has no disciplinary action against them in their current employment records.

DOI: 10.4324/9781003462316-26

Contributors Demographics. Two or three business experts were chosen from each of the 17 organizations, which resulted in 45 contributors in all being interviewed for this study. The demographic information on the study of the interviewed contributors is shown in the seven figures that follow: Figures 21.1, 21.2, 21.3, 21.4, 21.5, and 21.6.

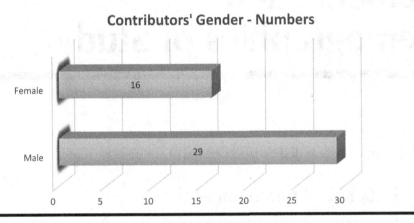

Figure 21.1   Contributors' gender (sex) by numbers in the two genders.

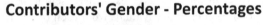

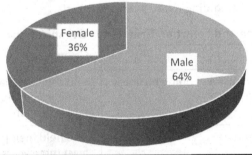

Figure 21.2   Contributors' gender (sex) by percentages of each of two genders.

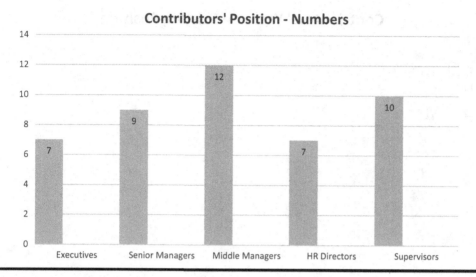

Figure 21.3 Contributors' present positions by numbers in each categories.

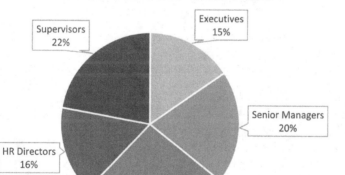

Figure 21.4 Contributors' present positions by percentage of each category.

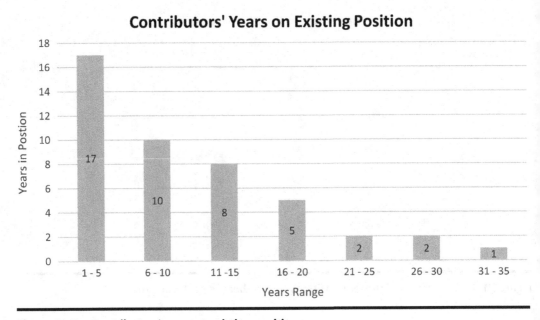

Figure 21.5   Contributors' years at existing position.

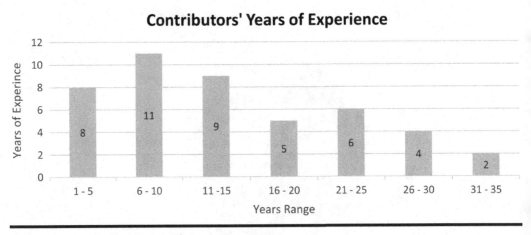

Figure 21.6   Contributors' years of professional experience.

Additionally, contributors completed a self-evaluation exercise and provided feedback on their knowledge of and use of the 4Cs while dealing with their workforce. The accompanying chart (Figure 21.7) shows the overall and average contributors' ratings on these four skills, with 0 being the lowest and 10 being the most. Given that no one gave themselves a rating of less than 5, we totaled the self-ratings from 5 to 10, then we averaged them using 5 scales (ranging from 1 to 5).

This self-assessment exercise was designed to (1) help contributors recognize that they have 4Cs abilities; and (2) help contributors reflect on the extent to which they apply those skills while interacting with their workforce.

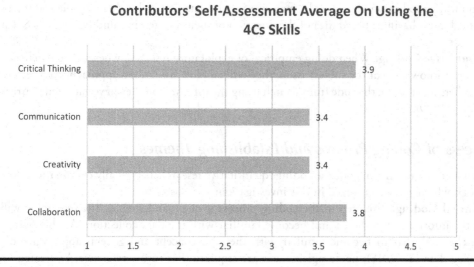

Figure 21.7   Contributors' self-assessment average on using the 4Cs skills.

Creating Codes and Recognizing Themes Based on Collected Data

One technique to quantify the information gleaned from several interviews is to code the qualitative data, which may transform a collection of data that might first appear disorganized into meaningful data (Yi, 2018). In qualitative research, developing and utilizing codes is just as vital and pertinent as the collection of quantitative research data. When presenting the findings to the customer or the general public, the quantified codes lend the researcher credibility and dependability (Yi, 2018).

A set of qualitative data can also be coded to produce a solid structure. The semi-structured interview methodology devised in this book can help researchers narrow down the questions, and the coding procedure aids in organizing and structuring the responses (Christians & Carey, 1989). However, not all interviews will go well or cover subjects that are pertinent, which raised concerns about how the same interview questions would highlight various aspects of the issue for different participants (perhaps from different industries). The option to arrange their interview scripts and identify relevant study topics is provided by the coding of the interview data (Christians & Carey, 1989).

Methods of Coding

Christians and Carey (1989) identified two different categories of coding techniques. Both approaches were employed in this study's coding of the information gathered from research interviews.

Deductive Coding. With this approach, the researchers have already created their codebook, which will serve as a guide while they code the data. When using this strategy, researchers typically begin the data collection procedure by investigating the data that is already accessible and their current fields after having a broad idea of the direction of their research in mind (Christians & Carey, 1989).

Inductive Coding. When doing empirical or exploratory research, when the researchers have little prior knowledge of the subject issue, they will employ this coding approach. As a result, the researchers must create the code from scratch using the information they have gathered (Christians & Carey, 1989).

Process of Coding Process and Establishing Themes

When it comes to carrying out the coding, quantitative researchers typically choose the following strategy, which was also utilized in this investigation:

Initial Coding. This step in the coding process is quick and simple. The researcher will go over the information gathered and become familiar with the data collection. At this point, the researcher only has to become familiar with the core concept and general appearance of the obtained data (Yi, 2018); no complex codes are required. For future reference, Yi created broad code sections and generic code names. She then utilized them to generate much more specific and detailed codes relevant to the research issue.

Categorization

When the initial coding has been completed and all of the interview transcripts read, typically a disorganized collection of codes remains. In order to discover a path that best reflects the study analysis at this moment, researchers group related codes by the same categories by shifting them around (Yi, 2018). After 1144 code extracts and 1436 code applications, this study had created 92 codes as a consequence of the coding procedure. In order to organize the codes and evaluate and identify consistent and predominate themes for this research, Yi (2018) classified the codes pertinent to the actual data obtained on the various impacts of 4Cs skills on businesses.

Themes

The themes give researchers the opportunity to present stories that are pertinent to the study issues and the conclusions they have reached (Yi, 2018). The codes are examined and categorized to provide themes. The lesser or subcategories serve to complement the main themes, while the bigger categories serve as the principal topics. Beginning at this stage, the researcher can construct the narrative using the information gathered and pertinent codes (Christians & Carey, 1989). The ideal application of these developed themes is to assist researchers in telling the same tale from many perspectives or in developing several unique stories that will connect to one another. Finally, using effective narratives developed via the process of developing themes can turn potentially chaotic qualitative data into insightful and valuable knowledge (Yi, 2018).

Study's Theoretical and Conceptual Framework

The theoretical and conceptual frameworks provide the foundation for credibility in any research by illuminating the investigation's directions (Dickson, Emad, & Adu-Agyem, 2018). Although these two terms appear to be similar, they reflect various ideas and serve various purposes in the research evaluation. Given these parallels, a lot of students have trouble telling these associated frameworks apart in their studies (Dickson et al., 2018; Imenda, 2014).

According to Dickson et al. (2018) and Imenda (2014), the overall goal of theoretical and conceptual frameworks is to provide the research findings more context, make them acceptable to the theoretical paradigms in the domains of study, and support generalizability. These two frameworks aid in stimulating the inquiry process, assuring the expansion of knowledge, and improving the empiricism and consistency of the study. According to Dickson et al. (2018), "Thus, it is no exaggeration for Imenda (2014) to say that both the theoretical and conceptual frameworks give life to a research" (p. 438).

Theoretical Framework

According to Grant and Osanloo (2014), the theoretical framework serves as the blueprint or direction for research. It is based on the most recent and widely accepted theories in an area of study that are relevant to and represent the research questions or hypotheses. According to Grant and Osanloo (2014), "the theoretical framework consists of principles, constructs, concepts, and tenants of a theory" (p. 13). A theoretical framework can aid researchers in defining their research methodology, epistemology, philosophy, and analytics in order to position their work in an academic and scholarly manner (Ravitch & Carl, 2016; Grant & Osanloo, 2014; Imenda, 2014), in addition to providing a path for the research inquiry.

Conceptual Framework

According to Camp (2001), a conceptual framework serves as a structure that the researcher or researchers are convinced can offer the standard explanation for the event or problem under study. According to Peshkin (1993), a conceptual framework is connected to the ideas and concepts that have been selected by the researcher(s) in order to support and organize the advancement of knowledge. It shows the researcher's explanation of how the phenomena or problem under inquiry would be investigated. The conceptual framework shows an integrated manner of seeing the challenges related to the study subject, as noted by Liehr and Smith (1999). The conceptual framework establishes the relationship between the fundamental ideas of the study from a statistical perspective. It sets up a logical framework to help show how the topics in the research study relate to one another visually (Grant & Osanloo, 2014; Imenda, 2014).

Table 21.2 represents a comparison between the roles of theoretical and conceptual frameworks in any qualitative research. This comparison will help readers better understand how theoretical and conceptual frameworks help produce valid research.

Table 21.2 The Characteristics and Roles of Theoretical Framework and Conceptual Framework

#	Theoretical Framework	Conceptual Framework
1	It offers a more comprehensive collection of concepts to which the research belongs.	It addresses a particular or more specific concept that is utilized by researchers in their investigations.
2	It is founded on the most recent hypotheses to be found in the relevant literature that have been tested and verified by other researchers.	It is founded on the fundamental concepts that serve as the primary determinants in research.
3	It is a paradigm that bases research on the findings of its proponents and the study that they have conducted.	It may be the researcher's own model or one that they have modified for use in describing the relationship between the primary variables in the investigation.
4	It has a solid foundation, a well-designed structure, and widespread approval among the academic research community.	It is a suggestion for how to approach the research topics that have been stated.
5	It offers a central point for traveling into the unknown research in a specified topic of inquiry, which is what it is doing right now.	It is the framework that demonstrates in a logical manner how the study is initiated.
6	It includes theories that have interconnected relationships with the assertions that they construct.	It comprises the research topics that are related to one another in order to describe the relationships between them.
7	Within the framework of research, it is utilized for the examination of hypotheses, as well as for the anticipation and management of situations.	It is hoped that this would encourage the development and evolution of a theory that will be of use to professionals working in the relevant subject.

Note. Adapted from Dickson et al. (2018).

What Is Next?

What comes next is Appendix A, a list including some selected resources to support readers in the knowledge and elements of this book and its related chapters and topics.

References

Camp, W. G. (2001). Formulating and evaluating theoretical frameworks for career and technical education research. *Journal of Vocational Educational Research, 26*(1), 27–39. https://doi.org/10.5328/JVER26.1.4.

Christians, C. G. & Carey, J. W. (1989). The logic and aims of qualitative research. *Research Methods in Mass Communication, 2,* 354–374.

Dickson, A., Emad, H., & Adu-Agyem, J. (2018). Theoretical and conceptual framework: Mandatory ingredients of a quality research. *International Journal of Scientific Research, 7*(1), 438–441. Retrieved from https://www.researchgate.net/publication/322204158.

Grant, C. & Osanloo, A. (2014). Understanding, selecting, and integrating a theoretical framework in dissertation research: Creating the blueprint for "house." *Administrative Issues Journal: Connecting Education, Practice and Research,* 12–22.

Imenda, S. (2014). Is there a conceptual difference between conceptual and theoretical frameworks? *Journal of Social Science, 38*(2), 185–195. https://doi.org/10.1080/09718923.2014.11893249.

Liehr P. & Smith, M. J. (1999). Middle range theory: Spinning research and practice to create knowledge for the new millennium. *Advances in Nursing Science, 21*(4), 81–91. Retrieved from https://journals.lww .com/advancesinnursingscience/Fulltext/1999/06000/Middle_Range_Theory__Spinning_Research _and.11.aspx.

Ravitch, S. M. & Carl, N. M. (2016). *Qualitative Research: Bridging the Conceptual, Theoretical and Methodological.* Los Angeles, CA: SAGE Publications, Inc.

Peshkin, A. (1993). The Goodness of qualitative research. *Educational Researcher, 22*(2), 23–29. https://doi .org/10.3102/0013189X022002023.

Yi, Erika. (2018). Themes don't just emerge: Coding the qualitative data. Project UX Website. Retrieved from https://medium.com/@projectux/themes-dont-just-emerge-coding-the-qualitative-data -95aff874fdce.

Appendix A
Supportive Resources

Books

- Bellanca, James and Brandt, Ron (2010). *21st Century Skills*. Bloomington, IN: Rethinking How Students Learn. Solution Tree Press.
- Bradberry, Travis and Greaves, Jean (2005). *The Emotional Intelligence Quick Book. Everything You Need to Know to Put Your EQ to Work*. New York, NY: Fireside.
- Cappelli, Peter (2012). Why *Good People Can't Get Jobs. The Skills Gap and What Companies Can Do About It*. Philadelphia, PA: Wharton Digital Press.
- Connors, Christopher, D. (2020). *Emotional Intelligence for the Modern Leader*. Emeryville, CA: Rockridge Press.
- Donahue, Wesley, E. (2022). *Resolving Team Issues and Challenges*. State College, PA: Centrestar.
- Gardner, H. (2006). *Multiple Intelligences: New Horizons*. New York, NY. Basic Books.
- Goleman, Brandon (2019). *Emotional Intelligence; For a Better Life, Success at Work, and Happier Relationships*. Middletown, DE: A Self-Published Title.
- Goleman, Daniel (1998). *Working with Emotional Intelligence*. New York, NY: Random House.
- Goleman, Daniel (2006). *Social Intelligence. The Revolutionary New Science of Human Relationships*. New York, NY: Bantam Books.
- Goleman, Daniel (2014). What it takes to achieve managerial success. *TD: Talent Development, 68*(11), 48–52.
- Goleman, Daniel (2015). *Emotional Intelligence; Why It Can Matter More Than IQ*. New York, NY: Bantam Books.
- Goleman, Daniel, Boyatzis, Richard and McKee, Annie (2002). *Prime Leadership: Learning to Lead with Emotional Intelligence*. Boston, MA: Harvard Business School Press.
- Hora, Matthew, T. (2016). *Beyond the Skills Gap. Preparing College Students for Life and Work*. Cambridge, MA: Harvard Education Press.
- Kite, Neilson and Kay, Frances (2012). *Understanding Emotional Intelligence. Strategies for Boosting Your EQ and Using It in the Workplace*. Philadelphia, PA: Kogan Page.
- Klaus, Peggy (2007). *The Hard Truth About Soft Skills. Workplace Lessons Smart People Wish They'd Learned Sooner*. New York, NY: Harper.

- Lindberg, Carl (2023). *Interpersonal Communication; Understand and Develop Your Inner Dialogue.* New Heaven, CT: A Self-Published Title.
- Miner, Nanette (2018). *Future-Proofing Your Organization; By Teaching Thinking Skills.* North Haven, CT: The Training Doctor.
- Neal, Stephen, Spencer-Arnell, Lisa and Wilson, Liz (2009). *Emotional Intelligence Coaching. Improving Performance for Leaders, Coaching and the Individual.* Philadelphia, PA: Kogan Page.
- Paul, Richard and Elder, Linda (2006). *The Miniature Guild to Critical Thinking Concept and Tools.* Santa Barbara, CA: The Foundation for Critical Thinking
- Rao, S., M. (2016). *Soft Skills: Your Step-By-Step Guide to Overcome Workplace Challenges to Excel as a Leader.* Melbourne, FL: Motivational Press.
- Sawatzky, Roxanne (2014). *21st Century Organization. How to Meet the 21st Century Skills Gap.* North Haven, CT: A Self-Published Title.
- Segal, Jeanne (2008). *The Language of Emotional Intelligence.* New York, NY: McGraw Hill.
- Smith Budhai, Stephanie and Mclaughlin Taddei, Laura (2015). *Teaching the 4Cs With Technology. How Do I Use 21st Century Tools to Teach 21st Century Skills?* Alexandria, VA: ASCD Arias.
- Tulgan, Bruce (2015). *Bridging the Soft Skills Gap: How to Teach the Missing Basics to Today's Young Talent.* Hoboken, NJI Jossey-Bass, a Wiley Imprint.
- Wall, Bob (2007). *Coaching For Emotional Intelligence. The Secret to Developing the Star Potential in Your Employees.* New York, NY: AMACOM.

Articles

- AIIM (2023). Association for Information and Image Management. Retrieved from https://www.aiim.org/what-is-collaboration#:~:text=Collaboration.
- Al-Shehab, N., AL-Hashimi, M., Madbouly, A., Reyad, S., & Hamdan, A. (2021). Do employability skills for business graduates meet the employers' expectations? The case of retail Islamic banks of Bahrain. *Higher Education, Skills and Work-Based Learning, 11*(2), 349–366. https://doi.org/10.1108/HESWBL-09-2019-0117.
- Common Sense Media (2020). What is communication? Retrieved from https://www.commonsensemedia.org/articles/what-is-communication.
- David, M. E., David, F. R., & David, F. R. (2021). Closing the gap between graduates' skills and employers' requirements: A focus on the strategic management capstone business course. *Administrative Sciences, 11*(1), 10. https://doi.org/10.3390/admsci11010010.
- Foroughi, A. (2021). Supply chain workforce training: Addressing the digital skills gap. [Supply chain workforce training] *Higher Education, Skills and Work-Based Learning, 11*(3), 683–696. https://doi.org/10.1108/HESWBL-07-2020-0159.
- Greer, S., Brown, K., & Raimondo, M. (2020). Gap Bridgers: Teaching skills to cross lines of difference. *Journal of College and Character, 21*(3), 221–233. https://doi.org/10.1080/2194587X.2020.1781664.
- Kamaroellah, A., Eliyana, A., Amalia, N., & Pratama, A. S. (2021). Investigation of ideal employability skills: A literature review on components and antecedents. *Journal of Legal, Ethical and Regulatory Issues, 24*, 1–9. Retrieved from https://heinonline.org/HOL/LandingPage?handle=hein.journals/jnlolletl2424&div=83&id=&page=.

- Kerr, Barbara (2023). Creativity. Retrieved from https://www.britannica.com/topic/creativity.
- Konstantinou, I., & Miller, E. (2021). Self-managed and work-based learning: Problematising the workplace–classroom skills gap. *Journal of Work-Applied Management*, *13*(1), 6–18. https://doi.org/10.1108/JWAM-11-2020-0048.
- Mahajan, R., Gupta, P., & Misra, R. (2022). Employability skills framework: A tripartite approach. *Education & Training (London)*, *64*(3), 360–379. https://doi.org/10.1108/ET-12-2020-0367.
- Ng, P. M. L., Chan, J. K. Y., Wut, T. M., Lo, M. F., & Szeto, I. (2021). What makes better career opportunities for young graduates? examining acquired employability skills in higher education institutions. *Education & Training (London)*, *63*(6), 852–871. https://doi.org/10.1108/ET-08-2020-0231.
- Nizami, N., Tripathi, T., & Mohan, M. (2022). Transforming skill gap crisis into opportunity for upskilling in India's IT-BPM sector. *Indian Journal of Laboure Economics*, *65*(3), 845–862. https://doi.org/10.1007/s41027-022-00383-9.
- Papyrina, V., Strebel, J., & Robertson, B. (2021). The student confidence gap: Gender differences in job skill self-efficacy. *Journal of Education for Business*, *96*(2), 89–98. https://doi.org/10.1080/08832323.2020.1757593.
- Rampasso, I. S., Mello, S. L. M., Walker, R., Simão, V. G., Araújo, R., Chagas, J., Quelhas, O. L. G., & Anholon, R. (2021). An investigation of research gaps in reported skills required for industry 4.0 readiness of Brazilian undergraduate students. *Higher Education, Skills and Work-Based Learning*, *11*(1), 34–47. https://doi.org/10.1108/HESWBL-10-2019-0131.
- Saini, K., & Saini, R. R. (2022). Bridging the employability skills gap: A review. *The ICFAI Journal of Soft Skills*, *16*(3), 43–50. Retrieved from https://www.proquest.com/docview/2732569974?pq-origsite=gscholar&fromopenview=true&sourcetype=Scholarly%20Journals.
- Scriven, M., & Paul, R. (2003). Defining critical thinking: a statement prepared for the National Council for Excellence in Critical Thinking Instruction. In 8th Annual International Conference on Critical Thinking and Education Reform, Summer 1987. Retrieved from https://www.scirp.org/reference/referencespapers?referenceid=2595525.
- The Foundation of Critical Thinking (2019). Define Critical Thinking. Retrieved from https://www.criticalthinking.org/pages/defining-critical-thinking/766.
- Yamada, S., & Otchia, C. S. (2021). Perception gaps on employable skills between technical and vocational education and training (TVET) teachers and students: The case of the garment sector in Ethiopia. [Perception gaps between teachers and students] *Higher Education, Skills and Work-Based Learning*, *11*(1), 199–213. https://doi.org/10.1108/HESWBL-08-2019-0105.

Videos/YouTube

- Showcasing Essential Skills: The 4Cs. Vermont Student Assistance Corporation. https://www.youtube.com/watch?v=lzjckWOOye8.
- 4Cs and Skills Based Learning. Learning Life. https://www.youtube.com/watch?v=4g295NL12pg.
- 21st Century Learning & Like Skills: Framework. Teaching in Education. https://www.youtube.com/watch?v=ixRBjEW_sFs.

- What are the 4Cs? Business Leaders Under Fire. https://www.youtube.com/watch?v =ABsJL1VrozI.
- What is the 4Cs? Common Sence Education. https://www.youtube.com/watch?v =QrEEVZa3f98.
- What Are the 4Cs of 21st Century Skills? 21st Century Classroom. https://www.youtube .com/watch?v=TwMvsuj3gU8.
- Implementation of 4Cs in Classroom. Teaching Partner. https://www.youtube.com/results ?search_query=4cs+skills.
- 21st Century Skills: The 4Cs. Shana Sewalt. https://www.youtube.com/watch?v=BXT2STtm _54.
- A Skill to Master Critical Thinking. Syed Samir Anis. TEDxMuscatSalon https://www.you-tube.com/watch?v=vswf_I1j_Ds.
- 21st Century Learning: Education Conference & Live Chat. Teaching in Education. https:// www.youtube.com/watch?v=AEjp1Gtf20Y.
- 21 Soft Skills for Teachers. Helpful Professor Explains! https://www.youtube.com/watch?v =NzwlDmMkEKs.
- 21st Century Skills & The 4Cs. Ikrasena Koyuncu. https://www.youtube.com/watch?v=dk _URoub2sI.

Blogs

- What are the 4Cs's of 21st Century Skills? ICEV. Bri Stauffer. https://www.icevonline.com /blog/four-cs-21st-century-skills.
- What are the 4Cs of 21st-Century Learning Skills? Torrens University Australia. Alison Lamp (January 9, 2023). https://www.torrens.edu.au/blog/what-are-the-4-cs-of-21st-cen-tury-learning.
- Exploring the 4Cs of 21st Centuery Learning. LANSCHOOL. Education Insights. (May 27, 2021) https://lanschool.com/blog/education-insights/exploring-the-4-cs-of-21st-century -learning.
- A Guide to the 4Cs of 21st Century Skills. KidsPARK. Jacqueline Samaroo (November 18, 2019).https://blog.kidsparkeducation.org/blog/a-guide-to-the-4-cs-of-21st-century-skills.
- How to Implement the 4Cs in Education to Teach 21st-Century Skills. Nearpodblog. Darri Stephens (December 4, 2023). https://nearpod.com/blog/4cs-education/.
- Adding 4Cs to the 3Rs: 21st-Century Skills in Today's Classrooms. Infobase, Stay Curious. Waneta Hebert (December 9, 2022) https://infobase.com/blog/adding-4-cs-to-the-3-rs-21st -century-skills-in-todays-classrooms/.
- The 4Cs (Education). The Keys for 21st-Centuery Schools. Europass Teacher Academy. Susan Gagliano (March 31, 2023). https://www.teacheracademy.eu/blog/4-cs-education/.
- Exploring the 4cs of 21st Century Learning. Ellipsis. Katie Baird (June 25, 2020) https:// ellipsiseducation.com/blog/four-cs-21st-century-learning.

Websites

- What are the 4Cs of 21st Century Skills? South Charlotte STEM Academy. https:// scstemacademy.org/4-cs-of-21st-century-skills/.

- What are the 4Cs of 21st Century Skills. ICEV Online. https://www.icevonline.com/blog/four-cs-21st-century-skills.
- The 4Cs of Organizational Success & Corporate Culture. Growth Tactics. https://www.growthtactics.net/4cs-of-organizational-success-corporate-culture/.
- The 4Cs to 21st Century Skills. Arizona Department of Education. https://www.azed.gov/sites/default/files/2017/08/The4Cs21stCenturySkills.pdf.
- Thoughtful Learning: What are the 4Cs of Learning Skills? University of Nebraska-Lincoln. https://newsroom.unl.edu/announce/csmce/5344/29195.
- The 4Cs of 21st Century Skills. BW Education. https://bweducation.businessworld.in/article/The-4C-s-Of-21st-Century-Skills-/25-05-2021-390783/.
- Complete 21st Century Skills for Educators. Udemy.
- Dynamic Works. https://dynamicinstitute.com/job-seeker-accelerator/?gclid=CjwKCAiAmsurBhBvEiwA6e-WPGuBWMVc81b6OKCzvjbYQx94HtypJk5jiHAGoAVSr-iFoaNJQDgKhxoCoosQAvD_BwE.
- 21st Century Skills for Workplace Success. Nocti Business Solutions. https://www.nocti-business.com/assessments/21st-century-skills-for-workplace-success/?utm_source=google&utm_medium=cpc&utm_campaign=act_workkeys&gad_source=2&gclid=CjwKCAiAmsurBhBvEiwA6e-WPDeXZuesePLGOECR3xbX8VjAfGMtIAz9bhReZKeXIYDe3Qy13dQVuxoCz3oQAvD_BwE.
- EvolveMe. Learn Skills Online For Free—Develop Your Personal Skills https://evolveme.asa.org/.
- Workplace Skills Test—Workplace Skills Assessment. https://www.noctibusiness.com/.
- Help employees with future skills. https://uk.indeed.com/.

Index

Printed in the United States
by Baker & Taylor Publisher Services